TERROR

AND

RESISTANCE

TERROR AND SOCIETY

I TERROR AND RESISTANCE:
A STUDY OF POLITICAL VIOLENCE

TERROR
AND
RESISTANCE

A STUDY OF POLITICAL VIOLENCE

WITH CASE STUDIES OF SOME

PRIMITIVE AFRICAN COMMUNITIES

———•———

Eugene Victor Walter

OXFORD UNIVERSITY PRESS
London   Oxford   New York

OXFORD UNIVERSITY PRESS

London   Oxford   New York
Glasgow   Toronto   Melbourne   Wellington
Cape Town   Ibadan   Nairobi   Dar es Salaam   Lusaka   Addis Ababa
Delhi   Bombay   Calcutta   Madras   Karachi   Lahore   Dacca
Kuala Lumpur   Singapore   Hong Kong   Tokyo

TO RUTH

coniugi carissimae, amicae dilectae, sodali forti

PREFACE

As far as I know, this inquiry is the first systematic effort to develop a general theory of terrorism. I do not presume to offer definitive conclusions about the nature and functions of political terror, but merely to initiate explorations in an uncharted domain and to go over more familiar ground with some new ideas in mind. The present volume does not investigate movements to overthrow established systems of power— I have named that kind of movement the *siege of terror*— but limits the study to the *regime of terror*, which is a system maintained by established power holders. The central problem of the book is to find out why some men who already have authority choose to rule by violence and fear.

After stating the problem in such global terms, I must explain why the empirical material in this volume is restricted to the phenomenology of terrorism in some primitive African societies. My historical explorations in ancient and modern regimes have convinced me that even though terror emerges in unique contexts and, in each case, is expressed and understood in a local idiom, conforms to specific values, and serves the needs of a particular power system, it is a universal process formed by recurrent elements and organized in systems with regular structural features. I was struck by the connection between terror, the possibilities of resistance, and crises of social integration. Certain empirical generalizations emerged from my preliminary investigations, but I needed to pursue them in a unified setting, and I needed to find a way to organize them in a coherent theoretical argument that would retain empirical roots. I did not want to confine the study to an abstract model of terroristic behavior remote from historical realities, and I wanted to share the adventure of extracting social theory from the substance of history. For these reasons, I decided to locate the process of terror in some simple societies and to show its pattern in their social-political life, clarifying its causes, conditions, and consequences. In that setting, the problem can be stated in plain terms. The variables are relatively easy to grasp, and one does not have to disentangle factors introduced by changing economic forces, elaborate stratification, or other complexities of modern social structure. In pre-modern, traditional societies, politics may be highly sophisticated, but the variables and the kinds of social relationship are limited. The scheme of the book, then, has the advantage of simplicity without the vacancy of an abstract model. Furthermore, to select a domain of observation in which technology is rudimentary contravenes the artless notion that extensive systems of terror are produced only by advanced societies.

From the dynamics of the political communities examined in this book, we may abstract typical features that will help us to understand the process of terror in different environments. The second volume will pursue the analysis of terrorism in other social conditions and will explore the intellectual history of the idea of terror as well as its psychodynamics. Although the present inquiry works toward a general theory, the explanation does not cover every typical regime of terror—revolutionary governments and totalitarian systems, for example, introduce factors that are beyond the scope of the first volume.

Early versions of some sections of this work have appeared as essays in journals. I acknowledge with thanks permission to use them here: to the American Sociological Association for "Violence and the Process of Terror," *American Sociological Review*, Vol. 29, 1964, 248–57; and to the editors of the journals in which the following articles appeared: "Power and Violence," *American Political Science Review*, Vol. 58, 1964, 350–60; "Rise and Fall of the Zulu Power," *World Politics*, Vol. 18, 1966, 546–63.

I am grateful for permission to quote several long passages:

to the University of Kansas for the quotations on pages 107–8 of C. A. Valentine, *Masks and Men in a Melanesian Society;* to the President and Fellows of Harvard College for the quotations on pages 116, 122–23 of George W. Harley, "Masks as Agents of Social Control in Northeast Liberia," *Papers of the Peabody Museum,* Vol. 32, No. 2, 1950; to Longmans Green & Co. Ltd for the quotations on pages 151, 243 of A. T. Bryant, *Olden Times in Zululand and Natal;* to Shuter and Shooter (PTY) Ltd for the quotations on pages 173, 187–88, 219, 220–21 of James Stuart and D. McK. Malcolm, eds., *The Diary of Henry Francis Fynn;* and to the Van Riebeeck Society, South African Library, Queen Victoria Street, Cape Town for the quotations on pages 196–97, 216 of Nathaniel Isaacs, *Travels and Adventures in Eastern Africa,* Vol. I.

I am grateful to the Rockefeller Foundation for a grant in legal and political philosophy, which enabled me to begin the inquiry in 1957–58. I am obliged to Brandeis University for financial assistance and to my friends there for their interest and loyalty. I am also grateful to Boston University for providing funds that helped me to complete the work, and I especially want to thank Philip Kubzansky, Dean of the Graduate School, for his friendly support. I thank Betty Griffin for elegant typing.

My greatest debt, which it is a joy to acknowledge, is to colleagues in the social sciences and to my students. Their enthusiasm sustained me, and even when their ideas did not help my investigation, discussion gave me a chance to clarify my own thinking. I am grateful to Benjamin Nelson, who is always ready to take up the conversation where we have left it, for several insights into the ways of social science. In the early stages of the research, I had the privilege of discussions with Hannah Arendt, David Cooperman, Julian Franklin, Edward Friedman, Peter Gay, Louis Hartz, David Kettler, Albert Salomon, Alfred Schutz, Maurice R. Stein, Leo Strauss, and Kurt H. Wolff. Herbert Marcuse and Barrington Moore, Jr., have been very helpful with advice and encouragement. Elizabeth Colson, Marion Kilson, Daniel McCall, Guenther Roth, Richard

Sklar, and John R. Seeley provided useful comments on the drafts of chapters. I am deeply grateful to Shula Marks of the Institute of Commonwealth Studies in the University of London for her criticism of Chapters VI–X. It goes without saying that I take full responsibility for everything I have written.

I learned a great deal from my students in seminars on terrorism I taught at Brandeis, Harvard, The New School for Social Research, and Boston University. Their company brightened the research, they grappled with the problems in their own ways, and they sometimes pointed out directions I would have missed. Larry Gross and Thomas Hanley were especially helpful.

The treasures of Widener Library and the Peabody Museum Library, as well as the courteous assistance of the staffs, helped to enrich this book.

Stuart Russell and Seymour and Paula Leventman helped to read the proofs. My daughter, Claudia, was a research assistant whose devastating wit relieved the tedium of documentation. My son, Ian, helped with the index. My wife, Ruth Ice Walter, shared my meditations with unfailing interest and never lost confidence in the value of the inquiry. It is a pleasure to dedicate this book to her.

CONTENTS

Terror in the compound is
the dread of dissolution.

—Plotinus

TERROR

AND

RESISTANCE

CHAPTER I

THE PROCESS
OF TERROR

When the overwhelming scourge passes,
You will be battered down by it;
As often as it passes, it will bear you away;
For morning by morning will it pass,
Both day and night;
And sheer terror will it be
To understand the message.

—The Book of Isaiah, xxviii.

RULE BY TERROR, a familiar process in history, has virtually escaped systematic analysis. Working for the modern state, this old scourge of human communities destroys men for the same ends it once achieved as the instrument of immemorial despots. This form of power remains at the edges of rational inquiry, but the experience of recent times, punctuated by terroristic outbreaks and burdened by regimes of terror, makes the world tremble with an awareness that seeks general explanations.

The phenomena of terrorism touch familiar issues and raise classic questions. To investigate terrorism is to study power *in extremis*, and, as it sometimes happens when extreme situations are probed for meaning and mechanism, the inquiry throws new light on the subject and reveals features that are ordinarily invisible in more tranquil conditions.

Terror is not confined to anomalous circumstances or exotic systems. It is potential in ordinary institutions as well as in unusual situations, and reigns of terror are not properly understood if they are conceived of exclusively as ephemeral states of crisis produced by adventitious events or as alien forms of control. Systems of terror, usually defined as "abnormal" by the conventions of Western social and political thought, may be generated under certain conditions of stress by "normal" political processes, and it should become evident in the course of this investigation that the problem of terror raises virtually every major issue of political sociology and political theory.

The idea of a reign of terror is commonly presumed to have emerged during the French Revolution. No one has explored the intellectual history of the concept or searched the classical tradition of social and political thought for the elements of a comprehensive theory. Similarly, few inquirers have compared the phenomenology of different terroristic regimes to find empirical generalizations. Stereotyped notions about terror are etched deeply in the habits of political thought.

One approach identifies terror with totalitarian systems. According to this way of thinking, terrorism is understood as a single feature of an abstract system, and its nature as a distinct process gets lost in a discussion of general totalitarian characteristics. It is true that the study of totalitarianism has been one of the few paths to recent theories of terrorism, but it has led to an incorrect identification of organized terror with systems of total power. To correct this distortion, it would be necessary to examine within their historical contexts several typical systems of power in which the process of terror is at home.

Another approach is impaired by a difficulty that Herbert Spencer called "the political bias." Ever since the French Revolution, "terrorist" has been an epithet to fasten on a political enemy. Burke and his followers have said that if you scratch an ideologue you will find a terrorist. On the other hand, revolutionary radicals have tended to think of terror as a defensive maneuver against counterrevolutionary forces. Both points of view are quick to label almost any kind of violence exercised by their opponents as terrorism. Still, when it is convenient, both also tend to dissociate terrorism from acts and threats of violence. Thus, when manifest violence diminishes in systems such as the Soviet Union, Communist China, or Cuba, the critics of revolutionary movements want to redefine terrorism as some process hidden in the interstices of the system. Similarly, when manifest violence is absent, the critics of bourgeois society want to identify terrorism with economic intimidation and—like their opponents—want to find it hidden in the interstices of the system. Used in this way, the term is vacuous, no more than an epithet for a system one hates.

Conventionally, the word "terrorism" means a type of violent action, such as murder, designed to make people afraid. In ordinary usage, however, the related word "terror" is ambiguous, often suggesting any kind of extreme apprehension, no matter what the cause. Moreover, it may mean, on the one hand, the psychic state—extreme fear—and, on the other hand, the thing that terrifies—the violent event that produces the psychic state. I shall try to avoid confusion by maintaining a precise usage, employing terms such as "terrorism" and "organized terror" consistently as equivalents to *process of terror*, by which I mean a compound with three elements: the act or threat of violence, the emotional reaction, and the social effects.

This usage makes it clear that the experience of terror differs in many ways from the experience of other kinds of fear and from that of anxiety. Whereas anxiety may have as its cause a number of factors, including intrapsychic tensions, interpersonal conflicts, and unsettled social conditions, the terror examined in this volume is restricted to an emotional state that has specific violent acts or threats as its cause. By "cause," I mean sufficient condition—that is, with its presence the effect will also be present.

To clarify my definition, I shall suggest briefly some limiting cases, showing that the process-of-terror concept excludes several situations that are loosely called "terrorism" or "reign of terror."

For example, imagine a revolution in which the successful

insurgents carry out mass executions of former officials and their associates. Suppose, for the sake of illustration, there is no confusion about identifying the revolutionary citizens, who, we shall assume, approve the executions, and the adherents of the old regime. In addition, assume that no suspicion of counterrevolutionary activity hangs over the citizens and that the executions do not make them afraid for their own safety. Then the situation can be clearly defined as destructive violence against former power holders, but not as a process of terror.

For another example, modify the first hypothetical case and imagine that at the same time the executions are taking place, the citizens are faced with widespread famine, disease, great social dislocations, and the threat of invasion. The atmosphere is full of fear existing simultaneously with the mass executions. Yet, the behavior of the revolutionary government is not terrorism, nor is the relation between leaders and citizens a system of terror if the fear is caused by these other factors and not by the executions or similar acts of government violence.[1]

A *system of terror* may be broadly defined to include certain states of war as well as certain political communities, as long as the term refers to a sphere of relationships controlled by the terror process. To designate such a sphere as a "system of terror," however, implies that all the individuals within it are involved, in one role or another, actually or potentially in the terror process. Hence, a system of terror should not be identified as any society that happens to have terror in it. Durable pockets of terrorism, restricted to specific kinds of behavior or to special classes of individuals, may be found in societies generally governed by more benevolent methods. For example, sedition may be expunged *in terrorem;* felons, slaves, or an ethnic minority may receive exceptionally violent treatment: in such instances we may speak of a *zone of terror*, within which the violence and fear are confined. Outside the zone, power relations follow the rules of an ordinary system of authority. Whether the sphere is considered as "zone" or as "system" depends on what is understood to be the domain of observation.

For example, isolated conceptually and taken as a closed system, slavery of a certain kind is a system of terror; however, it is also a zone of terror within the society that contains it. Of course, any zone is closely linked to the rest of the society in many ways, but this larger society is itself not a system of terror unless all the members are involved, in one role or another, actually or potentially in the terror process.

Systems of terror fall into two major categories, depending on whether they work against or coincide with the dominant power structure. One type is oriented toward overthrowing a system of authority—for example, a state—either to enable the directors in the terror staff to seize control of the state or to clear the way for some other group approved by them. In this type, the members of the terror staff may be recruited externally from foreign enemies of the political system under attack, or drawn from indigenous rebels or revolutionaries. Its purpose, in any case, is to destroy the authority system by creating extreme fear through systematic violence. The type may be referred to as a *siege of terror* and is not the subject of this book. In rebel groups not strong enough to overthrow a state, terrorism may be a technique—in some cases a ritual—which is part of their strategy to repudiate and remain independent of the authority system.[2]

Systems of terror in the other category coincide and coact with systems of authority and are directed by those who already control the ordinary institutions of power. Instead of relying entirely on authority, conventional rules, and legitimate techniques, the men in power, for reasons to be discovered, choose to initiate the process of terror. The form may be called a *regime of terror*, and the systems of terror examined in this study are of that type.

Regardless of its political orientation, the first element of the terror process, in a logical as well as a chronological sense, is the specific act or threat of violence, which induces a general psychic state of extreme fear, which in turn produces typical patterns of reactive behavior. The term "violence" will be restricted to the sense of *destructive harm*. As a general term it would include not only physical assaults that damage the body, but also magic, sorcery, and the many techniques of inflicting harm by mental or emotional means. One may turn to anthropological literature for accounts of magical and spiritual terrorism practiced by shamans, magicians, and priests,[3] and the reader will find that kind of terror mentioned in the chapters on African secret societies. However, physical violence is close to spiritual violence and by itself is more ponderable, historically more extensive, and organized on the widest scale. In most cases, the kind of terrorism examined in this study depends on the way physical violence is used.

The specific act or threat of violence may be a form of involuntary behavior, a deliberate action, or an intentional course of action. If the act or threat is not chosen or if it is produced by abnormal psychic processes and cannot be withheld, it is involuntary. If the act or threat is willed, it is deliberate violence. If the psychic effect and reactive behavior are also willed, then the act or threat is intentional terrorism. The concept, "process of terror," developed in this study, includes all three. Although the pattern of calculated terrorism is the one that comes most readily to mind, systems of terror are also established by persons who do not "want" them. Thus, the presence or absence of deliberateness is not crucial to the definition, although it is natural to associate terrorism with deliberate acts of violence and their consequences. Involuntary behavior, including psychotic acts of violence, must be included. The relative amounts of calculated action and involuntary behavior may be important in constructing a typology of terror processes, but the involuntary event cannot be taken as the limiting case.[4]

Thus, in some cases, the chain of events in a process of terror may begin with an emotionally disturbed overlord living in the midst of political tensions, who commands his agents to perform acts of violence which induce the fear reaction which in turn yields social effects upon which the political system depends. Some political conditions call forth continuous violent behavior of this sort, encouraging a kind of institutionalized rage, or supporting psychotic behavior. The image and definition of the overlord as a dangerous person may enable the power system to function in a set pattern that could not persist in other circumstances. As I shall point out in the Zulu case, it is uncertain whether the madness of one overlord was genuine or feigned, for the method was more striking than the madness. At any rate, because the fear and its social effects are caused by specific violence, the chain of behavior clearly fits the present concept, "process of terror." That the consequences may not be intended by the directors or agents of violence is irrelevant. The "useful" social effects of irrational violence may or may not be perceived and approved after they emerge from the terror process.

Intended terrorism is, of course, a much more obvious type. In this case, the directors resolve that terror is the order of the day, and they consciously design a pattern of violence to produce the social behavior they demand.

Stripped to the essentials, a dramaturgic model of the terror process would include three actors: a *source of violence*, a *victim*, and a *target*. The victim perishes, but the target reacts to the spectacle or the news of that destruction with some manner of submission or accommodation—that is, by withdrawing his resistance or by inhibiting his potential resistance. An expanded model, closer to the realities of a political system, would have a division of labor and specialization in the source of violence. Let us call the organization which is now the source, the *terror staff*, and within it distinguish between a *directorate*—men who can design, initiate, control, define, and justify the terror—and the *agents of violence*—executioners, warriors, and the "king's knives," who carry out orders and perform acts of destruction. The victims and the targets may or may not have special social identities, depending on the circumstances. Everyone in the system may be a target, but the process needs a regular selection of victims, who are dispatched according to variable rates of destruction. In a chiefdom where terror is continual but of low intensity, the available stock of evildoers, deviants, scapegoats, and candidates for legal punishment may be sufficient. A terroristic despotism needs a larger supply. They may be selected at random or else chosen by spies and informers. The informers may be specialists, or indiscriminate people who are potential victims themselves.

Organized terror as defined in this study has played an important role in the social and political life of many peoples. The evidence in this book is confined to some primitive Africans, and the next volume will consider civilized Greeks and Romans. I hope the analysis in both volumes will dispose of the old prejudice that still insinuates in subtle ways that rule by violence and fear is alien to the Western political tradition but natural to people who, according to some moral or technical standard of comparison, may be called "barbarians." Inspection of the evidence reveals that such an attitude has no rational ground. To think that some people—Oriental, Russian, German, or Bantu, for example—are culturally prone to terrorism and that others are culturally immune is an attitude as pernicious as it is false. Any complex political system can be transformed into a system of terror, which is not restricted to certain kinds of national character or to "barbaric" dispositions.

Although persons as well as societies work hard to screen off the experience of terror and to shut out the knowledge of its operation, many observers would have us believe that terror has become a global experience. They point out that the world lives in permanent crisis as the most powerful governments continue to mount against one another weapons that have a destructive energy beyond experience and beyond imagination. The mass media remind us continually that we are poised on a "balance of terror." Moreover, great numbers participate directly or vicariously in the fright of victims and witnesses to terrorism in areas shattered by internal warfare. Race conflict and the struggle over civil rights have made visible zones of terror in which acts of violence against black people support tactical resistance to social and political change. Furthermore, memories of many of the living store the dreadful experience of how systems of terror and extermination work in totalitarian regimes. Though the Nazi concentration camps were closed units, physically sealed, the terror in them, as its designers knew, penetrated far beyond the walls. Terror does not often stay within boundaries, and it is rarely provincial in its impact. Now, some writers ironically insist, it is a truly international social process, and it has helped to universalize an emotional climate—an international atmosphere dominated by fright.

Albert Camus suggested that our twentieth century is the century of fear. He wrote:

who can deny that we live in a state of terror? . . .
To emerge from this terror, we must be able to reflect and to act accordingly. But an atmosphere of terror hardly encourages reflection. I believe, however, that instead of simply blaming everything on this fear, we should consider it as one of the basic factors in the situation, and try to do something about it. No task is more important. . . . And if an atmosphere of fear does not encourage accurate thinking, then [one] must first of all come to terms with fear.[5]

An atmosphere is lived in long before anyone thinks of investigating it, but when it becomes disturbing enough to be noticed and defined as a hazard to normal life, rational beings are moved to bring it under analysis and reflection. Organized terror is only one part of the turbid mixture of fear, but to come to terms with fear we may begin by trying to understand the ingredients. The human hope of coming to terms with fear by analysis and reflection and the scientific task of formulating a general theory of terror both urge the inquirer over a broad field of experience, where it may be possible to uncover the hidden mechanisms of terror and, for practical as well as theoretical reasons, learn not only its causes and functions, but also the secrets of its termination.

CHAPTER II

THE USES

OF VIOLENCE

And in some cases if things which naturally have a
quality lose it because they have suffered violence, we say that
they are deprived.

—Aristotle, *The Metaphysics*.

SOME HISTORICAL PERIODS have the reputation of being filled
with violence. Jan Huizinga, in his study of the late Middle
Ages, meditated on the violent tenor of life then, its oscillation
between cruelty and tenderness, and the public joy in torture
and executions.[1] From the first age of feudal society, after the
Frankish Roman Empire broke up, Europe had experienced
widespread disorder, but violence was more than a reaction to
political disintegration. It was deeply rooted, Marc Bloch told
us, in the social structure and the mentality of the time. Violence was even an element in manners, and medieval men, emotionally insensitive to the spectacle of pain and having small
regard for human life, "were very prone to make it a point of
honour to display their physical strength in an almost animal
way." [2] Violence had become a class privilege for the nobility,
which reserved to itself the right of private vengeance and "as a
mark of honour any form of recourse to arms. . . ." [3]

Violence, then, is not exclusively an instrument of control; it
can also be a privilege of social rank. For example, among the
Anuak people of East Africa, who had no king or chiefs, nobles
claimed the privilege of attacking commoners who offended
them.[4] Moreover, some rulers, such as the kabaka of Buganda

and the Zulu king, in the nineteenth century, used violence as a means of control but *also* performed violent deeds as conspicuous symbols and privileges of awful majesty.[5] Thorstein Veblen observed:

> Epithets and titles used in addressing chieftains, and in the propitiation of kings and gods, very commonly impute a propensity for overbearing violence and an irresistible devastating force to the person who is to be propitiated. . . . Under this common-sense barbarian appreciation of worth or honor, the taking of life—the killing of formidable competitors, whether brute or human—is honorable in the highest degree. And this high office of slaughter, as an expression of the slayer's prepotence, casts a glamor of worth over every act of slaughter and over all the tools and accessories of the act.[6]

Since I am dealing with violence as an instrument of power, I shall exclude violence that occurs as a mark of status or honor, or for other reasons, such as a disposition to behave in a cruel or intemperate manner. Similarly, I shall exclude economic terrorism, ranging from armed robbery to systematic extortion, and the various methods by which violence may be used for economic gain.

When violence is employed in the service of power, the limit of force is the destruction of the thing that is forced. As Paul Tillich put it, "In this sense there is an ultimate limit to any application of force. That thing which is forced must preserve its identity. Otherwise it is not forced but destroyed."[7] A violent event, however, may be simply an act of destruction—for vengeance or other reasons, or for no apparent reason. In this case, violence is not an instrument of power, for the violent act is complete and the object destroyed.

We must distinguish, therefore, between the process of violence and an act of destruction which is complete and not an instrument of anything else. The former is incomplete, for it is directed to an end beyond itself—in the cases under discussion, the proximate aim is to instil terror; the ultimate end is control.

Thus, in civil terror we are dealing with two processes, one dependent on the other: the process of violence in the service of terror, and the process of terror in the service of power. Military terror is different. When terrorism is used in a war of extermination, the aim is to paralyze the enemy, diminish his resistance, and reduce his ability to fight, with the ultimate purpose of destroying him. In this case, we see the process of violence in the service of terror, and ultimately, terror in the service of violence. The great Zulu despot, Shaka, discussed in later chapters, is an example of one who perfected both civil and military terrorism.

As long as terror is directed toward an end beyond itself, namely, control, it has a limit and remains a process. Under certain conditions, terror becomes unlimited and therefore is no longer a process but an end in itself.

Violence may occur without terror, but not terror without violence. In examining violence designed to control, we should distinguish the process of terror from the use of violence to change conditions. In the case of terror, the regime does not eliminate the group that falls in the zone of terror, but controls it through violence and fear. A segment of the group may be destroyed to instil terror in the rest, but the group is not wiped out. In the case of violence to change conditions, the persons in the zone of violence are destroyed as a group, making a structural change in the society. The latter is an irreversible change, for the selective depletion of the population renders the society that emerges after the violence has ceased structurally different from the society that preceded it. In contrast, the process of terror is reversible, in this special sense, for by itself it does not alter the structural characteristics of the society. The very fact that the fundamental conditions remain unchanged makes the system of terror necessary in the minds of the directors. The following examples will illustrate the difference between the two types.

First, consider a violent process that changes the conditions of control by liquidating a group of persons. Take the hypothetical case of a tyranny opposed by a nobility, and imagine that instead of meeting their resistance by concessions or by terror, the regime decides to eliminate the intransigent nobles. When the dust settles, they are dead or have fled, the society is now structurally different, and the regime controls without the previous opposition.

In the second case, imagine that the resisters are food producers who cannot be eliminated as a class because they are indispensable. If violence is used against them, it is to keep them in control, and when it ceases, the society remains structurally unchanged.

The two situations are quite different, yet the second type in time may be transformed into the first. Imagine that a process of violence is initiated against a nobility with the intention not of destroying it but of keeping it in control. If the terror continues over a long period of time and a significant number of nobles perish as victims, the nobility is gradually depleted as a class. Their ranks may grow empty, or the places may be filled by the regime with new personnel whose political attitudes are different from those of the liquidated nobles. In this case, then, the violence has two consequences: control by terror as well as gradual change of conditions.

Several combinations are possible. The extinction of group A, for example, may be used as the process of violence that creates the terror that controls group B.

Violence and Resistance

Violence, then, may be used to destroy, to control, or to punish. Control and punishment are forms of power, whereas destruction is not, unless it is used indirectly to control or to punish. The use of violence in a system of power, we shall see, is significantly related to the presence or absence of resistance. In conditions of minimal resistance, unless other cultural or psychic factors create a disposition to act in a violent manner, men in authority tend to avoid destructive methods of power. Resistance or the expectation of resistance, on the other hand, increases the probability of violence.

This relationship may be seen not only in human power systems but also in several of those animal societies that are organized in hierarchical patterns of dominance. In these hierarchies, the behavior of effectively dominant animals meets no resistance, and the mutual relations among the members of the group are remarkably free of violence. When the dominant animal loses control—and the loss may be heralded by very subtle signals—it meets increasing resistance, begins to act in a violent manner, and meets violence in return. Generalized fighting breaks out, and the group is disrupted. A human power system, highly dependent on symbolic processes and rational goals, is different from an animal social hierarchy, which is shaped primarily by innate patterns, especially by the relative strengths of attack and flight drives. Yet, animal dominance hierarchies, providing an opportunity to examine formal relations between control, resistance, and violence, are interesting enough to draw close but cautious attention.

Reason and symbolic processes make possible in human power systems a wider range of techniques for resisting power and for eliminating resistance than the stereotyped patterns of subhuman dominance hierarchies. However, acts of resistance and measures to cope with resistance are simply acts of counterpower. The forms are not necessarily violent: they may employ techniques of persuasion and other kinds of influence.

An act of force initiates changes in the behavior of respondents against their will or inclination. The forms of resistance are either ways in which the respondents attempt to keep these undesired changes from taking place, or methods of retaliating in some other field of action. I shall mention a few kinds of resistance, using the example of an established power relation between a "superior" and "subordinates."

(1) The subordinates may try to persuade the superior to withdraw the action he initiated. (2) They may simply refuse

to obey, risking punishment. (3) They may obey with overt reluctance, creating obstructions that are expensive to the superior. (4) They may try to deter him by threatening punishment. (5) They may punish him by withholding advantages he ordinarily receives (e.g. taxes). (6) They may use violence against the agents who enforce his decision. (7) They may attack the superior himself. (8) By intrigue or some other means they may initiate controls over his conduct in some other field of action. (9) They may initiate actions to change the conditions that moved the superior to take action in the first place.

Resistance to power, then, takes the form of punishment and countercontrol, but a power relation is a dynamic interaction in which at least some control may be exercised by all parties. Of course, each does not control the others to the same degree, nor do they control the same thing. Simmel recognized that domination is a form of interaction in which the superior generally acts so as to make the subordinate react to him, but in a manner chosen by the superior.[8] Power relations vary in the degree to which the subordinate's act is actually controlled by the superior. The institutional forms through which men control and organize the energies of other men permit greater or lesser degrees of autonomy and freedom, and the degree of spontaneity and independence that subordinates bring to the total relation conditions whether they are limited in their reciprocal action or whether they are able to resist the superior's will. An established power system is a web of resistances as well as a circuit of controls, and innovators aflame with the *libido dominandi* often take drastic measures to cut through the web.

Even situations of absolute power often contain certain limits imposed by the claims of subordinates. Simmel observed:

If the absolute despot accompanies his orders by the threat of punishment or the promise of reward, this implies that he himself wishes to be bound by the decrees he issues. The subordinate is expected to have the right to request something of him; and by establishing the punishment, no matter how horrible, the despot commits himself not to impose a more severe one. . . .

[T]he *significance* of the relation is that, although the superordinate wholly determines the subordinate, the subordinate nevertheless is assured of a claim on which he can insist or which he can waive.[9]

Confrontation, Simmel contended, implies interaction, and, in principle, interaction always contains some limitation on each party to the process, although there are exceptions to this rule. History is full of techniques introduced by rulers to manage the conditions of confrontation so as to reduce the potential for reciprocal control by subordinates. One way is to increase the political distance between ruler and subjects: by deifying the ruler or finding other ways to make him unapproachable, or by any method of political mystification drawn from that ancient bag of tricks known as the *arcana imperii*. One of the tasks of the present inquiry is to discover the conditions in which these more subtle methods of dealing with resistance are abandoned for the processes of violence and terror.

Resistance may be countered by persuasion; by rewards and "buying off" leaders of the opposition; by negotiation, bargaining, and exchanging advantages; and by forms of coercion short of violence. Acts that are not violent but which control through fear may be distinguished from the process of terror and defined as "intimidation." This technique includes economic and social deprivation, and may be described as follows:

Intimidation as a means of achieving desired ends is a feature of behavior where power or authority is based primarily and essentially on force. . . . It calls for a technique calculated to evoke fear in the party which is expected to do or not to do certain things, without, however, resorting to direct violence, which would bring intimidation into conflict with established authority and law.[10]

In certain institutions that set the acceptability of resistance near zero, the men in control, frequently resorting to violence, stood at the edge of the terror process. Slavery was such an institution. Theodor Mommsen in his great history of Rome remarked that "slavery is not possible without a reign of terror." [11] Stanley Elkins persuasively compares some of the techniques of North American slavery with those of the Nazi concentration camp. [12] In the antebellum American South, Kenneth Stampp shows, slavemasters developed an elaborate power system that depended on complex techniques to minimize resistance. [13] Although most masters seemed to prefer persuasion and reward to punishment, violence was regarded as a necessary means of control and punishment.

> Without the power to punish, which the state conferred upon the master, bondage could not have existed. By comparison, all other techniques of control were of secondary importance. . . . But the whip was the most common instrument of punishment—indeed, it was the emblem of the master's authority. [14]

The violence of punishment, however, easily shifted over to the violence of terrorism, for the process was used not only to punish acts of disobedience and resistance but also to sap the potential for disobedience in advance and to break the power to resist. Brutality was common on large plantations, and the typical overseer preferred physical force to incentives as a method of governing slaves. "Some overseers, upon assuming control, thought it wise to whip every hand on the plantation to let them know who was in command." Slaves had to be flogged, it was sometimes maintained, until they manifested "submission and penitence." The lash was often used to "break in" young slaves and to "break the spirit" of insubordinate older ones. [15]

Violent treatment is encouraged by ways of thinking that dehumanize classes of persons or reduce them to objects. Resistance is not acceptable from an instrument. A tool that refuses to carry out the purposes of its owner is defective, and it is either discarded or hammered into shape. The technical concept of the slave classifies him as a tool—an idea clearly expressed in the theory of slavery found in ancient treatises on agriculture. The often quoted Varro, for example, classified implements of cultivation in three categories: (1) *genus vocale,* those having speech; (2) *genus semi-vocale,* those having voices that were not articulate; (3) *genus mutum,* the silent ones. The first category included the slaves; the second, the oxen; and the third, the wagons.[16] If the technical conception of the slave as an instrument of production prevails over other moral or humane notions, then economic factors determine his conservation or destruction.

Hannah Arendt points out the consequences when the notions drawn from areas of productivity invade the understanding of control and authority:

> an element of violence is inevitably inherent in all activities of making, fabricating, and producing, that is, in all activities by which men confront nature directly, as distinguished from those activities, like action and speech, which are primarily directed toward human beings. The building of the human artifice always involves some violence done to nature—we must kill a tree in order to have lumber, and we must violate this material in order to build a table.[17]

Therefore, when the idea of control is confused with notions of fabricating and building, people may be viewed not only as instruments but also as materials to be shaped according to design. From this viewpoint resistance may be interpreted as the unyielding property of a stubborn material.

From the point of view of one who uses violence to cope with it, resistance may be perceived as the premeditated activity of determined political opposition, or, on the other hand, it may appear as the irrational behavior of people too stupid, too backward, too barbarous, or too fractious to respond to methods of control more subtle than violence. For analytical purposes, resistance should be understood objectively as an organized response to a force that provokes it, and also subjectively, according to the meanings given to it by both parties to the conflict.

Violence and War

In the present age, governments have to deal with protest campaigns, mass demonstrations, and organized civil disobedience. These movements have been styled by the sociologist Clarence Marsh Case as forms of "nonviolent coercion." They seek to bring changes against the will of the powerholders, but with acts that are not destructive.[18] Although the participants may renounce coercion as well as violence, and though they may intend their efforts as a pure attempt at persuasion, such campaigns are nevertheless interpreted as organized acts of force opposing official actions. The resisters, of course, interpret the official actions they are opposing as initial acts of force.

Because a resisting group is generally weaker than the group that exercises power, and because in a modern power system the former group does not usually have effective instruments of violence, reactions to resistance are more frequently violent than acts of resistance. Discussing African resistance movements, Leo Kuper observes:

> Passive resistance and Mau Mau are very different forms of resistance adopted, in recent years, by the indigenous peoples of Africa against the domination of white settler groups. The response of the dominant group in Kenya to the primitive violence of Mau Mau is the counterviolence of modern warfare, while in South Africa the white rulers have responded to passive resistance, not directly by violence, but by the establishment of the necessary machinery for violent action.[19]

If organized resistance uses destructive techniques employing instruments of violence and those techniques are met with similar violent actions, then the confrontation may be defined as warfare; if it takes place within a single political community, then it is civil war.

War, according to the classic formulation by Clausewitz, is a duel on an extensive scale between armed combatants, each striving by physical violence to compel the other to submit to his will and each aiming to overthrow the adversary and to make him incapable of further resistance.

> War, therefore, is an act of violence to compel the enemy to fulfill our will.
> Violence, to encounter violence, equips itself with the inventions of art and science. . . . Violence, i.e., physical violence . . . is therefore the means; imposing our will on the enemy, the end.[20]

War is a political instrument, Clausewitz continued, carrying out political transactions by violent means, and it is an act of violence practiced without limits.[21] The aim of all action in war is to disarm the enemy and remove his ability to resist, and victory in battle consists in nothing less than the physical and moral destruction of the enemy's armed forces.[22] War resembles the process of terror in many ways, but Clausewitz provides the clue for distinguishing the two. "War," he writes, "is not the action of a living force on a lifeless mass, but . . . always the shock of two living forces colliding. . . ."[23]

VIOLENCE AND PUNISHMENT

Military terrorism, as a technique of warfare, is within Clausewitz's conception, but civil terror, as previously defined, is frequently practiced against unarmed, noncombatant populations by their own leaders. If the directors of the terror are interested in self-justification, the practice may take place under the guise of legal punishment and the enforcement of law.

This raises the question of when violence inflicted by men in authority is legal punishment and when it is not. As I have indicated, in the institution of slavery, punishment easily changes to terrorism. Since violent punishments do evoke fear and are often justified by their putative deterrent value, it is

Is terror possible or the
without violence
threat of. ?

sometimes hard to distinguish the administration of punishment from the process of terror. It is more difficult when political leaders use the violence involved in the act of punishment to extend their political control. In such cases, the violence *seems* to serve the separate processes of punishment and terror simultaneously.

When a violent process is socially prescribed and defined as a legitimate means of control or punishment, according to practices familiar to us, the destructive harm is measured and the limits made clear. Social definition as an authorized method often extracts it from the category of violence—at least from the standpoint of the society—and places it in the same domain with other socially approved coercive techniques.

Thus, violence is generally understood as unmeasured or exaggerated harm to individuals, either not socially prescribed at all or else beyond established limits. It is often socially defined to include processes that originate as authorized, measured force but that go beyond the prescribed conditions and limits. For example, in systems such as ours, a police officer may be authorized to exercise physical restraint in making an arrest, but he will be said to act in a violent manner if, without acceptable reasons, he attacks and injures a fugitive. In some cases, however, police brutality may be officially condemned as violence, yet socially expected and used unofficially as a means of control. In this study, any kind of destructive harm will be taken as violence, but specified as legitimate or illegitimate by social definition. Terrorism is distinguished by the conditions, the structure, and the effects of the violent process.

In the oldest forms of punishment, it has been suggested in some historical studies, the violent destruction of the offender serves the purpose of removing a source of danger from the community. In the earliest stages of primitive society, punishment is entirely defensive, and the violence is not intended to produce suffering or fear.[24] Deterrence, the argument continues, was introduced in a later stage by kings and despots, who tended to deal with crimes as offenses to the royal office:

The ruler is not slow to discover that one of the most effective means of safeguarding his interests is to strike terror into his subjects, and the principle of determent manifests itself in those horrible mutilations and refined cruelties characteristic of the penal system of absolutism.[25]

It is possible, however, to sort out civil punishment from civil terror; Hobbes, who wrought with great care the deterrence rationale of punishment, also provided the key to the distinction. In *Leviathan,* describing the characteristics of punishment, Hobbes distinguished it from an act of hostility. Punishment applies only to persons already in a condition of political obedience to the authority that inflicts it. Against enemies, including those who by rebellion renounce their status as subjects, any degree of violence is permitted:

> Harm inflicted upon one that is a declared enemy, falls not under the name of punishment: because seeing they were either never subject to the law, and therefore cannot transgress it; or having been subject to it, and professing to be no longer so, by consequence deny they can transgress it, all the harms that can be done them, must be taken as acts of hostility. But in declared hostility, all infliction of evil is lawful.[26]

Punishment, in contrast to an act of hostility, has certain limitations and defining characteristics, and its purpose is to strengthen the disposition to obey.

> A punishment, is an evil inflicted by public authority, on him that hath done, or omitted that which is judged by the same authority to be a transgression of the law; to the end that the will of men may thereby the better be disposed to obedience.[27]

Hobbes proceeded to list a number of conditions that extract inflicted evils from the class of punishments and give them the character of hostile acts. Among these conditions, penalties that are inflicted without previous public judicial process, or for an act that took place before there was a law to forbid it, or in excess of the penalties prescribed and published in the law, lose the character of punishments. Likewise, any evil inflicted without the intention or the possibility of disposing the offender, or by his example, other men, to obey the laws is not punishment but an act of hostility, "because without such an end, no hurt done is contained under that name." [28]

Punishment defined sociologically, I would maintain, is a penalty imposed for the transgression of a recognized norm established either by coercion or consent in the course of a social relationship. The features that distinguish violent legal punishment from other kinds of violence, including the terror process, are the fundamental conditions of legality. For violence to qualify as legal punishment, it must be imposed by duly constituted public authority for an act within its jurisdiction that is publicly judged to violate a legal rule promulgated before the act took place. In addition, the penalty must not exceed that stated in the law, and, according to Hobbes and to the utilitarians who follow him, at least, it must be inflicted with the intention or the reasonable probability that it will strengthen the disposition to obey the laws. These conditions of legality are limits to violence, and if they are indeed observed, no matter how harsh the punishment—although, certainly, severe punishment may be condemned on other grounds—it is excluded from the category of terrorism. Violence, in these conditions, would follow deviation from the rule, and no matter how destructive punishment might be, the individual who chooses to conform remains reasonably secure from official harm. In contrast, the terror process begins with violence itself, which is followed by intense fear and irrational, reactive behavior patterns.

In contrast to terrorism, deterrence implies the anticipation of a probable evil and the ability to avoid it. The fear of punishment is different from the fear generated in the terror process. There is a great deal of difference between the emotional state of a man who can calculate, "I fear that if I take this course of action, it will lead to violent punishment," and the turbulent, irrational fear, scarcely permitting thought, stirred up in the wake of unpredictable violence.

The conditions of legality imply that there must be a way of being innocent. If there is no path left open to avoid transgression, or if people are bound to be charged falsely with offenses they did not commit, then it is not possible to be innocent. In the terror process, no one can be secure, for the category of transgression is, in reality, abolished. Anyone may be a victim, no matter what action he chooses. Innocence is irrelevant.

SYSTEMS OF VIOLENCE

Terrorism differs from war and punishment in the way violence is used. The violent process may be a means of destruction, an instrument of punishment, or a method of control, and it may shift from war to terrorism, to punishment, and back. The mere presence of violence is not as significant as the degree of violence, the occasions for its official use, and its place in the temporal sequence of the process used in the service of power.

One could construct a typology of power systems based on the use of violence. At one pole are systems that use violence as a last resort; at the other, those that use it as a first measure. Somewhere between them we would place the Draconian systems, which punish the smallest infractions with the severest violence, yet do not extend the use of violence beyond punishment. Were we to fill out this skeleton with the flesh of historical experience, we could identify at one pole the systems blessed with concord, in which power is supported by minimal force, and in which violence is truly an *ultima ratio*. At the other extreme, we should find the terror systems, in which violence is a *prima ratio potestatis*.

The practice in authoritarian states of punishing definite acts of resistance and breaking up organizations suspected of sedition may be compared to a surgical procedure. In contrast, the process of terror, in its ideal form, may be compared to a chemical procedure. Independent social clusters and unauthorized political associations tend to dissolve in the medium of extreme fear. More than that, however, an emotional environment is created in which certain kinds of interaction cannot take place. The first efforts from which organized opposition might emerge are simply not made. The steps that might lead to confrontation with the agents of violence are never taken. Unless they are insulated in some unusual manner from the corrosive process, the people in such an environment are deprived, we shall see, of a capacity that naturally belongs to the members of other systems—the power of resistance.

No historical system, judging from the results, has managed to eliminate resistance completely. In the concentration camps, the Nazis came closest to perfecting the system of terror in many respects; still, the camps fell short of their intentions. No system of terror, despite its enormous horror and devastation, has proved to be entirely effective. Likewise, it should go without saying, no empirical system is congruent with the ideal type. But before any investigation turns to the historical variations with their unique characteristics and particular differences, it is important to grasp the ideal type. Then, to comprehend protean terror in its full complexity requires a broad, unrestricted, comparative approach, which means getting some distance from immediate historical experience and viewing the process at work in other times and in other cultures. Distance, objectivity, and new perspectives will contribute to a better understanding of the terror process, which has become so significant in the present age.

CHAPTER III

VIOLENCE

AND

AUTHORITY

The notion of force is far from simple, and yet
in order to state the problems of society it
is the first that has to be made clear.

—Simone Weil, "Reflections on the Causes
of Liberty and Social Oppression."

HAVING NOTED that Burke in one of his speeches on the American Revolution had exclaimed, "For heaven's sake, satisfy *somebody*," Whitehead declared that "governments are best classified by considering who are the 'somebodies' they are in fact endeavouring to satisfy." The dissatisfaction of a dominant class, Whitehead reflected, is an immediate source of danger.[1] Nevertheless, Whitehead did not observe that some governments cope with this danger in destructive ways, and the adviser to a terroristic despot, choosing an alternative just as logical as Burke's, might have exclaimed, "For the devil's sake, kill somebody."

According to the conventions of political thought since Plato and Aristotle, the "somebodies" whom governments were designed to satisfy have enjoyed the center of attention. The quest for information about power has been a locative pursuit, asking who exercises it and in whose interest, yielding—through the ages—typologies of rulers, a theory of the ruling class, or the description of a power elite. Few inquirers have sought out the "somebodies" who were being destroyed.

At the same time, it has always been assumed that a government bent on satisfying somebody would also be expected to preserve the same from harm, and according to our way of thinking it is inconceivable that a ruler might exercise violence against the very "somebodies" he was trying to satisfy. Therefore, our conventions of political thought have shut out the realities of terroristic systems, for our imaginations cannot grasp the paradox of a regime of terror—a government that destroys part of the community in order to control the rest. To make the matter even less intelligible, the part being destroyed need not have a social identity different from the somebodies to be satisfied.

We think of proper governments, moreover, as instruments to protect the community against violence, and although history is generous with examples to the contrary, we refuse to imagine a durable government, based on consent, that uses continual violence as a regular technique—not a last resort—on its own people. We identify order with consent, but we also equate violence with the absence of order. Therefore, from the self-evident half-truth that order is based on consent, we move confidently to the half-false converse that violent governments are not based on consent.

The case studies in this book challenge prevailing assumptions about the relation between violence and authority because they are systems of terror that were supported by authority, consent, and tradition. They are unintelligible to the conventional political mind and demonstrate the need for a new theoretical approach. Throughout the literature of social and political theory, writers of very different persuasions have held the common idea that violence sits on the grave of consent.

According to one perspective, violence is absent from political systems that function properly, and its presence indicates a breakdown—or to put it another way, the failure of power. Yet even in the point of view associated with *Realpolitik*, writers who claim that violence remains at the heart of any political system also assert that *raw* violence is an imperfect technique of control. The most effective rulers, they believe, conceal it with gentler skills, substituting persuasion for force, loosing violence only when it is not possible to get voluntary obedience. Both points of view tend to agree that obedience, whether it is based on reason or on mythical formulas, grows more vigorous as violence grows less visible. But neither position can furnish concepts to explain the features of a political community in which a ruler who secures enthusiastic obedience also exercises unremitting violence.

One might try to dispose of the apparent contradiction in a system of violent authority by calling it irrational and by postulating the madness of the rulers, but that attempt begs the question of why the system supports allegedly mad rulers. Or one might attack the contradiction, either by ignoring the violence or by denying the consent. Thus, on the one hand, one could argue that the violent system is integrated in the same manner as any other state, that the ruler is primarily an agent of redistribution and co-ordination, that the system holds together because it fulfills basic needs, and that the presence of violence is dramatic but not essential. On the other hand, to deny the consent, one could describe the system as a regime of naked force, devoid of principle, stripped of myth and rationale, and unadorned by the trappings of legitimacy. Yet, none of these approaches solves the contradiction, for they depend on stereotypes that do not fit the contours of reality.

Associated with the idea that violence and consent necessarily exclude each other, one finds the belief that regimes governed by violence are necessarily and inherently unstable. Men can do anything with bayonets—or spears—except sit on them, it is said, and violent rule is bound to change to another, more durable form. Expressing this way of thinking, Bertrand Russell identified "naked power" with military violence and with "the power of the butcher over the sheep" when he wrote:

As the beliefs and habits which have upheld traditional power decay, it gradually gives way either to power based on some new belief, or to "naked power," i.e., to the kind that involves no acquiescence on the part of the subject. . . . Periods of naked power are usually brief.[2]

Nevertheless, even if many—perhaps most—violent systems are unstable, our evidence shows that some may be stabilized by violence for decades and even for centuries. However, it would be foolish to go so far as to argue that violent systems are not vulnerable to stress or that they are more stable than other kinds.

Furthermore, if "naked force" is violent, it is not true that all violent systems are "naked," for some of them are covered by the full panoply of legitimacy. In one type, we shall see a solitary ruler whose position is legitimate exercising absolute power through organized fear produced by systematic violence against his own people. Many of the ordinary methods of rule are retained in this type of state, and in some respects the despots act like kings, but looking at the system as a whole, the pattern of violence and the behavior it causes eclipse the ordinary institutions, and terror distinguishes the regime from ordinary kingdoms. By comparing it with centralized kingdoms in which terror is absent, we can make some conclusions about the functions of terror in despotic systems.

To search for pattern and rationale in terrorism, it is important to clear away misconceptions about the conditions of stability as well as to dismantle stereotypes of the relation between violence and authority. For clarification, I shall use this chapter to explore familiar concepts such as "power," "force," and "authority." The last term, it is generally agreed, means power that is based on consent. There is less agreement about the precise meaning of "power," and sharp difference of opinion about how violence fits—or does not fit—in a system of power. Since I have already identified "violence" as the principal element in the terror process, the term will be distinguished from "force" and "coercion," for it is important to understand how terrorism differs from the ordinary political practice of coercion. But before asking how violence is related to power, probing the concept of power will help to clear the way.

THE CONCEPT OF POWER

Power may be experienced as inspiring, wholesome, tolerable, or oppressive, depending on the circumstances. It may release creative energy, heightening vitality;[3] it may destroy motivation, generating a pall of depression; or it may stimulate conflict and rebellion. It may induce a sense of freedom or a sense of tyranny. Ortega has shown that sometimes the state may be shaped by the community's vital preferences and life within it felt as exhilarating freedom, whereas at other times the whole weight of regulative institutions is oppressive and life is converted into "spiritless adaptation of each individual existence to the iron mold of the state."[4] From an historical point of view, the way in which power is experienced is a critical matter, for it determines the motivations of people to keep or to change the system in which they live.

To have a conception broad enough to cover all types, elementary and complex, I would define a *power system* as a pattern of actions, performed by specific persons, which controls a range of behavior in a specific group and deals with instances of behavior, within a given range, out of their control. This generic definition is formal and does not specify methods of regulation or the way in which power is experienced. Before expanding this definition to take up the problems of violence and authority, I shall try to clarify the meaning of activities such as initiative, control, punishment, and co-ordination, which are the essential transactions in a system of power.

Initiative. The ancient Greeks rarely fail us when we turn to them in a receptive but cautious spirit for conceptual clarity, and their treatment of the abstraction "power" and terms related to it is relevant and suggestive. In Greek, a root contained in several words associated with political power has two meanings. The verb *archein* means both "to rule" and "to start"; the noun *arché* means both "sovereignty" and "beginning." J. L. Myres, in his analysis of Greek political ideas, suggests:

> It is now clear that in compounds the prefix *arkhé* (as in our words "architect" and "archbishop") describes not merely the first or chief man of a company or organisation, but the initiatory function of him who "starts" the others to work, and originates the design which they are to complete. And this appeal to Greek practical life confirms the view that what is essential in the notion of *arkhé* is just this initiatory "push" or "drive" with which the gifted man imposes his will-and-pleasure on the rest.[5]

If we follow Myres, we may infer that where Herodotus reports the wealthy noble, Otanes, to have said he had no wish "*archein kai archesthai*," as well as where Aristotle writes that the good citizen must have the knowledge and the ability "*archesthai kai archein*," the words mean "to start and be started" as well as "to rule and be ruled." [6] In Aristotle's definition of terms in *The Metaphysics*, one of the six meanings of "beginning," following the Ross translation, is the group or individual "at whose will that which is moved is moved and that which changes changes, e.g. the magistracies in cities, and oligarchies and monarchies and tyrannies, are called *archai*. . . ." [7]

"To have power" covers a broader range of activity than *archein*, which means "to govern" or "to rule," but the concepts have two factors in common; namely, initiative and causation. Defining *dynamis*, Aristotle says, "the beginning of a change or movement is called a power. . . ." [8] In social interactions, we may say that if the source of an action performed by an individual is to be found in a prior act of another individual, then the latter has power over the former with respect to that act. By "source" we also mean "cause" in the sense that it must be the sufficient condition for the action; if the prior act does happen to occur, then the subsequent action will take place also. When action is "caused" in this way, then we can speak of one individual or group "controlling" the action of another. As I shall explain, however, there is more to power than "control," for power processes frequently deal with actions that are out of control. If an individual or group we shall name "P" intends to cause a respondent designated "R" to perform an action "X," and R does not perform X, then if P proceeds to change R in some way—for example, to penalize or to "reform" R—because of the failure to perform X, this procedure is a form of power, since with respect to X, P is the source of changes in R.[9]

Aristotle states, moreover, that the tendency to resist change is also a kind of power,[10] and the observation that resistance, or the ability to withstand attempts at control, is a form of counterpower, is a central idea in the present investigation.

One must bear in mind the cases that would be excluded from the conception of power; for example, instances in which an individual acts on his own, without the act being initiated by some other specific person or group. To avoid confusion, power should be distinguished from interactions similar to it, especially the process that is usually called "social control" in the more narrow sense. (I am excluding altogether the very general sense in which social control means regulated behavior of any kind.) In the course of socialization, the inclinations and dispositions of individuals are shaped in ways that cause them to want to do the things that are expected of them—that is, to act in an institutionalized manner. This social conditioning yields acts that stem from the individual's own initiative. In cases of deviant behavior, excluding illegal acts, the right to levy social sanctions such as criticism or ridicule is usually exercised by an indeterminate number of persons within a given range of social relationships. What differentiates this kind of social control from power is that first, conventional behavior comes from the individual's own initiative and, second, deviant behavior is not punished by specified persons charged with the task of enforcing the socially prescribed conduct. In contrast, a case of conformist behavior, caused by the demand for a conventional act by a specific person, is indeed an instance of power. So also is a case of legal punishment carried out by a specific staff.

This is not to deny that social control and socialization are related to power as auxiliary forces. Individuals are conditioned to obedience in most societies, with lesser or greater degrees of rigor, so that in ordinary circumstances when acts of power do come their way, men are disposed to obey them. If these acts come under the aegis of legitimate authority, obedience is usually voluntary and resistance minimal. As MacIver put it, "Men obey because they are social beings—or, if you prefer it, because they are socialized beings." [11]

Control, Punishment, and Rehabilitation. The concept of power is often confined to acts of control, or to "the production of intended effects," as Russell defines it.[12] The notion of an intended effect is too limited, and the idea of power should not be restricted to the action of control. When controls are exercised and penalties imposed by individuals who did not think of doing so in the first place, or by those who did not foresee the consequences of their actions, they are unintended acts of power. Moreover, Felix Oppenheim has shown that control is a domain too narrow to be identified with power, and he extends the latter to mean the ability to influence, to restrain, or to punish. To have power, in this sense, means "to be able to subject others to one's control or to limit their freedom." [13] If a person is ordered to perform a specific act and refuses, his behavior is *not controlled* with respect to that act, for the commander did not cause the person to perform the act. Yet, if the commander of the act punishes the person for not performing it, he still has power over him. One has power over another with respect to a particular act if he can control (cause) the act or make it punishable to perform or to withhold it.[14] Penalizing is the major form of exercising punishment, and penalties—involving pain, privation, or some other kind of unpleasantness—are experiences that are disliked and avoided because they are considered harmful, or because of some other obvious reason. I would go beyond Oppenheim's scheme to include, along with penalties, procedures of "reform," "treatment," and "rehabilitation." These, too, may be imposed by persons in power as responses to acts they are unable to control. In some cases, these practices are disguised forms of penalty. In others, they may help an individual rather than harm him—add something valuable to his life rather than take something away. Yet, regardless of whether the experience given is baneful or beneficial, it constitutes a form of power if it changes the individual whose conduct was out of control. Oppenheim's taxonomy of power relations is based on the microanalysis of particular transactions, but it may still be used to identify events and processes after we move from the interpersonal to the macrosocial level of inspection, although it has certain limitations on that level.

Control of an individual's act is exercised in two ways: through determining his choice or through managing his body or environment in such a way that he has no choice. The former way is called "influence," and its several methods include "persuasion," which means convincing him in some manner that it is to his advantage to perform (or withhold) the act in question, and "deterrence," which means making him withhold (or perform) the act out of apprehension for the consequences of his refusing to obey.[15] Deterrence bears a superficial resemblance to the terror process because it employs fear; but it is different, as we have noted in the previous chapter. All cases of control—with the consent of the one who is controlled as well as against his will—imply a causal relation, meaning that the act of the controller is the sufficient condition for the response of the individual controlled. "Whenever one actor exercises control over another, he causes him to behave in a certain way."[16]

In addition to "exercising control," there is a category of "having control": potential action which includes "having influence" and "preventing." The former means that a controller stands in such a relation to an individual that if the latter *were* to intend performing a given act, then the controller *would* dissuade, deter, or otherwise influence him not to perform it. "Preventing" means not actually causing an individual to withhold a specific act, but closing the alternative in advance, making it impossible—whether he decides to act or not—for him to perform the act. Oppenheim explains:

> Prevention is usually not mentioned among the various forms of control and power; yet, making it impossible for others to act in a certain way constitutes the most effective device of gaining control over their actual behavior. Would-be controllers usually want to establish control over their respondents in such a way that the latter make no attempt at evading it.[17]

Leadership: Satisfaction and Co-ordination. In elementary systems of power with a solitary head, the leader, chief, or king generally performs a configuration of functions that involves both controlling and punishing: initiating collective action, legitimating, co-ordinating particular acts, integrating the group, adjudicating disputes, and dealing with disruptive behavior. Some characteristics of control and integration in an elementary system of power are revealed in William F. Whyte's classic study of the Cornerville gang:

> The leader is the focal point for the organization of his group. In his absence, the members of the gang are divided into a number of small groups. There is no common activity or general conversation. When the leader appears, the situation changes strikingly. The small units form into one large group. The conversation becomes general, and unified action frequently follows. The leader becomes the central point in the discussion. A follower starts to say something, pauses when he notices that the leader is not listening, and begins again when he has the leader's attention. When the leader leaves the group, unity gives way to the divisions that existed before his appearance.[18]

The leader provides co-ordination and initiative, but reciprocal obligations and the exchange of services, Whyte shows, also bind the group, and built into the leader's role is the expectation that he will be generous.

George Homans has noted in Tacitus' description of the German tribes how the relation between the king and his companions resembles the relation between the informal leader and the small group.[19] If we turn to Tacitus, we find also that the king's power is limited, and "the generals do more by example than by authority." In assembly, the king or chief is heard "more because he has influence to persuade than because he has power to command." The leaders with the largest following are those whose exploits promise the largest advantages.[20] Similarly, in many African traditional systems, it is the practice for large followings to adhere to popular chiefs who rule well, and for poor rulers to lose their people. Even among the Southern Bantu, where loyalty and patience have been cardinal virtues, Eric Walker indicates that if a chief "ate up his men" by confiscating their property and otherwise meting excessive punishments, he might wake up to find his people gone over to a more moderate rival.[21]

Whereas the traditional chief typically holds power in relatively peaceful conditions, the king is a figure more often found in conditions of repetitive, organized warfare. Weber suggests, "The king is everywhere primarily a war lord, and kingship evolves from charismatic heroism."[22] The Israelites, according to the First Book of Samuel, wanted a king to "judge us, and go out before us, and fight our battles." The king typically combines in his person several functions: military, judicial, religious, and civil executive. Since they have little division of function and not much constitutional machinery, primitive monarchies resemble one another, despite cultural differences, in a striking way.[23]

Kingship of the simple kind requires ritual control over the royal ancestors and other spirits, making possible the control of nature by magic; military might, involving a staff of armed

dependants; judicial skill; and the techniques of civil administration. Some ruling houses tended to develop this configuration of abilities as a specialty which they would bring to any
people they could rule by force or by invitation. During the
heroic age of Greece, there is evidence that some Achaean
princely families moved about, thrust out of one area, winning
a throne in another, fleeing vengeance from one people to establish a dynasty in the midst of another. Exercising power
through a typical, elementary configuration of control and punishment techniques, and by the force of their personalities,
kings managed to hold together in a single political unit several
diverse kinship groups.[24] Many primitive people have believed
that the power configuration is the exclusive property of a royal
family, and that a single sacred source of control and punishment is the only alternative to internal fighting and other kinds
of disorder. A. W. Southall in his study of some traditional
political systems in Western Uganda, describes how power—
especially rainmaking and judicial skill—is a quality possessed
exclusively by the lineage of Alur chiefs. Members of the
chiefly family would be invited, bought, and even stolen by
neighboring people who yearned for welfare and order, but
knew of no other method to establish a political head.[25]

FORCE AND VIOLENCE

The heads of states and some chiefdoms have force at their
disposal, commanding staffs that can exercise coercion, and
therefore they do not have to depend exclusively on voluntary
co-operation or influence. Forms of influence, such as persuasion, we have seen, are not instances of force because through
them the controller changes intentions, causing people to
choose to perform acts initiated by him. Deterrence, preven-
tion, restraint, and punishment, when they work against the
will of the respondent, are instances of force. When people do
something according to their own will, we ordinarily say they

are acting voluntarily. When they act against their will, desire, inclination, or intention, we say they are being forced to do something. This is the sense in which the word "force" will be used in the present study—a general term to include any agency that compels someone to do something that he does not want to do. The term "coercion" will be limited to mean any social form of compulsion—usually some kind of institutionalized force. The term "violence" will be restricted to the sense of *destructive harm*—hence, a destructive kind of force.

Aristotle did not distinguish between force and violence, but used the term *bia*, which, like the German word *Gewalt*, may mean both. In his works, *bia* is used in a very general way, standing for the physical concept referring to inanimate nature as well as for "compulsion" in human behavior. As he defines it in the fifth book of *The Metaphysics, bia* is a kind of necessity that hinders and impedes the course of impulse and purpose.[26] The notion of force "as an agent of compulsory motion," Max Jammer shows, is the core of Aristotle's system of mechanics.[27] To force something means to make a thing move against its own "natural internal tendency," and the same conception appears in his ethical theory as well as in his theory of physics. In human conduct, *bia* refers to cases where the cause of action lies in things outside the actor, and when the actor contributes nothing.[28] Jammer explains that in physics, the notion of force evolved through the Peripatetic and Scholastic stage, where it was encumbered by animistic formulations. In this stage, the notion of force was rooted in the everyday experience of push and pull, but it is easy to see how close it was to the sociological notions of conflict and power.[29] Paul Tillich, too, has indicated that the notions of power and force when expressed in words by physicists are anthropomorphic metaphors. "Power is a sociological category and from there it is transferred to nature . . ." he observes.[30] Indeed, when the concept of force in physics is liberated from confusion with the sociological notion, it tends to disappear, and although modern mechanics still tolerates it as a "methodological intermediate," Jammer argues, "the theory of fields would have to banish it even from this humble position." [31]

Another Greek term associated with political power, namely, the word *kratos*, often appears in the same context with *arché*, which was discussed early in this chapter. It signifies "strength" or "might," and just as *arché* is found in terms such as "monarchy" and "oligarchy," *kratos* appears in the suffix of such terms as "aristocracy," "democracy," and "plutocracy" —in each case referring to a system in which the strongest element is, respectively, the best-born, the people, and the wealthy. In other contexts, however, where *arché* suggests initiative and the voluntary side of obedience, *kratos* indicates force and the involuntary side. [32]

The poetic tradition, differing from Aristotle in this respect, offers a provocative distinction between force and violence. As mythological personifications, Kratos (Might) and Bia (Violence) are individuated spirits, but they are both forms of force, and they appear together on the same team, servants of divine power. In Hesiod's genealogy of the gods, Kratos and Bia are the "wonderful children" of Pallas—whose name perhaps means the "brandisher" or "shaker," thereby representing threat—and Styx, who represents horror. Kratos and Bia dwell only in the house of Zeus and go where he directs them. [33] In *Prometheus Bound*, they are the first to appear on stage, dragging Prometheus to his rock. In this play, Aeschylus conveys that Zeus is ruling as a tyrant who has seized power, having overthrown the old order of gods and having displaced the previous king, Kronos. Whenever rule is new, it is harsh, we are told. A tyrant's orders are his own private business, and the new steersman on Olympus controls by rules that have no law to them. [34] Kratos (Might) is the first to speak in the play; he discusses the fate of Prometheus and later rebukes him for rebellion. Bia (Violence) is silent throughout the play. [35] The words of Kratos are consistently tough and bitter, and he is told that he is always ruthless and without pity. [36] Even though both are instruments of force in the service of tyrannical power, the difference between the roles of Might and Violence is instructive. Might uses words and directs itself to reasoning processes. Violence remains mute. It suggests that force in the sense of Might is similar in some way to leadership, since it employs persuasion. But persuasion for what? If leadership induces voluntary action, how can Might exhort involuntary action? If the content of Kratos' speeches is examined, an answer emerges: the persuasive mission of Might is to manage the impression of irresistibility and to diminish resistance. No one can escape obedience and service; only Zeus is free. Resistance is foolish and dangerous. The message of Kratos is that one should learn endurance and resignation in the face of superior strength.[37] Violence, the other instrument of tyrannical power, acts, but has nothing to say.

VIOLENCE AND POWER

Although men universally agree that violence and other kinds of force are perennially associated with the exercise of power, there is anything but agreement over the question of the proper (in both a technical and a moral sense) relation between violent methods and the power system. Among the several ideas of political power in the vast literature on the subject, two prominent conceptions appear, superficially at least, to contradict each other. One, considering violence as the failure of power, would exclude it from the definition; the other, considering violence as the specific property of political associations, makes it central to the definition of political power.

One position considers "authority" as the authentic form of power, based on consent, voluntary obedience, and persuasion, and considers violence as a symptom of the breakdown of authority. The nuclear ideas in this venerable notion may be found far back in the Western tradition: in Homer's and Hesiod's beliefs about the antagonism between violence and right, in the Socratic opposition to Thrasymachus, and in Plato's conviction that persuasion is morally superior to force, to mention only a few sources. This notion of power is held by many writers in the modern period—by Rousseau in *The Social Contract*, for instance—and expressed in the recent literature of social science by writers such as Charles Merriam and R. M. MacIver. Merriam protests that many observers "make the same fundamental error in analysis of the power situation in society, of overstating the role of violence." He argues:

> In most communities the use of force is relatively uncommon in proportion to the number of regulations, and the success of the organization is not measured by the amount of violence in specific cases, but by the extent to which violence is avoided and other substitutes discovered. The monopoly of force, which is so often declared to be the chief characteristic of the political association, is not meant for daily use, but as a last resort when all other measures of persuasion and conciliation have failed.[38]

Similarly, MacIver declares:

> Without authority force is destructive violence, spasmodic, undirected, futile. Authority is responsive to the underlying social structure. The force of government is but an instrument of authority, vindicating the demands of an order that force alone never creates.[39]

Though writers who hold this point of view recognize that violence may be used as an instrument of force by men in authority, they think of it as a last resort and tend to diminish its significance in the organization of controls. They are inclined to deny not only its moral value but also its effectiveness as an instrument.

The contrary idea was expressed recently by C. Wright Mills, who stated succinctly, "All politics is a struggle for power; the ultimate kind of power is violence." [40] Although Mills and others who view power in this fashion may deplore the bitter reality they perceive, a number of writers holding similar points of view have drawn more positive conclusions. The tradition that includes many of the Sophists, Machiavelli, and Hobbes is a familiar one, and writers within it may not only describe the instrumental worth of violence but also defend its moral value, arguing that it contributes to the termination of discord, the maintenance of order, and the safety of the ruler. The "Mirror of Princes" genre, which is to be found in many civilizations, frequently combines advice in the form of rules for cultivating personal virtue with a manual of refined violent techniques. In the literature of India, the combination is seen in the classic *Kautilya Arthasastra,* probably written at the end of the fourth century B.C. shortly after the death of Alexander. It was composed, according to the tradition, by the Brahman who engineered the downfall of the low-caste Nanda dynasty, placed the great Maurya Chandragupta on the throne, and served as his chief minister. In this book, an introductory section on the personal conduct of the saintly king is followed by an elaborate handbook of systematic deception, violence, and internal espionage.[41] Max Weber observes, "In contrast with this document Machiavelli's *Principe* is harmless." [42] It is useful to select this kind of writing in the Indian tradition to illustrate the point of view under discussion because the contrary Indian strain with its idealism and nonviolence is more familiar.

In India's Code of Manu, which tradition places at the dawn of civilization,[43] violence is described as an instrument of punishment, which in turn is declared to be the most important technique of power. The chapter on kingship goes so far as to state that "Punishment is (in reality) the king. . . ." [44] Fear of punishment maintains social order and holds all beings, including the gods, to their duties. Above all, social order depends on the integrity of the caste system, and, indeed, "the king has been created (to be) the protector of the castes (var*n*a) and orders, who, all according to their rank, discharge their several duties." [45] The picture Manu paints of what the world would be like if the ranking system were violated reminds one of the speech Shakespeare gives to Ulysses in Act I, Scene iii of *Troilus and Cressida:*

> O, when degree is shaked,
> Which is the ladder to all high designs,
> The enterprise is sick!

> Take but degree away, untune that string,
> And hark what discord follows!

> Then everything includes itself in power,
> Power into will, will into appetite;
> And appetite, an universal wolf,
> So doubly seconded with will and power,
> Must make perforce an universal prey,
> And last eat up himself.

Punishment, according to Manu, keeps the social hierarchy intact:

> The whole world is kept in order by punishment, for a guiltless man is hard to find; through fear of punishment the whole world yields the enjoyments (which it owes). . . .

> All castes (var*n*a) would be corrupted (by intermixture), all barriers would be broken through, and all men would rage (against each other) in consequence of mistakes with respect to punishment.

> But where Punishment with a black hue and red eyes stalks about, destroying sinners, there the subjects are not disturbed, provided that he who inflicts it discerns well.[46]

Hence the most important function of the king is to correctly measure and administer penalties in the form of violence and deprivations.[47]

Recognizing that violence inspires fear, Manu recommends that the king punish severely those offenders who have committed violent acts. A king must not "let go perpetrators of violence, who cause terror to all creatures," and a king who desires glory shall not, even for a moment, neglect (to punish) the man who commits violence.

He who commits violence must be considered as the worst offender, (more wicked) than a defamer, than a thief, and than he who injures (another) with a staff.

Official violence is indispensable, however, and in the scale of punishments, the degree of violence administered is proportional to the gravity of the offence. Since the purpose of punishment is to maintain the social system with its castes intact, the most violent punishments—penalties *in terrorem*—are to be meted for actions that most seriously threaten the system. For example:

Men who commit adultery with the wives of others, the king shall cause to be marked by punishments which cause terror, and afterwards banish.

For by (adultery) is caused a mixture of the castes (var*n*a) among men; thence (follows) sin, which cuts up even the roots and causes the destruction of everything.[48]

It is clear, then, that according to the ancient text of Manu, the effective and proper use of violence as an instrument of punishment is essential to the exercise of power.

The contrast between the two ideas of violence in the system of power may be further illuminated by turning to the social thought of another political culture, namely, the literature of China during the latter half of the third century B.C., in which orthodox Confucianism is pitted against the so-called Legalist revision of that doctrine. Describing the confrontation, which takes place during the Ch'in empire and continues in the revolutionary period which follows, H. G. Creel observes, "Seldom have two political principles been so clearly opposed and so plainly tested. . . ."[49] The Confucian principle maintains that government must be judged by the degree to which it satisfies the people, considers the state as a co-operative venture, and declares that the proper technique of rule is education and persuasion. The opposite doctrine maintains that it is foolish for the ruler to seek the good will of the people, and that their "wisdom" is useless, for "they are like babies." The Legalists hold that the only way to govern is through force and fear, and in the book named after one of their leading theorists, the *Han Fei Tzu:*

> They set forth, with ruthless clarity and astringent logic, a system of totalitarian despotism. Han Fei Tzŭ recognizes the supremacy of nothing but force, and aims at making the ruler rich and powerful. The people are to be used completely as instruments of the ruler's designs, living or dying as suits his purpose. . . . The ruler need only keep [his ministers] and all of his subjects in such a state of fear that they will dare to do no wrong.[50]

Moreover, they offer a highly refined, repressive system of *shu*, or "methods," and insist that to rule properly, the sovereign must "monopolize the handles which control life and death."[51] After the *Han Fei Tzu*, Creel remarks, "the policies of Machiavelli's *Prince* seem timid and vacillating."

The administration of proper punishment is as crucial a matter to Han Fei-tzu as it is to Manu.[52] However, the purpose of the king, according to Manu, is to maintain the established order; he is not interested in absolute control. The ideal ruler of Han Fei-tzu, on the other hand, is content, the philosopher Fung Yu-lan indicates, with nothing less than celestial omnipotence. The "methods" guarantee strict enforcement, *"and nothing that he encounters resists him."*[53]

The extreme attitudes concerning the proper place of violence in the power system—one minimizing, the other maximizing its importance—are perennial positions, expressed in diverse cultures. They are the opposite poles of a continuum, with several alternative positions between them. Among the ancient Greeks, for example, Solon of Athens apparently believed that good order was based on the concord of classes and that the state was a co-operative venture, but, disagreeing with Hesiod, he did not think that violence and right were irreconcilable opposites. Instead, he thought they were co-ordinate elements in the power system, working together in the cause of good order, and that violent force was sometimes necessary, because it separated warring factions and prevented them from destroying one another and the state.[54]

The extreme positions are based on presuppositions which may be understood as two different social models. The viewpoint that minimizes violence reasons from a model of co-operation,[55] and seeing violence as an indication that co-operative activity has broken down, infers that violence signifies the breakdown of power as well. The other viewpoint begins with a model of social conflict and reasons that in many cases if conflict were absent, then power would be unnecessary. Violence from this perspective may be seen as a decisive form of power responding to conflict.

Coercion, Violence, and Politics. The use of violence as the decisive instrument in conflict and decision has been regarded by some writers as the specific characteristic that distinguishes political structures from other kinds of social organization. Force, physical coercion, and violence, according to this point of view, lie at the heart of politics. As the anthropologist Radcliffe-Brown states in his Preface to *African Political Systems:*

> In studying political organization, we have to deal with the maintenance or establishment of social order, within a territorial framework, by the organized exercise of coercive authority through the use, or the possibility of use, of physical force. In well-organized states, the police and the army are the instruments by which coercion is exercised. Within the state, the social order, whatever it may be, is maintained by the punishment of those who offend against the laws and by the armed suppression of revolt. Externally the state stands ready to use armed force against other states, either to maintain the existing order or to create a new one. . . .

The political organization of a society is that aspect of the total organization which is concerned with the control and regulation of the use of physical force.[56]

In the encyclopedic *Wirtschaft und Gesellschaft*, Max Weber ascribes to the state certain formal characteristics, namely, compulsory membership, territorial jurisdiction, continuous organization, and coercive enforcement, but he clearly singles out the use of violence as a *specific* characteristic giving an organization political identity. In the text of a celebrated address given in Munich in 1918, he makes his ideas on this subject clear.

In that address, he observes that since there is no task that some political association has not taken up, and since there are no special ends that are exclusively political, the state and its historical antecedents can be defined in sociological terms:

only by a specific means peculiar to it as to every political association: that of physical violence. "Every state is founded on force (*Gewalt*)," declared Trotsky duly at Brest-Litovsk. That is in point of fact correct. If there existed only social structures for which violence were unknown as a means, then would the concept "state" be abolished, and then would emerge what is defined as "anarchy" in this special sense of the word. Violence is naturally not the normal or only means of the state —that goes without saying—but indeed a means specific to it. Today the relation between the state and violence is especially intimate. In the past, all kinds of different associations—beginning with the sib—have known physical violence as an altogether normal means. On the contrary, today we have to say that a state is that human community which, within a given territory—"territory" is one of its characteristics—claims for itself (successfully) the legitimate monopoly of physical violence. Specifically, at present the right of physical violence is assigned to all other associations or individuals only to the extent permitted by the state; it is supposed to be the exclusive source of the "right" to use violence.[57]

In this passage, Weber uses the word, *Gewaltsamkeit*—which means "violence"—eight times, modifying the noun four times with the word meaning "physical." Only at one point in the passage, and in a quote from Trotsky, does he use the term *Gewalt*, which may be translated either as "violence" or as "force." *Gewaltsamkeit* is more stark and less equivocal. It may not be identical with the still more restricted meaning, "destructive harm," that I have assigned to "violence" in this study, but certainly, methods of destructive violence are more closely associated with the sense of extreme coercion and forcefulness in *Gewaltsamkeit* than they are with the wider term, *Gewalt*. In my opinion, the English translations of Weber's work lose a point that he is trying to make by his consistent use of *Gewaltsamkeit*. The Gerth translation of the 1918 speech renders it five times as "force" and three times as "violence." [58] In the section on political and hierocratic associations from *Wirtschaft und Gesellschaft*, Henderson and Parsons translate it each time as "force," obscuring Weber's intention, since they render *Zwang*—meaning "coercion"—as "force" too.

In this section, which Weber places immediately after the section in which he defines "power" (*Macht*), hierocratic and political associations are treated as structures of domination and as different species of the same genus, namely, corporate groups with a head, staff, and members, organized according to a coercive principle (*Zwang*). But where hierocratic organizations employ psychic coercion, political groups use a physical kind, and Weber names *violence* (*Gewaltsamkeit*) as the specific form of coercion used by political groups exclusively.[59] He makes it clear that other methods besides physical coercion are widely used by political groups, including the state, insisting, nevertheless, that the threat or use of violence is a special characteristic that identifies associations as "political."

Weber's idea of power includes conflict as an important element in it. He explains, "A social relationship will be referred to as 'conflict' insofar as action within it is oriented intentionally to carrying out the actor's own will *against the resistance* of the other party or parties." [60] Then he defines "power" as "the probability that one actor within a social relationship will be in a position to carry out his own will *despite resistance*, regardless of the basis on which this probability rests." [61] Thus, it is clear that two kinds of power are possible: one kind in conditions where conflict and resistance are absent; the other in conditions where there is a conflict in which one party successfully overcomes resistance. Since Weber is careful to distinguish power from other forms of social control in which co-operation is more crucial, his approach at least suggests that in the exercise of power, resistance and conflict in one degree or another are highly probable, and perhaps even expected. This idea of power, therefore, tends to imply a process of *overpowering*. Reinhard Bendix has perceptively observed that "Weber's definition of power is very similar to Clausewitz's definition of war." [62]

Although Weber stresses that violence is the characteristic that technically distinguishes political organization from other groups, he makes it clear that political systems use all the techniques of any social organization and that in some states the use of violence may be negligible. Moreover, the presence of conflict in his definition of power does not exclude the importance of co-operation.

Nevertheless, a number of writers have reacted sharply to the point of view that stresses coercive sanctions. They would prefer to emphasize co-operation, authority, and peaceful methods of control instead of conflict, coercion, and violence. David Easton, a political scientist who views the political structure as a distributive system authoritatively allocating values for the entire society, protests that Radcliffe-Brown "overemphasizes the role of coercive sanctions, especially force." Easton agrees that at one time or another all kinds of different organized groups "have used both violent and non-violent means of persuasion with varying degrees of legitimacy attached to this use," but whereas Weber claims that when they do employ violence legitimately, the use of this method gives such groups a "political" character, Easton comes to the opposite conclusion that "governmental institutions can no longer be differentiated from others merely by virtue of the sanctions that they are able to impose." [63]

Few writers will commit themselves to an exclusive choice between authority and violence as the essential principle of political action, for it appears more sound to work out formulas that keep them both in some preferential ratio. Likewise, few would, in the manner of Heinrich von Treitschke and Franz Oppenheimer, insist on force as the primary principle in formulas of the state; it is more usual to balance the principles of coercion and consent. Thus, MacIver writes:

> force holds nothing together. Force is a substitute for unity. . . .
>
> Coercive power is a criterion of the state, but not its essence. . . . When force is much in evidence it is a pathological symptom. . . .
>
> It is true that there is no state where there is no overruling force. This is the *differentia* between the state and all other associations. There is no state where other associations arrogate to themselves the exercise of compulsion. There is no state where there is anarchy. But the exercise of force does not make a state. . . .[64]

Except for a subtle difference of emphasis, this statement is not far from Weber's view of how *some* states operate.

The most useful concept of the state would not be restricted either to moderate or to violent states, for history is full of both. Nor is it reasonable to confine ideas of the political process to organized negotiation, bargaining, exchange, competition, and other peaceful transactions, omitting violence. Both extremes should be included and conceptions framed in a manner that will lead the investigator to uncover the empirical conditions determining the presence or absence of violent methods.

None of the perennial approaches to the subject of violence and authority comprehend the dynamics of terroristic regimes.

There is no place for them in the schemes of writers who perceive violence and authority as contradictory principles. And those who detect mixtures of violence and authority in the structure of political life have not devised a way to distinguish and to analyze the differences between the system that employs violence as a final resort and the type that uses it as the principle method of control.

Terroristic Despotism. To the terroristic primitive states examined in this book, I have given the name "despotism," because their political features may be distinguished from those of a "tyranny," but the heads of both types do have some characteristics in common. The tyrants of the archaic period in ancient Greece were often moderate, but by the time of Plato and Aristotle, the term came to mean a wicked ruler. Both tyrants and despots are expected to use violence, and if their actions depart from that role, the epithets are modified: witness Aristotle's makeshift term, the "half-wicked" tyrant, and that hero of the Enlightenment, the "benevolent" despot.[65] The very words "despot" and "tyrant" are ancient vehicles for hostile feelings about specific individuals in positions of power, and Hobbes observed that "tyrant" is a term for a ruler one dislikes. Yet, the objective reality to which the loaded terms refer is almost always a solitary overlord exercising arbitrary power, who in every sphere of behavior is limited by few institutional restraints. The technical difference between despot and tyrant depends on the historic role of each in a particular power system and the meanings given to that role. In each case, the definition turns on the way the ruler came to power, the character of his legitimacy, and the sources of his support.

The Greek word "despot" means "lord" or "master" (equivalent to the Latin *dominus*), and, according to Aristotle, despotic rule is based on the primary relationship between master and slave, in which the former uses the latter as an instrument of action for his own benefit. The despotic relationship is unpolitical, for Aristotle reserves the concept of the political to associations of free men. Since free men do not willingly endure despotic rule, only barbarians, who are slaves by nature, have despotic governments that are natural or based on consent. The tyrant rules *like* a despot (*despotikos*), but in different social conditions and over unwilling subjects who are deprived of their natural constitution.

Therefore, the tyrant is not a legitimate ruler, and the Western political tradition since the time of Aristotle has considered tyranny not as a constitutional form but as a departure from constitutionalism altogether. The tyrant comes to power by force or fraud, and although he is supported by a segment of the community, he is opposed by another segment which is, in most cases, loyal to the traditional system which was overthrown. If the resistance disappears and he finds himself ruling over willing subjects, then, according to Aristotle at least, he is no longer a complete tyrant but more of a king.[66]

The methods of the tyrant, unless he conceals the true nature of his power by techniques described by Aristotle and Machiavelli, are usually considered unnatural or immoral, and his regime often understood as an abnormal episode in the political history of the people he dominates. If he does happen to begin his reign as the legitimate ruler, he abandons that role by performing actions that are defined as unconstitutional and illegitimate.

The despot, on the other hand, is always legitimate, and despotic regimes may experience rebellions, but they are not typically punctuated by the political revolutions that mark the beginnings and ends of tyrannies. Moreover, the methods of the *terroristic* despot, despite their destructive consequences, are often considered natural by the people he dominates. Although they may hate the experience of oppression, they seldom dispute his right to rule or his right to the methods he employs. Individuals ordinarily object or try to escape when they are singled out as victims of his cruelty, but not always. A number of victims accept their fate with passive resignation or even with the show of enthusiasm, in some cases praising the destructive power of the despot while being led to places of execution. In terroristic despotism, we shall observe, violence is culturally syntonic. In tyrannies, violence is usually experienced as culturally alien.

I would agree with the definition of despotism as a system of arbitrary, unmediated power—adding the qualification that the power is legitimate—but I do not accept Montesquieu's proposition that the principle of despotism is terror. There are cases of despotism without terror, and it is more accurate to think of terror as a principle that distinguishes one form of despotism from the other. Indeed, it is the purpose of this book to discover the conditions in which despotism—or any other state —chooses to adopt the process of terror.

Nevertheless, the use of terror is not confined to states. The following two chapters examine the nature and functions of terrorism in some chiefdoms, which lacked the degree of centralization and the public coercive apparatus associated with the state.

CHAPTER IV

SOME ASPECTS

OF POWER

IN SIMPLE SOCIETIES

Social laws were the work of the gods; but those
gods, so powerful and beneficent, were nothing
else than the beliefs of men.

—Fustel de Coulanges, *The Ancient City.*

IN THE PRIMITIVE WORLD, the process of terror may be discovered in some kinds of warfare, in the violence of some chiefs, and in the frightfulness of secret societies. Moreover, it worked episodically in some kingdoms, and regularly in some despotic states. According to one point of view, however, political terrorism is associated with rudeness and simplicity, presumably to be replaced by milder forms of rule when a society evolves to a higher order of complexity and the way of life becomes more mannered or civilized. Not long ago, terroristic despotism was fancied in the oldest and simplest imagined group—the primal horde. The Victorian fantasy of the primeval despot, described by J. J. Atkinson in his *Primal Law,* then elaborated and given immortality by Freud in *Totem and Taboo* and by H. G. Wells in *The Outline of History,* pictured a monstrous patriarch who ruled by violence and fear, monopolizing women and expelling males, and who became a "tribal god" after his death. Nevertheless, setting aside speculations about prehistoric life and setting aside the psychological truths in the fantasy of the primal

horde, terroristic controls are not to be found in the simplest
societies known to man. Yet, it does not mean that terrorism
springs from complexity in any simple fashion, or that it is the
necessary product of a movement toward advanced stages.
Complexity provides new opportunities of many kinds, and it
opens new alternatives for social action and organization, including violent alternatives. Moreover, social complexity, im-
plying more differences among people, also implies more occasions for conflict and resistance, which may be encountered by
violent "solutions." In addition, political specialization provides the means for holding absolute power—which is virtually
unknown in the simplest societies—and a social apparatus for
destroying or neutralizing limitations.

Although tensions and conflicts generated by the inner dynamics of the state and great changes in the form of the state are
probably the most frequent historic source of terrorism, the
state is not necessary for terrorism. For theoretical purposes,
we should inspect every form of political community and examine generally the conditions and consequences when one or
more corporate groups use violence frequently or employ terror
as a regular procedure. The process of terror, we shall find, is
one mode of action that leaders and rulers may choose to deal
with limitations on their power.

In the terms used in this study for the different kinds of political community, I adapt the usage suggested by E. R. Service
in *Primitive Social Organization*.[1] A "band" is the most rudimentary structure: a political community identical with the
face-to-face residential group. Although it may follow a leader,
it has no offices or specialized political roles. The members ex-
ploit a territory together, following a paleolithic style of life
and usually fed by hunting and gathering. A "tribe" is a larger
community that includes several residential units. Lacking officers and specialized political roles, it is integrated by segmentary lineages, clans, age grades, religious associations, or other
corporate sodalities, which dramatize relationships that extend
beyond the local units and bind them together. The members of

a tribe are usually occupied with herding or agriculture, and they live in neolithic style. I reserve the term "tribe" for this specific form of political unit, and do not use it, as many writers do, to refer to ethnic, linguistic, or cultural units.[2] Bands and tribes are egalitarian societies, which shun formal distinctions of rank, but all the others are organized hierarchically.

A "chiefdom" is the community of all the people who acknowledge the authority of a specific person who occupies the office of chief. Although some observers may carelessly describe any leader as a chief, including ephemeral leaders who may emerge in bands and tribes and whose powers and responsibilities depend on personal abilities, in this study I restrict the meaning of the term. The chief of a chiefdom is the incumbent of a permanent position that has been socially defined by rules independent of the person who fills the office. The procedures and sanctions that regulate his official activities do not depend on his particular qualities. The chief has authority to initiate actions, to command, to administer justice, and to keep order, although his powers of coercion are limited. For a staff, he may rely on the elders of the community to mobilize the young men under their authority when the need arises, or he may select messengers and other assistants at will. In some societies that have age grades, if a body of men is required for some action involving physical force, the chief may call on a corporate set of young men, who were initiated at the same time and who maintain their collective identity, to serve as a mobile squad and to function according to the need as an emergency force, as police, or as an agency to execute his orders. He organizes the labor of his people for public tasks, collects revenue, and redistributes wealth, his office circulating property in a manner that conforms to the unequal order of social relationships. His relatives often constitute a nobility, and rank is frequently measured by genealogical proximity to the chief, determining higher and lower categories of social persons, the forms of privilege, and the relative positions of individuals, families, lineages, and villages, although simple technology limits the extent to which life styles can differ. Chiefs are not remote from everyday life, and in most cases it would be more accurate to say that the chief was at the center and in the midst of the system, rather than at the top of it. Chiefdoms are denser and more complex than tribes, having local residential groups generally larger than those of tribes, and they are more productive, yielding a surplus that supports the offices of chief and his limited staff. Larger chiefdoms are divided into territorial units under subchiefs, but the central staff of a chief is usually something between a retinue and an enlarged household. Not many individuals are free of the need to make a living, and the system cannot support an extensive specialized staff engaged solely in command and administration. A "paramount chief" commands the allegiance of several chiefs, but he is often not much of a monarch. He may determine the external relations of his vassal chiefs and may even initiate important activities in the chiefdoms under his suzerainty, but in many cases he has scant authority or capacity to control the people within the subordinate chiefdoms except the one under his immediate control. It is true that the term "paramount chief" was coined by British administrators, but as Richards has observed, it "was often an apt description of the conditions they found." [3]

A "state" is socially more complex than and politically distinct from a chiefdom. Size is only a rough criterion, for some great chiefdoms are larger than some tiny states. What distinguishes a state from a chiefdom is the nature and means of coercion authorized and exercised in the political community. In contrast to a chief, who can mobilize an armed force if necessary, the head of a state claims the legitimate monopoly of force and commands a special body of men organized to use it. This defining characteristic differentiates the state from other kinds of political community, but the state commonly exhibits other attributes as well. In chiefdoms, differences in rank and privilege are more prominent than political distinctions. In states, political differentiation is associated with social stratification. Central machinery of command, administration, and justice develops to a greater or lesser extent, and wherever possible the processes of branching and specializing make visible many different kinds of office. Large states are teeming with civil bureaucrats, military leaders, princes, priesthoods, title holders, liaison officers, noble chiefs, commoner chiefs, and hosts of administrative officials. Therefore, where a chiefdom has a specialized, permanent leader, the state has a specialized, permanent staff. Very often, full-time professionalization in arts, crafts, and commerce develop as well, with the accompanying emergence of other classes in the population. Civil society transcends the more elementary units of kinship and sodality. Political communities that have not made the transition to this larger, "national" unity, but are merely a system of lineages or other similar corporate bodies controlled by a central administration may be referred to sometimes as "protostates" or "segmentary states."

In a typical African state, a king ruled over many chiefdoms, which were not independent communities but territorial divisions of the kingdom, and the chiefs were subordinate officers, with varying degrees of power. In his relationship to the people, generally speaking, the head of a kingdom was more remote than the head of a sovereign chiefdom. The concept of a king implied a solitary role that was supreme and unique, and the symbols of kingship, even though they included the idea of fatherhood, also dramatized forcefully that the position was unique, distant—sometimes closer to the ancestors than to the people—and qualitatively different from the positions of chiefs. In determining whether the indigenous term for an African ruler should be translated as "chief" or as "king," one should take into account the nature of his relationship with the people, but ultimately it depends on whether his resources included the command of a specialized staff.

The right to rule was generally hereditary, although in a few cases it was elective, and restricted to a royal lineage. Depending on the rules, the individual of that lineage chosen as king was usually the senior male, or the strongest, or the one judged to be the most capable representative of the royal family. The only kind of state to develop in primitive Africa was a monocratic form of rule in which either a king or a despot stood as the formal head of the governmental structure. When communities grew more complicated than bands and tribes, social identity was almost always expressed through allegiance to a chief, or king, or despot, who represented the unity of a social body that extended beyond the scope of lineage and sodality. The chief—and, in states, the king or despot—was usually defined ideologically as the "owner" of the land or the "father" of his people. Kings were limited monarchs, but a few rulers were despots, that is, arbitrary rulers without substantial institutional controls on their power. Kingdoms, we shall see, were systems integrated and stabilized by balanced relationships, distributed power, institutionalized limitations, and patterns of conditional resistance. Despotisms were held together, paradoxically, by institutionalized caprice and absolute power, and in some of these systems despots regularly used violence to inhibit potential resistance. Although primitive states were confined to the monocratic type, they were anything but uniform, and they displayed all kinds of organizational permutations and subtle constitutional nuances. The historical range of African kingdoms probably shows richer diversity than the more familiar kingdoms of European experience. An analysis of the functions of violence in these traditional states will be reserved for later chapters.

Writers who examine the politics of stateless societies— bands, tribes, and chiefdoms—often neglect the evidence that some of the most important "political" activity of the people in those communities was directed toward limiting or inhibiting actual and potential leadership. On all levels of social organization, from complex states to simple bands, we shall find limits, checks, and inhibitions on violence, aggression, and ambition, as well as social institutions that guarantee conditional resistance to the exercise of power. We shall examine the nature of these controls in each kind of political community, beginning with the simplest. Leaders and rulers who exercised arbitrary power or who could initiate the process of terror were men who had found some means to overcome the limits and resistances that were natural components of political life in every community.

BANDS

The social life of bands was furthest removed from the conditions of both terrorism and despotism. In one type of band, the political community was almost identical with the family— adult men were equal in status and power, and all members were bound to one another by the sentiments and obligations of kinship. In another type, the composite band made up of refugees and the fragments of shattered communities, the members were held together by their dependence on a leader, and he was essential to the very existence of the community. As Lévi-Strauss describes the Nambikwara in Brazil, the band owed its form, size, and very origin to the leader. Yet, he had "no powers of coercion," and if he was unsatisfactory, the followers simply left him to find another leader:

> There is no social structure more fragile, or shorter-lived, than the Nambikwara band. If the chief is too exacting, if he allots to himself too large a share of the women, or if he cannot find enough food for his subjects during the dry season, discontentment follows immediately. Individuals, or whole families, will break away from the group and go off to join a band with a better reputation.[4]

Still another kind of band depended on neither a leader nor kinship for its solidarity, but was integrated by a religious ideology that animated the environment, turning it into a mystic force that was loved and worshipped. As Colin Turnbull describes the organization of the Mbuti, forest pygmies in the Congo, authority was dispersed throughout the community, drawing on different leaders for different fields of activity. No single individual could claim respect in all fields, and one found neither chiefs, headmen, councils of elders, nor ritual specialists. Men with outstanding authority in a field—such as hunting—could at most, in camp discussions, where decisions on public issues were made, claim the right to be heard. But even then they might be shouted down and ridiculed. One great hunter, who had the personal attributes that Lévi-Strauss found in the leaders of the Nambikwara band, said: " 'It is never good for one man to talk too much, particularly if he is right.' " [5] Turnbull also describes how another man, aggressive and ambitious, tried to draw special attention to control his peers, wanting to get the hunt started when he was ready. Either ignored by the others or ridiculed, he was finally publicly criticized for his behavior by an elder and disgraced. Since such limitations were rooted in the whole pattern of shared expectations, they were clearly social institutions with political functions.

TRIBES AND VILLAGE COMMUNITIES

Proceeding from bands of hunters and gatherers to more complex societies living in tribal organizations and in village settlements, one found a greater variety of institutions that checked leaders and inhibited the emergence of specialized political roles. One of the most interesting may be perceived in the polity of the Tiv in northern Nigeria, a tribe organized in a segmentary lineage system. Within this community there were traditionally no offices of leadership, but every local unit had influential men.[6] The Tiv system "granted political authority, that is, legitimate institutionalized power to no one. There were no offices to which authority could adhere." [7] But even though men with informal power in the indigenous system or formal leaders established by the British were "natural and necessary," according to Paul Bohannan, they were profoundly distrusted, and their ability to control others was attributed to *tsav*, a witchcraft substance, which grew naturally in the hearts of born leaders but which could also be cultivated artificially, it was believed, by cannibalism. Thus, wicked men of power could unnaturally augment the *tsav* growing naturally in their hearts by a diet of human flesh. Symbolically, Bohannan observes, this belief indicated that power was obtained "by consuming the substance of others." The most powerful men, therefore, "no matter how much they are respected or liked, are never fully trusted. They are men of tsav—and who knows?" Historically, Tiv society was convulsed by extended witch hunts—social movements that emerged periodically, yet outside the processes of normal institutions, to detect and eliminate powerful men who might have had wicked *tsav*. As the normal processes of political activity gave rise to inequalities and "a rigidity in power relationships which Tiv find threatening to their constitutional ideas," the "regular series of movements" purged the system, leveled the tendency toward hierarchy, and ensured the preservation of institutions "based on the lineage system and a principle of egalitarianism." [8] The manifest activity of hunting for cannibalistic witches had the latent function of preventing concentrations of power.

In other parts of the world as well as in Africa, societies in which power was evenly distributed had less dramatic social institutions than those of the Tiv that nevertheless yielded the same kind of result. In the typical Turkish village, for example, several processes and institutions, including the form of legal inheritance, the means of acquiring wealth, and the highly individualized networks of power, worked together to yield a system in which concentrations did not endure. As Paul Stirling observes, "The system worked to prevent a stable hereditary hierarchy."

The success of each powerful man depended on bringing up many strong, competent sons to help with the farming and on establishing a network of friends and allies bound to him through patronage and personal favors. Control over his own village and perhaps other villages depended on personal influence with merchants, officials, and the elite in the towns as well as the leaders of other villages. As this personal power increased, it provoked rivals who were "prepared to use violence," and in the face of this opposition, "only he himself personally would be able to hold his supporters together." On the death of each powerful man, the concentration dissolved. The multitude of sons instrumental in building the power in the first place divided the inheritance, and the wealth of each was consequently relatively small. Secondly, none of the heirs, beginning his independent career with a modest portion, could preserve the social network of personal relations that had reinforced his father's power. Even the most loyal supporters of his late father were not likely to accept leadership automatically from a member of the younger generation. Thus, a cyclical leveling process made it impossible for any one household or line of households to maintain wealth and power beyond a single generation.[9] The power of the central government was remote, that of the formal village headman negligible, and that of community leaders ephemeral.

Other traditional village communities did have specialized political roles and a hierarchical social order. Nevertheless, the structure of executive action in those villages inherently restrained the formal authority of headman or chief. The staff of a typical village chief was usually drawn from the members of his own lineage as well as, in some cases, clients and other dependants, and he also shared power with a council of elders, who were the heads of other families. The elders represented their families, they were expected to exercise moral control over their people, and they also controlled the economic resources of their households. Their co-operation was essential if the village was to function as a unit. An elder assumed a double role, working both as a representative of his family group and as an official agent of the village community as a whole. The authority of the head of a kinship group on this scale was almost universally confined to moral and ritual spheres. One may generalize from Paula Brown's statement about the features of this authority in West African societies: "Whatever sanctions they controlled, kin-group heads were never autocratic, since they depended upon the support of their kin groups, and especially of the elders, for effective administration." [10]

The inner circle of a village council in Africa was usually made up of the chief and a few elders of the highest rank, who represented the important households. In large villages, of course, where householders were organized in wards, the political structure was more complex. A typical small village, however, may be found in Nadel's description of a traditional Nupe community in central Nigeria. Policy was often initiated by the inner circle, but all the elders were executives of the village. Through their mediation, the decisions of the chief and the leading elders reached the various kinship and local groups, and in turn, through all the elders, these groups registered claims and interests that called for action by the community.[11]

In most cases, the village chief, as formal head of the community, symbolized its collective identity and represented it externally; internally, he initiated, co-ordinated, and sometimes financed collective activities of various sorts, controlled land resources, collected taxes for the higher political authority, and settled certain classes of disputes. In all matters of local government he was institutionally bound by the advice of the elders and dependent on their co-operation. Moreover, local government was tempered by the limits of village jurisdiction, and its voice was usually confined to persuasion, warning, and advice. Conditions that permitted the emergence of despotism did not exist on the village level. Still, the dynamics of power that led to despotism or to institutions that prevented it in political communities of larger scale may be detected in the village.

Village chiefs who would have liked to be autocrats tried various devices to evade institutional limitations. They might try to stack the village council with favorites, and if they were successful in bypassing the claims of legitimate candidates to eldership, the council became a rubber stamp, composed of friends and sycophants. In most cases, however, the elders remained the most important source of potential resistance. If a chief taxed excessively or refused a legitimate claim to land, they appealed to higher political authority, but if the king refused to hear them, they might withdraw their support from the village chief and go on strike. Then the chief was faced with a situation in which important ceremonies went unattended—a serious blow to his prestige. Moreover, his power was undermined, for certain collective activities could not proceed without the ritual associated with them, and since the elders and the congregations under their authority financed ceremonies, provided the magic, and organized the ritual, the resistance brought normal activity to a standstill. Several other forms of resistance were familiar, and they were not necessarily restricted to leadership by the elders. Other family heads or outlying segments of the community might refuse, for example, to give an overbearing chief a tax, gift, or some other form of income that was customarily due to him.

The chief's position of economic superiority was probably the most decisive means of counter-resistance available to him. He had more sources of income than anyone else in the village, and bribes, gifts, and rewards, as well as threats of deprivation and other kinds of economic intimidation, might be used to compel submission. Once again, however, the conditions of village life set boundaries to this tactic. In Nupe, for example, although the chief had higher rank and more wealth than anyone else in the village, he was, as Nadel observed, "the most prominent in a graded order of prominence." His income did not erect an insurmountable barrier between the others and himself; he possessed more of what others possessed, and from his surplus he had to pay expenses required of his office. Chiefs who were not generous were always disliked, and it was probably impossible for one who was both overbearing and niggardly to retain any followers. According to Nadel, "the surplus capital which he derives from his office is not . . . large enough to be turned into an effective instrument of political ambition." On state occasions, the costume and insignia of the chief distinguished him conspicuously from all other people, but in everyday life he looked no different from any other farmer. His position, Nadel concluded, "economically privileged though it may be, is not *meant* to lead to the formation of an essentially different, sharply separated, permanently privileged ruling class . . . [for] the political organization of the village is meant to preserve the social homogeneity of the community." [12] The situation was different in heterogeneous polities that were stratified, with a ruling class dominating an exploited population. But even there, the exploited peoples often lived under the direct control of their own village chiefs, and institutions, especially on the local level, frequently placed some limits on the power of the exploiters.

In homogeneous village communities, then, the structure of the common life fused together political authority, religious activity, kinship, economics, neighborhood ties, education, recreation, and so forth. The fusion explains why the chief was so vulnerable to religious and kinship controls, to mention but two. As we shall see when the community grows less homogeneous, men and events may dissociate the political executive from the network of institutions with all their informal imitations, either permitting it to work with less restraint or else relocating the executive in a new machinery of formal and informal controls.

Since villages were rarely sovereign communities, and the instruments of coercion, including the right to kill, were restricted to higher jurisdiction, a village chief with a yen for autocracy had to work under serious deprivations. Even in sovereign chiefdoms, however, where the head of the political community had *force majeure* at his disposal, the same dynamics of power and resistance, as well as the constraining structure of executive action, worked to limit the power of the chief. He had to satisfy his people to hold their loyalty; he depended on his own lineage for political, military, and economic support;

and he needed the co-operation of others—especially the heads of other lineages—to execute his orders.

CHIEFDOMS AND PROTOSTATES

As A. W. Southall generalizes from the case of the Alur people, who live around the Nile and Lake Albert in Uganda and the Congo, small chiefdoms provided a focus for a heterogeneous polity, but their governmental structure tended to be "half-enlarged household, half embryonic state." [13] The chief or chieflet's position was stabilized by his own lineage, which also helped to restrain his authority. Since his office guaranteed superior wealth—usually cattle—he could take more wives than anyone else and beget more children, so that successful chiefs actively expanded their own lineages. Beyond their lineages, chiefs could command labor service from their subjects, but they were expected to reciprocate with generous supplies of food and drink. A chief's success depended on how he exercised power. If he were to abuse his subjects by harsh demands, or to show weakness by not using his power to protect them from others, he would fail. He did not use force to impose authority on those who did not voluntarily accept it in the first place, or to prevent people from leaving him. Among the Alur, Southall reports, "There is no mention in the tradition of any groups of chiefs or chieflets ever having tried to prevent the transference of allegiance by force, just as there is also no mention of any chief ever having tried by physical means to enforce recognition of his suzerainty on derivative chieflets or on any other chiefs." [14] E. R. Service makes the general observation that the authority of chiefs and nobles in a chiefdom is not backed by a monopoly of force but by stable, legitimate expectations. Men obey the chief because it is the right thing to do and because he fulfills their needs. "Chiefdoms have centralized direction and problems of governance, but no true government to back up decisions by legalized force." [15] This political order tended to be flexible, with much political responsibility left to the heads of local groups, the chief intervening in cases of violent disruption or when directly petitioned. In the Alur society, which had many features typical of chiefdoms in general, chiefs did not enforce strictly defined authority within precise territorial boundaries, but relied on ritual and magic to maintain their positions as pivots of the economic system, gathering tribute and expecting services, and regulating spheres of political and juridical power that were less secure at the peripheries than at the centers. As Southall indicates, "They had no military organisation to oppose against direct challenge to their political authority. But they could usually rely on the loyalty of a sufficient number of clan sections to muster an extempore force stronger than any that was likely to challenge them," and their miscellaneous dependents constituted an informal bodyguard. [16]

Other chiefdoms with some typical political features may be observed among the Mandari, a Nilo-Hamitic pastoral people who live in the savanna of the Equatorial Sudan. Traditionally, they were organized in small sovereign units under rival chiefs who co-operated in herding activities when the season made it necessary, and relationships among the large numbers of political communities covered the range from friendship to agonistic hostility. As in every chiefdom, the *Mar*, or chief of each Mandari community, was the pivot of economic, jural, and political relations, but his right and means of coercion were limited. The office was hereditary within a single lineage, and the position supported by religious beliefs, although if the lineage grew too weak to exercise power effectively, the office might be usurped by another line. Moreover, as Jean Buxton explains:

> While a *Mar* assumes office by hereditary right, the successful fulfillment of his role is largely dependent on whether he can please his people and build up a strong group of retainers. Although, once installed, Mandari say a *Mar* can never be deposed or killed by his own people, his position can, how-

ever, be weakened by the non-cooperation of the elders of the council, or the withdrawal of support of powerful collateral lineages, who in the past sometimes fragmented away to found new chiefships, particularly as a result of quarrels between powerful siblings.[17]

There was a close bond between the *Mar* and his elders, and though they mutually supported one another's authority, the actions of each also limited and checked the power of the others. Another check, as well as an instrument of political integration, was found in a practice familiar to heterogeneous chiefdoms and many kingdoms too—the first officer or "prime minister," who played a crucial role in executive power, came from the unprivileged class: commoners or clients. In the case of the Mandari, the elders chose a client—a member of the class that was excluded from owning land—to be the "close assistant and mouthpiece" of the *Mar:* to issue his commands, keep order in the council place, and act as chief in his absence.

One of the most important restraints in all political communities was the concept of the "good chief." As H. A. Junod observed in his classic study of the Thonga of Southeastern Africa, "A chief who wants to succeed in his government must have a good character." [18] Among the Thonga, the ideal was institutionalized by the behavior of two court personages, the herald (or praise singer) and the jester (or public vituperator), who continually reminded the chief and everyone around him what the traditional expectations were. Every morning, before sunrise, the chief was awakened by the herald's loud song, which praised the deeds of departed rulers and disparaged the incumbent. In the light of predecessors, the singer cried, the present chief was a coward and a child, not to be compared with his father, his grandfather, and their glorious ancestors. The court jester, in addition, acted as a public censor, freely insulting everyone and enjoying perfect immunity when he loudly criticized the chief.[19]

It is often said that the essential qualities of a good chief were "beer, meat, and politeness," and in all chiefdoms the ideal included protection, provision, and decorum. A chief who could not feed his people or protect them, it was agreed, or who was too weak or too abusive, would in one way or another lose the community. The concept of the good chief, however, was more than an ideal, for it sometimes included a range of expected deviation from the ideal. Sometimes violence was associated with chieftaincy, and, although it was not ideal, within limits violent behavior might be tolerated. In the traditional Bemba system in Rhodesia, Audrey Richards observes, "a chief practiced savage mutilations on those who offended him, injured his interests, laughed at him or members of his family, or stole his wives. A number of these mutilated men and women still survive in Bemba country today." The line of chiefs came from the Crocodile clan, and the people explained that the ruling family was so named because " 'they are like crocodiles that seize hold of the common people and tear them to bits with their teeth.' " Thus, Richards concludes, "there is no doubt that the greatness of the [Crocodile clan] rested to a large extent on fear." [20] Chiefly violence on all levels, however, was limited not least by the closest relatives of the paramount chief, especially his mother, his eldest son, and the senior members of his family. Bemba history records the case of a subchief named Fyanifyani, whose outrageous violence—apparently "a sort of blood lust"—was ended by the intervention of the paramount's family, and the man removed from office.[21] For the paramount himself, the most important limitation was the *bakabilo*, a hereditary council with oligarchic features, who could control the chief by refusing to perform ritual functions necessary for his work. In 1934, Richards found the paramount chief living in grass huts because the *bakabilo*, indignant at his behavior, had refused to perform the ceremony necessary for him to begin building his new village.

In the old days, the Bemba chiefs, with their army and staff of executioners, had effective apparatus for violence. When chiefs were expected to be violent, this characteristic was understood as a sign of their superiority, but the association of chieftaincy with violence was usually accompanied by some dissociation of the political executive from the communal network of ordinary institutions, so that the chief lived with a specialized retinue in a social environment that resembled a court. The productive level in chiefdoms was high enough to yield a surplus that supported a staff of persons who were detached from ordinary pursuits and whose activity might be restricted to the chief's household: wives, shamans, entertainers, weavers, potters, and so forth.[22] However, chiefdoms ranged in size from small residential units to large protostates. The Mandari *Mar* relied mainly on the men of his own lineage and the clients attached to it. His following made up the superior force of the chiefdom, but if the other lineages wanted to band against him, they would have prevailed.

In larger systems, the chief controlled numerous courtiers, including administrators, attendants, messengers, and executioners, and in such a staff one may discern the germ of state organization. Lucy Mair suggests that the first, rudimentary essential of state power is "a leader who can keep permanently associated with him a body of retainers whom he can call on to enforce his wishes, and who identify themselves more closely with him than with any of the divisions of the population."[23] Since the members of ruling lineages competed among themselves, they had to find support outside of their own kin. Therefore, an important part of their following was made up of strangers: "refugee clients, people detached from the societies where their kinsmen would help them to stand up for their rights and so wholly dependent upon their lord's protection."[24]

Mair's conclusion about the nucleus of state formation illuminates the stages in successful centralization. However, to pursue our special line of inquiry into the dynamics of chiefdoms and states, we must examine an earlier approach, which turned out to be less conclusive, but equally revealing in unexpected ways.

CENTRALIZATION

Robert Lowie, in his well-known book *The Origin of the State*, looked elsewhere for the nucleus of state power—not in retinues of strangers, which were familiar to the East African societies that Mair examines—but in unions of fellowship; namely, in the secret societies that dominated the politics of traditional West Africa. He was struck by some functional resemblances between these groups and certain men's organizations among the Plains Indians in America, and he suspected that the state might be found latent in sodalities or "associations"; that is, corporate groups with permanent, continuous organization based on neither kinship nor propinquity, but on a set of purposes, which had the capacity to transcend the parochial exclusivism of blood and neighborhood ties. The formation of the state required some centralizing force strong enough to counteract "primitive separatism," and Lowie wondered "how far associations, which ostensibly and primarily serve specific purposes of their own, incidentally tend to organize society on territorial lines." He reasoned that if the state is identified with maintaining political order within fixed territorial limits, "then the associations uniting *all* members of an area evidently prepare the way for the political integration of that area," while associations of more limited scope might contribute to that effect.[25] Moreover, associations exercised police functions in many societies, and they provided a staff of men who were authorized to carry out coercive sanctions—another element in state power.

Among the Plains Indians, Lowie observed, individuals were generally free from interference with their actions, and nothing was more alien to them than the idea that a chief should wield power over life and property. Yet, during the period of the hunt, certain men's societies were vested with the authority to use force to prevent premature attacks on the herd, and they could deal with offenders by confiscating their property or by

corporal or capital punishment. Thus, for a brief time, the unchallenged supremacy of this police force "unified the entire
population and created a state 'towering immeasurably above
single individuals,' but which disappeared again as rapidly as
it had come into being." [26] In a later article, Lowie added that
the seasonal disintegration of the social units rendered the coercive agencies ephemeral and precluded a permanent state. In
the whole of America, he generalized, sundry gropings toward
centralization of power were undermined by opposite trends.[27]

For more durable gropings toward centralization by similar
agencies, Lowie turned in *The Origin of the State* to West
Africa, and selected the Kpelle people in Liberia, who had several secret societies of a religious and magical nature that carried out secular functions. The greatest of them was the Poro
Society, which permeated culture and social life, dominated
politics, and through universal initiation of males—females
were initiated in the corresponding Sande Society—served as a
prerequisite to entrance in other important secret organizations. The outstanding feature of the political structure was a
dual system of controls, with the Poro Society carrying out religious, educational, social, and political functions, depending
in no small measure on violence and terror, and with the
"king" standing at the head of the formal political, administrative, and judicial structure. Although Lowie followed the usage
of Diedrich Westermann, who made the classic study of the
Kpelle, and referred to the *Kalon* as a "king," it is clear from
an examination of Westermann's description of the office that
the incumbent would have been described more accurately as a
paramount chief, which indeed was one of the several terms
that Westermann used along with "king." [28]

The two systems of power—the Poro and the formal government—were connected through the paramount chief and other
public officials who were all high members of the Poro Society,
but the chief did not control the Poro by virtue of his office, nor
did the Poro attempt to organize or administer the entire political community. The precise relation between Poro officials and

public officers varied from one community to another. Power was shared by the two centers of authority, but the ultimate decisions rested with the Poro. As Lowie explained:

It is in the Poro bush that all important affairs of public life are debated and settled; and new ordinances are announced in the name of the organization. Though the King is theoretically privy to all its activities and is sometimes referred to as its real head, the Grand Master appears as a dangerous rival even in normal times and seriously curtails the royal power during the [King's] four years' probation, assuming a large part of the administrative powers otherwise lodged in the sovereign, maintaining bridges and roads, summoning councils, and generally controlling the population. To these national functions connected with the Poro must be added international ones: during the probationary period no wars are tolerated, and even litigation within the tribe is outlawed.[29]

In southern Nigeria among the Ekoi people, Lowie added, the power of the chief was severely limited, and the major decisions were made by a council of old men. The head of the Egbo, which was the secret society corresponding to the Poro of the Kpelle, was by far the most powerful man in the community. The Egbo took over practically all the functions of government and exercised a deep influence on religion and cultural life. In addition, the Egbo Society "punished theft, collected debts on behalf of its membership, and flogged uninitiated people who had offended the organization."[30]

In *The Origin of the State*, Lowie concluded, "Associations do not play the preponderant role in political development which I was at one time inclined to ascribe to them." The evidence that in many chiefdoms secret societies exercising police functions and vested with coercive authority held the lion's share of executive power persuaded him to abandon an earlier conviction that associations were necessarily the rudiments of the state. Men's organizations among the Plains Indians, he now recognized, were sometimes disruptive as well as unifying forces, and the power of secret societies in Africa sometimes prevented centralization. Therefore, if "associations succeed in overcoming the separatism of kin groups by bringing together men of different families and sibs, they are quite as capable of dividing the community along associational lines, and additional factors are required to establish the territorial bond." In that case, "associations are not inherently centralizing or disruptive agencies. Everything depends on the correlated factors of integration."[31]

Although he never pursued "the correlated factors of integration," Lowie made it clear that communities with secret associations in them could move in alternative directions:

> a survey of West African data suggests two alternative lines of development with all intermediate degrees of power distributed between the chief and the associations. Either the men's societies are the real seat of power, dwarfing the royal influence, or the king may utilize the organization of a secret society for purposes of his own.[32]

Where associations were the real seat of power, their activity inhibited centralization, for their control of executive functions prevented a paramount chief from gathering the powers that would have transformed him into a king. Lawrence Krader adds that where chiefs in West Africa failed to centralize power, they were blocked by other factors besides the secret societies: bonds between master and client as well as the tribal councils added formal or informal obstacles to the concentration of power in a single office.[33] The institution of clientship, familiar to ancient and medieval European society as well as to primitive Africa, perpetuated relationships in which dependent persons pledged loyalty and service to masters who in return provided protection and the means of subsistence. These relationships sometimes worked against loyalty to the sovereign and the forces of centralization. The various effects of councils will be taken up in later chapters, but they also sometimes served to inhibit centralization.

In societies where a chief did manage to gather separated powers and to establish a kingdom and a state, the members of the secret orders became the personal agents of the king. This kind of transformation, Hutton Webster observed, was concluded only after a struggle.[34] Yet, the outcome of the struggle never destroyed the associations or took away their powers, but changed the definition of those powers and moved the secret societies to a different position in the political system. The Mende people of Sierra Leone would provide examples of communities in which secret societies played a subordinate but important role. There the typical political community has been described as a centralized monarchy "in which most political positions are vested in members of hereditary groups and with the additional factor of associations. These perform important political and administrative functions, especially in economic and cultural fields and in the general maintenance of social control." In such a community, it was the prerogative of the Poro Society, "as main custodian of tribal tradition, to watch the chief; to ensure that his actions as ruler conformed with customary practice."[35]

If the head of a community turned the political structure into a kingdom and managed to control the secret societies as part of his staff, that transformation redefined but did not end the dynamic tensions between the public offices and the invisible order of the associations, and only shifted the balance between them. Centralization was a trend made up of several processes, and "the state" is a concept that may be applied usefully to a stage in a continuum, but it is too vague to illuminate the social processes involved.[36] The political structure was shaped by the dynamics of corporate groups within the community—in states as well as in chiefdoms where executive power was split and the polity bicentralized. Lowie's investigation of the relation between associations and the formation of the state may have come to a dead end. But if we turn our attention away from the anatomy of the state to the dynamics within it, and if we examine the processes that sometimes yield states and sometimes prevent them, his work opens up a different line of inquiry. The nature of Lowie's interest made his conception of secret societies too narrow, and he neglected the significance of their characteristic terrorism. I would never contend that these associations were exclusively agents of terror, but through their capacity to produce and organize fear—one of their most obvious features—secret societies worked as a means to inhibit, within and without the state, some natural controls and limits to *centralized* power, which were described earlier in this chapter.

In a chiefdom, we have seen, the relation between chief and elders was crucial for many reasons, one being the dependence of the chief on the elders for an executive staff. As chiefdoms grew in size and complexity, the chief might gather a personal retinue with minimal ties to the local community and thus by degrees grow less dependent on the elders. The relations then formed a system of dynamic tension, in which elders and chiefs co-operated, bound by mutual needs, claims, and obligations, yet strained apart by trying to protect or build independent bases of power, and also worked to impose, preserve, or throw off controls of different kinds on one another's actions. In states, the tension was of a different order and magnitude, as elders were incorporated with subordinate chiefs in a unified system of command and administration. Where neighborhoods and local communities were organized around lineages in states that had a king, administrative machinery, courts of law, and other centralized agencies, these local lineages—led by elders —were often sources of tension and stress. Feelings of identification with the kin groups and the internal rivalries arising out of the divisions between the lineages tended to keep the political structure unstable.[37] In addition, the very palace organization that began as the arm of the king, could become a large social body with divisions and contradictions in it that might either contribute to the tensions or else be used as counterforces to help balance the system. At this level of complexity, when stability was menaced by potential conflict and the tendency to fission, there were two typical ways to achieve integration.

One was to fashion a constitution that would allow all the groups with different social identities to live together in peace. The system depended on compromise, distribution of power, delegation of authority, reciprocal adjustments, the mutual acceptance of limitations, forbearance, devising institutions to minimize the occasions of conflict, finding ways to satisfy rather than to deny claims, and the deliberate effort to respond to resistance in some manner that was not destructive. This system thrived in an emotional atmosphere of moderation, and in Europe the pattern was named "constitutional monarchy."

The other alternative was to destroy all forms of overt resistance, contradiction, and opposition, to eliminate the traditional sources of instability and tension by changing the corporate structure of the state, and to inhibit potential resistance by recurrent violence. This was the pattern of terroristic despotism, and one example of it is explored in the later chapters on the Zulu system.

Ultimately, the ruler of a state who chose the violent alternative depended on the loyalty of a disciplined staff that was structurally dissociated from local institutions. Thus, in classical antiquity it was often observed that tyrants of the most violent sort did not trust their own people for unconditional obedience and systematic destruction, but instead engaged mercenaries and surrounded themselves with foreign bodyguards.[38]

POLITICAL FUNCTION OF ASSOCIATIONS

Still, the state was not inevitable, and the course of development that led from small chiefdom to large chiefdom and then proceeded to constitutional monarchy, or else branched off to terroristic despotism, was not the only line of political evolution. Another alternative—returning in our analysis to the crucial relation between chief and elders—was for a group of elders in a chiefdom to obtain supreme power and to exercise it as an oligarchy. This alternative of collective rule by such a group was possible, in notion and in fact, only before a state had formed. In a *kingdom*, the official function of elders was to advise and assist, and there was no way open for them to claim the right to rule. An oligarchic revolution in a kingdom would have been imagined or supported by no one. In those *chiefdoms* where elders did have supreme power, they held it not by virtue of their public office but by indirect means and, as we shall see, by their relation to the ancestral spirits. Their positions in the invisible order of secret societies opened a way to overcome the formal limits of their public authority as elders and to control the incumbents of public offices, for the highest formal authority remained with the chiefs.

Chieftaincy was a political office that in its early stages remained distinct in many respects from other spheres of social control. In certain chiefdoms, Lestrade suggested, social lines of organization and the political organization were independent variables.[39] The powers of elders and the heads of households were broad and undefined, but limited to the group, and their authority was moral and persuasive rather than compulsory and legal.[40] Moreover, the way of making decisions in this sphere emphasized the search for harmony rather than the coercive closure of issues. The procedure tended to register prevailing opinion, to crystallize the sense of the meeting, to avoid conflict, and to find a compromise. Finally, the presence of kinship inhibited the use of violence. According to generally observed rules, the closer the relationship, the greater the restraint on belligerence and violence.[41] Thus, the very rules that placed social controls in the hands of elders and headmen also depoliticized their power—and here I am giving "political" power the familiar meaning, classically expressed by Weber, of the capacity to make a final decision that can be legitimately enforced by physical coercion or violence.

In the secret associations, a sphere that transcended the kin group and the local community, elders exercised another kind of power. The secret associations were cults that had their origin in universal puberty rites that were organized and conducted by the elders, who, from time immemorial, were the responsible guardians of the political community.[42] Hutton Webster observed:

> In Melanesia and Africa, political centralization has resulted to a large degree in the establishment of chieftainships powerful over a considerable area and often hereditary in nature. But this process has not continued so far as to make possible the entire surrender to the tribal chiefs of those functions of social control which in the earlier stages of society rest with the elders alone. The secret societies which have everywhere arisen on the basis of the puberty institutions, appear in Africa and Melanesia as organizations charged with the performance of important political and judicial functions.[43]

In some communities, the development of secret societies gave elders an opportunity to politicize their power, providing them with a legitimate source of coercion and violence. This power, with its freedom from public limits and the capacity to make final decisions with coercive force was greater than the public authority of chiefs. It attracted a coalition of chiefs and elders sitting as a college of equals in the religious cult and, in effect, united as an oligarchy. In the political system, this small circle of peers worked as specialists in terror—although that was not their exclusive function—and dominated the system by virtue of their high positions in the secret societies. As George Harley put it, public affairs "rested in the hands of a few privileged old men of high degree . . . who worked in secret and ruled by frightfulness." [44]

Fear was produced and organized by the use of carved wooden masks, carefully worked and polished, which were handed down through generations of officials in the secret orders, sometimes with an accumulated patina of blood or magical substance. The masks were fashioned according to stereo-

typed images that represented ancestral spirits or other supernatural forces. They also served as dramaturgic devices that
helped men to dissociate their acts performed as agents of the
secret society from their roles in public life. Thus it was possible for a venerable, kindly patriarch to be also a bloody terrorist. The use of a mask to separate and define the differences
between an individual's role in a sacred drama and his role in
familial life is known to a great number of societies all over the
world.[45] It is widely recognized, moreover, that masks possess
great emotional force to inspire expected patterns of behavior.
A student of masks in the Southwest Pacific observes:

> Wherever they come from in time or space, and whatever
> their shape or component materials, masks have long been
> recognized as casting a spell which is peculiarly their own. . . .
> The feeling is often expressed that these objects are endowed
> with a singular preternatural quality. The beholder of the mask
> is moved to attribute a life of its own to the object. The feeling
> arises that a masked performer has somehow undergone a
> metamorphosis and assumed in living form the qualities of his
> disguise. The watching audience, knowing that what it sees
> is a person wearing something that he can again take off,
> nevertheless is captured by the illusion that the mask somehow
> belongs to the figure and expresses its nature. Wearers of
> masks, on the other hand, often report that they feel more or
> less transformed by the image they are wearing, so that they
> are moved to act according to the characteristics which are
> associated with it.
>
> [In New Britain] Lakalai men say that as soon as they don
> one of the masks known for violent behavior, they begin to
> feel strong and fierce. . . .[46]

This emotional effect helps to explain the impression the dis-
guises made even on the initiates of the secret societies, who
knew that the masks were worn by men, as well as the impact
on the uninitiated, who believed the masked figures were gods.
Furthermore, as a member of a secret order, a man could, if

necessary, commit acts of violence against his own kinsmen, even though such acts were taboo according to the rules of public life. The secret societies created relationships and obligations that were dissociated from the ties of kinship and neighborhood. For example, when a boy was initiated into the Egungun Society, a masked association of the Yoruba people in southwestern Nigeria, he was asked:

> "Are you prepared to go even against your brother?"
> He replies "Yes."
> "Are you prepared to go even against your father?"
> "Yes."
> "Are you prepared to go even against your mother?"
> "Yes."
> Then he puts on an *egungun* dress for the first time.[47]

In the West African chiefdoms examined in the next chapter, terror was not exercised by a ruler's executioners, and it depended on dissociations different in kind from those we may observe in a terroristic despotism. The form of terrorism, then, is structurally different from the type examined in the subsequent chapters on the Zulu system. Finally, the examples given in Chapter V should dispose of the persistent fallacy that tradition prevents terrorism or that terror follows only the breakdown of tradition. The officials of the secret societies were kindly patriarchs who were also traditional terrorists, and the purpose of their terror, it was widely understood, was to uphold tradition.

One may object to my description of secret associations as instruments of terror because the work of their members often resembles the conduct of agents who enforce law and custom in many societies. Wearing masks to punish offenders, one may contend, is not much different from putting on a police uniform or judicial robes to enforce the law against criminals. In the role of judge or policeman, the agent of the law, like a Poro masked official, may be responsible for acts of violence he would never perform in a private capacity.

I would argue that the resemblance is arresting but superficial, although the work of secret officials does shift between terrorism and legal punishment, making the issue complex and difficult.

Everyone knows that the effect of a mask is different from the effect of a uniform. Although some people may take fright at the appearance of policemen and judges, terror is not the socially expected response to the sight of a uniform. The effect of a grotesque mask, however, is socially defined as fear, but the fright goes deeper than social definition. It may be a primordial response to any device that transforms and disfigures the face and body, and Hebb's experiments with chimpanzees suggest that the terror reaction produced by a frightening mask may be wired into the anthropoid nervous system and have biological origins older than mankind. In a very interesting series of experiments, the psychologist D. O. Hebb has shown that these primates respond with an unlearned, spontaneous "paroxysm of terror at being shown a model of a human or chimpanzee head detached from the body" or at being shown a distorted image of a head. The evidence indicates that both men and chimpanzees have a similar spontaneous fear, and Hebb's experiments lead one to speculate that the severed head and the grotesque mask is not merely a symbol but what an ethologist, or social biologist, might call a sign stimulus, which triggers an innate releasing mechanism in the anthropoid nervous system and produces the terror response.[48]

The only factor that a uniform and a stereotyped mask have in common is that they both identify a role. Nevertheless, the uniform is not intended to conceal the social identity of the judge or policeman, and the continuity of social identity, which defines "who" the role player "is," makes him accountable—in principle—for his actions in any role. Despite all the psychological truths about how persons are absorbed in the roles they play, and all the microsocial truths about how life is exhausted in an agenda of games, it is still true that a performance assumes the existence of a performer who has a social identity that transcends the sequence of performances. Society is not the stage alone, but the audience and the stage together, and it is usually possible to learn the identity of the person playing a role. In other words, there is ordinarily a visible, public link between the role and the person socially responsible for the acts performed in the role. The function of the secrecy enjoyed by secret associations is to destroy the link between the role in the association and the member's public identity. Whereas public officers are responsible for their acts to the society as a whole— or to special representatives—the secret association denies that connection and occludes responsibility within its own boundaries. The terror helps to sever the connection, preventing challenge or any other kind of resistance to the actions of masked officials.

Finally, the terror helps to facilitate the enforcement capacity of the secret association as well as to support public authority. Spirits from the invisible world are enlisted in the service of power, and a spirit is a supernatural force immune to resistance because it is invisible and unpredictable. By exploiting the fears of supernatural forces, and by further eliminating resistance through unexpected visitations and the threat of violence, the secret associations clear the way for the operation of ordinary controls. They augment the scope of duly constituted authority through terror, expanding its resources beyond the limitations of public offices.

CHAPTER V

INVISIBLE

GOVERNMENT

Though in many of its aspects this visible world seems
formed in love, the invisible spheres were formed in fright.
—Herman Melville, *Moby Dick.*

SECRET SOCIETIES extended all over West Africa. The scope
and nature of their work were known to one and all, and the
wide range of their activities made them the dominant social
force in many places. They were spread throughout southern
Nigeria, the Ivory Coast, Liberia, Sierra Leone, and parts of
Ghana and Guinea, although in some large states—Ashanti,
Dahomey, and Nupe—the central government's control of ritual and force deprived associations of public functions.[1] In
many communities secret societies took the responsibility for
administration, supervision, and adjudication in several
spheres, and outside the political realm they supervised economic life, took charge of education, regulated sexual conduct,
provided medical treatment and social services, and organized
entertainment and recreation.[2] The Poro Society, which was
the most powerful and pervasive association, active from time
immemorial, has a recorded history of over four hundred years.

What were kept secret by these associations were the ritual,
magical formulas and medicinal recipes, the mysterious relationships to the ancestral spirits, the closely guarded details of
internal organization, and the sources of their political power.
The extent of a member's information depended on his position

within the organization, and some things were restricted to the few old men who had ascended to the highest degrees. The published work of George Harley, who worked as a medical missionary in West Africa for over three decades, reveals a sympathetic understanding of the culture and a great deal of information about the secret societies. He studied the Poro Society in Liberia among the Mano, Geh, and Gio—neighbors of the Kpelle, who were discussed briefly in the previous chapter. His observations make it clear that the success of the Poro depended on its effectiveness as a terroristic organization—that the "final secret of the Poro was frightfulness." According to Harley, the leaders of the secret order held sway by virtue of the widespread fear of their magical powers and through the violence associated with their acts. "This fear lies behind all chiefs and political leaders, behind all heads of families and men of standing. It has an enormous influence in regulating the social and economic life of the people." [3]

Poro officials controlled ordinary social and political life through the intervention of masked and costumed figures, who were understood to be ancestral spirits. Some of them acted as clowns, dancers, and entertainers, and provided occasions for hilarity, but when a mask of a serious nature appeared, always worn by a lord of the higher orders with his body also disguised by a traditional costume, and when the voice of a spirit was heard in the village or in the bush, ordinary life was suspended. People crawled away and hid themselves, trembling with terror of the dreaded spirit of the mask, or else they behaved submissively in stereotyped ways prescribed by the identity of the specific mask. Harley reported that the Poro spirit masks

> were used in all important events: to stop village quarrels, or control fighting warriors; to catch, try, condemn, punish or even execute social criminals; to intensify the holiday spirit of great occasions; to promote fertility of the fields and bountiful harvests; to cultivate public sentiment, regulate hygiene, build

bridges and sacred houses; and to conduct and administer the Poro school which was all things to all men.[4]

Thus, agents from an invisible realm intervened in ordinary life at moments of crisis or solemnity, even to perform certain administrative tasks.

THE CONTROL OF CHIEFDOMS

Therefore, in some bicentralized and polycephalous chiefdoms such as those found among the Kpelle, Mano, Geh, and Gio of Liberia, political life was divided between visible and invisible spheres. The visible, public realm was typically organized in families, quarters, towns, and clans, all under the formal but limited authority of a paramount chief, with the clan as the most significant political unit.[5] Office was usually hereditary, and on each level, family heads, quarter chiefs, town chiefs, clan heads, and the paramount chief shared power with senior men and councils of elders, the visible system being marked by the great extent to which chiefly powers were circumscribed. The town chief was "little more than executive head of his council of elders," and the councils had "a manner of ridding themselves of autocrats—a fact few chiefs allow themselves to forget." The paramount chief had a court with several functionaries who had a certain degree of independence. His prime minister or "speaker" was a powerful clan chief and usually the first one in line for the paramountcy. Each clan chief as "father of his country" had supreme authority in principle but limited power in practice. "An actual despot, ruling without reference to the cult and war leaders, would be very unpopular and would not last long." [6]

The ordinary, secular management of civil affairs carried on by what Harley called "the external organization of chiefs and minor officers," operated primarily as an administrative and judicial mechanism, proceeding through visible relationships of mutual responsibility with open, public discussion and lively participation taking place on every level and involving the entire population. This sphere was "perfectly evident to casual observers. It was known and understood by all members of the group, including women and children. It was based upon a patriarchal system that controlled the people in a more or less democratic manner." But the jurisdiction of the visible government, the open discussion, and the reciprocal responsibilities of chiefs and people were confined to specific routines, and the open system of public regulation gave way to the invisible government in critical matters or when issues required decisions of policy. As Harley explained:

> The head of the family ruled his immediate household. It was an easy step from this domestic rule to the authority of the "quarter chief" who heard complaints and settled petty palavers in a few families living side by side in the town and united by close ties of kinship. He would not hold formal court, but would talk matters over with interested people, sitting around almost anywhere. Everyone present had freedom of speech and of opinion. If there was a disagreement of a more serious nature, or if anyone objected to the quarter chief's decisions, a more formal hearing would be held by the town chief. From here appeals could be carried to the clan chief. . . .
>
> Town chiefs and clan chiefs had the custom of calling in the elders to help decide matters of complicated or obscure nature. They might sit in the town council and express their opinions openly and informally, but as a matter increased in importance, the meetings of the elders became more and more secret until they reached the final high council. This met at night in a secret part of the sacred Bush, presided over by a high priest with a simple but highly effective ritual.[7]

The invisible government deliberated in secret to formulate policy, and it intervened in the civil order by means of masks. When a "masked spirit" came to town, Harley says, "the chief stood in the corner." Presenting different faces and bearing many functions, all the masks were understood to be images of ancestral spirits, but they were generally used as badges of office. The masked figures worked as ceremonial leaders, messengers, police, instructors, war leaders, judges, and executioners. When masks were worn, they were treated as living gods; when they were not worn but present, resting passively on the ground at secret palavers, they were treated as oracles and petitioned for authoritative judgments. The atmosphere of fright inspired by certain masks was based on their cultural significance—their meaning in the tradition—and the emotional reaction amounted to nothing less than a terror by convention. The effect of the terror was to make the power of the mask unilateral and free of reciprocal influence, in stark contrast to the limited powers of every public official. In the visible, secular realm, a chief experienced reciprocal controls and limitations imposed by elders and by public opinion, but one of the higher masks encountered on a mission was not even to be gazed on, and certainly not to be challenged or influenced by ordinary people. Kenneth Little observes, "Doubtless the terrifying effect of these 'spirits' derived largely from the violent way in which the individuals impersonating them were licensed to behave. Several earlier writers . . . have described how such a Poro party of masked officials descended with irresistible force upon any community rash enough to ignore the society's dictates." [8]

The dissociation of the invisible government from the social relations of ordinary life made systematic terrorism possible. By attributing their acts to the work of spirits, the masked officials were liberated from ordinary responsibility for those acts, although, we shall see, they were held responsible to the highest orders of the secret association and to custom. As masks, they were not bound by the ordinary ties of family, clan, or civil hierarchy. The greatest mask of the Poro in the old days was "fed" regularly by the blood sacrifice of animals, but when it was transferred from one generation to the next, the new owner sacrificed his eldest son to the mask and, accompanied in the ceremony by his ritual consort, ate the sacred parts of the body. Harley explained that the sacrifice dispatched the son as a messenger to inform the ancestors of the transfer of the mask, but the sacrificial murder and ritual cannibalism, depriving the mask's new owner of his eldest son, also signified that the owner was beyond the claims of kinship and that his office transcended the relationships of the civil world.

When the masks intervened in the visible realm they acted as spirits uncontrolled by social relationships, but the internal order of the invisible realm—the structure of the Poro Society —both reflected and reorganized the ranks of the civil order. The secret society was stratified in three broad segments: commoners, chiefs and nobles, and the class of specialists called *zo*. The ranks within each class have been compared to the stages of Freemasonry, each with its lore, ritual, secret communication, special obligations, and program of advancement to the rank above. Locally, Poro initiations would often wait for a chief's son to reach puberty so that he might serve as the leader of his age set. In the Poro schools, commoners learned their trades and received other training useful for their station, nobles and chiefs learned the arts and mysteries of their rank, and the class called *zo*—ascribed for some, achieved by others—made up the higher degrees. The word *"zo"* includes the meanings of specialist, doctor, professional, and expert, and in ordinary life it could refer to a master blacksmith as well as to a priest or physician. The *zo* were an elite who knew the higher secrets of any organization, and in the Poro Society, an hereditary *zo* knew many secrets from his father before being initiated. However, a child of commoners who was marked by certain physical or emotional characteristics could become a *zo* if a diviner ordained it.[9] The highest *zo* were at once priests, doctors, professors, magicians, master terrorists, and sagacious oligarchs. At the apex stood the head of the organization, sometimes referred to in English as the Grand Master, but named by English-speaking Liberians as the "Big Devil." The members of the highest degrees, whose specific rank and function were known only to their peers, formed a social aristocracy that inspired admiration and fear and enjoyed a prestige that was once coveted throughout West Africa.[10]

Almost any chief might also be a *zo*, but as such he might or might not own a spirit mask. When the highest chiefs were both *zo* and the owners of the greatest masks, their positions in the invisible government augmented their secular power immeasurably. Harley described four men he had known who had held the highest positions in both worlds. One was the paramount chief and an hereditary clan chief as well as the owner of the greatest mask and the greatest fetish. No one in the community had any greater authority, yet he was not a despot, for his power was not solitary, and policy was made in concert with other *zo*, his peers in the highest secret council. This august body would be composed of other men who were secular chiefs and magistrates, greater and lesser, as well as elders from the levels of clan and town. The dual roles integrated the secular and invisible orders, and conflicts between the two systems were minimized because the most powerful men in the community held key positions in both.

Other secret societies, such as the Antelope Horn, the Snake, and the Leopard associations, overlapped the Poro and the visible, public domain. They had special functions, but since all men were initiated in the Poro and all women in the Sande Society, they were connected in many ways, and it would not be wrong to consider them as specialized offshoots of a single, invisible order. Disruptions and controversies in the secular realm would invite the masked intervention of a spirit. Any issue of a critical nature might fall into the jurisdiction of a specialized secret association for investigation and resolution. Although women had little to say in public discussions, unless called as witnesses, their role was changed considerably when they acted as the agents of the spirits, and the secret association composed of the old women enjoyed a great deal of prestige and power. They had the responsibility for smelling out witches, they were consulted by the chiefs on many matters, and the consent of the old women's cult—as well as the Poro's —was required before a chief could declare war. If an issue were beyond the scope of the specialized secret orders, it would be taken up in the highest and least visible palaver of all, that is, in the council of men who owned the greatest masks, known in Mano as the *Ki La mi*. Harley was not sure if this group was confined to the Poro Society, but he believed that if not exclusively within the Poro, it was located "within the cult of the *masks*, of which the Poro was the most highly developed form for manifesting the power of the ancestors toward the people." [11] The group formed "an inner society of patriarchs," who were immune from chiefly power and who could act through the council of elders in the political sphere. They could even depose a chief if necessary, and their decision in all matters was final.[12] In ordinary life, the *Ki La mi* was visible as a kind of peerage, and the title meant the "skin people," because they were privileged to carry animal skins to sit on. At the very summit of this peerage was the innermost circle enjoying supreme status, "called *Ki Gbuo La mi* [the 'big skin men'], against whom personal insults or violence was considered no less than treason." [13]

Therefore, the upper degrees and inner circles of the invisible order made the crucial decisions concerning government, politics, war, and relations with other communities.[14] The formal civil chief had authority in ordinary matters, but the masks intervened when potential conflict threatened stability, and cases could be appealed from the secular courts to the tribunal of the Poro, which had final jurisdiction. When a chief was also a high-ranking Poro official, according to Harley, "He was something of a king, and had power of life and death over his subjects provided he worked through the Poro, never against it."

The initiates in the highest degree, according to Harley, were "postgraduate" terrorists—experts in the final mysteries of " 'frightfulness,' or the art of the innermost circles of the Poro itself." [15] Yet, Harley marvelled at the contrast between their work as masked spirits and their character as ordinary men. Regarding two whom he had known well, he remarked:

> If the messenger carried Zawolo's razor in his hand instead of the usual tongs then the big men knew that a culprit was to be tried for his life. . . . [Yet] I have never known a man more dignified and gentle, and I was a little surprised to learn that in the old days he had literally had the power of life and death over his people, for, as keeper of the great mask, he was a judge from whose decisions there was no appeal.
>
> Gbana . . . was a grand old man with pure white hair when I last saw him. He always had a kindly smile. At the height of his influence he was judge for a total of nine towns. . . . It is hard to reconcile the gory history of [his] blood-stained mask with the benign clear-eyed patriarch under whose tutelage I myself once joined the blacksmith's guild. I can only do so by regarding him as a high priest, worshipping his ancestors in the manner which custom demanded.[16]

Indeed, the entire organization of masks, Poro and others, worked as a kind of cultural police force, preventing and punishing deviations from custom. In addition, custom and tradition framed the limits of what a mask could do, prescribing the occasions for intervention and its style of action. The masks were offices, their functions continuing without interruption from one generation to the next. In the invisible order, by a rule of universal succession, the owner of a mask performed its duties as a corporation sole, which means, following Maine's usage: "The capacity or office is here considered apart from the particular person who from time to time may occupy it, and, this capacity being perpetual, the series of individuals who fill it are clothed with the leading attribute of Corporations—Perpetuity." [17] As Harley reported:

> If the wearer of a mask died, his place was taken by another and the mask continued to function without interruption. Thus the equilibrium of the community suffered a minimum distur-

bance, being that occasioned by the loss of an individual not especially important as such, rather than the loss of an important official whose individual character could not be replaced, whose successor might be activated by policies divergent from those already established. The mask thus provided continuity of authority, regardless of the personal attributes of the current wearer.[18]

Thus, the boundaries of social behavior were maintained not by formal laws or by declarations of policy but by the fixed functions of the masks and by the terror they inspired. The boundary keepers themselves were kept in bounds by their peers. *En rapport* with the spirit, the wearer of a mask could not improvise very much, and his interpretation was guided by a traditional concept of what the mask must represent. "If he should act out of character, he was liable to swift and final punishment at the hands of the *Ki Gbuo La mi,* who took all these things very seriously." [19]

When men wore the masks, the violence and terror of their actions were dissociated from their social identities and attributed to the spirits. Similarly, violence was dissociated from some routine activities of the secret cults. "The Poro was a place of abstinence and peace. Within its sacred precincts all personal enmities were supposed to be forgotten. While the Poro or Sande (the girls' school) was in session war was taboo." In its ordinary aspect, the cult was a place for peaceful teaching and worship. The terrors of initiation, where boys were supposed to be devoured and reborn, the sacrificial cannibalism in the old days, the secret executions in mysterious places of the forest, deaths by poison for those who betrayed the cult, and the sense of unknown danger lurking in the forest were all attributed to the work of the spirits. Furthermore, in their visible aspect, the *Ki La mi* were men of peace, immune from arrest and civil trial, exempt from war service, and bound by strict taboos against fighting or quarreling. Nevertheless, in their invisible roles, the taboos did not restrict their fine art of poisoning rivals.[20]

Even though power was not distributed equally within the elite, rivalry prevented excessive concentrations, and each *zo* lived with the danger that he might be poisoned by one of his peers. Everyone knew the *zo* were experts in the use of toxins, and no one interfered with their privilege of keeping or using poisons for which antidotes were unknown. The favorite *zo* poison would be used "only by big men to kill big men." A *zo* believed that if he did not kill his rival, the rival would do away with him.[21] The *zo* ate together frequently, "one never knowing when the other might get the drop on him." An especially successful *zo* might be taken on by another who was jealous of his reputation and who would say, " 'It is about time something happened to spoil his good luck. I will see what I can do.' " One of that kind became known as "the *zo* killer," and eliminated seventeen rivals before he succumbed. The reputation of his mask, even after it had passed to his successor, struck such terror

that a dog was supposed to fall dead on seeing it. An uninitiated person, especially a woman, would also "fall dead." When it was worn into town, a messenger gave warning. All women gathered children and dogs and scuttled inside the houses, kneeling and clapping their hands behind fastened doors. Even the initiated men crawled around at their duties on hands and knees.[22]

Sometimes the rivalry penetrated to the visible government, and a chief who did not own a spirit mask but still was a *zo,* after some preliminary arrangements, might publicly defy a mask. A chief's prestige would soar if he did not "stand in the corner" when a spirit mask came to town and if he refused to permit a mask to settle a palaver. However, in a case reported by Harley, the career of one chief—a warrior *zo* who defied a spirit in this way—ended fatally when he indiscreetly violated one of the taboos of that mask during a petty war.[23]

The general effect of the masks as a political executive and as agents of social control was to prevent concentrations of power and to get rid of deviants. As Harley put it, "the rugged individualist was very likely to be eliminated and his 'estate' divided among the surviving peers." [24] Moreover, the struggle over policy matters was removed to the invisible realm, leaving to the ancestral spirits the responsibility for decisions as well as the responsibility for justice. The visible government, then, was little more than an administrative apparatus.

As M. G. Smith has shown, the ways in which societies divide, distribute, join, and dissociate political and administrative powers and functions are bound to be crucial matters for the nature of their structure and for their stability. [25] In typical chiefdoms that did not have secret societies to discharge political functions, the visible structures contained both administrative and political activities. Competition for power and conflicts over policy took place more or less openly between the chief and the members of his lineage, between subordinate chiefs, between the heads of territorial units, or between the heads of lineages. Discontent with leadership was expressed as action against the incumbent, producing complaints, obstructions, defections, moves to eliminate the chief one way or another or to reduce his authority, and other forms of resistance that extended to secession and rebellion. Fission was the common result of competition for power. Frequently, the formation of a state, with an apparatus for coercion and violence under the direction of a single ruler, brought the drives toward fission under control.

In Alur society, where chiefdoms remained uncentralized, at the most growing to protostates—or segmentary states, to follow Southall's usage—the fissiparous tendencies were brought into the service of expansion, with unruly sons or disgruntled kinsmen of the chief moving out to organize politically undefined areas as new chieflets. Yet, even this solution had obvious limits. When the boundaries of expansion were reached, the permissive attitude toward fission would have had to change. The frontiers would have become more precise and the powers of chiefs and chieflets more strictly defined. If the Alur had faced such limiting conditions before the coming of the Europeans, Southall concludes, the expansionist energies would have been turned into rivalry for political power, and it is probable that one chief would have risen to dominate the others. "Clearly this would have meant larger and more centralized political units having more and more the quality of states." [26] In the following chapters, we shall examine this historical process in Southern Africa, observing the formation of the Zulu state and its consequences.

In West Africa, the dual system that confined issues of policy to a secret council and restricted competition for power to the private combat among *zo*, eliminating it from the public sphere, produced a relatively stable situation that managed to hold off centralization—at least among peoples such as the Kpelle, Mano, Geh, and Gio—without falling prey to the forces of segmentation and fission. Any kind of state would have turned the Poro oligarchs into lesser powers. As we shall see, in cases where kingdoms did form, the secret societies adapted to the change but were transformed into subordinate, though important, agencies.

States and chiefdoms can get along without associations, but secret societies with secular power must depend on the existence of a visible government to provide an arena for intervention. Although it may assume the responsibility for many administrative functions, the association cannot organize the entire community or take on the routine of daily administration. Constant presence would destroy its effectiveness, which depends on mystery, dramatic intervention, and the sudden return to invisibility. The men in the masks are only temporarily dissociated and not socially removed from ordinary life. To establish a system in which the visible government is regularly controlled by spirits would be to construct a theocratic order with an elaborate apparatus to maintain distance between people and divine rulers, which would require a social system as productive and complex as the kind that supported the ancient Egyptian or the Inca state. Such a system would in turn produce a socially distinct ruling class.

In the simple, bicentralized chiefdoms of West Africa, chiefs could increase their power only *through* secret associations such as the Poro. This power depended to a large extent on character, opportunity, and position within the Poro—not on the office of chief. Therefore, the office as such did not serve as a focus for unitary centralization. Since the very work of the mask depended on dissociation, a man who gathered the highest powers in his lifetime—an hereditary clan chief who was elected to paramountcy and who owned the great mask—could not always pass the cluster of powers intact to his heir. Moreover, as long as he had to work through the Poro, he was controlled by his peers on the great council. As a peer, he deliberated on equal terms with the others, unattended by his following—a procedure that separated him from the source of his secular power, since in the visible realm a big man was distinguished by his wealth and by the number of his followers. Within the Poro he could use as a staff certain lesser masks to carry out orders, but they were not under his exclusive control, regulated as they were by custom and working under the scrutiny of the other peers. Furthermore, the pledge of secrecy in the highest councils minimized factions, removing from the arena of public controversy the issues around which important chiefs might gather and mobilize followers.

Yet, the political relationship between the Poro Society and the chiefs was not uniform. Schwab observed:

> In Gbunde, Loma, and Mano the Big Devil can countermand or make inoperative any course of action of which he does not approve, even if the paramount chief, the council of elders, and the whole community are in accord that it should be done. Persons who have ventured to dispute his decision have been known to die suddenly.

But in Gio, the head of the Poro is not superior to either the paramount chief or the town chief: "Rather, he supplements the chief's authority." [27] Among the Sherbro of Sierra Leone, the Poro asserted its authority at the beginning of a chief's reign. A new chief was kept in seclusion for weeks or longer in a building erected on the outskirts of the Poro Bush. The Poro, for the period of confinement, constituted a kind of regency, and the chief was instructed by the elders who directed Poro affairs. In Sherbro, the Poro also retained control over economic affairs and certain matters associated with crises of the life cycle.[28]

Despite the high degree of stability achieved in the relation between visible and invisible spheres, the balance was probably tipped by external factors such as the opportunity and the requirements of warfare. It is difficult for a secret society to dominate generals in the field, and through the command of armies, warrior chiefs probably found a basis for power that was more independent than any other position. The power of these chiefs now worked beyond and above the secret society, although they were still influenced and limited by the associations in many respects. Kenneth Little suggests that individual chiefs gained and kept extra power through military success. He believes that great warrior chiefs, backed by mercenaries, may have won quick victories, but sought some means of control more effective than physical force. They may have exploited beliefs in spirits and medicine that were common to all peoples in the region by using the Poro as an instrument of government in the conquered territories.[29]

In the Mende chiefdoms of Sierra Leone, Little observes, the chief had no ritual or religious functions and hence no magical controls. His function as a ruler derived from his role as a war leader, and his power to command was based on physical capacity and the force of his personality, not on the mystical forces from which the Poro drew its strength. One may surmise that he turned to the Poro for assistance. In the secret society, moreover:

> He would have at his disposal a body of secret agents, well disciplined and already under oath, to police the particular territory in which they belonged. These agents would keep the

head chief continuously informed about what was going on, and he would be able to use them, if need arose, to stamp out disaffection or civil unrest.[30]

In the Mende system, one also finds a political and administrative apparatus more elaborate than that of the Liberian chiefdoms discussed previously, but spheres of jurisdiction were divided between the high chief and the associations.[31]

EFFECTS OF CENTRALIZATION

In kingdoms, the role of the secret association varied in importance. It ranged from being a position as central as the Council of State, which was the most important agency in some Yoruba kingdoms, to being a mere influential force known to be a useful check on the greed and violence of chiefs.[32]

In the Grassfields kingdom of Kom in West Cameroon, which had a sacred kingship and a royal lineage, the *kwifoyn*, a regulatory society of masked initiates, worked as a secret society, a police force, and the king's retinue. Quartered on the palace grounds, it recruited palace retainers from the commoners and served as the executive arm of the government. One day of the week was reserved to it, during which certain acts were taboo. The impression of awe and the production of terror were managed largely by the use of named and dreaded masks and by sacred gongs. Similar to other secret societies, invisibility helped to dissociate its controls from the countercontrols and the resistances that adhere to ordinary public relationships:

> In the execution of its state duties its retainers appeared clothed in net gowns which masked face and body; its authority was of an impersonal kind, and its agents could not be held to account by the populace. It was everywhere seen as supporting the chief; without it there would be disorder.[33]

If we turn to the Yoruba kingdoms of southwestern Nigeria, we find that the position of the secret society is less central in a large state than in small kingdoms. Let us compare the kingdom of Oyo, a great centralized state flourishing in the eighteenth and nineteenth centuries, with its vassal kingdoms in a region further southwest known as Egbado.

The Yoruba term for king is *oba,* and the title of the Oba in the great kingdom of Oyo was the *Alafin.* The *Oyo Mesi* was a group of lords who were nonroyal title holders in the kingdom of Oyo, but not in Egbado, and they served as the Council of State in Oyo. The *Ogboni Society* was a cult of the Earth and a dreaded secret association. Other secret societies were the masked associations of the *Egungun* and the *Ora.* The information in the following discussion is drawn mainly from several articles by Peter Morton-Williams.

The Oyo kingdom was an aggressive, expanding state, and in the nineteenth century it established a trade corridor to the sea, setting up members of the royal dynasty as vassal rulers of the Egbado towns in this corridor. The towns were tiny, separate kingdoms dependent on Oyo. Among the several religious associations, besides the Ogboni Society, which were an important part of the political system in these small kingdoms, the masked Egungun Society as well as the Oro cult worked through magic, violence, and fear as agencies of social control, creating an atmosphere of danger, calling forth the ancestral spirits, and bringing the gods to town. Morton-Williams has described how the visitations of invisible spirits in an Egungun ceremony "generate an atmosphere of terror, and of vengeance by spirit forces." [34] They exercised considerable power, working as a police force and searching for witches and sorcerers, but their violence also helped stabilize the political order by liquidating concentrations of power outside the official hierarchy. The Oro and Egungun cults threatened or eliminated rich or powerful men with independent resources that might have allowed them to challenge the constituted authorities. [35]

In the Oyo kingdom, the Egungun Society was prominent, but not as powerful as in the Egbado towns, and it was controlled by government officials. A lord of the Oyo Mesi—the

Council of State—directed the cult, and the most powerful mask was owned by the Alafin, who assigned it to a slave or a eunuch in charge of detecting witchcraft. The dogma that the Oba "owned" all the cults was interpreted to mean, in the Oyo kingdom, that it was the duty of the priesthoods to serve the gods in order to satisfy the needs of the king, and that the work of the secret societies was to be placed in the service of the public good.[36] The dogma justified binding the cults into the palace apparatus.

Both types of kingdom had evolved a constitutional order based on principles of check and counterpoise. Yoruba people could not conceive of government without kingship, Morton-Williams claims, but they also believed that uncontrolled kings would abuse their powers. The powers of the king were limited and balanced by an organization known as the Council of State, but the composition of this council was not the same in both types of kingdom. In the Egbado towns, the leaders of the Ogboni Society served as the Council of State, providing the structural opposition to the king and his palace officials, and the head of the Ogboni could demand the suicide of the king.[37] Within the Oyo kingdom, however, the Ogboni Society had a different constitutional function. The political authority of the Alafin as the secular and ritual head of the state was limited by ritual restrictions and checked by the Oyo Mesi, which served as the Council of State, in structural opposition to the king and palace. The function of the Ogboni Society was to limit the Oyo Mesi and to mediate between it and the king. Thus the king in Oyo was checked by one corporate structure—the Oyo Mesi—which in turn was checked by a second corporation— the Ogboni Society—which also mediated between the first corporation and the king.[38]

Mediating between the two positions, the Ogboni could impose ritual sanctions on both the Alafin and the Council of State. Their support was a crucial matter for the Alafin, since the Bashorun, the head of the Oyo Mesi, held the king's life in his hands. Once a year, the Bashorun divined to ascertain the quality of the relationship between the Oba and his double, or spirit counterpart, in heaven; a bad relationship could justify a command that the king should commit suicide. Collectively, with the Bashorun as spokesman, the Oyo Mesi could pronounce the rejection of the Alafin, which was followed by his suicide. The king had no equivalent to the council's power of life and death over him, for he could not remove the members collectively from office, although in certain circumstances he had control over individual members of the Oyo Mesi.[39]

The Ogboni Society supported the king in another way as well. As a secret corporation of political and religious leaders and special priests, the Ogboni spread terror among the population in the manner of other secret societies. In Oyo, the terror inspired by this association was understood to support the power of the Alafin. It was said, " 'Every Oba must have Ogboni so that the people may fear him.' " [40]

The institutionalized co-operation of the Ogboni with the Oyo Mesi had other political consequences besides limiting the power that checked the power of the king. In the Ogboni, it was felt, the Oyo Mesi sat with the wisest people in the community, and the great chiefs in the Council of State shared in the Ogboni ritual on equal terms with other initiates, unattended by their usual followings. The pledge of secrecy in Ogboni deliberations and the procedure of seeking to achieve unanimity went far to reduce factionalism within the kingdom and to stabilize the political order.

A pattern emerges if we compare the positions of the secret society in political communities of different sizes and different orders of complexity. In some small, bicentralized chiefdoms, the Poro Society was more powerful than the chiefs; in centralized chiefdoms, the chiefs had an advantage over the Poro, but the set of political functions and administrative responsibilities was divided between the secret society and the high chief. In some small kingdoms, a secret association worked as the executive arm of the government or as the Council of State. In larger, complex kingdoms, it served as only a part of the executive and administrative apparatus or as a mediator between agencies more powerful than itself. As the ancestral spirits moved from the forest to the palace, their nimbus faded. Moreover, from the superiors of chiefs, they turned into the servants of kings. They lost the exclusive privilege of coercion and were rivaled as agents of violence by other, more specialized staffs in the palace organization. Secure in his authority, the king relieved the ancestors of the responsibility for legitimate violence.

However, the pattern does not agree in all respects with Hutton Webster's theory of the origin, growth, and decline of secret societies. Webster discovered that in several parts of the world, especially Africa and Melanesia, a puberty institution would grow into an association exercising police functions, "ruling by the terror it inspires," using religious mysteries as instruments of social control, and imposing penalties of heavy fines or death for infractions of their rules.[41] I believe that the element of *mysterium tremendum* in its impact on the community would probably differentiate this kind of organization from the associations with police functions among the Plains Indians, despite Lowie's effort to bring them together in a single concept. Webster believed that the growth of population and the rise of large communities are "necessarily associated" with the decline of secret organizations as regulatory agencies and that "the establishment of the power of chiefs [and kings] on a permanent and hereditary basis" as well as other factors contributed to "the undermining of such crude institutions." [42]

The evidence indicates that the effects of centralization and complexity did not "undermine" the secret societies or cause them to "decline." They simply adapted to the new realities of power, not disappearing as political forces or agencies of social control but indeed losing their former positions of supremacy.

The mode of adaptation varied with the type of political structure. Among the Mende, secret associations were linked together as a network of control in a large federation of centralized chiefdoms. Among the Yoruba, the associations helped to link up a hierarchy of kingdoms. It appears that the Yoruba

people joined together secret societies in a system of social control that extended at times to an area that included some mil-
lions of people. By restricting the size of units, limiting jurisdictions, and confining organizations to specific categories of
social relationships, they arranged for associations in different
towns to overlap, and by fictitious kinship linked the leaders in
the towns with the leaders of the associations in Oyo. In the
towns, the leaders came together in a single council, formulating policy that was expressed by their king as the will of the
community. Far from declining, they added flexibility and du-
rability to an extensive system of political power. Morton-Williams concludes, "they produced a system of social control capable of working in a small community or in many thousands
and, most important, adapted to the hierarchy of kingdoms
built up by Oyo. They kept this vast society together for a long
time; it broke down not because of internal conflicts, but under
military invasion." [43]

In states, therefore, the secret society's terroristic activities
were important but not primary. Associations worked as part of
an elaborate constitutional mechanism, and the resources of the
king included other agents and staffs whose violence might be
used with greater precision. To understand the functions of terror in states, then, we must turn from the secret society and
search in another direction.

Some large states in West Africa, such as Ashanti, Nupe,
and Dahomey, made no political use of secret cults. Likewise,
throughout the rest of the African Continent, with notable exceptions, organizations in communion with the invisible world
did not tend to absorb major political functions. Other associations, such as age regiments, were more important in the East
and in South Africa. The political use of secret societies proved
to be a social invention having special affinities with West African cultures, but the dynamics underlying that particular adaptation showed features that were universal.

When a political community is formed from elements that
are less complex—for example, when a chiefdom combines sev-

eral clans or tribes, or when a kingdom unites several chief-doms—some means are found to deal with crises of political integration. Invisible government by a secret society is one "solution"—one choice among several alternatives—one mode of dealing with these problems by means of terror in chiefdoms and in small kingdoms. But in states, beyond the various patterns of more or less peaceful, constitutional arrangement, another form of the violent alternative is possible—that of terroristic despotism.

CHAPTER VI

THE RISE

OF THE

ZULU STATE

The absolute stands even above the reasonable.
That is why sovereigns often choose to act unreasonably,
in order to retain their sense of absolute freedom.

—Goethe, *Conversations.*

THE ZULU KINGDOM is not extinct. It survives in the imaginations of many Bantu-speaking people, and remains latent in
their social practices.[1] Historically, it is as old as modern
France, but it remained an independent system for a brief
seven decades, its glory ending in the Zulu War of 1879. The
period of independence was spanned by the reigns of five monarchical figures: Dingiswayo (c. 1808–18), who laid the
foundations; Shaka (1816–28), who established the despotic
state and ruled at the zenith of Zulu power; Dingane
(1828–40), who continued the despotism as European settlers
began to entrench upon the Zulu domain; Mpande (1840–72),
whose sovereignty was limited by accommodation first to Boer,
then to British, power; Cetshwayo (1872–79), who sought to
break free but lost independence in a war against the British.
Shaka stands out as the greatest of them all—both Romulus
and Napoleon to the Zulu people—and his legend has captured
the imaginations of both European and African writers, inspir-

ing novels, biographies, and historical studies in several tongues. As a violent autocrat he is both admired and condemned: admired by those who love conquerors, condemned by those who hate despots.

For the later part of its history, the Zulu state, like most African kingships, may be described as a limited monarchy. The period of terroristic despotism was limited to two dozen years, from about 1816 to 1840, and to only two rulers. Even the most jaundiced historians of the Victorian age, Boer as well as British, obsessed with the putative ferocity and rudeness of the Bantu-speaking people, agreed that despotism among them was "abnormal." George McCall Theal, the exemplar of those historians, observed that in contrast to the unusual "pure despotism" observed under Shaka and Dingane, "the normal system of government" was patriarchal rule in a familiar, indigenous pattern of checks and balances.[2] Although the dramatic features of African despotism have left strong impressions on history and literature, the type of rule is infrequent and cannot be understood as a common species in the wide range of African kingship.[3]

Despite its uncommon character as a political community, the evolution of the Zulu state in the reigns of Shaka and Dingane illuminates the relationship between terrorism and despotic power. Notwithstanding the limitations of a primitive technology, Shaka was able to utilize violence on such a scale as to create what some social scientists have called a proto-totalitarian system. Without gas chambers, machine guns, or a guillotine, Shaka managed to establish one of the most effective regimes of terror on record. He modified the traditional assegai, which was a long throwing spear, by reducing the length of the shaft and turning it into a short, thrusting weapon. With this material instrument he constructed a pattern of terroristic controls more efficient, although smaller in scale, than the techniques of totalitarian states with all their deadly apparatus. His regime proves that a system of terror depends not on the instruments of violence, but on the techniques of social control.

The secret weapon of a terroristic regime is its social organization.

Nathaniel Isaacs, who observed Shaka closely in the last two years of his reign, declared, "The world has heard of monsters —Rome had her Nero, the Huns their Attila, and Syracuse her Dionysius; the East has likewise produced her tyrants; but for ferocity, Chaka has exceeded them all; he has outstripped in sanguinary executions all who have gone before him, and in any country." Other observers have agreed with the historian Theal that the Zulu developed "the most perfect despotism the world has ever known," but it is not necessary to accept that judgment of its perfection to recognize its heuristic value.

The system began when Shaka, in the second decade of the nineteenth century, fused the Mthethwa[4] and the Zulu people into a single nation, which reached imperial proportions after he established a regime of military and civil terror. The empire continued but declined under the rule of his fratricide successor, Dingane, terminating with another assassination, after which Zulu power was limited by European pressure and subsequent conquest. The internal transformations wrought by the despotic regime were accompanied by enormous devastation and dislocation throughout South and Central Africa, disrupting a third of the continent, although it appears from recent interpretations of the evidence that other inchoate states along with Shaka's forces must share some of the responsibility for the disruption.[5] A mythical aura envelops the *Mfekane,* or the great "Crushing," which is the name given to the period in which people were set into motion by the wars among nascent states. According to legend, fragments of communities banded together—such as the Mantati horde, the subject of much fantasy—and moved as a ferocious swarm, reduced by battle and starvation, yet crushing their way to new locations. The numbers destroyed in the *Mfekane* are probably exaggerated, but Fynn surmised that the deaths caused by Shaka's wars exceeded a million, and some estimates of the slaughter in the wake of total wars and mass migrations have placed the dead at close to two million.[6] If the number of deaths and Shaka's responsibility for them are both highly exaggerated, it is nonetheless an historical fact of political life in nineteenth-century Southern Africa that both the Zulu and their enemies believed that Shaka had caused this enormous devastation and dislocation. The idea enhanced the terror of his name and influenced the actions of his successors as well as the Europeans who eventually crushed the Zulu state.

It is also estimated that by 1820 Shaka had deprived some three hundred chiefdoms of their independence, had commanded a force of more than one hundred thousand warriors, and had brought half a million souls under his rule. Fugitives from his violence fled with their armies to make empires of their own.[7] Even after his day had passed, Shaka's influence remained, for his system was remembered as a model of terroristic military despotism, coupling internal absolute power with external military terrorism.

ORIGINS OF THE ZULU STATE

Among the numerous African people who speak the Bantu tongue, one configuration of language and culture known as "Nguni" has the reputation of being a distinct group with a remarkable political destiny. Settled in South Africa on the southeast coast between the Drakensberg Range and the Indian Ocean, more aggressive than the people of the interior, and, as van Warmelo puts it, "more deeply persuaded of their inherent superiority," the Nguni formed relentless military organizations and powerful states, produced mighty rulers and distinguished statesmen, combining a talent for efficient destruction with the ability to integrate disparate peoples in larger social frameworks. Attesting to this distinctly political vocation, Bryant declared, "Of all the Bantu race probably no single tribal family has produced so many great and famous political stars

—conquerors, statesmen, social organizers, and wise, progressive, high-minded rulers—as has this of the Ngunis." [8]

European investigators are struck by the homogeneity of culture and language in this configuration,[9] but the people were not conscious of a Nguni identity. Shula Marks suspects that the word "Nguni" may be a "convenient fiction for the days of migration and small independent chiefdoms," and that the term may stand for "an amalgam of different clusters of clans, each with its own history, customs, and genealogy." [10] The early history of the group is conjectural and buried in myth and fantasy, which were not restricted to the indigenous tradition, for the Europeans invented fabulous tales or merely jumped to conclusions about Nguni wanderings.[11] Two massive compilations of indigenous traditions, published by Byrant and by Soga, tell contradictory stories, but until recently the uniform tendency of historical statements about the Bantu-speaking people was to date their arrival—sweeping Hottentots and Bushmen before them—no earlier than the sixteenth and seventeenth centuries.[12] There is no reason to impugn the motives of historians such as Bryant and Soga, for they simply accepted the unexamined historical premise of their time. But it is no surprise that prevailing assumptions about the date of Nguni settlement should support the political claim that European immigration in Southern Africa was no more recent than that of the Bantu-speaking peoples. The strategies of European expansion would hardly have welcomed an historical assumption that black claims were more ancient than white. Historical thinking is a political act, and if men do not deceive themselves about history, they often have to lie about it. And as Momigliano, writing about the sources of Roman history says, "Men lie about the past because the past is not dead, because they are still struggling with it." [13]

From European records, we know that political communities occupying Natal in the seventeenth century were in the same locations and had the same names they were known by in the nineteenth century. Statements of seamen wrecked on the southeast coast and forced to traverse the land testify that the inhabitants, later given the invidious but vague name "Kaffirs," were numerous, rich in cattle, and at war with Bushmen and Hottentots but disposed toward peace among themselves.[14] As early as the middle of the sixteenth century, Monica Wilson shows, we get a picture of a sparsely populated coast but a countryside with many villages farther inland. It leaves the impression of scattered, small-scale societies and chiefdoms with plenty of open land between them and no dense population. Farther north of the Natal area, the Portuguese records indicate, "the country was thickly populated and provided with cattle." No one knows how long the people had been living on the southeastern part of the continent, but Wilson concludes, "There is nothing in the recorded traditions to indicate any substantial movement of Nguni people . . . since 1300, and it may well have been centuries before that." [15] Recent archaeological evidence from Swaziland, identifying the signs of iron workers, supports the hypothesis of early settlement by Bantu speakers there—since Hottentots and Bushmen did not smelt iron—perhaps as early as the fifth century A.D.[16]

The Nguni probably drifted south over a long period of time, and the vanguard of the long series of migrations—made up of groups that would be known as amaXhosa and abaThembu— was finally checked in the latter part of the eighteenth century in the vicinity of the Great Fish River by another migration moving north, namely, European settlers extending the frontier of the Cape settlement. As Eric Walker described the confrontation, "there were in 1779 on either side of an ill-defined and totally unpoliced border, white men and black, at very different levels of civilization it is true, but both rough and ready agriculturalists, both essentially cattle-farmers, both migratory and both greedy of land." [17] The Nguni offered the white settlers serious and durable resistance.[18] Superior weapons made it possible for the momentum of European colonization eventually to overcome the far more numerous Africans, and a long series of wars leading to conquest and domination transformed a military problem into the social and political problem that grips South Africa today.[19]

Considerably behind the Xhosa vanguard confronting the white settlers on the eighteenth-century frontier, the Nguni people living in the cradle of the Zulu state in South Africa occupied the country between the Tugela River and Delagoa Bay. The Tugela was over four hundred miles of difficult terrain up the coast from the Great Fish River, and the first white men to settle in Zululand and Natal sailed off the coast from Cape Town, arriving in the years 1823–25, which was after the Zulu state had been formed and at the zenith of Shaka's despotic regime. Although Shaka's predecessor had established trade with the neglected post at Delagoa Bay, the Portuguese rarely entered Zululand, and it remained unknown until observed by the adventurous English traders led by Lieutenant King, Henry Fynn, Lieutenant Farewell, and Nathaniel Isaacs, and publicly revealed in the lively reports of Fynn and Isaacs.[20] Nevertheless, the traditions that describe the making of the Zulu kingdom, although they preserve contradictory anecdotes, agree that Shaka's predecessor, Dingiswayo, Chief of the Mthethwa, was influenced by some contact with European civilization. The actual source of that influence varies with the narratives.

FORMATION OF THE STATE

The traditions agree that the link between two rejected sons— Dingiswayo, son of Jobe, Chief of the Mthethwa, and Shaka, son of Senzangakhona, Chief of the Zulu, who were cast out by their fathers and who returned from exile and wandering to claim their respective chiefdoms—proved to be the relationship that established the Zulu kingdom, which soon became a despotism. Thus, obscure events somewhere between 1750 and 1805 set in motion the chain of actions that led to the creation of the state.

In those days, before the mighty nation was formed, the name "Zulu" referred to an undistinguished and relatively small lineage. According to Bryant's reckoning, the Mthethwa population was over four thousand at the time, and the Zulu half that number. According to some traditions, Jobe, Chief of the Mthethwa, as it sometimes happened to chiefs who had grown old, was slow to designate his heir, and, feeling the tension among the rival huts of his several wives, resisted the pressure to make public his choice and to clarify the succession. Tana, the senior son of the principal wife, was the heir presumptive, but, either because of outright rebellion or as a result of suspicions planted by a rival party, he and his younger brother Godongwane came under a cloud, and the chief ordered them killed. Tana perished; Godongwane was wounded but escaped and hid in the bush. The number of years in his subsequent exile varies with the narratives, but at the end of that time he dropped his old name and assumed the name Dingiswayo, which means, "He who was caused to wander." During this time, according to all the traditions, he made some contact with European civilization, either by hearing about it or by actually observing a European settlement, and brought away ideas that later inspired him to reconstruct the Mthethwa chiefdom.

One story was that he traveled south and encountered white people in the Cape of Good Hope,[21] but Bryant roundly condemned the tale, claiming that it had no basis in native tradition but was fabricated by Sir Theophilus Shepstone, the well-known Secretary for Native Affairs in Natal during the early and mid-Victorian period. Bryant argued persuasively that Dingiswayo could not have reached a white settlement in the south, since the nearest one was fully 450 miles away as the crow flies.[23] Another account is that he went north to Delagoa Bay and made contact with the Portuguese.[23] It appears that this story is subject to the same kind of criticism, but it is given more credibility by the fact that Dingiswayo established trading relations with the Portuguese after he assumed chieftainship. A third tradition, which was preferred by both Bryant and Soga, states that he gained his knowledge from a white traveler, probably a physician-explorer, who was equipped with a horse and gun and whom he served as a guide through the bush. According to the story, when the white man was killed by the Qwabe people, Dingiswayo, having heard that his father was dead, returned to his community with a considerable following, which, Bryant argued, "could have been nothing else than the white man's carriers." Perhaps they had served as interpreters, or perhaps they had transmitted the ideas directly to Dingiswayo, or perhaps a smattering of some language other than Nguni or English had passed between the white man and Dingiswayo, but it is difficult to understand how in a period of time that was relatively brief, as it appears from all accounts, the language barrier could have been overcome sufficiently to communicate complex ideas, such as the details of regimental organization and disciplined warfare.

The importance of the contact was stressed by Bryant, who wrote:

> The significance of so seemingly trivial an incident as the flight of Dingswayo and his return in company with a European traveller lay in its consequences. . . . Certainly the progressive ideas and activities subsequently displayed by Dingiswayo do suggest such extraneous influence; for, as a pure initiation of the Bantu mind and a product of purely Bantu training, they would have been decidedly extraordinary.
>
> Here we seem to be at that insignificant spring which marked the starting-point of the deluge of bloodshed soon to devastate all this part of the African continent, driving thousands upon thousands to homelessness and misery, thousands upon thousands to torture and death; the tiny seed from which grew forth that many-branched disturbance of the Bantu race which had as its direct results the foundation of the Zulu nation. . . .

Had there been no flight and no return of Dingiswayo with a thinking and talkative white man, there might have been no subsequent Mtetwa aspirations and conquests; no Mtetwa conquests, no Shaka impelled to martial and imperial ambitions; no warlike Shaka, no Zulu nation, no Zulu war; no Sutu nation or Basutu War; no Tebele nation, or Matebele War. Nor would our own [Natal] have been born so soon.[24]

Yet, there is no conclusive evidence about the nature of this contact, and all the inferences drawn from the conflicting traditions do not stand up to critical scrutiny. First of all, the complex ideas behind Dingiswayo's innovations—e.g. discipline and drill, regimental organization, massed attacks, encircling tactics—could hardly have been impressed on him in the course of a journey through the bush, given the probable language barrier between the men, no matter how curious Dingiswayo may have been about how the Europeans carried on warfare. To guess that he might have observed troops on the drill field and have learned about their methods of fighting during a sojourn in a white settlement, as Shepstone suggested, is certainly more plausible. Yet, British settlements are ruled out because of their distance. A Portuguese settlement seems more probable, but it is not certain he could have obtained the information there. Fynn described Delagoa as he saw it in 1822:

> The fort and settlement of Delagoa were as contemptible as can well be imagined, though they had been occupied for a period of perhaps 60 years. The inhabitants consisted of the Governor, four or five sub-officers, a priest, five or six licensed traders, who, with the exception of a couple of sergeants, were Portuguese from Europe. The soldiers were all dark coloured natives; they had been collected on the spot and drilled on military lines. The officers, especially the Governor, wore dashing uniforms on gala days; the clothing of the native soldiers, however, was incomplete, many of them being without jackets or shoes, while a number of their muskets were fastened with rope yarn to their stocks; and other makeshifts were resorted to so as to bring them under the name of "guns." [25]

Still, the spectacle of this native rag-tag army—perhaps some of them even equipped with assegais, since there were not enough guns—could have given Dingiswayo the idea of organizing and training the Mthethwa along similar lines. It seems a more likely source than conversations in the bush. In any case, although it is not unreasonable to guess that European influence may have been behind Dingiswayo's innovations, we cannot be certain about it; what evidence we have is not sufficient to tell exactly how the influence did work, and we cannot rule out the possibility that the changes came without European influence. Confronted with inexplicable changes in primitive society, one is all too tempted to introduce as deus ex machina the European.

Omer-Cooper observes that similar changes were taking place simultaneously and spontaneously in a number of Nguni communities and suggests that they were "a natural reaction to changing conditions," making it doubtful "whether Dingiswayo should be regarded as the sole originator." [26] Shula Marks points out that the "very remarkable process of state formation that went on in the area towards the end of the eighteenth century" has received insufficient analysis, and she believes that as an explanation, "Dingiswayo's white man simply will not do. . . ." [27] Until further work is done on the problem it is probably best to suspend judgments about the legends of European contact and to keep in mind Omer-Cooper's conclusion that "These great movements were independent of European influence in origin, though as they developed they interlocked with expanding European activity affecting and being affected by it." [28]

The legends of Dingiswayo's return say that he rode on a horse—a fearful creature unknown in those parts—and carried a gun, both perhaps the property of the murdered white traveler, or that a false rumor was spread to the effect that he had taken over the dead European's horse and gun, and that with a company of retainers gathered on the way, he easily wrested the leadership of the Mthethwa from Mawewe, his reigning brother. It is also possible, of course, that the horse and gun, if they were real, came from Delagoa Bay.

Fynn, whose informants, it must be remembered, included Shaka himself, reported that the first act of Dingiswayo after he seized power was to form his people into regiments, subdivided in companies. As soon as he had organized this system, he began attacking all the surrounding chiefdoms. He opened trade with Delagoa Bay, which was afterwards developed on an extensive scale, although Portuguese rarely entered his territory in person. The chief, according to the system instituted at this time and continued by Dingiswayo's successors, maintained a monopoly of trade, and he also established manufactories, encouraging primitive artisans to produce articles of clothing and furniture, utensils, carvings, and, as Fynn put it, "many curious specimens of excessively neat workmanship." His changes in the system of power meant centralization and increased control, but his manner of exercising power, according to the tradition, was mild and even chivalrous, and his memory is treated not only with respect but with reverence.

Successful wars of conquest brought neighboring chiefdoms under his control, but they were treated with restraint. The wars were justified by the claim that he wished to end the continual fighting of the communities by bringing them under a single government, establishing a supreme head to settle disputes. Incessant conflict, he declared, could not have been the design of Mvela, the First Being. Instead of several kings equal in power, he said, those who first came into the world intended that there should be one great king reigning over the little ones. Singularly, Dingiswayo's apologia is virtually a primitive form of Dante's argument for universal monarchy, and no one knows for sure whether the author was really Dingiswayo or Mr. Fynn.

Defeated communities offering submission and tribute were left intact under the immediate control of their own chiefs. Nor were they deprived of their cattle: the oxen were distributed among Dingiswayo's warriors, but the cows were restored. The commanders had strict orders to prevent plunder and to avoid unnecessary destruction. Vanquished people were accepted as equals and intermarriages with them encouraged. As Fynn observed, "By such mild means he conciliated his enemies, upon which several tribes voluntarily became tributary to him and assisted him in his battles. Before long he so enlarged and improved his army as to make himself respected by his friends and feared by his foes." [29]

Before Dingiswayo, the military force of each chiefdom was a small "standing army" made up of young bachelors in the warrior age grade. Adolescent boys lived a barracks life in military kraals, serving as aides and herd boys until their age set was organized ceremonially as *iButho*, a new guild or regiment, and they were elevated to the status of warriors. Carrying out military and police functions and for certain purposes acting as a labor gang, the warriors constituted the staff, not permanent but assembled according to circumstance, which enforced the chief's will. They fought the battles of the chiefdom, executed judgments by killing people accused of crimes, confiscating their property in the chief's name, and when the supply of the chief's cattle was low, replenished the bovine treasury by making raids on other communities. They cultivated the fields of the chief, built and maintained his kraals, and manufactured his war shields. No provision was made for their subsistence, except for a few of the chief's oxen slaughtered perhaps once a week. The men in the barracks had to provide for their own needs, with help from family and friends. The cords that bound the system were traditional discipline and moral authority. Bryant wrote that "each and every individual of the Nguni clan, boys and girls, maids and men alike, [was] taught, first to father, then to king, to be ever obedient, docile, disciplined, self-sacrificing unto the last, unto the supreme test of offering one's life on the field of battle." [30] These fundamental attachments were in later days incorporated in larger, more centralized organizations, and, in articulation with the process of terror, they remained as the voluntary component—the moral adhesive—in the regimes of Shaka and Dingane.

Nguni military techniques, before Dingiswayo's reconstruction of the Mthethwa army, did not lend themselves to systematic destruction. Old men who remembered those days recalled to inquirers such as Shepstone and Bryant that a life of ease and plenty was punctuated occasionally by quarrels, which were settled by armed combat, and that such periodic fights were not serious matters. The quarrel was settled usually by a single encounter on a day ceremonially arranged, and armies never slept away from their homes. Unlike later times, the men said, "The sun that saw tribes fight never set till their quarrel was ended." Internal quarrels over succession to the chieftainship were more bitter and protracted, but they almost always ended in fission, and a section of the community moved to another place. In the case of conflict between chiefdoms, agonistic combat served as a visible test of strength, and when one side, to the satisfaction of combatants and spectators, emerged as the superior force, the defeated army conceded, the other claimed victory, and the dispute was settled in its favor. As Shepstone reported:

> The few old men still living, who lived then, delight to tell how that in those good old times they did not fight to shed blood, or burn houses, or capture cattle, or destroy each other, but to settle a quarrel, and see which was the strongest: how that their women looked on while the men fought; that prisoners taken in battle were not killed, but kept till ransomed; and especially how that many a young warrior, when the day's strife was over, would hand his shield and assagai to a companion to take home for him, that he might accompany his late foes to renew his vows to some daughter of the rival tribe.[31]

In the old style of fighting, combat between single selected warriors settled the conflict, or else both sides approached each other, shouting war cries and insults, until they were in javelin range, and then the warriors hurled their own spears and all they could find on the field until one army fled. Each man was an expert in the use of his assegai, but he was never drilled to act in concert with the others, nor did the warriors as a unit perform even in the simplest military evolution. A campaign was little more than an unorganized swoop, quickly ended. Dingiswayo changed the technique by drilling his men to fight in units, then marching his regiments forward in massed attack, training them to hold their fire as they moved through the fusillade, covered by their large shields, until they confronted the enemy at close range. It was not long until warriors fighting in the old style would break and run at the sight of the massed impi—the Zulu word for a force of armed warriors—and since it was not possible to withstand this kind of attack, chiefdoms eventually were compelled to adopt the new tactics. For the Nguni, the new system carried important implications. On the one hand, it constructed an organization and method that made possible systematic destruction, forging an instrument of military terrorism. On the other hand, it fashioned a military discipline and network of controls within the community that was not possible under the old system.

Many writers have assumed that Dingiswayo's military system merely reflected European example.[32] Others insist that he revived an institution that had fallen into desuetude. Bryant believed that the "regiments" were survivals of original circumcision guilds—no more than age sets of youths to be circumcised at the same time. Each guild had its own distinguishing name and insignia, and they were universal Nguni institutions before either Dingiswayo or Shaka was born.[33] It is not clear whether Dingiswayo or Shaka or even their predecessors had abolished the rite of circumcision, but after it fell into disuse, chiefs continued to assemble and name sets of young men who had reached warrior age. The historians Walker and Theal considered the massed impi to be a revival, and Theal went so far as to state that the tactic of fighting in crescent formation with "horns" on the flanks, the "bull's head" in the center, and a massive "chest," or reserve, waiting in the rear with their backs to the fray, was not an innovation at all. According to Theal, whose military information was often accepted by Walker and other later historians, in Zululand and Natal, the ancestors of Dingiswayo

> were acquainted with the regimental system and with the method of attack in the form of a crescent two centuries before his time, and he may have heard accounts from antiquaries of what had been the custom in those respects in the olden days, if the practice itself had died out, which seems somewhat doubtful, though in tribes under feeble chiefs such knowledge might soon be lost.[34]

Another explanation, which is mentioned in the following chapter, suggests that the military tactics developed out of indigenous hunting practices.

When Dingiswayo began his reign, he was surrounded by scores of independent chiefdoms, which settled their disputes according to trial by arms. Such fights resulted in few deaths and no atrocities. He ended the feuding, however, by a program of conquest, and also reduced the independence of the separate communities. A chief who resisted was put to death or to flight, and his position occupied by a favorite of Dingiswayo. Chiefs who submitted were allowed to retain their territory and internal sovereignty unimpaired. In all cases, whether their territory was temporarily occupied or not, chiefdoms were neither destroyed nor dispersed. Controlling a network of chiefs who were his favorites or who had more or less voluntarily accepted his dominion, Dingiswayo created a new political order which was a system of suzerain-vassal relationships.[35]

The Zulu people were one of the smaller conquered chiefdoms that acknowledged his suzerainty, and Shaka, the outcast son of Chief Senzangakhona, took refuge with the Mthethwa and made a distinguished career as an officer in Dingiswayo's forces. Shaka's early life is now a well-known Zulu myth. The legends stress his illegitimacy, and they say that after Senzangakhona belatedly accepted Nandi, Shaka's mother, as a wife, he found her so disagreeable that she was ordered to leave the community. She and her son lived in several places until Shaka eventually enrolled in the Mthethwa army. The chronicles of Shaka's ordeal vary in details, but they consistently relate that he was tormented by his peers. As a mature warrior his physical appearance was magnificent, and observers were impressed by his strength and dexterity when leading either the dancers in the royal kraal or the impi in the field. As a boy, however, he was subjected to physical assaults as well as mockery and, Bryant related, "his little crinkled ears and the marked stumpiness of a certain organ were ever a source of persistent ridicule among Shaka's companions, and their taunts in this regard so rankled in his breast that he grew up harboring a deadly hatred. . . ." [36] All the narratives of his early sufferings seem to provide a psychological explanation for the rage and destruction in the years of his despotism.

GROWTH OF THE STATE

When Senzangakhona died, Shaka claimed the Zulu as his patrimony and made himself chief. Some stories tell that the old chief died naturally and that Shaka, with the aid of a Mthethwa detachment, had to defeat his brother, the heir apparent, by force of arms. Other chroniclers say that the chief was overcome by poison, and still others suggest that sorcery was employed by Shaka and his partisans and that his father's spirit sank under the spell of *ukuthonya*. The practitioner of this kind of magic sought to

> gain or possess some occult, hypnotic-like ascendancy over another by some process of charming, etc., as one court-favourite over another, a young-man over his father or sweetheart so that he can manage them as he likes, or as a dog is supposed to do by voiding urine over that of another. [37]

If Shaka did use sorcery in his effort to seize power, it helps to explain his own elaborate precautions and violent defenses against magic later, when he occupied the throne of the Zulu state.

With the support of Dingiswayo, Shaka reorganized the Zulu along Mthethwa military lines and trained his impi in the new methods of fighting. Together the two chiefs extended the campaign against all neighboring chiefdoms that stayed within range, yet adhering to Dingiswayo's strategy of limited warfare and the policy of requiring no more than submission, fealty, and indirect rule.

At the same time, occupying half of northern Zululand, the large Ndwandwe community initiated an aggressive campaign, led by their crafty and unscrupulous chief, Zwide, whose mother, according to the chroniclers, was even more ambitious and ruthless than he, decorating her hut with the skulls of fallen chiefs and other vanquished heroes. Possibly stimulated by Dingiswayo's military program, Zwide had decided to make conquests of his own, and he emerged as a rival of Dingiswayo, contending with him for Nguni paramountcy. Incensed by Zwide's actions—particularly the murder of Dingiswayo's sister's husband, who was a subject of Zwide—Dingiswayo marched against him. It is said that Zwide, knowing he could not match the Mthethwa armies, overcame Dingiswayo by trickery and magic and that the great chief perished as the victim of a sorcerer's spell, his skull to occupy the place of honor in the museum of Zwide's mother. Reflecting on the life and death of Dingiswayo, Bryant eulogized:

> from the meagre traditions still obtainable, we know him to have been a man of progressive and praiseworthy ambitions; enlightened and constructive in his policy of social improvement and political reform; an able military organizer and a clean fighter. Magnanimous in his wars of conquest, benevolent in his rule at home, the fair name of Dingiswayo remained unsullied by deeds of barbarism and tyranny—a noble record, indeed, of a statesmanlike, if barbarian and Negro, monarch.

If Shaka was the consolidator of the Zulu nation, Dingiswayo was its first and real founder. If Shaka was the Timur and the Attila of his race, Dingiswayo was its Menes and its Alfred the Great.[38]

Shortly after the death, on a pretext of personal offense, Shaka had the legitimate heir, a half-brother of the late chief, killed, and in his stead placed a cousin of Dingiswayo, his own favorite, Mlandela, an old companion who had been serving in one of his regiments, at the head of the Mthethwa. In this manner, that chiefdom remained under his direct control, the regiments becoming part of the Zulu impi. The kingdom was at hand: a system in which a solitary paramount with unique powers and privileges, receiving a unique salute and special praise chants, whose position was defined as incomparable to all chiefs and leaders, commanded a network of subordinates, who in turn controlled social units placed under their authority by the king. In the decade that was to follow, Shaka's career moved up the scale of power: from a chief like other chiefs to a king unlike any chief; thence to an absolute ruler unlike a traditional king; and finally to a despot claiming omnipotence.

For present purposes, that decade may be divided into three periods. From about 1818 to 1820 Shaka fought for control of the area that was to be known as the core of Zululand: about 12,000 square miles extending from the Indian Ocean to the Buffalo (Zinyati) River on the west, and from the Pongola River on the north to the Tugela River on the south. From 1821 to 1824, having eliminated all external opposition to his rule, he "swept up the rubbish" in and around Zululand, penetrated Natal, and created a vast, almost uninhabited wasteland or traffic desert around his domain. He also consolidated his regime, making several fundamental innovations, eliminating traditional restrictions that might limit his power, and developing a system of terror within the Zulu state. From 1824 until his assassination in 1828, he probed as far south as his respect for the British forces would permit, and pushed as far north as the biological limitations of his impi, toughened as they were to the fatigue of long marches, would allow. In these last four years, Europeans were often present in the royal kraal, and on some occasions even accompanied him in the field. The center of interest during this period, as well as the best source of information about the Zulu state at the meridian, is in the relationships between Shaka and the Englishmen Fynn, Isaacs, Farewell, and King.

At the beginning of the first period, just after the death of Dingiswayo, the most powerful chiefs did not accept Shaka as the successor to leadership of the Nguni federation. He was hemmed in by the Ndwandwe on the north—ruled by Zwide, his most formidable antagonist—the Qwabe in the south, and the Thembu in the west. Fighting a brilliant defensive action against a massive invasion by the Ndwandwe, led by five sons of Zwide, he demolished this force, and then, before Zwide could recover from the destruction of his army and the loss of his sons to organize sufficient reinforcements from allies in the north, Shaka defeated the Qwabe in a swift, decisive campaign, securing his southern frontier. In less than three years, thirty chiefs and their people were gathered into a single political system, and the former enemy troops incorporated in the Zulu military forces, not only making up for the Pyrrhic victory in the First Ndwandwe War, but also replenishing the impi beyond the losses of all campaigns and expanding the Zulu army to new proportions. Throughout the decade, military activity continued with little respite. When the army was idle, not accumulating men and cattle, Shaka complained that it was eating him up. Besides, Bryant explained:

> Had the British Army in 1879 found Zululand occupied, not by a single united nation requiring only a single concentration of attention, but by a hundred independent kingdoms, each demanding separate treatment; and had that British Army consisted of but a single battalion of a few hundred strong, which was all Shaka at first could muster; and had it been equipped with a single assegai per man and lacked all commis-

sariat, we should have been enabled to understand more clearly the vastness and the complexity of the task undertaken single-handed and accomplished without hitch or hindrance by the mighty Shaka in his conquest, not only of Zululand, but of the whole region between Delagoa Bay and Mtata. We are no longer surprised at his untiring activity. To achieve such a tremendous result, and that within the space of a short reign of less than a decade of years, uninterrupted warfare was of absolute necessity. Hence it was that almost every succeeding autumn or winter season witnessed the inauguration of its own campaign of aggression.[39]

Around 1819, after Zwide was defeated in a Second Ndwandwe War and the people scattered, no forces remained to work for a restored balance of power. The large chiefdoms in the west melted before the impi, the Ndwandwe were dispersed, and the Qwabe incorporated. By 1820, the political character of Zululand was transformed into an imperial domain.

The flight from Shaka set up two patterns of migration. Bands of fugitives with varying degrees of strength and organization, coalitions of fragments, and other masses of people in search of plunder or simply safety tended to move west or south, in the latter case often seeking European protection wherever they could find it. Some reversed the immemorial path of migration and crushed their way north. Potential resistance to Shaka's rule decreased as strong chiefs fled great distances to found new states, gathering heterogeneous peoples in the course of long marches. Mzilikazi, a former Zulu general and originally a chief of the Kumalo, who followed Shaka's methods (even to the point of naming his royal kraal "Bulawayo," after Shaka's capital), settled down in what was to become Rhodesia, eventually controlling an area of 500,000 square miles, which was an expanse even larger than Shaka's territory. Soshangane founded the Gasa kingdom in Portuguese East Africa, and Zwangendaba the Ngoni kingdom in what is now Zambia. In 1822, the Ndwandwe fragments led by these two rulers paused in the vicinity of Delagoa Bay in their flight from Shaka's wrath. They sojourned to plunder the Thonga before resuming a long march to the sites of future states. During that episode, they attacked the party of Captain Owen, who was making a hydrographic survey for the British Admiralty.[40] With the record of that encounter, written Zulu history begins, and we need not depend exclusively on the oral tradition to reconstruct the external impact and the internal pattern of Zulu social and political life from that time on.[41]

Subsequent reports were made by a number of Englishmen from the Cape, in pursuit of ivory and other commercial treasure, who paused in their mercantile adventures to tell the wonder of Shaka's kingdom. The best sources are the records of Fynn and Isaacs. The descriptions of Isaacs, who arrived in October 1825, are the closest to immediate experience, for he quoted directly from his journal, in which he had made detailed, sometimes daily, entries.[42] Fynn was one of the first white men to visit Shaka, arriving at the royal kraal in the company of Farewell in July 1824, fifteen months before Isaacs, and he "rapidly acquired a perfect knowledge of Zulu and cognate dialects . . . travelled and lived among natives more than any of his companions, and was by far the best informed as to the conditions of the country and its inhabitants." [43]

By the time he had acquired a thorough knowledge of Zulu language and customs, he was spending a great deal of time in friendly conversation with Shaka, who always demanded his attendance during leisure moments. These frequent occasions made possible an understanding of Shaka's disposition and, as Fynn later wrote, gave him "an opportunity of minutely ascertaining the basis on which he acted." His notes contained observations made by himself as well as the first written records of Zulu memories, although the work that eventually reached publication was written from recollection, years after his original notebook had been lost in his absence, having been interred in his younger brother's grave by faithful attendants following imperatives of Nguni custom.

The first visits occurred during a relatively peaceful interval, and the Englishmen were in a position to note features of Shaka's rule which are mentioned vaguely or incompletely in the traditions, especially the phenomena of violence.[44] In his history of the Zulu based on tradition as he gathered it, Gibson expressed bewilderment over the mixture of benevolence and cruelty in Shaka's character. The manifestations of Shaka's system of terror puzzled him, and he wrote:

> The character of Tshaka, as it is known to the descendants of the people over whom he ruled, was largely made up of the two qualities of generosity and wanton cruelty. He is reputed to have been liberal in his gifts to those who had been so fortunate as to earn his favour, whilst acting towards the generality of the people in a manner to make it appear that he derived a kind of amusement from seeing them killed or placed in situations of such danger as to preclude almost all hope of escape. His object in practising the first of these attributes might have been that of securing support, but his aim in indulging the second is not so easily to be perceived. Tradition is vague in regard to it. It merely refers generally to the nature of the things he was in the habit of doing, wthout specifying any act in a manner which might afford a possibility of authenticating it, or assigning a cause.[45]

A recent history of the Zulu state similarly fails to comprehend the significance of Shaka's violence. Donald R. Morris writes of Shaka's regime:

> His rule was based on a fear so profound he could afford to ignore it; his subjects would no more think of resisting him than a mouse would gainsay an elephant. He moved through his daily routine surrounded by a retinue that included a group of executioners, who, a dozen times daily, bashed in skulls or twisted necks at a flick of Shaka's hand. The lives he snuffed out in this fashion were guilty of no great crimes; they might have sneezed while he was eating, or made him laugh when he was serious. *It was not set policy that made him act like this,* nor was it cruelty, which implies a desire to inflict pain. It

went beyond cruelty, it ignored pain, and the people he killed meant no more to him than so many ants.[46]

The notion that his violence was devoid of policy is contradicted, we shall see in the following chapter, by the judgments of men who observed Shaka's behavior and experienced his regime. It is important to correct statements that fail to admit Shaka's intent, because they lend support to the prejudice that primitive rulers are not capable of sophisticated policy and to the false theory that systematic terrorism is exclusively a function of advanced technology.

Terrorism depends on the effect deliberate violence has upon those who witness it or learn of it indirectly. Morris misses the point as he writes,

> Time and again, for no discernible reason, Shaka, with a flick of his hand and no further attention, ordered the execution of some member of his entourage. It was a phenomenon that was noted on every occasion on which a European paid a visit to the royal kraal, and despite the initial impression that Shaka merely wished to impress his visitors with his absolute powers, it gradually sank in that the executions were a normal part of Zulu court life, and that *Shaka gave as little heed to the impression left on his visitors as he did to that made on the victims or their families.* The power was indeed absolute, and it had reached the ultimate corruption.[47]

Actually, the impression left by the violence was the linchpin in Shaka's system of power. Terroristic despotism depends on the impact that violence makes on the consciousness of witnesses and on the communication of their fear to others more remote.

CHAPTER VII

THE TERROR

UNDER

SHAKA

They lived in perpetual alarm lest the finger of the despot
should be held up as a signal of death or of devastation.
—Nathaniel Isaacs, *Travels and Adventures in Eastern Africa.*

THE PROCESS of terror was one of the facts of Shaka's regime
noted but only dimly understood by the Englishmen during
their initial visit to the royal kraal. It was observed the day
after their reception. The journey inland had been delayed, for
Shaka, on hearing of their arrival from the sea and learning of
their desire to visit him, kept them waiting at Port Natal under
close surveillance by his spies, but well supplied with gifts of
cattle, until he gave the signal for them to begin the 200-mile
trek. They proceeded circuitously, led by Mbikwane, a high-
ranking kinsman of Shaka—no one less than his chief induna, or
prime minister—who treated them with extraordinary tact.
Their welcome at the capital was a festive occasion celebrated
with elaborate display. Shaka later insisted that they appear
astounded by the exhibition of Zulu power and grace—and,
indeed, they were impressed by the spectacle. He also extracted
assent to the proposition that they had never seen such order in
any other state, and that he was the greatest king of all, his
people as numerous as the stars and his cattle innumerable.
They witnessed dancing and singing, warriors and regiments of
girls on parade, and endless droves of the royal cattle on dis-

play. Fynn noted that when they had first entered the kraal that Shaka "was so surrounded by his chiefs that we could not distinguish him."[1] On a signal from him, all his people smartly left the scene to execute complex ceremonial maneuvers, leaving the king alone with the visiting party in a corner of the kraal.

The next morning they attended the ruler as he performed his daily ritual of ablution and decoration in public, while the singing, the dancing, and the cattle exhibit proceeded as the day before. Meanwhile, Fynn reported, "it became known to us that Chaka had ordered that a man standing near should be put to death, for what crime we could not learn: but we soon found it to be one of the common occurrences in the course of the day."[2] They saw the action repeated several times:

> On the first day of our visit we had seen no less than ten men carried off to death. On a mere sign by Shaka, viz: the pointing of his finger, the victim would be seized by his nearest neighbours; his neck would be twisted, and his head and body beaten with sticks, the nobs of some of these being as large as a man's fist. On each succeeding day, too, numbers of others were killed; their bodies would then be carried to an adjoining hill and there impaled. We visited this spot on the fourth day. It was truly a Golgotha, swarming with hundreds of vultures.[3]

It was perceived that this violence was part of Shaka's routine, and Fynn described a typical scene:

> Cattle and war formed the whole subject of his conversations; and during his sitting, while in the act of taking a pinch of snuff, or when engaged in the deepest conversation, he would by a movement of his finger, perceivable only by his attendants, point out one of the gathering sitting around him, upon which, to the surprise of strangers, the man would be carried off and killed. This was a daily occurrence. On one occasion I witnessed 60 boys under 12 years of age dispatched

before he had breakfasted. No sooner is the signal given, and the object pointed out, than those sitting around him scramble to kill him, although they have good reason to expect the next moment the same fate themselves, but such apprehensions are far from their thoughts; the will of the King being uppermost. I have seen instances where they have had opportunities of speaking while being carried off, but which they always employed in enthusiastically praising the heroic deeds of their King.[4]

Shaka took special note of the vultures in constant attendance and frequently threatened his people with the saying that the king's birds were hungry and needed to be fed.[5]

Isaacs too described many episodes of violence similar to those recorded by Fynn. On 5 December 1825, during his first visit to Shaka, he witnessed the arrival of a body of around three hundred Zulu, every one saluting the despot as he went on and declaiming the royal praises.

> On a sudden a profound silence ensued, when his majesty uttered one or two words, at which some of the warriors immediately rose and seized three of the people, one of whom sat near me. The poor fellows made no resistance, but were calm and resigned, waiting their fate with apparently stoical indifference. The sanguinary chief was silent; but from some sign he gave the executioners, they took the criminals, laying one hand on the crown and the other on the chin, and by a sudden wrench appeared to dislocate the head. The victims were then dragged away and beaten as they proceeded to the bush, about a mile from the kraal, where a stick was inhumanly forced up the fundament of each, and they were left as food for the wild beasts of the forest, and those carnivorous birds that hover near the habitations of the natives.[6]

The next day Isaacs received as a gift from the despot some of the cattle that had belonged to the victims.

Such violent episodes sometimes took place during military exercises, but they were commonly observed as civil phenomena, since they occurred most often in the midst of great assemblies. On 4 April 1826, Isaacs reported that the despot was surrounded by about two thousand of his people and that he was

> discussing affairs of a warlike tendency. As soon as we had taken our seats on the ground, as near as we could discreetly, we heard him give orders for the execution of seven men, all of whom were taken from near the spot where we were seated. They were instantly seized and beaten to death, with other barbarous cruelties too revolting to detail, and which operated on me so painfully, that I was compelled to retire from so horrible and inhuman an exhibition.[7]

The means of killing varied: strangling seemed to be reserved for royal persons, and sometimes warriors could claim death by the spear in preference to more lowly forms. For the rest, victims were dispatched by dislocating the neck, clubbing, stoning, various mutilations, or pounding sharpened stakes through the rectum. In general, victims accepted their deaths with resignation. On one occasion, a number of herd boys accused of drinking the milk of the royal cattle were ordered to report to an executioner to be slain for the forbidden act. They obeyed the order, repeated the despot's message, and were killed. Isaacs reported seeing the ruler's chief domestic knocked down and dragged away, and hearing him "distinctly thanking the savage monarch as they were beating him to death." Victims were often led to their deaths chanting the praises of the despot.[8] Still, such obedience *in extremis* was not universal. On 16 September 1828, exactly a week before Shaka's assassination, Isaacs, preparing to leave the royal residence for Port Natal, found Shaka

> with about two hundred people, forming a half circle, with a few chiefs sitting near him, trying six prisoners for stealing corn. We had scarcely been seated a few moments when the despot ordered the prisoners for immediate execution. Two of

them, stout, able fellows, tried to make their escape by leaping over us with great agility, and making good use of their speed: but the warriors finally secured them, and stoned them to death.[9]

Perceptively, Isaacs commented on this occasion that the executions were "merely done to terrify us." Shaka's use of violence was so extensive that it is often dismissed as mere butchery and the frenzy of a madman without rhyme or reason. Even those who have devoted themselves with consummate skill to the exact analysis of latent forces in Zulu society have overlooked the pattern in Shaka's violence, tending to regard it as psychotic behavior. Yet, Fynn and Isaacs, who knew Shaka intimately, pointed out the method in acts that later commentators thought madness. A rationale for his apparently promiscuous violence may be found as we sort out the occasions and the identity of the victims, as well as the witnesses affected by the spectacles of destruction.

TERROR OF ARMS

There were two turning points in the development of Shaka's practice of violence: first, after the defeat of the Ndwandwe around 1819, when the internal system of terror was apparently initiated; second, after the death of his mother in 1827, when the terror seemed to be out of control, exceeding all limits and threatening to devour the society. Before the system of terror was established within the state, however, Shaka had committed himself to a policy of military terrorism, from which he never wavered, having discarded the limited warfare of Dingiswayo's era for the *impi ebomvu*—literally, "red impi"—or war of extermination. The chroniclers say that as a regimental commander under Dingiswayo, Shaka had chafed at the policy of limited warfare and in the councils of war had unsuccessfully argued for the strategy of *impi ebomvu*.[10] In any single battle, the technique resembled, to some extent, immemorial Nguni hunting methods: the crescent formation or "horns" of the Zulu impi encircled the enemy—similar to the way in which lines of hunters enclosed the prey—and killed every living thing caught within the circle. Bryant suggested that Shaka had adopted the policy of extermination as soon as he became chief of the Zulu, even before Dingiswayo was out of the picture. Early in his career, Shaka

> after overcoming the Butelezis had conceived the then quite novel idea of utterly demolishing them as a separate tribal entity by incorporating all their manhood into his own clan or following, which brilliant manoeuvre immediately reduced his possible foes for all time by one and at the same time doubled the number of his own army.[11]

Admitting the young warriors into his regiments, he usually destroyed women, infants, and old people. Sometimes he spared the girls, who, presumably, entered the royal seraglios, and the stout lads, who became herd boys, baggage carriers, and, ultimately, Zulu warriors. All who were admitted into Zulu society in this way were absorbed as individuals, giving up their formal tribal loyalties and assuming a Zulu identity. The case was somewhat different for the communities of chiefs who voluntarily became tributaries and were permitted to remain intact. Nevertheless, it is clear that the Zulu system was quite different from those "conquest states" such as the Matebele (Ndebele) which maintained a caste structure.

One element in Shaka's strategy was to create a vast artificial desert around his domain. The area was depopulated and anything that might serve as food was destroyed. There are several descriptions of this wasteland on record and, Shepstone observed, "The object, of course, was to render existence impossible within the reach of his arms, except under his rule." Bryant added that "to make the destruction complete, organized bands of Zulu murderers regularly patrolled the waste, hunting for any stray men and running them down like wild-pig."[12]

The desolation not only made escape from Shaka's domain precarious, to say the least, but also would have imposed an equally difficult logistic problem for invading warriors. Fynn reported that a belt of more than 25 miles around Natal was uninhabited except for a few living skeletons who stayed alive by eating roots and who played the antelope to the Zulu lion. An area 200 miles to the north of the center of the state, 300 miles to the west, and 500 miles to the south was ravaged and depopulated. Some people turned to cannibalism, and one narrator recalled fleeing through the wasteland to a deserted village where crops were still intact, but "They found the gardens all cultivated, and the crops ripe; but the cannibals had been there, had eaten the cultivators, and placed their skulls on the top of their huts." [13] Robert Payne, as he said in his book on terrorism, believed that "The German Army under Keitel invented the 'traffic desert,' " [14] but it is clear that in this respect as well as others, Shaka had anticipated the Nazis.

Shaka responded to resistance of any kind with destruction, and the only alternative he offered a community that refused swift capitulation and enthusiastic subordination was total war. Flight was impeded by the determination of people beyond his domain to defend their territories against invasion, and in the later period the possibility of escape was reduced further by the presence of the traffic desert. In the earlier campaigns, it seems, after a Zulu attack, Shaka held out the captured women and cattle as inducements for the fugitives to return and enter the ranks of the Zulu. Bryant believed that in this stratagem lay the secret of Shaka's military success:

If a foe were worth conquering at all, he was worth crushing out of existence once and for all. Whatever was to fear in the tribe must be eternally removed; whatever was good and serviceable must be appropriated by the victor as a reward of triumph and applied as a further strengthening of his own position. In this way something could be gained and then securely held. Shaka's army, therefore, would charge the enemy, and, when it fled in panic, as inevitably it would, they would follow it vigorously home, kill its chief, and return with its cattle and women as booty. Thus reduced, without a head, without women, without cattle, a vanquished clan had no recourse but to avail itself of the "clemency" offered it of incorporation with the victor's own people.[15]

In his later campaigns, Shaka grew more destructive. Sometimes explicit instructions were given to spare no one. Fynn witnessed such an order after Shaka was stabbed in an attempted assassination. It was supposed that the assassins had been sent by Zwide, Shaka's distant but only powerful enemy, who may have been gathering forces to reoccupy the homeland from which the Ndwandwe had been expelled. Bryant speculated that Zwide may have actually died at this time, and the attempted assassination may have been part of his *ihlambo* ceremony: the "washing of the spears" in blood that concluded a month of mourning after the death. When Shaka recovered from his wound, an impi was mustered against the Ndwandwe. The chief induna, Mbikwane, made a speech urging revenge, and the order to march was given. The warriors, Fynn reported, "were directed to spare neither man, woman, child, nor dog. They were to burn their huts, to break the stones on which their corn was ground, and so prove their attachment to their King."[16] The opportunity to find and exterminate the Ndwandwe arrived soon enough.

Zwide was succeeded by his son, Sikunyana, who led the revitalized Ndwandwe back to the Zulu frontier in 1826. Shaka forced a small detachment of Englishmen to accompany him as musketeers as he marched an army of 50,000, according to Fynn's reckoning, to engage Sikunyana in the Third Ndwandwe War. In a battle that did not last more than an hour and a half, the Ndwandwe threat was extinguished. According to Fynn's report, their numbers, including women and children, "could not have been less than 40,000." He looked on as "The remnants of the enemy's army sought shelter in an adjoining wood, out of which they were soon driven. Then began a slaughter of the women and children. They were all put to death." Isaacs also noted that Shaka appeared "to have destroyed in this last encounter nearly every human being of the tribe, man, woman, and child." [17] Soon after this battle, Shaka, enraged at the crime of Michael and John, two Hottentots who had raped the young wife of an important Zulu chief while in the service of the Englishmen, insisted that to make amends for the offense and to avert a general execution of all the foreign visitors, a detachment of ten muskets march with an impi against Beje, chief of a Kumalo segment. This small community formerly pursued by Zwide had also eluded the Zulu for years by hiding in the rocks. Isaacs, who was severely wounded in this conflict, reported that when Shaka instructed them in the mode of attack, he commanded them

> not to leave alive even a child, but exterminate the whole tribe. We remonstrated against the barbarity and great impropriety of destroying women and children, who, poor unoffending innocents, were not culpable, and could do no injury. "Yes they could," he said; "they can propagate and bring children, who may become my enemies. It is the custom I pursue not to give quarter to my enemies, therefore I command you to kill all." [18]

That this practice was a matter of policy and not the product of an adventitious rage, was indicated again in an argument with Fynn, in which Shaka maintained that the Cape colonists were foolish to deal with the frontier tribes on a friendly basis. He argued, "By destroying a tribe entirely, killing the surviving chiefs, the people would be glad to join you on your own terms." [19]

In an interesting essay comparing the Zulu and the Spartan systems, W. S. Ferguson, the classical historian, described Shaka's practice of total war, correctly observing that he waged war "not against the armed forces of the enemy alone, but against his entire moral and material resources. . . ." [20] It is clear, however, that there were two parts to his military policy:

first, the destruction of any tribe engaged in combat; second, the effects that the violence—or even the reputation of this violence—had on the emotions of people within striking range. The violence was wrought by highly disciplined impi, similar to hoplite formations, executing massed attacks in precise evolutions, using the short, stabbing assegai. The combination, which was a revolution in weaponry and military technique, could not be defeated by anything less than firearms, and was powerful enough, as the Zulu War proved half a century later, to give a modern British army serious resistance. The secondary effects of this violence were skillfully used by Shaka, like other marauding conquerors known to history, to spread the terror of his name. Fynn testified that "the barbarous cruelties he practised struck terror into many who had never seen his force and fled at his name."[21] Likewise, Shepstone declared that his new mode of warfare caused such terror that chiefdom after chiefdom gave way at his very approach to their frontiers.[22] Ferguson, in his careful assessment of the Zulu system, wrote:

> In summary, we may say that the Zulu impis owed their irresistibility among the surrounding natives, and their successes over the whites, to the following characteristics:
> 1. The merciless discipline maintained by Chaka.
> 2. The high training of the men in physical endurance and in effecting mass movements.
> 3. The use of the stabbing assegai and hand to hand fighting.
> 4. The tactics of surrounding the enemy and thus destroying him utterly.
> 5. The well organized system of espionage.
> 6. Their reputation for invincibility and the terror which their pitiless massacres of the entire population of the enemy inspired.[23]

There is evidence that Shaka considered the terror process at least as important in his strategy as the ability of his impi to overcome antagonists by force of arms. Although he recognized the superiority of firearms, if the English should invade his territory, he told Fynn, "they would be terror-struck at the magnitude of his army." [24] Shaka's English friends registered doubts that the Zulu prowess, apart from the success of their technique, was inherently superior to that of other communities. Fynn believed that the Zulu were confident in their system as long as they were successful, but that a few defeats would have demoralized them. Near the end of Shaka's career, in the campaign against the amaMpondo, Fynn listened to speeches made by a number of chiefs to Ngomane, then chief induna, in the course of which

> One in particular said that the whole army, during such time as they had served under Shaka, every time a war was proposed had expected to be defeated, but, under his command, they had become so used to conquering and to seeing the enemy entirely defeated on every occasion, that they were now ready to face whatever the enemy might offer, and that as soon as possible.[25]

Isaacs noted that Shaka had struck the surrounding communities with terror and that they were alarmed at the sound of his name, but that the Zulu tended to avoid direct confrontation wherever possible and to rely on terror and deception. The soldiers of Shaka, he said, "knew full well that their renown was enough to make their enemies crouch before them, and they gained more by the terror of their name, than they achieved by their prowess in arms." Moreover, "It is not the Zoola's system of warfare to meet their enemy openly, if they can avoid it: they like to conquer by stratagem, and not by fighting; and to gain by a ruse what might be difficult for them to achieve by the spear." [26]

DISCIPLINARY TERROR

For generations, Africans and Europeans have extolled the heroism and gallant spirit of the Zulu armies. Hence, it is surprising that these virtues are not mentioned in the recorded impressions of Fynn and Isaacs. Perhaps the historical sagas of the Zulu people, making a heroic age of Shaka's reign, have imaginatively translocated the military spirit of the impi in the Zulu War, sixty years later, to the earlier period. One suspects that the virtues were active in the era of Cetshwayo but inchoate in the time of Shaka. In any case, Fynn wrote that the superior technique of Shaka's troops gave them military success, and "they have become daring, though not brave, as I firmly believe that one repulse would so completely throw them back as to dispossess them of their remaining courage." [27] Similarly, the experience of Isaacs in engaging the enemies of the Zulu convinced him that they were equal in ability to the troops of Shaka and that the latter "possessed no innate courage." The key to Shaka's military success, if one takes the evidence of Fynn and Isaacs seriously, was terrorism against other tribes and terroristic discipline within the impi. Lacking moral courage, the Zulu warriors, Isaacs thought, fought to avoid being massacred—by the enemy and by their own officers. Their only alternatives were to return triumphant and participate in the spoils or to be named cowards and suffer a cruel death. On 13 April 1826, having attended the despot, Isaacs observed:

> Chaka was then engaged in conversation with his chiefs on the subject of the last war, and commanded them to point out all those who had proved themselves to be cowards, as they had now to contend with a brave and formidable enemy. The chiefs assured him that all of them had been killed, not one having been spared who had so disgraced himself. [28]

Armed with the large shield and the short, stabbing assegai, each warrior must return from the fight with his arms or else die in battle. Still, if he violated no rules in battle and even if he fought with valor, he was not thereby assured immunity from the violence of his officers. After the battle, each regiment was expected to "bring forth the cowards," who were executed without delay. It seems that commanders often killed men who had fought well but whose sacrifice was needed to fill some expected quota of victims. After the defeat of Sikunyana's Ndwandwe army, Fynn observed:

> Early next morning Shaka arrived, and each regiment, previous to its inspection by him, had picked out its cowards and put them to death. Many of these, no doubt, forfeited their lives only because their chiefs were in fear that, if they did not condemn some as being guilty, they would be suspected of seeking a pretext to save them and would incur the resentment of Shaka.[29]

Isaacs commented that in cases of alleged cowardice the guilt need not be established, "for merely from suspicion, the poor object of it is led away to suffer a cruel death by impalement, at the mere nod of a tyrant."[30] If a regiment were actually defeated in battle or forced to retreat from superior numbers, the entire organization would be massacred together with the families of the warriors. To celebrate this practice, the imperial residence was given the name *kwaBulawayo,* or the "place of slaughter." Witnessing disciplinary violence not only on parade but also in the field, Fynn reported:

> We proceeded on our journey, and in three days arrived at Port Natal. On the fifth day Shaka rose very early. I overtook him when he was ascending a hill, on the side of which, on the bottom, the Mbelebele regiment happened to have bivouacked. When he, Shaka, perceived that the regiment was not yet moving he ordered his servants to run and stab a few of them. They did so and killed five. The regiment then ran on ahead with all possible speed to lead the way and clear it of thorns, the omission to do which, in accordance with the usual

practice, they supposed was the reason why the servants were killing them. In their haste a group of men passed within five yards of Shaka, not having noticed him until they got within that distance. He looked at them so fiercely as to make them run back, whereupon he vociferated his usual oath . . . in so violent a manner as to bring them to a momentary stand. He then ordered an attendant to single out a man and stab him. They sat down, about 80 in number, when the attendant for some moments looked about for a bad-looking man; he found one, then stabbed him in the left breast and, by Shaka's orders, left the assegai in the body that it might be seen by passers-by. The moment the assegai pierced the body Shaka averted his head, his countenance betraying something like a feeling of horror, but we had not proceeded more than a mile when two other unfortunates experienced the same fate.[31]

Civil Terror

Since warfare was the predominant activity of the Zulu state, no part of social life was entirely free from the vicissitudes of military action. The economy required hoe cultivation, carried on by women, but it depended more on the influx of cattle seized from conquered people. The impi was the dominant organization in the state, tending to exclude all others. As Gluckman showed, the "military organization of Zulu culture under the king . . . largely unified his people. . . . The dominant values of Zulu life were those of the warrior, and they were satisfied in service at the king's barracks and in his wars." [32] Even the durable pattern of traditional family life was fundamentally altered by Shaka's military innovations. Men who reached warrior age were to remain bachelors until retired from active service by the despot. The importance of this change was stated eloquently by Mofolo, the Sotho writer:

The reader must remember that above all else on earth the Black Races love to marry. Often in speaking of the good things

of life people do not mention marriage, because marriage is
life. Therefore we can understand well how hard the warriors
of Chaka worked to gain this reward. To set his regiments an
example Chaka remained a bachelor till the end of his life.
This is . . . the most important thing that Chaka did.[33]

Every part of the kingdom was geared to perpetual conquest,
and the routine of social life fluctuated with the military campaigns. Nevertheless, it is possible to trace the work of the
terror process in situations that were relatively independent of
military functions.

Violence was a standard penalty in the old Bantu culture, for
fines and death were the only two modes of punishment for
specific civil offenses, torture being reserved for cases of witchcraft. Even benevolent rulers ordered the death penalty for certain crimes, especially those that were considered offenses
against the king. To give one example, death was the penalty
for anyone found cutting corn without the king's permission
before the First Fruits ceremony. Since the ceremony regulated
the harvest season, premature cutting was a threat to the community, but it is also true that the offense had political significance, for it was so clearly a violation of the royal prerogative
that it constituted an act of rebellion. Nevertheless, as argued
in a previous chapter, the use of violence to punish specific
civil offenses is qualitatively different from its use in the terror
process. In the Zulu state, two notable instances of civil terrorism were Shaka's defense against magic and his violence
against proscribed sexual relations, which was consistent with
his general policy of shattering the loyalties of primary relationships.

Gluckman tries to explain Shaka's behavior in the latter case
by postulating abnormal personality:

Shaka himself had no children. He said that a son would
kill him for the throne. He had many concubines but no wives,
and any concubine who became pregnant was killed. I believe
that this, and other data on his sexual life, show that Shaka

was at least a latent homosexual and possibly psychotic. Very likely this motivated another of his military innovations: he forbade his men to marry or have sexual relations with women until he gave them permission to do so in middle age, and he quartered all his men in great barracks, as in any modern army. It is significant that his regimental barracks system was not retained by his successors and imitators, though they used his other inventions.[34]

This explanation is shaky indeed, for every item may be explained with equal cogency as a product of calculation rather than the outcome of impulses that were abnormal in a clinical sense. Shaka's refusal to generate heirs, fearing they would covet the throne and be potential patricides, is well known. It is reported that he destroyed one infant who was presented as his child; still, the chronicles tell a story of his permitting another child, obviously his own, not only to live but to escape to Tembeland. His brother, Dingane, who succeeded him to the throne, also refused to marry and to beget heirs. Moreover, like Shaka, Mzilikazi forbade marriage to the Matebele warriors. It is difficult to know what "other data on his sexual life" Gluckman means, but there is ample evidence, from the descriptions of his conduct as well as from anecdotes in the chronicles, that Shaka enjoyed his women.[35] The organization of bachelor warriors is nothing unusual, since it was a widespread institution to be found in the military systems of people as diverse as the Nilo-Hamites and ancient Dorians as well as in that of the Bantu. What Shaka did was to assume control of his warriors' career, extending the time they remained unmarried and making a matter for his decision the sequence of age grades that was previously regulated by the natural progress of the life cycle. The rule of celibacy forbade impregnation but not sexual contact, and the warriors were expected to have sweethearts and to gratify desire by *ukuhlobonga*, a traditional method of external intercourse.[36] The problem of the *ikhanda* system, or the pattern of barracks life in military kraals, is more complex than Gluckman here suggests, and its introduction under Shaka and subsequent fate under Dingane are more reasonably explained, it will be argued, by the vicissitudes of the power system than by Shaka's presumed sexual attitudes. An interpretation of Shaka's relationship to women similar to that of Gluckman is given by Donald Morris. Morris asserts that Shaka "was unquestionably a latent homosexual" and "probably impotent." Against the tradition that Shaka limited his sexual activity to *ukuhlobonga*, Morris conjectures, "in view of the utter lack of control that characterized every other facet of his personality, it is probable that he never managed to consummate a full relationship." Then what of Dingane, Shaka's successor, who also kept a seraglio but refused to marry and to beget? Unwilling to stretch the assertion of impotency to include the next reign as well, Morris blithely declares that Dingane "was most likely sterile." [37]

If the evidence is examined with care, it leaves one skeptical about the question of Shaka's abnormality, unless one follows the circular line of reasoning that any social innovator is "abnormal." The same issue is often raised in regard to Shaka's use of violence. Fynn and Isaacs, who were intelligent, reflective men as well as keen observers, though outraged by Shaka's cruelty, never raised the question of his psychic abnormality, but instead suspected that certain acts were political tricks. As Fynn put it, Shaka's puzzling and atrocious actions were part of "a political scheme in furtherance of Shaka's vain imaginations and to keep the minds of his people filled with wonder." [38] One need not argue that Shaka was "normal" in the sense that he was free of delusions: on the contrary, there is evidence that he was driven by fantasies that we would consider grotesque. Nevertheless, to oversimplify the relation between personality and power system leads to a false picture of despotism as well as to misleading theories about the function of terror in a despotic system.

In Gluckman's brief analysis, social conditions in Zululand, under the pressures of acute overpopulation, were such that a conqueror could easily centralize the communities and emerge as an overlord of the region. Shaka had the appropriate personality for the task, but after he established himself as head of the kingdom, his abnormal "emotional outlook" caused him to destroy the traditional system and to set up the barracks organization of unmarried warriors. According to this viewpoint his violent behavior as well as the new institutions may be explained by his abnormal emotional outlook, and although they were imposed on the people, the discomfort was endured because Shaka's system of domination satisfied important social needs.

Gluckman's explanation ignores the official, collective fantasies that matched Shaka's "abnormal" outlook, and it also fails to show satisfactorily why the people chose to support his behavior and to co-operate actively with the violence. In later chapters I shall try to give a *social* explanation of terroristic despotism that does not find it a crucial matter whether or not the overlord is *ab initio* "abnormal" in a psychological sense. A psychological investigation of Shaka's behavior would be interesting as a separate inquiry, but its methods should not be identified with political sociology. A sociological explanation, even though it may use psychological information, should uncover the forces that activate violent roles and the conditions that support them. Certainly, much more is required than an understanding of the overlord's character to comprehend the structure of violence in a despotic system.

Yet, violent autocrats are intriguing subjects for biographical interpretation, and Shaka has captured the imaginations of both European and African writers using a variety of literary forms. In most cases, the biographical approaches to Shaka's rule, concentrating on his character, when confronted with the evidence of his violent acts, have tended, on the one hand, either to deny their terroristic function, in order to exonerate him, or, on the other hand, to consider those acts as the "natural"—that is, removed from the need for further explanation— manifestations of a psychotic or evil character.

Ritter, although he recognizes Shaka's use of terror, especially in the latter days of the regime, argues in his sympathetic essay that Shaka has been maligned by history, that he was not responsible for the great wars that racked the subcontinent, and that he was in reality a judicious empire builder, who used violence where it was necessary to impose the Zulu *pax*. The responsibility for devastation, Ritter claims, may be found in the acts of Shaka's enemies, especially Zwide.[39] In contrast, Thomas Mofolo, a Christian Sotho, in his novel of Shaka's life, originally written in Sesotho (the language of the people who live on the other side of the Drakensberg Range, west of Zululand), indicated that "Chaka, the originator of all that was evil," started all the wars and migrations that tormented Southern Africa.[40] In this highly dramatic novel, Shaka sells his soul to a diabolic person appearing as a witch doctor, and in the grip of the black magic given to him, commits greater and greater atrocities, until, at the end of his life, he becomes the representation of total evil. In an introduction to the English translation of the novel, Henry Newbolt wrote that in the book, "Chaka's irresistible career is the perfect and unanswerable example of the ruin of human life by the rule of force, deliberately adopted and consistently followed." The tragedy becomes "the apocalyptic vision of a monstrous beast, consumed by an all-destroying blood-lust." [41] Similarly, H. Rider Haggard, the well-known Victorian novelist, attempted in *Nada the Lily*, his romance of Shaka's time, "to set out the true character of this colossal genius and most evil man,—a Napoleon and a Tiberius in one. . . ." [42]

Even if insanity or moral wickedness were the cause (sufficient condition) of Shaka's violent behavior, it would be difficult to maintain an identical argument to explain the behavior of Dingane, his fratricide successor, who continued the system of terror, and to explain that of Mpande, who retained similar, but more limited, practices. Nevertheless, the temptation to cling to such a line of reasoning is strong, even if it means constructing an entire line of "mad" or "wicked" rulers: witness the historical reputation of the Julio-Claudian emperors from Tiberius to Nero. However, even if we assume (without conceding) the fact of Shaka's madness or evil character, we cannot go on to explain why his behavior was not merely permitted but indeed supported by the political community, nor can we indicate the consequences of his irrational acts for the system of power. Shaka carried to their furthest extremes the principles of terroristic despotism, and it is possible to examine the objective features of his rule without full knowledge of his psychic state.

To augment his despotic power, Shaka struck at the primary loyalties of kinship ties and personal attachments, not permitting those sentiments to compete with the total loyalty that he demanded from his people. When Shaka was stabbed, and when persons close to the throne, such as the chief induna, his grandmother, and his mother died, the people were forced to put on a great display of mourning. Individuals whose public grief did not appear sufficient were killed. At the same time, his people were forbidden to grieve for the loss of their own relatives—especially if the latter had been slaughtered by the despot. Isaacs wrote, "I have known several instances of people having been suspected of crying for the loss of relations, who were, by the king's order, put to death on the instant." [43] Men were sometimes forced to kill their own children and in turn were killed if they showed reluctance. As reported by Isaacs:

> In ordering any of his subjects to be killed, Shaka never gave his reason for consigning them to death until it was too late to recall the sentence of execution. A sign, given by the pointing of his finger, or by the terrible declination of his head, was promptly obeyed, and as promptly executed, by anyone present. Thus a father did not hesitate to be the executioner of his own child; the ties of consanguinity availed nothing with the tyrant, his decrees must be carried into operation, and that unhesitatingly; and if after perpetrating the revolting deed the feelings of nature should predominate, and manifest themselves to the inhuman savage, the party was instantly ordered to be despatched, with the atrocious remark, "Take the Umtugarty [*umthakathi*] away: let me see if loving his child better than

his king will do him any good. See if your clubs are not harder than his head." The executioner was then permitted to repair to the kraal of the poor dead and mutilated creature, and there destroy everyone who might be connected with it, to take the implements of war as his booty, and drive the cattle to the king, who orders its distribution among his warriors then present.[44]

In these ways, and by other means, Shaka sought to bring Zulu life under his control, loosening ties of kinship and not permitting anything like a private sphere to exist. The controls imposed on intimate personal relations were supported not only by the despot's circle of induna and counsellors but also by the people. The rules were breached often enough, but leaders and people responded with swift violence whenever violations, real or imaginary, were disclosed.

After the death of Shaka's mother, Ngomane—then chief induna—made a speech, Fynn recorded, which was received with unanimous approval. In it he declared:

as it was probable that the heavens and the earth would unite in bewailing her death, the sacrifice should be a great one; no cultivation should be allowed during the following year; no milk should be used, but, as drawn from the cow, it should be poured upon the earth; and all women, who should be found with child during the year, should with their husbands be put to death.[45]

After three months, large offerings of oxen having been made to the despot by all the chiefs, the first two restrictions were removed, but the prohibition of sexual intercourse—or, at least, of impregnation—was strictly enforced throughout the year. One reason for the rule seemed to be that since the death of such a great person was a calamity, and since the grief of Shaka was inordinate, any sign of joy was an offense to the despot.

Just as the unmarried men lived in military kraals, the

choice maidens lived in ten or fifteen seraglios commanded by adopted royal mothers or queens. Like the royal cattle, the despot's young women were objects of pride to be displayed, and they also served as his concubines, although he referred to them as his "sisters." Each seraglio was a restricted area located in the upper part of a royal kraal, the largest being at the principal royal residence. The girls were selected according to beauty, served with abject submission, and lived, as did the regiments of warriors, on rations provided by the despot. Fynn estimated that Shaka had 5000 young women organized in this fashion, and was served personally by 400 or 500, drawn mainly from his principal residence but augmented by hundreds from other seraglios. The other unmarried girls of the kingdom were apparently organized in age sets that were analogues of the regiments. Occasionally, Shaka relaxed the code and declared a holiday, allowing the warriors to sport with the girls. Moreover, when a regiment was relieved of celibacy and granted the privilige of wearing the head ring, symbol of the adult man, he arranged marriages with a specific regiment of girls. Krige observes:

> In the days of the great Zulu kings when no man could get married until his regiment had been ordered by the king to put on the head-ring (the sign of full maturity), all the marriageable girls that had accumulated since the previous order for marriage were given a name and simply told off to marry those men. Such an order was very often the cause of great sorrow in the lives of many of these girls who had already formed attachments with boys of their own *intanga* [local age set]. In Shaka's days there were sometimes women of thirty years of age unmarried, just because he refused to allow the men of his regiments to get married until the best of their fighting days were over.[46]

By arranging marriages, Shaka reduced even further the authority of the kin groups. Through the separate organizations of young men and women, he maintained control over their intimate lives, just as he was able to place lesser restrictions from time to time on the lives of married men and women. The design was perceived by Fynn, who observed:

> Shaka's innovations were not confined to the expansion, organization, discipline and efficiency of his army, vast, complex and mobile as it was, nor was his time and attention wholly occupied by the campaigns or deeds of his warriors and the numerous direct and indirect consequences thereof. He was shrewd enough to see that the success of his system, as a whole, and the many far-flung and exacting operations he was always engaged in depended to no small degree, on the way in which the relations between the sexes were controlled. Among his extraordinary developments in this connection were the royal *izigodlo* or seraglios, and, once organized and developed by Shaka, they were maintained by later kings, very much on similar lines, though not on so large a scale.[47]

The girls in the seraglios chafed under their restrictions, and when the despot's back was turned, risked death by intrigues with men who dared to approach them. Undoubtedly, Shaka heard reports of their behavior, and in typical fashion asserted his control by a violent act. Isaacs gave a full account of what was later called "the slaughter of the innocents" on 11 November 1826. Shaka had dreamed that the boys in the royal kraal were having intercourse with the girls of his seraglio. By a ruse, he led a group of warriors some distance from the kraal, told them of his dream, and declared his intention to punish the offense. His people responded: "Father kill them for they are not fit to live." The dream of mass cuckoldry stirred him to "beat his aged and infirm mother with inconceivable cruelty," because, he claimed, "she had not taken proper care of his girls." Marching the party back to the kraal, he ordered the men to surround it:

> He then ordered the victims intended for destruction to be brought to him, and those whom he selected his executioners

immediately despatched. He began by taking out several fine lads, and ordering their own brothers to twist their necks, their bodies were afterwards dragged away and beaten with sticks until life was extinct. After this refined act of monstrous cruelty, the remainder of the victims in the kraal were indiscriminately butchered. Few of the poor innocent children cried or evinced any sorrow, but walked out as if inwardly conscious they were about to be removed from a state of terror to "another and a better world." [48]

When the slaughter was ended, Isaacs reported that Shaka addressed his warriors, saying, "You see we have conquered all our enemies and killed a number of Umtaggarties, I shall now consult Umbeah, and find out the rest." Shaka was referring to Mbiya, his dead foster father who was advising him in dreams, and the word he used to name the victims, as recorded ungrammatically in Isaacs's orthography, was *"abathakathi,"* which takes the singular form, *"umthakathi."* [49] Then Shaka turned to his chiefs and said, "To-morrow I shall kill all those who have offended since I have reigned, there will then be nothing wanted to make you and me happy."

CONTROL OF MAGIC

Although Shaka probably named these victims *"abathakathi"* because he accused them of a serious sexual offense, and indeed the term is sometimes used in this sense, the word *"umthakathi"* is usually translated as "wizard" or "sorcerer," but it is an ambiguous term that contains other meanings as well. Some of the meanings have political implications which may be understood in the context of Zulu history, and they help to reveal the measures employed by Shaka to develop the despotic regime. The social importance of magic in the Zulu system is well known, but the concept of the *umthakathi* is one of the most important links between magic and power. It also provides the clue to another extensive use of civil violence, namely, Shaka's terroristic measures to protect himself against sorcery on the one hand, and his efforts, on the other hand, to break the independent power of the witch detectors and other *izinyanga*, or "doctors," and bring the practice of magic under his control. Magical practices touched every part of Zulu life, and the reality of magic was never questioned. In most cases, the use of charms and medicines was limited to chiefs or to duly initiated specialists (*izinyanga*), and if ordinary people were to practice magic, they would run the risk of death by incurring the suspicion of sorcery, the foulest vice and most heinous crime.[50] In all the chiefdoms and kingdoms of the old Bantu culture, nothing was dreaded more than the harmful use of magic, and when anything went wrong, the influence of the sorcerer was suspected. Calamities and disease, it was thought, were produced by malevolent spirits or by hostile men or women.[51] Even the most powerful chiefs and kings were frightened of sorcery. Indeed, they more than anyone lived in terror of death by secret magic.[52] As Krige describes, just as the *inyanga* was the protector of society, curing the sick, averting evil omens, and "smelling out" evildoers, the *umthakathi* was the enemy of society.

> He is the man or woman who uses the powers of the universe which he has learnt to employ by means of magic, for antisocial ends. The *umthakathi* uses his power for evil and against the welfare of society; he injures people's health, destroys life, prevents rain, occasions lightning, makes the cows become dry, and is the cause of all manner of misfortune. Once he has been discovered, therefore, he is shown no mercy, but is got rid of as speedily as possible.[53]

Kidd declared that when he first visited Pondoland, it was calculated that on the average, one person a day was executed on charges of witchcraft.[54] In Shaka's era the number must have been beyond reckoning, since anyone singled out for destruction might be given the epithet *umthakathi.*

Although "*umthakathi*" seemed to stand for "the enemy within," the term had four meanings that were more specific.

First, when it meant "sorcerer" or "wizard," it referred either to murder by the physical act of secret poisoning or to magical violence by medicines used in charms and secret rites. Sorcery was almost always blamed for the death of a chief. Isaacs told the story of a time when white metal had been discovered and used to make bangles, which were insignia of distinction:

> At this period a number of chiefs died; the inyangers [*izinyanga*] . . . wisemen or soothsayers, were ordered to assemble, and immediately discover the cause of their death. Several people were suspected of having administered poison to them, and were all killed without discrimination, or without proof of guilt. The prevailing malady by which the chiefs had been carried off still continuing, and innumerable natives having been destroyed under the impression of being the cause of their death, or being according to their designation, "Umtu-gartie," [*umthakathi*] that is, "evil-disposed persons," they decided that the white metal worn by the chiefs was the cause of the death of that class of persons, which put an end to further executions of the innocent. The individuals, however, who had discovered the metal, and those who had fabricated it into bangles, were condemned and executed.[55]

Second, the term, *"ubuthakathi,"* meaning sorcery, also meant "surprising skill or cunning." [56] This meaning should not be a linguistic shock to us, for in our own usage we say that a highly skilled person who produces surprising things is a "wizard" in some special activity: Thomas Edison, for example, was known as "the wizard of Menlo Park." When Dingane massacred the party of Boers led by Piet Retief in the royal kraal, he is supposed to have said, "Seize the wizards!" and he may have been referring to the firearms and other implements that gave the Europeans technological superiority. In the Zulu usage, however, the skill had to be unexpected, and therefore suspect. An expert whose skill in a craft or profession was legitimate and expected would never have been referred to as an *umthakathi,* but rather as an *inyanga,* or specialist.

A third meaning of the term applied to the malefactors of the greatest criminality: murderers, adulterers, and persons who violated the rules of consanguinity.[57] Perhaps Shaka had this specific meaning in mind when he called the victims in his "slaughter of the innocents" at the royal kraal "*abathakathi.*" Moreover, in the olden times, when a warrior broke the orders of the war doctor, who treated the impi with medicines to make them invincible, his act declared him *umthakathi*, and his village was destroyed with him.[58]

Finally, the reproach of being *umthakathi* attached to general bad character or persistent bad conduct, and in this usage the term signified "evildoer," [59] a notion which has counterparts in the ideas about witchcraft shared by many African societies.

Shaka destroyed all the individuals he accused as evildoers with the intention that this massive violence should prevent others who might be tempted to take up magic against him. It is clear that the terrorism was based on his own fear of intangible violence: his dread of sorcery and precautions against magical harm were well documented by the chroniclers as well as by the European observers. Even if the deterrent effect of his violent campaign against sorcery is questioned, its effect on Shaka should be taken into account: it gave him confidence that the danger of sorcery was reduced when potential sorcerers were terrorized and inhibited by their terror from entertaining thoughts or taking measures to plot against the ruler.

In the early and middle periods of his regime, Shaka relied on his war doctors to work magic against his external enemies, and on the specialists in the art of divination—otherwise known, when their work was detecting, as *izanusi*—to smell out the enemy within, who were turned over the "secular arm" and executed immediately. The *isanusi*—the singular form of *izanusi*—using the gift of divination to unravel mysteries, was the person in greatest demand in the old Zulu society. He or she was needed to interpret omens, diagnose disease, explain misfortune, and find lost cattle, as well as to reveal sorcery and to practice magic in legitimate ways for the social good. The protector of society, the *isanusi* was the link between the ancestral spirits and the living as well as the dedicated enemy of the *umthakathi*. The highly respected role was so important that Krige has declared it to be "one of the pivots upon which the welfare of the society rests." [60] Although the jealousy of the military organization prevented the existence of separate religious or political associations in Zulu society, the power exercised by the diviners allowed them to remain a kind of sacred order. [61] The custom of smelling out and destroying sorcerers, universally supported by traditional sentiment, was deemed necessary to the well being of society, and it was felt that if the custom were breached, the spirits in their rage would bring disaster on the people. [62] Even the ruler was powerless to interfere with the process of smelling out, so that in Rider Haggard's novel, which is based in part on the chronicles, Shaka speaks bitterly, "The witchdoctors rule in Zululand, and not I. . . ." [63]

Shaka was vulnerable to the *izanusi,* even though the ruler was immune from accusations of sorcery himself, because his circle of lieutenants—induna, generals, and trusted councillors —was fair game to the diviners. The implicit threat of smelling out a favorite of the despot functioned as a limitation on his power. According to the chronicles, Shaka's struggle with the *izanusi* extended over several years, leading to his establishing immunity from detection for the army and culminating in a scheme contrived to break their power once and for all. [64] He could not go so far as to deny the principles of divination or to impugn the role of the *isanusi*—besides, once he had full control of the process, it would be a useful instrument—but it was possible for him to repudiate the incumbents as false diviners. To that end, he played a trick, which is recorded by the oral tradition.

Secretly, he smeared the walls and the ground in front of the royal hut with blood, an act, if committed by any of the people, of sacrilege and lese majesty. After the outcry, all the *izanusi*

were summoned to a great assembly to discover who had perpe-
trated the outrage. A large number, including several members
of the king's inner circle, were smelled out, but their expected
execution was delayed by the despot's order. Only one *isanusi*
—Ritter's account mentions two—had the wit to say that the
act had been committed by *izulu*. Shaka, a great punster himself, was pleased by the double entendre—for the word signified either "heaven" or a praise name of the Zulu king—and he
spared him, ordering all the others to be slain by their would-be
victims. It is said that from that time Shaka would not execute
anyone smelled out by an *isanusi*. Mzilikazi, a despot of the
Matebele (Ndebele), who emulated Shaka in many respects,
once played a similar trick, putting a stone in his mouth to
make it appear that he had a swollen cheek. He called all his
doctors to smell out the person responsible for his affliction,
and after their victims had been picked out, spat out the stone
and exposed the diviners as frauds.[65]

The effect of Shaka's policy of reducing the power of the
izanusi, according to Ritter, had been to make life in Zulu society more attractive to the people of other tribes. Since the army
had been immune from the process of smelling out and liber-
ally treated with gifts of cattle, it drew volunteers from other
societies. Similarly, rich men, who realized that their wealth
would some day make them the target for an accusation of sorcery, moved with their entire kraals to Zululand.[66] After his
mass destruction of the *izanusi*, it is said that Shaka used to
declare that "he was the only diviner in the country, for if he
allowed rivals his life would be insecure." [67] Moreover, he declared himself to be the only legitimate rainmaker in the kingdom, giving the order, "Let all the heaven-doctors be killed." [68]
His policy against diviners was followed later by other chiefs
and kings, but to a lesser extent. Bishop Callaway described the
izinyanga as a priesthood with the duty of consecration, and
observed that a new ruler called celebrated diviners to invest
him with chiefly virtue so that he might be truly a ruler and not
one merely by descent. They installed him on the throne with

charms and medicines, and later, when he obtained from the diviners their medicines and secrets, he often ordered them to be killed, lest they turn their magic against himself.[69]

At the end of his life, Shaka had virtually a monopoly of the most important magical practices, and those *izinyanga* allowed to practice clearly took no thought of challenging the power of the despot. Isaacs wrote:

> Chaka ruled his people by perpetually keeping them in a state of terror, and his command over them was also greatly facilitated by his continually impressing them with the power of charms, witchcraft or necromancy, which he practised, with inconceivable effect, on his poor, abject, deluded, and oppressed subjects. This he carried to such an extent as to excite a belief in their minds, that he had the power of knowing all their thoughts, and of seeing all their most secret actions.

His employment of magic, Isaacs thought, was intended to "inspire them with something like awe, and strike terror into them (by his seeming unearthly character and hidden power), that should check any disposition to revolt among them for his inhuman massacres." [70] He took on the title of dream doctor, and while the army was away on its last campaign in the north, he was busy smelling out evildoers.[71] He gathered hundreds of women and questioned them about their ownership of cats— presumably, he was hunting sorcerers who worked magic through animal familiars.[72] Regardless of their response, the persons singled out for questioning were doomed, and he slaughtered these hundreds of women in the absence of their husbands. This last destructive action, it is said, helped to mobilize the growing sentiment against Shaka's violence, and the repugnance it caused contributed to the popular approval of his assassination.

CONTROL OF LEADERS

The major targets of Shaka's violence were individuals and groups who, if left unchecked, would naturally act to limit or even challenge his power. The most serious threat to a ruler, he knew, was the potential rebellion of his own sons. Thus, he refused to marry or to beget heirs. The women of the seraglios as well as the appointed "queens" supervising them were prevented by the fear of violence from producing children. Fynn related that he had heard of an occasion when Nandi, Shaka's mother, who governed the concubines in the principal royal kraal, presented an infant and its mother, claiming that Shaka was the father of the child:

> He immediately seized the little innocent, and, throwing it up in the air, it was killed by the fall; the mother was instantly ordered to be put to death, whilst Shaka so severely beat his mother, Nandi, with a stick, for presuming to accuse him of being the father that she was lame for three months. When she recovered, she had the ten concubines put to death who had agreed with her proposal to show Shaka the infant.[73]

The first collective targets of Shaka's violence were the old men of the kingdom, who were marked for destruction about the time the system of terror was established. The elders, as in any traditional society, not only served as living archives of custom and law[74] but also exerted moral influence on the ruler. In the simplest societies, the elders are frequently the most powerful set of men, and in the more complex primitive societies, under ordinary conditions, they hold considerable authority, not only participating in important decisions, but also exercising restraint in various ways on the power of the ruler. Any innovating chief or king who seeks to rule without traditional limitations must deal with the resistance of the elders.

Shaka dealt with this resistance by redefining the status of the old men and then slaughtering them. Instead of respected persons who had passed from active service to venerable authority, they were declared to be useless "old women" who were unfit for fighting. It appears that before their extermination, Shaka had changed their status by instituted ridicule. It is said that he had compelled them to wear petticoats of monkey skins, shaped like the garments of old women, for battle dress. A song that Shaka had composed for the occasion of his seizing the Zulu chieftainship included the following lines:

> The aged must be separated and placed in the rear.
> Do you not see they impede the King's army?
> They were men formerly,
> But now our mother's mothers,
> We must find petticoats to wear.[75]

Around the time the Ndwandwe were defeated, he gathered the aged men and had them killed. Even if some were spared, it is clear that their power as a group was ended and that those who survived were prevented by terror from attempting to influence the king. Significantly, the seat of power was named after the violent act that had changed the structure of controls. To commemorate the event and to keep alive its lesson, he named the principal royal kraal "*Gibixegu*," which means "drive out the old men." [76]

When the terror of military discipline was instituted, the name of the royal kraal was changed to commemorate the destruction of "the cowards." Shaka gave it the name "*kwaBulawayo*," meaning "place of slaughter," [77] and Mzilikazi, who copied Shaka's system of terror, gave his principal kraal in Southern Rhodesia the same name. By giving the seat of power names with violent meanings, Shaka made clear to all the nature of Zulu rule. In the previous name, *Gibixegu*, he commemorated the rise of absolute power; the second name, *Bulawayo*, indicating that the seat of power was a place of death, signified that the royal power was based on continual violence.

The remaining source of possible limitation on Shaka's

power was the group referred to vaguely by the Europeans as "the chiefs." These *amaphakathi*, literally meaning the members of the inner circle, often surrounded him in the royal kraal and accompanied him on marches. In many respects they were similar to what the Romans had called *comites*—namely, officers, companions, and attendants making up a retinue. Some were *izinduna*, ministers chosen by the despot, whose personal loyalty had rewarded them with office and whose power and survival depended entirely on him. Others were the heads of chiefdoms and lineages formerly independent, whose original authority had not been created by the despot but who now gave him fealty and attended his presence. In addition, the generals were among the most important members of the circle.

The *amaphakathi* attended the king with the strictest ceremony. As Fynn described:

> The chiefs and regiments belonging to the kraal, as well as those coming on and going off duty, no sooner heard of his rising than they collected and approached him. When they got within 30 yards of him they would salute with respectful fear by saying: "Bayede!" a salutation due only to kings. They would then seat themselves on the ground before him in silence and proceed to listen with great attention and anxiety. They caught with great eagerness every word that escaped him in course of conversation and answered him only with acclamations of praise or by expressing astonishment at his talents.[78]

Shaka depended on the higher officers of the inner circle to execute his will, particularly the ministers, generals, and subordinate chiefs, who were also called upon for opinions on matters of state. He counteracted their potential limitations on his power by a method of division. For example, each of the three armies had a military council made up of generals and regimental commanders. The despot, at his pleasure, would call on one or more of these bodies for counsel, stating his own opinion first on whatever the issue happened to be and calling for theirs. They were cautious in their response and rarely opposed his stated position. If they did express opposition, he would summon another council: if it agreed with him, the members became his favorites, and the group that had fallen out of favor was expected to present a solatium to the despot for offending him. This procedure, which seems on the surface absurd, in effect was a clever technique by which Shaka managed to make full use of the councils while at the same time he prevented them from uniting and acquiring solidarity. The rivalry induced them to check one another but not the despot. Isaacs observed that Shaka was generally at variance with half of his military advisers and prevented their getting together by having the regiments move in opposite directions and locating them in positions that were some distance apart. Meetings in general were not formally or explicitly proscribed, but it was well understood that they were subject to Shaka's anger and suspicion and that those who dared to participate in assemblies without his knowledge would be dispatched without excessive delay.[79]

When Shaka came to power, Bryant showed, he made a clean sweep of all "uncles, nephews and such like against whom he harboured a grudge." [80] He killed chiefs and other important persons whose loyalty he suspected and replaced them with kinsmen and other favorites. Throughout his reign, suspicion was enough to cause the violent removal of any lieutenant, and getting the despot's ear to plant suspicions was an important move to be made in the complex intrigues of the inner circle. Ferguson believed that there were indications that Shaka lived in fear of his several induna.[81] Certainly, the pattern of violence that ravaged the circle around the despot in great assemblies had terroristic effect on the *amaphakathi*.

Thus, the Zulu despot used the process of terror to inhibit potential resistance from the leading men in the state. When the agents of violence were ordered by the king to carry out an execution, they knew they would lose their own lives if they refused, but when Shaka ordered the death of a chief, they were "willing instruments, knowing that the confiscation of the property of the chief and his tribe would be the reward of their infamous labours." [82] Violence, however, was used to control the chiefs, not to eliminate them, for they were needed as a staff to administer the despot's will, and Shaka employed the process of terror not only to control but also to protect them. A leading person, it was believed, could not die naturally unless he were killed in battle. Other forms of death—even if they assumed the appearance of age or disease—proceeded, it was thought, from the magic power of evildoers. On the occasion of such a death, Shaka would hunt for the sorcerer, believing that he must expose himself by an inability to shed tears. Therefore, all persons who did not weep satisfactorily were massacred. Isaacs observed:

> That the king himself does not feel any loss in the death of a chief, and that he never grieves, were pretty evident to us. The present is merely a usage or barbarous custom, instituted to enforce sorrow on the people for the death of a principal native, and cause them to use every means to protect him and preserve his life, or prevent their having recourse to charms to destroy him. . . . Several of the people were knocked down in our presence and killed; all the huts were searched, and those found within were forced out to share the fate of those who had been previously killed for not weeping. Our lives were alone held sacred amidst this scene of sanguinary executions, for it appears that a general feeling pervaded the natives, even in the moment of terror and unrestrained massacre, of our being the king's white people, and that our presence was a most favourable omen. [83]

Chiefs who were favorites of the ruler were permitted, and probably even encouraged, to build great establishments with numerous herds and many wives. Without such fond indulgence this opulence would be dangerous, since the display of a great lord might be considered to rival the unique role of the despot. After the assassination, Dingane took the obvious precaution of liquidating Shaka's supporters, but destroying Zihandlo, great Chief of the abaMbo, who had waxed expansive as a vassal prince under Shaka's "armpit," was more than usually agreeable. Zihandlo had offended, Dingane claimed, by "playing the little king" and by "boasting a harem as great as mine!" [84]

Occasionally, Shaka placed the responsibility for certain actions on the inner circle. It is possible that despite the terror, Shaka felt pressure from his lieutenants. After the rape committed by the Hottentot servants (see p. 141), he explained to the Europeans that "the cause for his being so enraged in the morning was to gratify the chiefs, who had met to consult him on the subject of the insult to the violated girl." He assured Farewell that he was still friendly, but insisted, " 'something must be done to appease the chiefs, or they will say I am not fit to command; you must, therefore, go and fight [umBeje].' " [85] It is possible, however, that the signs of apprehension were a pretense. Shaka may have introduced a strategem that is more familiar in later Zulu history. Sometimes the kings would absolve themselves from the responsibility for an action by blaming it on one or more of their induna. [86]

After the episode of the slaughter of the innocents (see p. 155), Shaka was observed to threaten his chiefs. Isaacs reported that he told the assembled warriors that "they had hitherto witnessed the deaths of common people, but they would soon behold that of chiefs." [87] No wholesale slaughter did follow, however, and on the next day Isaacs reported nothing more extraordinary than the execution of the ruler's chief domestic, who thanked the despot as he was being beaten to death, and the murder of three girls, two of them king's women and the other the daughter of a chief.

The inner circle remained the most dangerous locus of potential resistance, and indeed it produced the final danger: conspiracy against the ruler. The trio that assassinated Shaka was composed of two royal princes—Dingane and Mhlangana, his half-brothers—and a principal induna, Mbopha, who served as a kind of Mayor of the Palace. Another half-brother, Mpande (not born of the same mother as the two assassins), was not in the plot. He had survived Shaka's violence, it is said, because he seemed to be a fool. Why Dingane and Mhlangana had been spared is not clear, but the chronicles tell that Shaka's intimates were urging him to guard against them, and it is suggested that his suspicions would have led to their execution had they not struck first.

It seems that he was taken by surprise. The armies were away in the last disasterous campaign to the north, and only a handful of men were present in the kraal. The chiefs who supported Shaka were killed without delay. We have no details apart from the oral tradition. As he was dying, pierced by assegais, it is said, Shaka turned to his killers and asked, "What is wrong, children of my father?"

THE TURNING POINTS

From the evidence, it appears that Shaka's regime of terror was inaugurated at the time the Ndwandwe were destroyed. Fynn observed that prior to this expedition, the ruler had behaved with restraint as compared to his subsequent conduct:

> His inclinations, until the defeat of the Ndwandwes, had been restrained by fear lest his subjects should detach themselves from him. Having, at length, defeated the only remaining formidable enemy, with nothing to fear from any other quarter, and when he imagined that his extensive power placed him in a state of perfect security, his real character began to develop itself. Up to this time he had, in great measure, acted in accordance with the system of his late protector, Dingiswayo, but, owing to his increased sense of security, his former tactics began to be blended with a more rigid despotism. He kept his subjects in perpetual awe and continual astonishment from the variety of his exploits and brilliancy of his achievements. But after the annihilation of the Ndwandwe people a reign of terror commenced, when his excessive cruelties overleaped all bounds.[88]

The severity of his violence increased, reaching a peak in the year 1827, culminating in the episode of Nandi's death, which was not only a climax of the terror but also a turning point in South African history.[89]

In Zulu social life, death was ceremonialized by rituals of purification and attended by convulsive demonstrations of grief.[90] Ordinarily, the death of a royal person was a great event, and, as we have seen, Shaka used the occasions for political ends, but, as the passing of Shaka's mother was absorbed in the system of terror, it surpassed the limits of custom and turned into an extraordinary massacre. Those who did not seem to be weeping or mourning loud enough were slaughtered. Huge crowds gathered at the scene—Fynn, who was present, estimated a number of 60,000. After a period of silence, Shaka had broken out into frantic yells, which had been a signal to the chiefs and people, who commenced "the most dismal and horrid lamentations." Fynn reported:

> Shaka ordered several men to be executed on the spot, and the cries became, if possible, more violent than ever. No further orders were needed. But, as if bent on convincing their chief of their extreme grief, the multitude commenced a general massacre. Many of them received the blow of death, while inflicting it on others, each taking the opportunity of revenging their injuries, real or imaginary. Those who could not force more tears from their eyes—those who were found panting for water—were beaten to death by others who were mad with excitement. Toward the afternoon I calculated that not fewer than 7,000 people had fallen in this frightful indiscriminate massacre. The adjacent stream, to which many had fled exhausted, to wet their parched tongues, became impassable from the number of dead corpses which lay on each side of it; while the kraal in which the scene took place was flowing with blood. . . . Late in the evening, on being informed of the dreadful loss of souls that had taken place, Shaka put a stop to the outrage, it only requiring a single word from him to do this.[91]

These massacres and their place in the despotic system may
be misunderstood unless one examines the observations of men
who knew Shaka and who experienced his conduct. Even sophisticated social scientists have overlooked the method in
Shaka's violence. For example, commenting on the great
slaughter at the death of Shaka's mother, Barrington Moore
has concluded that "this outburst of cruelty, even if on a mass
scale and triggered by the actions of a despot, does not appear
to have been part of any over-all political objective. Cruelty
here seems to have come mainly from outbursts of rage instead
of being primarily a deliberately chosen instrument of
policy." [92] This conclusion is contradicted by the judgments of
Isaacs and Fynn.

Nandi died on 11 August 1827, and according to the diary
of Isaacs, the crisis of mourning ended on 7 October, having
lasted fifty-eight days. Isaacs wrote in his journal that immediately after the death,

> horrible and fiendish slaughter was continued for a fortnight,
> to strike the people with terror, and make them approach the
> insatiable monster with awe. He had an impression also, that
> by a decree so ferocious and bloody the people would live in
> fear of his dying, when similar massacres would ensue; and
> that to avoid them they would not encourage the [*umthakathi,*
> or wizard] but would do all in their power to preserve the life
> of their monarch.

As the days went by and the loud public mourning continued,
Isaacs reflected that "The king is a dissembler and a most professed hypocrite." [93]

During the year, lamentations on a smaller scale were carried on from time to time, and Fynn observed:

> Whenever Shaka shed a tear, which he often did, the howlings
> were renewed. This, I think, he often did from political motives.
> After mature reflection I think I may safely assert that the

whole thing was nothing more than a political scheme. . . . The whole scene was a political scheme in furtherance of Shaka's vain imaginations and to keep the minds of his people filled with wonder. During the twelve months following the death of the female elephant [Zulu epithet of majesty given to the Queen Mother] the whole tribe were three times called together to repeat their lamentations. On the last occasion, the cattle of the whole tribe were collected, the bellowings of which was to be figurative of their lamentations.[94]

After a year had passed, a final ceremony was completed, and Fynn reflected:

And thus this memorable lamentation ended—in which, however, I cannot help suspecting that reasons of state policy had as much to do as any feeling of regret for his dead mother; and that he wished his people to infer, if such a sacrifice was necessary upon the occasion of her departure, how frightfully terrific would be that required at his own. Such considerations as these might possibly tend to prolong the life even of such a tyrant. And yet he fell at last at the hand of an assassin.[95]

The death of Nandi was also used as a pretext for the invasion of Pondoland in the south, Shaka saying that since tears could not be forced from foreigners, their cattle should be taken as substitutes. He intended to exterminate the tribes living between his domain and the Cape Colony, making an open road for intercourse with the European settlements. A diplomatic mission, with Lieutenant King in charge of two Zulu chiefs and their entourage, turned out badly, but Shaka had hoped it would establish diplomatic relations with the British and prepare them for his conquest of the tribes that lived on their nothern frontier. The warriors, anticipating plunder, were eager for conquest of the amaMpondo, and spies were sent out to inspect the enemy positions. Shaka felt that the campaign was needed to keep the military machine occupied, for when the impi were not fighting, he declared, they were "eating him up." Moreover, he seemed consumed by a restlessness that was reduced, at least temporarily, by massive destruction. At the end of the mourning and before the Mpondo campaign, Isaacs wrote:

> The restless monarch then took a walk round his premises, as if in deep contemplation, and on his return sent for me; when in conversation, he said "I am like a wolf on a flat, that is at a loss for a place to hide his head in;" the Zoolas had killed all his principal people and his mother, and he said he would now go to the other side of the water and see King George.[96]

The campaign against the amaMpondo was justified as the mourning hunt for his mother—the ritual of washing the spears in blood. Shaka stayed at Fynn's kraal on the Umzimkhulu River, which was as far south as he had ever ventured. The campaign ended when Shaka gave orders to his generals to withdraw and avoid engaging British troops marching north to meet the Zulu invasion.

Without even a day's respite, Shaka sent his armies from Pondoland in the extreme south to the extreme north of his domain and on to Delagoa Bay to attack Soshangane, who was growing strong and promising to become a rival power. This campaign was too much for the exhausted impi. The warriors succumbed to a dread disease they called "blood sickness," which may have been a species of cholera, or possibly dysentery, attacking them in a famished and weak condition.[97]

The reaction to terrorism was mounting. Bryant noted that Shaka's rule had "become so recklessly brutal, that his Zulu subjects, most docile and long-suffering of peoples, for the first time commenced to kick." Shaka had overreached himself. "The great revulsion had come about since Nandi's death, fanned to a devouring conflagration by the wholesale endless butcheries succeeding it."[98] The baggage boys on the march were called home to form a new regiment, and all the warriors in the northern campaign, including the officers, were forced to carry their own gear. This privation seemed to be the last straw.

Pretending illness, the fratricides Dingane and Mhlangana left their regiments to return to Dukuza, and linked their fates with Mbopha, having been urged to the desperate conspiracy, the chroniclers tell, by the fierce tongue of Shaka's aunt. In his last days, Shaka was depressed and anxious, disturbed by dreams of his own death. Near Dukuza he had built a small kraal, which he named *Nyakomubi*—Ugly Year. There the three conspirators took him by surprise and stabbed him to death.[99]

Near sundown on 22 September 1828—accepting the date given by Isaacs—while the armies were occupied in the north, Shaka was sitting in this small kraal with a few attendants, listening to the report of a detachment of messengers returned from an errand in the south. Suddenly, Mbopha—the "Mayor of the Palace"—ran at them, holding an assegai and waving his stick, shouting for them to be gone with their false tales and to desist from annoying their sovereign. The men scattered in surprise, and at that moment, Dingane and Mhlangana rushed forward from behind the fence and pierced Shaka with their assegais. According to the legend, he turned to his brothers before he fell and gasped, "Children of my father—what is wrong?" Mbopha ran to him and gave the final thrust, striking him through the back.

It appeared to Isaacs that the murder had been long premeditated by the two brothers, "and that the late savage massacres had hastened a resolution, which might, otherwise, have been stayed for a time." The assassins, Isaacs learned, addressed the people of the royal kraal as follows:

> "Don't you know it is the sons of [Senzangakhona] who have killed Chaka for his base and barbarous conduct, and to preserve the nation of the Zoolas, the sons of our fathers, that you may live in peace and enjoy your homes and your families; to put an end to the long and endless wars, and mourning for that old woman [Nandi] for whom so many have been put to a cruel death?" Thus saying, they went to the palace, where they dared not enter an hour before. . . .[100]

To the white people, Dingane announced that

> his brother Chaka had been killed for his inhuman conduct,
> having become no longer supportable to his subjects. The nation
> had too long groaned under his tyranny, and had submitted to
> his atrocities until they could not find safety from his savage
> and insatiable decrees; they had, therefore, in order to put an
> end to so much spilling of innocent blood, accomplished the
> destruction of the man who had occasioned it, and indulged in
> its barbarities.

It was hoped that the death of Shaka would "give to the natives
a period of repose from the vexations and casualties of war, and
from the terror which the savage decrees of the late king constantly created." [101]

Dingane murdered his brother and fellow conspirator,
Mhlangana, and succeeded Shaka as King of the Zulu. Fynn
registered his doubts about the future of the new regime and
suspected that the system of terror was an important element in
the power structure and too durable to be cast out by Shaka's
assassination. He observed:

> Dingana promised to set the minds of his people at ease by not
> imitating the conduct of Chaka, in such matters as he con-
> sidered to be hurtful of them. He composed, or caused to be
> composed, national songs, containing the denunciations against
> the former state of things; he adopted mild measures, and
> thought that he was establishing himself freely, when obstacles
> occurred which showed him the true state of things, and the
> motives that had driven his predecessor to such extreme lengths
> of severity and cruelty. I shall not be in the least surprised
> to see repeated by Dingana the very acts for which he punished
> Chaka with death.[102]

The hopes of liberation from the process of terror soon faded:

> Not three months after the return of the army from Soshan-
> gane's, the people became convinced that Dingane's promises

were nothing but words. Numbers were put to death for the most trivial offences, and many for having expressed disappointment at non-fulfilment of the promises he had made. Then did the destruction of human beings begin to go on as a matter of daily routine, as it had done in Shaka's day, and many of the former objectionable customs were retained, contrary to the expectation of the people in general.[103]

It appears that the Zulu people have tried to explain the process of terror by the idea that tensions in the political system could not be contained by other means and that control without violence was not possible. The traditional explanation of the terror contained in the chronicles is reported by Ritter in the form of a conversation, undoubtedly imaginary, between Shaka and Pampata, the despot's favorite concubine, transmitted by Njengabantu EmaBomvini, the son of one of Shaka's comrades in arms. In this traditional account, Pampata told the despot: "There was a time when the whole nation loved you, but now you only inspire terror."
Shaka is said to have replied:

Terror is the only thing they understand, and you can only rule the Zulus by killing them. Who are the Zulus? They are parts of two hundred or more unruly clans which I had to break up and reshape, and only the fear of death will hold them together. The time will come when they will be as one nation, and the clans will only be remembered as their izibongo (surnames). In the meantime my very name must inspire them with terror.[104]

Pampata answered that he would always need a bodyguard, for the people would not endure so much violence, and Shaka is said to have declared:

I need no bodyguard at all, for even the bravest men who approach me get weak at the knees and their hearts turn to water, whilst their heads become giddy and incapable of thinking as the sweat of fear paralyzes them. They know no other will except that of their King, who is something above, and below, this earth.

After indicating this exceptionally precise knowledge of how the terror process works, Shaka continued:

> There is a reason for everything that I do. When I look up and see the vultures circling and say that the birds of the King are hungry, it gives me an opportunity of "smelling out" those whom I consider to be a danger to the nation, and at the same time providing a drastic example to the others.[105]

When Fynn criticized Shaka for his excessive violence, the chronicler says, the despot claimed that the entire nation was held together by his command, and that he would not allow the slightest disregard of the ruler's wish. Comparing the state to a shirt, he argued that if the first rent in the fabric were left unattended, the entire garment would soon be in shreds. According to the chronicle, he declared to Fynn:

> If I should put you in my place for the space of a moon, Zululand would fall to pieces; for with your stupid White man's reasoning you would first condone the little offences. . . . [Therefore,] do not try to teach me how to rule the Zulus; for your ideas on that subject are as foolish as a man who urinates against the wind. . . .[106]

Thus, the Zulus seemed to believe that the process of terror overcame the tensions in the system and held the state together. Yet, perpetual violence had exhausted the people's obstinate affection for Shaka and their traditional loyalty. The assassination promised relief from chronic fear. They welcomed the new ruler, but the stresses in the power system remained. The scourge was dead; nevertheless the old forces kept alive the memory of the terroristic despot. It was not long until the new ruler, who began his reign as a king rather than as a despot, made the decision to reshape himself to that image.

CHAPTER VIII

ZULU TERROR

AFTER

SHAKA

As fear is the principle of despotic government,
its end is tranquillity; but this tranquillity cannot be
called a peace: no, it is only the silence of
those towns which the enemy is ready to invade.

—Montesquieu, *The Spirit of the Laws.*

SOON AFTER the assassination, a messenger appeared in Natal
with word that the settlers might live easy, for Shaka, who had
menaced them all, was dead.[1] Fynn's papers, written at a much
later date, claimed that he had felt skeptical about Dingane's
intentions, but Isaacs, recording his feelings at the time, expressed the highest enthusiasm for the successor. In the first
years of the new regime, Isaacs never lost an opportunity to
compare Dingane favorably with his predecessor, and he declared that having lost Shaka, the Zulu "have now a ruler who
has begun to govern with judgment, and to exercise his power
with discretion."[2] He was excited by the prospect that the
Zulu people would be allowed to trade freely with the Europeans and that the king would keep his country tranquil and
his people happy. He expected that Dingane would be loved
where Shaka had been feared, that benevolence would replace
cruelty, and that peaceful commerce would take the place of
predatory warfare. Moreover, he believed, "Dingan certainly is

destined to please his people, for he has the ways of a savage courtier, and seeks every moment to show that he wishes rather to reign in the good opinion of his subjects than to rule over them with the arm of terror." [3]

The enthusiasm of the Zulu exceeded that of the Europeans, for they embraced Dingane as a liberator. Fragments of the shattered army, straggling in from the northern campaign, expected to be greeted by Shaka's rage, but were instead welcomed by the regicide who reminded them that his act of murder spared them from destruction. Mhlangana, the brother who had shared the killing, was already eliminated, having been killed at Dingane's order soon after Shaka's death, and no one challenged Dingane's claim to the throne. His legitimacy was supported by the underground opposition to Shaka, which had been activated during the peak of the terror but had remained invisible until now. In a recent book on the reign of Dingane, Peter Becker identifies this opposition as a party of influential people who were "strict adherents to tradition" and therefore offended by Shaka's innovations and the misery caused by them.[4] Dingane denounced Shaka's conduct and promised to restore happiness to the land: to end the domestic slaughter and perpetual warfare, to disband the seraglios and release the royal women, to permit marriage, to restore judicial procedure to the chiefs, and to establish fair trials according to tribal law. Swords were to turn into plowshares—or, as Fynn reported the Zulu equivalent: shields and spears would be laid aside and the dancing stick taken up in their stead.

Shortly after his installation, Dingane left Dukuza, Shaka's last capital, with a retinue to set up in Nobamba, the ancestral royal kraal. In that location, Senzangakhona's kraal and burial place, it is plausible to think, he sojourned to absorb further legitimacy from the sacred ground and the spirits that dwelled there. Cowie and Green, two Europeans from the Cape, visited him at Nobamba and recorded impressions that are preserved in Mackeurtan's history of Natal:

They were much impressed by his popularity and wrote of him in flattering terms. He was "anxious to anticipate their wants, hospitable without ostentation," and displayed "a magnanimity and capacity befitting the chief of a great people." He told them that "his conduct should be of an opposite character to that of his predecessor, and that his only ambition was to make his subjects free and happy." . . . The monarch, his people, and his realm thus presented an idyllic picture that charmed the travellers.[5]

Nevertheless, looking back at the early period of the reign, Fynn noticed changes in the emotional tie between ruler and subjects. He wrote: "It is true that the people at large under Dingane were released from the state of perpetual terror they had experienced during the reign of his predecessor. At the same time there appears to be a want of affection and respect which Shaka always engendered or commanded." [6]

Two historical alternatives lay open to the Zulu kingdom. One was to break up into several tribal fragments. The other was to proceed toward a responsible monarchy limited by chiefs and people. Eventually, the power of the king was restricted and curtailed, and, as Max Gluckman observes, the monarchy as it developed after Shaka and Dingane, was quite different from "the early chequered history of the kingship." After the time of these despots, Gluckman writes, "in general, rulers accepted the same values as their subjects and acted on the advice of their councils of chiefs and wise men, without whose assistance rule would have been impossible." [7] Instead of allowing the kingdom to break up and instead of inaugurating a limited monarchy, Dingane, despite early expectations to the contrary, chose a third alternative—to renew the system of terror and to restore the despotic regime. It excluded the other alternatives, preventing the disintegration of the kingdom at the same time it inhibited institutions that would have established limited monarchy. "To choose" means here to select deliberately a course of action, even if the full consequences are not foreseen. To understand a choice, one must trace in detail the circumstances, perceptions, feelings, and ideas that gave it pattern. Moreover, exploring the conditions of terrorism under Dingane should reveal factors sufficient to deny the hypothesis that terror is a function of innovation, or, more specifically, that terroristic regimes are restricted to certain kinds of innovating rulers and charismatic founders.

THE QWABE REBELLION

Soon after the visit of Cowie and Green in March 1829 (see page 179), Dingane began to experience resistance, and the kingdom was threatened with fission. The occasion was a revolt by the Qwabe people which was actually stimulated by Dingane's own conduct. It turned into a general crisis because it exposed several unresolved issues: the ambiguity of Dingane's promise to release the privilege of marriage—especially the marriage of chiefs—from royal controls, the thrust toward independence of conquered segments that retained old identities, the problematic nature of the relation between the king and the chiefs of those fragments, and the need to define more precisely Dingane's still inchoate style of rule.

The Qwabe had been one of the largest independent chiefdoms in old Zululand. Exterminating the Ndwandwe, Shaka had conquered and incorporated the Qwabe. After killing Pakatwayo, he allowed them to live under the leadership of the chief's brother, Nqetho, who was permitted a considerable amount of local authority. Although Zulu patriotism quickly replaced old loyalties for small groups of conquered people distributed throughout the kingdom, tribal identities endured in those fragments large enough to preserve their social systems intact. Although Nqetho had pledged fealty and had paid tribute to Shaka, it was suspected that he might repudiate the paramountcy of Dingane and strike out for independence. Everyone knew that the relation between new ruler and subordinate chief was delicate. Dingane chose to deal with the potential resistance of the Qwabe by demanding the absolute subordination of the chief.

The incident provoking the rebellion took place at the time Dingane was implementing his promise to disband the seraglios and to restore the right of marriage. Actually, under Dingane marriage never did become a right, but remained a privilege granted by royal order, although the king did extend the privilege to include greater numbers of people. In 1832, Andrew Smith reported that only in the past few months had Dingane given extensive permission to marry, and that those previously without wives were getting eight or ten. He also noticed, however, that the privilege might be rescinded, observing: "Dingan frequently orders the entire men of a regiment to turn away their wives and let their hair grow. The master of a kraal where we halted one night (Friday) once received such an order." [8] In 1835, Gardiner reported that Dingane, like his predecessor, had never married, and although he placed no limit on concubines, continued to limit marriage among his people. The head ring—symbol of adult status—could be assumed only by order of the king.[9] At no time did Dingane give up the despotic control of marriage, although he was more generous than Shaka in extending the privilege.

The immense number of girls collected by Shaka were released from seraglios and given as wives to chiefs and elders, Dingane retaining only about three hundred. The widow of Pakatwayo, late Chief of the Qwabe, was one of the women released, and, consistent with traditional practice, declared herself the wife of Nqetho, brother of her deceased husband. Dingane seized the occasion to condemn Nqetho for a breach of protocol that amounted to lese majesty, saying that the marriage had not been ordered by the king and was unreported to him, going so far as to take into custody a messenger from Nqetho and handing him over to the chiefs for trial, alleging that he had made a false report about Nqetho's matrimonial condition. The issue amounted to a nice point of law, and the chiefs actually decided for Nqetho, Fynn recorded, "giving it as their opinion that he was not obliged to report his having taken to wife a woman who was already married to him by an ancient custom." [10] Nevertheless, since the king was offended, Nqetho concluded that his life was in danger, and he organized rebellion and flight.

The episode proved to be a critical moment in Dingane's regime. He could have chosen to deal with Nqetho tactfully; instead, he had demanded subordination. The Qwabe revolt spread quickly and raised the prospect of independence for a number of tribal fragments. In three days Nqetho gathered a large force without interference from the Zulu, raided cattle which were to remain symbolically important later in Dingane's reign, and presented the king with a new political crisis impossible to ignore. The energy and success of the uprising was much greater than anyone had expected. It was being said that the king was slow to put down the revolt because he feared a test of strength.

When the Zulu impi eventually did encounter the Qwabe, the two sets of former comrades-in-arms stared at one another, and each retired from the field. The reluctance to fight might have been encouraged by Dingane's announcements in past months that he would terminate Shaka's practice of executing cowards and liquidating defeated regiments. The episode made visible a contradiction between all the promised reforms and the integrity of the kingdom. Unless he committed himself to an entirely new style of rule, Dingane was faced with the dilemma of either resorting to Shaka's methods or losing control of the state. He chose the despotic alternative, and the middle period of the reign was devoted to reconstructing the terroristic system us well as efforts to recover Shaka's glory. At the end of the reign, he was defeated by new crises—a war with migrating Europeans armed with guns and a schism in the state.

LIQUIDATION

After the Qwabe revolt, Dingane became less hesitant about political assassinations. Earlier, as soon as Shaka had been dispatched, Ngomane, the prime minister, had fled beyond reach, but Nxazonke, an old sycophant, and Nomxamama, the court praise crier, were killed, to be followed by Ngwadi, Shaka's maternal half brother. Then Mhlangana, brother and fellow conspirator, who disputed the succession with Dingane, was eliminated. Still, these murders, committed in the heat of the regicidal act, were not taken to represent a policy of regular liquidation, and Dingane promised to spare the lives of those who had served Shaka loyally. The promise was made difficult by the presence of a Shaka faction, a source of persistent opposition to Dingane's succession.

During the Qwabe episode, a Zulu force driving home some recaptured cattle halted at the kraal of Magaye, Chief of the Cele, who had been a favorite of Shaka and who, it was reported to Dingane, opposed the succession. The induna tricked Magaye into expressing his hatred of Dingane and killed him. News of the murder served to redefine the king as a dangerous overlord, and a number of chiefs considered flight beyond his grasp. Another group took the bull by the horns and confronted Dingane at Nobamba to ask why peace-loving Magaye had been killed. The king professed ignorance of the murder and offered a reward to anyone who would point out the assassin. Mdlaka, Shaka's commander-in-chief, condemned him as a liar, continued to vilify him, and pointed out that the murder of Magaye proved that none of the chiefs or their dependants were immune from the threat of destruction.[11] Soon after the *iHlambo* ceremony—the "washing of the spears" which purified the king and confirmed his legitimacy—Mdlaka was killed. It is said that Mpande, the king's brother, would have been killed as well, save for the restraints of induna who said Mpande was a harmless fool and that too much royal blood had been spilled already. Mbopha, the third regicide, was appointed to a high post, but killed a few years later. The favorites of Shaka held important positions until Dingane's power was secure, and then they were gradually removed. An exception was Ndlela, "the Road," a Ntuli whose father had taken refuge with the Zulu in Senzangakhona's day. Ndlela had risen to military eminence under Shaka and was later appointed prime minister and commander-in-chief, remaining the most important officer in the kingdom until he was killed at the end of Dingane's reign. As the old favorites were eliminated, a body of chiefs loyal to Dingane himself replaced them. They were given full judicial responsibility and were at first expected to carry out the king's promise that all the disputes of the people were to be settled by an impartial tribunal according to law, without interference from the throne. The tribunal, Fynn observed, amounted to little more than a show of justice, for cases were reported to the king before any proceedings. The trivial cases were disposed of by himself; others were referred to the bench of chiefs for adjudication, but only after the judges were informed of the king's opinion. "So it happened," Fynn concluded, "that all these decisions were invariably biased to the extent of being made to conform to the king's will, pleasure or personal caprice." [12]

In connection with his promised reforms, Dingane had restricted the authority to order executions. During Shaka's reign, every principle induna had the power of life and death, but the new king, Gardiner pointed out, curtailed this power, limiting it to three induna. Nevertheless, executions for trivial offences once again were common, and many were killed for expressing disappointment in Dingane's failure to keep his promises. Again the royal kraal was occupied, to use Fynn's phrase, with the "daily routine of human destruction."

THE SPREAD OF FEAR

In the summer of 1829, Dingane left Nobamba with a large retinue to establish a new royal kraal. He chose the ancestral Valley of the Zulu, made sacred by the bones of the legendary founder of the clan as well as by the spirits of other royal ancestors, near the site of Shaka's first royal kraal. There he built a great kraal named emGungundlovu, "the Place Surrounded by Elephants," in the grand style of Zulu despotism, equipped with a retinue made familiar by Shaka's regime: royal women, servants, regiments, induna, body guards, executioners, an inner circle, retainers, and the royal herds. In this new setting, Dingane's style of rule changed dramatically from its earlier form. The system of terror, gradually renewed at Nobamba, was clearly institutionalized at emGungundlovu. The place of execution there was called "kwaMatiwane," named after a chief who had fled from Shaka and returned to Zululand shortly after the great kraal was occupied. Matiwane had escaped from Shaka's violence and returned to Dingane, expecting more lenient treatment. Killing him demonstrated that what had been expected of Shaka might also be expected of Dingane. The chief and his followers were executed in a manner suggesting that the slaughter ceremonially inaugurated the reign of terror in emGungundlovu. The hill of execution, perpetually attended by circling vultures, steadily accumulated deposits of victims until it received the bodies of Piet Retief and his party of Boers, the execution that brought an end to the regime. Becker, in his recent book, comments:

> The abhorrence and fear inspired by emGungundlovu—the Place Surrounded by Elephants—soon become a legend that was to spread all over Southern Africa; in particular, kwaMatiwane, Dingane's place of execution, was to arouse a feeling of horror in the imaginations of people living far beyond the shores of Africa. For the slopes of this stony ridge were destined to be strewn with the bones of many tribesmen and it

was here, at kwaMatiwane, that the lives of many white men were to end by order of Dingane, King of the Zulu.[13]

At no time were violence and fear considered departures from legitimate authority, for they might be traced back to the ancestral system of controls, which had preceded Shaka's regime. The pattern of terroristic despotism never lost its legitimacy, therefore, although the chief's right to kill and the subject's duty of fearful reverence were no longer fixed in the network of limitations and restraints that had been part of the patriarchal organization. No longer subordinate parts of a system of controls, violence and fear took on exaggerated proportions, becoming the central features of terroristic despotism. The elements had always been present; what changed was the frequency and extent of their use and the way in which they were organized.

In the ancestral system, Bryant wrote:

> The one great law that governed there was the law of complete submission to parental authority; and that authority was drastically enforced. Unquestioning, unanswering obedience to the supreme power was demanded without distinction, of all alike, of mothers, of sons (some of them already middle-aged men with families of their own), of every child. Every failure to obey was immediately followed by a penalty inflicted without mercy; while persistent insubordination might lead to the disgrace of expulsion, and open revolt might even terminate in death. And what each inmate of the kraal saw practised by the father, he in turn practised in his own regard, demanding of all his juniors the same measure of obedience as was demanded of him by those above. Alongside, or out of, this practice of complete submission was gradually evolved something more than mere respect, almost a holy awe—*ukw-esaba* or to fear, as the Zulus call it—for those above one. And this again was mutual and universal, the little boys revering the bigger boys; the bigger boys, the men; and all, their parents.[14]

This process of socialization produced an obedience that was adapted originally to a political system made up of kraals and clans ruled by fathers and chieftains. The kraal was the basic unit of the polity and a microcosm of the whole clan system, the entire structure of kraal, village, clan, and tribe, being built up with perfect symmetry.[15] Within the kraal, everyone was "ruled by a common head, at once father and kinglet, who governed all alike with unrestricted power of life or death, a *benevolent despotism* of protection, discipline and care."[16] Still, this power resembled the Roman *patria potestas*—absolute in principle but restrained in practice. While the supreme control of fathers and chieftains remained unchallenged, it was the prerogative of elder sons and of local headmen to be consulted in matters of general management. Executive power was carried out in a network of conciliar judgments.

The sentiment of obedience to authority, as Bryant showed, was a kind of fearful awe. In Zulu thought and language, the words for reverence and for fear are identical. One term— "*ukwesaba*" (to fear or to respect), "*ukwesabeka*" (to be feared or to be respected)—signifies both fright and obedience, suggesting that fear is the central idea in the concept of authority.[17] The "fear" in this word is a feeling about specific persons and is not a generalized or diffused emotion. Like other languages, Zulu distinguishes between the emotion that responds to a specific external object and the feeling associated with internal anxiety or dread. Therefore, the word "*uvalo*," meaning anxiety, nervous apprehension, or internal uneasiness, is entirely different from the term that means fear or respect.

In his discussion of Zulu custom, Fynn said that awe of and obedience to the chief were the mainstay of social control. In the ancestral system before Shaka, however, the fear-respect sentiment was located in a structure of segmental, intermediate authorities, arranged symmetrically from kraal to clan, and, after Dingiswayo, from kraal to state. In the despotic system beginning with Shaka, as the intermediate authorities—fathers, elders, headmen, chieftains, chiefs—lost their autonomy, they were still respected, but the ruler became a magnified center of fear and awe. As the frequency of violence increased beyond measure, the people's fear not only augmented in degree but also changed qualitatively. The sentiment of fear-respect associated with legitimate authority, was no longer imbedded in a stable structure of segmental, intermediate authority, so that it combined with the fear produced by violence and flooded the society with apprehension. Because the terror was mixed with the sentiment of fear-respect, it did not produce a feeling of outrage or lose the sense of legitimacy. Instead, the emotional climate was a compound of servile, inhibiting fear, preventing the desire to resist or even the thought of doing anything new. Gardiner recognized this pervasive "fear of doing amiss" and pointed out that the Zulu "are so afraid of doing wrong, or of displeasing Dingaan, that they dare not venture on any new course without his express permission. This servile fear pervades all classes. . . ." [18]

THE CULTURE OF DESPOTISM

The despotic style witnessed at emGungundlovu by visitors such as Andrew Smith in 1832 and Captain Gardiner in 1835 makes a dramatic contrast with the picture of the liberal king rhapsodized by Isaacs and observed by Cowie and Green in the early years. Smith declared that he had never seen such grandeur "in a Kafir tribe" or anywhere else. Along with the grandeur, the royal kraal conveyed an impression of awful majesty, supported by rituals of subservience performed by the people and by atrocities committed by the despot. As in the days of Shaka, the people were "the king's dogs." They used his name as a sacred oath and they groveled in his presence. When the despot sneezed, everyone exclaimed, "May he grow greater!" When anyone else coughed, spat, belched, sneezed, or blew his nose while the ruler was eating, he was beaten or killed. Anyone involuntarily committing the slightest offence or giving displeasure to the despot—especially if the culprit was the master of a kraal—was obliged to make a peace offering before he could hope to be restored to favor. No one dared utter an opinion if it differed from the one held by the despot. If a chief or the master of a kraal was killed, all his dependents were also killed and their cattle taken to the ruler, who distributed a portion to the warriors executing the order.

Not only honor and position but every kind of socially approved conduct depended on the despot's will. The whole style of life made it possible for people sometimes to consent—and always to appear to consent—to their own injury. Gardiner reported an incident that took place as the despot was playing with a burning glass:

> beckoning one of his servants near, he desired him to extend his arm, when he firmly seized his hand, and deliberately held it until a hole was actually burnt in the skin a few inches above the wrist. Crouched before him in the humblest posture, the unfortunate man seemed writhing in pain, but dared not utter even a groan, and, as soon as this wanton infliction was over, was directed to go round to the company and display the effect. . . . I was necessitated to witness a repetition of the same torture on another servant, whom he held in the same manner, and who appeared to suffer more intensely, yet without any further indications of his feelings than a nervous writhing of the whole body. No sooner was he liberated, than he confessed that the pain extended through every part from his head to his feet, and that he was convinced he must have fallen had it been prolonged. He too was ordered to exhibit his arm to all present, and really, from the expression of many of the countenances as he went round, a stranger might have imagined that some honorary badge had been conferred.[19]

The heralds of the ruler filled the air with praise chants—an unbroken string of deeds and attributes of the overlord. The chants emphasized his terrible aspect, crying: "Thou that art black, thou that art frightful, thou that art like a lion," or "Arise, vulture! Thou art the bird that eateth other birds." When the despot ordered his people to sing, he had them begin with the words, "Friends, are ye not afraid of the king?" His commands were obeyed with the utmost alacrity, a favorite device being to spit on a messenger as he sent him on an errand, with the understanding that the man would be executed unless he accomplished his task and returned before the royal spittle was dry. The principle behind this apparently capricious behavior was guessed by Andrew Smith:

we could clearly discover that he thought that his mere wish, if properly expressed and urged, would be sufficient to ensure its being complied with, and that non-compliance could only arise from the apathy of the messengers, who therefore were always blamed guilty or otherwise. So well do such messengers understand the dangers that await them that when they find the white man heedless of their importunities they fly to the best method of ensuring his compliance by telling him that their lives will in all probability pay the penalty of his inattention to the king's wishes.[20]

When dealing with non-Europeans, messengers would use violence if they were confronted by delay or recalcitrance.

It would not be an exaggeration to say that legitimacy was identified with the pleasure of the despot. The administration of public affairs proceeded by carrying out his expressed will and by anticipating his wishes. His caprice prevented the evolution of a system in which officials could develop autonomous procedures. He was never expected to act rationally or consistently. Gardiner recorded one occasion when the ruler appeared suddenly, adorned in a grotesque manner:

he had caused his whole body, not excepting his face, to be thickly daubed over with red and white clay in spots, and had but his figure corresponded with the character, he might have passed . . . for the genuine harlequin of the night. Thus adorned, a dance and a song were the least I expected, but he contented himself with receiving the acclamations of "Byate," "Thou who art forever," "The great black one," &c. &c.; and again retired as unaccountably from the sight of his wondering subjects, who none of them could devise the import of this singular exhibition. All I could collect from them was, that it was a new thing, that he had done it because he was the King and could do what he pleased.[21]

Paradoxically, social integration and political co-ordination depended on the despot's conduct—and, *in principle,* his actions were not subject to ordinary rules or expectations. Caprice, taken seriously, was at the heart of the state.

That is not to say that the system was chaotic. Traditional norms still regulated conduct, social institutions shaped people's lives, and the military organization maintained its own kind of formal rationality. Yet, none of the rules limited Dingane in any substantial way. His apparent caprice, it will be argued in Chapter X, was something less than chaotic impulse and something more than the absolutism implied in the maxim, *princeps legibus solutus.*

Nor should it be assumed that the despot's power depended exclusively on violence. At the same time that the royal kraal was a place of danger, it attracted those in search of honor and wealth. Favorites of the ruler received the cattle redistributed after executions, and, in the reign after Dingane's, Delegorgue observed that the king (Mpande) would order without hesitation the death of men lukewarm in his regard, distributing their property to his partisans. Military expeditions promised further acquisitions as well as glory. The warriors as well as the administrative staff and the royal household were largely released from the necessities of ordinary work and maintained at state expense. As an American missionary observed, the royal kraal seemed to be "little else than a camp of soldiers. The chief is always talking of some warlike expedition, and inspiring them with a desire for plunder and blood. They live, as it were, at the king's table, and not on the fruits of their own labour."[22] Andrew Smith had also observed that at the royal kraal there was usually a great collection of corn supplied by the people for the use of the regiments there. The large war shields were the property of the ruler and stored until the men were called to arms. When food supplies ran low, rich men might be assessed. In the days of Mpande, Delegorgue described:

Whenever it happens that the royal herds are diminished by a too rapid consumption of beef, in excess of the natural increase, messengers are sent to the wealthy captains to demand in the king's name that they will part with a specified number of cows. Hesitation is not permitted. Refusal would result in the death of the recalcitrant subject. The rich man must affect a gracious and well-pleased air, and leave the royal purveyor to choose from his best possessions. In pressing emergencies, the king causes anything that he thinks suitable to be seized at once, but ordinarily it is on the rich only that the tax is imposed. As a set-off for this, at the conclusion of a successful campaign, when the king has chosen his share of the booty, the surplus is divided in large lots among the grandees, and in more diminutive portions among the people.[23]

Chiefs and rich men held power and wealth in precarious possession, which depended on the ruler's feeling about them. His spy system would detect inchoate resistance and sometimes convey unfounded suspicions. Moreover, the despot's anxiety and extreme sensitivity to potential opposition frequently produced acts of violence. Delegorgue explained:

During the leisure of peace, when the mind of the chief, not employed in external matters, retires within, the fear of death is not slow to seize the most powerful and wealthy men of the nation. Indeed, the king, whose only diversion is to review and count his herds, to inspect his warriors, or to listen to his women sing—the king, whose acquaintance with elephant hunting is merely the pleasure of looking on from some prominent height—the king ere long feels weary. Surrounded by flatterers, unable to reckon a single friend, he conjures up a thousand anxieties: such or such a captain, who lives grandly, overshadows his power. He fancies that this man intends to make an attempt on his life; his sleep is troubled by the thought, a dreadful nightmare lies heavy on his breast. When he awakes, he names him, adding the terrible sentence: *umtakati bulala* [kill the evildoer]. A body of armed men sets out at once. It surrounds the victim's kraal and puts everyone to death. Then it wipes out the group of huts by fire; seen from a distance, their location seems no more than the shape of a large, black circle. The report of the expedition reaches the king, who only then feels he is breathing more freely. In the following days, the attached herds are brought before him, no one disputing their ownership with him, because to him alone belongs the heritage of wealth from those whose death he has caused. Thus, if a man is rich, that is often sufficient for the king to set himself up as his heir by this abominable means.[24]

He controlled concentrations of wealth and power, his office serving as a redistribution agency for the kingdom. The terror of the despot was balanced by his dispensing advantages, giving rewards, and providing a liberal supply of food. Andrew Smith, whose party benefited from this bounty, could not at first understand the surplus he continued to receive from the despot, but, when enlightened, commented on Dingane's policy:

He did not expect that I or my people would be able to eat all he might send; his object was to enable me to be generous to his people in order that they also might love me. Here was a man thoroughly acquainted with human nature; he knew well from experience that nothing secured the attachment of such persons as those he had to rule so effectively as an ample allowance of food; and it was from his liberality in that respect that he rendered his own residence which on other accounts was the spot specially desirable to his warriors.[25]

Thus, life in the royal kraal held attractions as well as dangers. Still, the beneficent features of Zulu despotism never concealed the primacy of violence, and the meaning of government to Dingane may be summed up in a pithy reference to a chief who had fled Zululand and was living under the protection of Europeans in Natal. The despot said, "But he is still under my government, and I have the privilege of killing him if he offends me. . . ." [26]

The royal kraal defined the state and gave meaning to its predominant activities, maintaining collective impressions of grandeur and royal omnipotence as well as the illusion of irresistibility. The rituals, tales, songs, gestures, expectations, hopes, fears, and all the elements that made up the culture of the royal kraal provided a rationale and justification for subordination and co-operation.

THE DESPOT AND HIS STAFF

The staff of the royal kraal included "the slayers," who were the royal executioners, a praetorian regiment, and other agents of violence as well as spies—domestic and military. Controlled by the despot and his several induna, this staff eliminated potential opposition, whether real or imaginary. The military organization, as extensive as the kingdom itself, with *amakhanda* or military kraals placed in strategic positions to police territorial chiefdoms, worked in the service of the royal kraal and also continued to reduce the environment to Zulu claims. The military force worked not only to absorb whatever plunder was available, but also, as one might expect, to generate insatiable demands for a continual supply of people to fight, cattle to seize, and warriors to incorporate. The entire system was set in motion and co-ordinated by the will of the despot, which was expected to be absolute, capricious, and irresistible. In principle, the ordinary people were "the king's dogs," and every member of the kingdom, high or low, was an instrument of his will. Commoners, warriors, chiefs, and induna could claim no course of action except to execute commands with the utmost precision. Potential resisters were eliminated, chiefs and headmen suspected of disloyalty removed without delay, and only men who inspired the highest confidence were appointed as induna.

Yet, the evidence indicates that the actual relation between despot and higher staff was more problematic, ambiguous, and fraught with contradictions than either Zulu principles or the European theory of despotism would admit. Observers painted a picture of an omnipotent despot ruling a population totally inert and obedient—the picture consistent with both Zulu and European ideas of despotism—and still presented contradictory observations, sometimes in the same report. Pondering the contradictions might have revealed the true nature of despotism, but the traditional idea was preserved and the contradictions were not dismissed or explained away but simply ignored.

On the one hand, observers regarded Zulu society as a system in which the despot effectively exercised total control over the entire population, including his immediate staff. Like other absolute rulers, Dingane controlled his chiefs and nobles by requiring them to attend him at court. Gardiner wrote:

> evidently with a political view of state surveillance . . . the most influential . . . are formed into [a] bodyguard, and . . . all in rotation are obliged to appear and reside for some time in the capital, where they become not only hostages for the good conduct of those dependent upon them, but are thereby prevented from plotting any scheme for the subversion of the existing government. It may be unnecessary to add, that the King has spies in all directions—an office which is here held in no ill repute. . . .[27]

Yet, inconsistent with the picture of total control and inconsistent with the European concept of despotism, Gardiner, Isaacs, Fynn, and other observers reported actions of induna, chiefs, and warriors, which, taken in the aggregate, constituted a constant pressure on the ruler. This pressure, when examined in the context of historical events, paradoxically worked as an independent force—indeed, one is tempted to say, an irresistible force—first, to re-establish the despotic system, which presumably was not in the self-interest of the same chiefs and warriors, and finally, to drive despot and staff to a conflict with the Europeans, which was the system's catastrophe.

Isaacs insisted on fixing the blame for the return of despotism not on the king but on his staff. He referred to "the fiery spirit of some of the chiefs, who are more impetuous than rational," and who often "break out into turbulence," frequently provoking the despot to violent acts.[28] Similarly, the missionary Owen felt less afraid of the ruler than of "the zeal of his captains and people, who are not influenced by those restraints which in some measure tie up the hands of the monarch himself. . . ."[29] Fynn thought that the despot "felt he was unable to restrain his army once it had arrived at its destination." He believed that even if the despot had given express orders to the contrary, the impi would not be content with less than total destruction.[30] Working against the intentions of the ruler, Isaacs named not only the "fiery chiefs" but also the military organization:

> One of the great checks to the advancement of the Zoola monarch in cultivating the sweets of peace, and in encouraging commerce, are his warriors; a powerful body of savages trained up to war from their youth, and to indulge in all the rapacity to which their various predatory excursions naturally tend. These, under the command of chiefs, whose ferocity is almost unrestrainable, keep the monarch always in awe of their power, and goad him to the commission of deeds, which I feel persuaded he would not have executed, but to keep them tranquil.[31]

They had become so used to living off plunder, Isaacs explained, that ordinary toil was not acceptable to them, and they constantly urged the ruler to pursue warlike expeditions. He asserted, in flat contradiction to the picture he had drawn of Zulu society passively subordinated to an omnipotent despot, that under these pressures, "the Zoola monarch has merely the shadow of power." The ruler, he stated, could only refuse or assent, "but under circumstances so peculiarly awing, he usually assents; though, with Dingan, I believe this proceeds, not from choice, but from apprehension." [32]

Isaacs believed that Dingane had changed Shaka's rule of celibacy because marriage and family attachments would soften the belligerent dispositions of the warriors and their chiefs. Until they were calmed down, he felt

> the monarch will always be existing between two opposing elements; that is to say, between his warriors vehemently urging him to engage in hostilities to gratify their propensities; and his people (under the influence and direction of the Europeans, whom they respect), who call on him to cultivate the sweets of peace, to enable them to live in repose, and to pursue those habits for which they now begin to feel a desire, being indebted to the European settler for their present knowledge.[33]

The missionary Gardiner also felt that Dingane was balancing the influence of Europeans and the desire to cultivate relations with the white settlement on the one side and the hostility of the chiefs and induna on the other side. Dingane disclaimed responsibility for the insults Gardiner received from the induna, yet rarely intervened on his behalf against them. Indeed, the puzzle is to determine the exact nature of the relation between the despot and his induna. After Dingane, in Mpande's time, Delegorgue gave an impression that the relation was consistent with the conventional idea of despotism:

> The king, in the daily discharge of his functions, is constantly assisted by three councillors, to whose expressions of opinion as to what should be done he listens. Unfortunately, under the immediate will of the despot, these men never dare to offer any opposition. I have seen them quail under Panda's glance, and always speak eloquently as he would wish, applaud the conclusions arrived at by him, and flatter him in every way afterwards.[34]

Many observers of Dingane's reign agreed with this impression. Yet, the induna seemed to exercise power over the ruler. Gardiner reports the execution of a brother of the despot, a case in which royal blood was shed against Dingane's will. The missionary was especially grieved by the killing because this prince was one of the most intelligent-looking men he had ever seen, because he had behaved in an extremely friendly manner, and because he had inspired in the missionary the hope that he (the prince) might be the first convert to Christianity. However, the characteristics that drew Gardiner to him undoubtedly rendered worse the prince's precarious political position. Gardiner saw him and his servants led to the hill of execution. He reflected:

A mystery hangs over his death; but whether true or false, the alleged offence is an intrigue against the King, in which two other of his brothers were also said to have been implicated, and about a year ago suffered the same fate. Dingarn, according to report, had hitherto spared his life, contrary to the wishes of the two Indoonas, but so determined was Umthlella [Ndlela] to effect his death, that, because his recommendations in this particular were not attended to, he had for some time refrained from visiting the King, excepting on matters of business; and the other day plainly told him that it was impossible that they could ever go out to war while the poisoner [probably *umthakathi*] (as he termed Goujuana) lived.[35]

The charge that the accused plotted against the despot was the form in which royal kinsmen or favorites were condemned. The failure of the despot to counter the allegation indicates not that he necessarily believed the accusation, but that he lacked the power to prevent the execution, or—what amounts to the same thing—that he feared the consequences of opposing the induna in this matter.

Gardiner was more aware of the problematic nature of the relation between ruler and induna than other observers, but he tried to explain it in a way that would imply—if the explanation were accepted—a theory of self-limitation. He wrote:

> Although the government is absolute, a considerable share of power is vested in the hands of two principle indunas of the nation, who are always consulted, and generally supposed to sanction every important measure of their sovereign, and in this manner it becomes a convenient triumvirate, contracting and expanding its powers within itself, according to the humour of the ruling despot.[36]

In later Zulu history, when the king was presumably more limited by institutional checks and expected to follow the advice of his council, Gluckman has shown that something like the flexibility and self-limitation suggested above by Gardiner did prevail, the king sometimes choosing to act autocratically, at other times behaving like a limited monarch. In dealing with Europeans, he would use the decisions of the induna as an excuse for backing out of commitments. Gluckman concluded that "The king's power and the councillors' insistence on their rights and jealousy of one another might all affect the course of discussion and the decision on any matter or case."[37] Thus, reasoning back in time from the reigns of Mpande and Cetshwayo accentuates the ambiguity of the relation between king and staff and shows that several interpretations of the nature of that relation are plausible.

Right after Dingane, in the reign of Mpande, even Delegorgue, who described the king as a despot, recognized one picturesque limitation on the king's power and said, "Notwithstanding the exercise of the most absolute despotism, there are three days in every year when the nation has the right to call the king to a severe account for his actions." The days fell at the time when the maize was ripe and the First Fruits Ceremony took place, previous to which it was a capital offense to cut corn. At that time, Delegorgue described:

> lively discussions occur; there are free interrogations, to which the king is bound to reply, and so as to satisfy the people. I

have seen simple warriors rush out of the ranks, transform themselves into orators full of warmth, energetic to excess, not only withstand Panda's scorching glance, but even denounce him in the presence of all, blame his acts, stigmatise them as infamous, as cowardly, oblige him to explain, destroy the reasoning in his answers, dissecting them and unmasking their falsehood; then threatening him proudly, and ending with a gesture of contempt. I have also seen, in consequence of such discussions, the king's party and that of the opposition on the point of rushing on each other. I have seen the voice of the despot disregarded, and that a revolution might have broken out on the spot, if only a single ambitious man had taken advantage of the indignation of those opposed to the king. But that which did not less surprise me was the order which ensued after the termination of this kind of popular tribunal.[38]

Although the chronicles trace the ceremony to Shaka, there is no European record of the "ritual of rebellion"—as Gluckman terms the custom—taking place in his regime. However, Isaacs noted it at the First Fruits Ceremony in the time of Dingane. He wrote: "At this period the chiefs are allowed to converse unreservedly with the king, speaking with great freedom, and in some measures to be dictatorial. After this is done, the whole dance, disperse, and return to their respective kraals." [39] Gluckman has argued persuasively that the function of the ritual was periodically to ventilate hostility to the throne and thereby to increase the solidarity of the regime.[40] Thus, the presence of the ritual sheds no light on the question of the dynamics of power or of the precise relation between ruler and staff, for taken by itself the ritual may be interpreted as a real check by the chiefs on the authority of the ruler or as a pressure-releasing mechanism that reinforced despotic controls. What all the theorists of Zulu despotism have failed to see is that the pressures and influences moving from staff to king worked not in the direction of limited monarchy, according to the European stereotype, but, paradoxically, as forces that restored and strengthened the despotic regime. A theoretical explanation of this process must be reserved for a later chapter. For the present, it is sufficient to point out that ruler, staff, warriors, and people all co-operated, from different but compatible motives, to support the official image of the head of the system as an omnipotent and irresistible despot.

MILITARY DECLINE

The bellicose dispositions of chiefs and warriors seemed to increase as the military prowess of the Zulu forces steadily declined. The army had never recovered from the disastrous northern campaign at the time of Shaka's assassination. In the early days at emGungundlovu, after Nqetho was dead and the Qwabe revolt had ended, the ruler—influenced by his warriors and chiefs, Isaacs insisted—was constantly engaged in military matters. In the old despotic style, Dingane used European muskets against the will of Isaacs to execute Nqetho's widows in public. Then he planned a number of military campaigns, which did not succeed. An attack against Mzilikazi and the Matebele forces once again failed. Dingane, forgetting his declaration that he had done with war, Isaacs observed bitterly, also prepared an attack against Ncaphayi, chief of the Baca people, to recover the large herd of Zulu cattle taken from the Qwabe who had originally seized the animals during the rebellion. As long as these cattle were unrecovered, their loss remained an affront to the ruling despot. The march against the Baca halted and turned back when the impi reached very cold country and many died from exposure. The decision to retreat was made by the chiefs, even though they feared Dingane's wrath, for it was whispered that if Zulu military efforts did not improve, the despot would begin to punish the leaders in the manner of Shaka. To ward off Dingane's anger, they reported that the spirit of Shaka had appeared to all the principal chiefs in a dream, warning that if the Zulu forces persisted on their march, they would be destroyed. The ghost also demanded to know what they were doing at such a distance from their homes, especially since they had killed him in order to enjoy peace and tranquillity. The specter reminded them that their presence in that remote region was inconsistent with the oath of Dingane to lay down spears and shields and go to war no more. Impressed with the report of this spectral visitation, Dingane spared the impi and its leaders, but continued to plan new expeditions. None of them succeeded except for an attack on the small community of the amaCele, the only successful effort since the death of Shaka. Failing to make new conquests and pressed by the restlessness of the army, Dingane began to prey on communities that were already tributary to the Zulu, attacking them and taking their cattle. These forays took place as the terror mounted in the center of the state. In attacking the tributaries, Fynn explained, Dingane

> had no difficulty in inventing reasons for destroying them one by one, so that he might derive from the conquest of people already his subjects that glory which he was incapable of winning in wars against admittedly hostile neighbours—incapable because of the Zulus having, when under his control, lost that daring and prestige for which they had been so conspicuous in the reign of Shaka.[41]

THE CRISIS OF PORT NATAL

In the early period of emGungundlovu, despite the reign of terror in the kingdom and despite hostile engagements with alien communities as well as tributaries, Dingane remained cordial to the Europeans. An account of gracious behavior toward a party of shipwrecked Portuguese—even though they were despised as slave traders—was recorded early in 1830.[42] Relations with the white settlement at Port Natal did not deteriorate until 1831, the change being marked by the destruction of John Cane's kraal, ordered by Dingane in April of that year.

John Cane, a trader who had been a member of the first European party to visit Shaka, was ordered by Dingane in the winter of 1830 to lead a goodwill mission to the colonial government in the Cape. The despot also commanded Jacob, "the Swimmer," to accompany Cane as interpreter. Originally of the Xhosa people in the eastern Cape Province, Jacob had been imprisoned by the Europeans for cattle rustling, but was turned over to Lieutenant King, who needed an interpreter. Although he saved Farewell from drowning when their boat capsized during the landing, Jacob fled into the bush after being attacked by another member of the party. He reached Shaka before any of the Europeans, became his interpreter and confidant, played an important role in Zulu-European relations, and after the death of Shaka also had the ear of Dingane. In the trip to Grahamstown with Cane, however, he resented having to return to the jurisdiction in which he had been arrested years before, and indeed was detained for the old charges. Convinced that Cane was responsible for the new indignity, he swore revenge. On his return, he told Dingane that Cane was plotting with the British army an invasion of Zululand. The despot was already offended because the mission had not succeeded. Moreover, Cane failed to report directly to him upon his return, sending bearers with a few presents and a lame apology. This disrespect not only increased the suspicion that he was arranging an invasion, but also constituted a serious breach of etiquette. Enraged, the despot dispatched an impi to wipe out Cane's kraal. The attack made a decisive change in the attitude of Isaacs toward Dingane and initiated the siege mentality of Port Natal. Isaacs remarked:

> The conduct of the king in this transaction at once shook our confidence, and led us to apprehend that he was a complete dissembler. His affectation of sorrow, his desire for peace, his anxiety for repose, and his determination to cultivate a good understanding with Europeans, we now conceived to be so many arts to delude us . . . [John Cane had] excited his wrath by not having performed his mission to his satisfaction, and for having very indiscreetly, and it must be said, unaccountably,

forgotten how important it was that he should have gone on to the monarch, and have rendered some explanation of the failure of this mission.[43]

No one believed the ruler's declaration that Cane was the solitary object of his wrath. Fynn observed:

The false information maliciously communicated by Jacob to Dingane produced a remarkable change in the King's attitude towards the European settlers. At first it appeared as if only Cane was the person affected, it being generally known that Jacob had openly quarrelled with him only. But whilst having every reason to be dissatisfied and angry with Cane, who had certainly been negligent and dilatory in the execution of his duties, the nature of the rumours was such as to make Dingane suspect not only Cane but every other white man in the country of being actively disloyal towards him.[44]

For the next seven years, until the conflict with the immigrant Boers brought Dingane's regime to an end, relations with the settlement remained turbulent, the Europeans living in continual fear of a Zulu attack. In 1834, even the intrepid Fynn, fearing that there was no future for Europeans in Natal and convinced that Dingane intended to destroy them all, left Natal forever to become an interpreter for the government in the Cape Colony.

The change in Dingane's attitude toward Europeans has been explained by observers and by later historians as a victory of the several induna and chiefs who were hostile to the white settlers and traders. They succeeded, it is said, in replacing his originally cordial feelings with their own fears of European domination. Many of those who were not hostile to the whites fled to Port Natal, where they lived under European protection. The usual explanation for Dingane's reversal is probably correct as far as it goes, but it does not take into account the structural features of the Zulu system, which were important factors in the change of policy.

A tight border sealed by a traffic desert and patrolled by the impi had maintained the ecological conditions for Shaka's system. The sealed border checked the natural tendency of fission and migration, and the people confined to the domain were deprived by violence of any kind of resistance to despotic rule. Subordination and co-operation did not guarantee preservation, however, for a large number of victims were sacrificed regularly to the process of terror.

The growth of Port Natal and the development of an escape route to the European settlement there undermined the conditions of the despotic regime. In Shaka's day, the trickle of fugitives seemed no serious threat, and the despot, after a moment of rage when he learned of the first refugees, shrugged off the problem, saying they had gone to live with his friends and not with his enemies.

Considered by the despots as an enclave in the Zulu domain existing at royal sufferance, the port, in Dingane's reign, grew to threatening proportions, not only as the terminus of an escape route but also as an independent political system, rivaling the Zulu power and competing for the resources of Zululand. Disquieted by the tension between Port Natal and the kingdom, Fynn remarked:

> about 3,000 refugees from Shaka and Dingane are computed to have been living under the settlers. All these knew well that Dingane had begun to resent intensely their being where they were, constituting, in his estimation, practically an *imperium in imperio*, and, therefore, regarded not only as a standing but a constantly growing menace to his authority.[45]

The ecological conditions of Zulu despotism would be destroyed if the people could escape from the terror and find asylum. Besides this structural reason for conflict with the European settlement and the threat of a rival political system, growing competition for resources increased the feeling of enmity. To Shaka, the small band of mercantile adventurers had inspired wonder and excitement. In Dingane's time, the larger population of Europeans, with the British forces of the Cape Colony behind them, was seen as an outpost of invasion, led by English traders who wanted to collect ivory, and later by Boer farmers who wanted to take the land. Coexistence was precarious, both sides believing that even though it might be deferred, violent conflict was inevitable. The merchants were continually frustrated by the despot's monopoly of all trade. Supply as well as prices were controlled by him, and, under pain of death, independent transactions were forbidden. Furthermore, the prospects of accumulating property and establishing ordinary business conditions were prevented by the menace that the Zulu might sack the port settlement at any time. Fynn complained:

At present it would be folly for anyone to attempt a residence, the security of property being so doubtful. Port Natal has for this nine years past been open, and has not been wanting in persons capable of opening a trade with the Zulus to advantage, had there been a government protection, without which no persons, with the least prospect, can with spirit enter into business of any kind under so despotic a government, the like of which I don't believe exists on this earth.

He deplored "the doubtful state we have been living in for the last three years, which must continue to remain so til some great change takes place in the Zulu government," but expected that "the time will, no doubt, produce a profitable market at Natal, and that as soon as the despotic government is suppressed." [46]

As the terror had mounted within the state and as military campaigns continued to fail, the flow of refugees increased. If a large tribal segment or an entire regiment defected en masse, it did not head for the settlement but struck out in another direction, sometimes crossing the Drakensberg Range to roam the highveld of the Transvaal. However, many small fragments of clans and other weak groups continued to seek protection from the Europeans. In the winter of 1832, after the failure of the second campaign against the Matebele (Ndebele), induna and warriors were dispatched at kwaMatiwane, the hill of execution, and a daily stream of fugitives trekked to Port Natal. They increased after the ill-fated Baca expedition, when Dingane killed more induna and plucked out the eyes of the scouts. It was rumored that Dingane would end the desertions to the port by massacring every soul in the settlement.

Jacob was killed in 1832, the despot ordering the Europeans to hunt him down after hearing reports that he had stolen royal cattle. Nevertheless, his warnings remained alive. The Xhosa people in the south, according to Jacob, had learned to their sorrow the tricks of the white men, and Dingane might expect that missionaries and traders would enter his domain as the vanguard of invading armies. The fears were exacerbated by the legend, often repeated, of Shaka's last words. It was said that as he lay dying, Shaka had gasped that Dingane would not rule long, for soon the white men would overrun Zululand. The induna took the legend and Jacob's words seriously, and they adhered to a policy of restricting the movements and the influence of the Europeans. Their suspicions inspired the despot's refusal to grant Captain Gardiner permission to open a mission station in Zululand. His petition rejected, Gardiner was called to preach the Gospel to the residents of Port Natal.

Deeply involved in the political and military problems of the settlement, Gardiner observed, "The natives at Port Natal are, almost to a man, refugees from the Zulu nation, goaded by a rigorous government to desert for protection to our settlement, their very existence, therefore, depends upon their combining to defend the asylum they have chosen." [47] Responding to the intense fear of an attack, he led the movement to make a treaty with the Zulu, and in the spring of 1835 entered negotiations with Dingane.

The reaction to Gardiner's offer of a treaty revealed Dingane's eagerness to solve the problem of Port Natal without risking an attack. The agreement stipulated that Dingane would guarantee the lives and property of all the present residents, but no new refugees would be received at the port and all future deserters would be given up.[48] Dingane expressed pleasure at the arrangement and, as quoted by Gardiner, " 'he granted all; that he would never molest any of his subjects now at Natal for past offences; that he should keep fast to his word; but that he knew the white people would be the first to break the treaty.' " [49]

Actually, the treaty was eroded by both sides, Dingane demanding the return of fugitives who had settled at the port before the treaty date and the Europeans continuing to entice and smuggle Zulu into the settlement. Enraged by this practice, the despot proclaimed that the treaty was canceled. The duplicity of Jacob remained as a popular explanation for Dingane's hostility, but Fynn understood the underlying reason:

> Although the present doubtful state of Natal is attributed to the falsehoods of Jacob, I am satisfied that the principle cause is the jealousy occasioned from so many natives being with us, and although it may not be Dingane's intention to murder all the whites at Natal, I have no doubt he is at the bottom of the reports, and many instances might be adduced which would show how he was interested by them.[50]

A new factor in the situation was introduced as the Boers, trekking from the south in search of land and attracted by the depopulated areas of Zululand, started arriving in 1834.

DINGANE'S CATASTROPHE

At the time the Boers first appeared at Port Natal, there were signs that Dingane was being pressed by demands for cattle and warfare. Shaka's praise chant had inquired rhetorically: "Thou hast overcome the tribes. Now where will you wage war?" Dingane had not resolved the contradiction. Forays against tributaries were insufficient, and the pressure to raid Port Natal was increasing. In 1837 a party of Boers led by Piet

Retief arrived. The port settlement was now a township re-named Durban, and Gardiner had returned after an unsuccessful attempt in England to plead for its protection by the Crown and adoption as British territory. The settlers welcomed the Boers, even though they recognized that the immigrants had trekked to escape British rule in the first place and that they would violently reject it if it were ever extended to Natal. They dreamed of an independent republic.

Retief's party visited Dingane with a request to settle on Zulu territory. In February 1838, the despot received them cautiously. The sequel is one of the best-known episodes in South African history. Dingane deceived the Boers into riding off on a mission to recover some cattle stolen from the Zulus. Omer-Cooper claims that the Zulu induna who accompanied them

marvelled at the powerful sorcery of the whites, their unscrupulous treachery and their lack of respect for chiefs. Dingane became more alarmed than ever at the thought of such dangerous neighbours. . . . If the Boers were allowed to consolidate their position they would be too strong for him, but if he could catch them unprepared the danger might still be averted.[51]

On their return, the despot contracted to cede the requested territory, then tricked them into entering the royal kraal without their guns, and at the cry, "Kill the wizards (or evildoers— *abathakathi*)!" the warriors slaughtered every one. Men, women, and children in the Boer laagers camped within range were also massacred. When a Boer commando reached emGungundlovu the following December, Dingane had already fled, having put the royal kraal to the torch. The remains of Retief's party were found on kwaMatiwane.

Perhaps the Boers had really impressed Dingane as wizards and not as ordinary Europeans; perhaps he was reacting to what he and the induna felt was a band of sorcerers, but it is clear that he understood their plans to invade the land. Another explanation, found in Boer sources, is that he murdered the

Retief party because two Englishmen set his mind against the Boers, calling them deserters from the King of England.[52] Certainly, Dingane seems to have thought that he could drive out the Boers without disrupting already strained relations with the settlers at Durban. He did not expect that the massacres would turn all the Europeans in the region and their black dependants against him and also create schism in the Zulu state. His brother, Mpande, rebelled and threw in his lot with the Europeans, contributing a Zulu force to the armies in the field against Dingane. Steadily losing, and having given up hope of regaining his power, the despot retreated to Swaziland, where his continued violence against his own staff provoked those induna who survived to arrange for him to be murdered by a local chief. He was killed by a Swazi detachment in March 1840.

MPANDE

Toward the end of October in 1839, Mpande had crossed the border of Zululand and had entered Natal with 17,000 followers, afraid that his brother had made plans to destroy him. The Boers permitted him to settle temporarily with his following, and a deputation from the Volksraad proclaimed him "Reigning Prince of the Emigrant Zulus" until he should be confirmed as the successor to Dingane. When the despot fled to the north, the Boers named Mpande King of the Zulu. Returning to Zululand, he received the people who had gone with Dingane and, after the despot was killed in Swaziland, trekked back to pledge allegiance and to settle under the new king's rule, which, it was understood, would be subordinate to the Boer Volksraad. His kingdom was a vassal state controlled by the Boer republic. That the British took Natal in 1841 and drove out the Boers made little difference to the Zulu kingdom. The Boers had been too weak and divided to make their suzerainty effective; the British did not want the responsibilities of annexation. Mpande reigned in peace for a period of thirty-two years, most of which were uneventful, and in 1872 he was the first Zulu monarch to die a natural death. The tranquillity of his reign had been interrupted by two violent episodes. In 1843, reacting to an alleged conspiracy by his brother, he sent his regiments to kill Gqugqu and his followers. In 1856 two of his sons contended for the right to succession, and the kingdom was wracked by civil war between their forces, ending in the triumph of Cetshwayo.

Zulu military action dropped to nothing, for Mpande made only a few raids to the north.[53] Two important features of the Zulu state—military aggression and territorial expansion—were contained, making fundamental changes in the power system. These changes and Mpande's adaptation to them have not been understood. The commonly accepted version of his reign pictures the king as an inept ruler and is based on his seeming mildness as compared to the mien of his predecessors, Shaka and Dingane, and on his political accommodation to the Europeans. His conduct is usually attributed to weakness and indolence. As Becker typically expresses this questionable interpretation, "He was content to devote himself to feasting and drinking, to gossiping with courtiers, to admiring his treasured herds and to flirting with his large collection of seraglio women." [54] Even Bryant, trying to explain the outbreak of hostilities between Cetshwayo and Mbulazi, the king's sons, was tempted by this point of view and wrote: "Mpande's natural weakness of character soon manifested itself in his utter inability to maintain discipline in his own household." [55] In his recent history of the Zulu, Morris elaborates the interpretation, claiming that Mpande "was almost totally ineffectual and constantly ignored by his own relatives, indunas and subjects," and "was tolerated as a leader simply because he rarely interfered with his subjects and because his commands could be ignored with impunity," that "he exercised little direct influence on domestic affairs, but he made a satisfactory figurehead," and that he "had paid craven fealty first to the Boers of the

Natal Republic . . . and then to the British who had replaced the Boers in Natal." [56]

In contrast to these pictures of Mpande, an entirely different perception is found in the two-volume work by the French traveler Adulphe Delegorgue.[57] This work is unmatched for information about the culture and social organization of the Zulu in the time of Dingane and Mpande. What is especially useful is Delegorgue's perspective—so different from that of the English and American missionaries as well as of the Boers, who provided the other sources of information for the period. Delegorgue was not Victorian but Rousseauean in his outlook, and he did not perceive the Zulu as a backward race or as depraved heathen, but admired them as a great people full of intelligence and dignity. For him, Mpande was not a fool, as one historical interpretation makes out, but the very prince of noble savages. As Delegorgue saw him, "An ample cloak, in Roman fashion, with which he draped himself in an eminently majestic guise, gave an exaltation to his features, in which the habit of command was boldly traced." He compared the king to the Boers, much to the disadvantage of these traveling companions, whom he considered as no more than "people made to drive oxen and to hold converse with them." [58] Even while discussing what he considered to be evil practices in the Zulu system, he recognized their place in the configuration of social institutions, and reflected, "To change customs of this kind one would first have to remodel everything, and establish everything anew; and, as a consequence, to impose on such a people the burdens borne by civilized communities." [59] Any history of Zulu society in this period that does not take Delegorgue's vision into account to balance the outlook of other European observers, suffers from the omission.

The commonly accepted picture of Mpande as an inept—or at least indolent—ruler has some basis in fact, but it has reached exaggerated proportions. It is true that, according to Zulu tradition, Mpande survived the violence of Shaka and Dingane by playing the fool, but his story suggests the legendary account in Roman history of Lucius Junius Brutus, who feigned stupidity to escape the tyrannical violence of Tarquin the Arrogant. There is sufficient evidence to contradict the judgment made by Morris and others that Mpande lost political control of his own people in the early days of his regime. Had these writers consulted Delegorgue they would have at least had to struggle with a different version.

On the occasion that Mpande fled from Dingane and entered Natal to seek protection from the Boers, receiving then their support to establish his authority over the Zulu, an incident took place which was significantly ambiguous and which has lent itself to two different interpretations of Mpande's rule. The leader of the deputation from the Volksraad asked Mpande to produce three induna who were to bear responsibility for the conduct of the prince. Delegorgue reports that Mpande sent for two, and then, after reflection, called for a third. Roos, the Landdrost in charge of the Boer deputation, reported that shortly thereafter a throng of several hundred men were observed to surround one of the induna just appointed and beat him to death.[60] Mpande appeared and publicly condemned them for this act, claiming that it would jeopardize the position of the refugees. Morris interprets the episode to mean that "his subjects showed the visitors what they thought of the new prince by murdering under their eyes an inDuna he had just appointed," [61] a judgment that fits the picture he draws of Mpande as a nominal ruler with no control of his people. In contrast, Delegorgue writes of the event as follows:

> Panda [Mpande] was called upon by us to explain the scene which we had witnessed with regret. He came, pretending to be in great anger. . . . In our eyes Panda had cleared himself of the crime. His eloquence made us believe him innocent. Some days elapsed before we learned that the act had been his first exercise of kingly authority, which had a cause quite recent and concerning us nearly. On the day when we acknowledged him chief of the tribe, it was necessary that a man should die by his order, and the forfeit was paid by the unhappy Pangazoaga:

and the blood of the man was to serve as an ointment for his limbs that night; the heart was to be roasted and presented to him to be eaten, as if to strengthen his body and double his heart. Such are the influences actuating the Zulu Kafirs. I know that several with whom I have been acquainted in Natal will not admit these things to be true; but I may state that I am the only one who has lived nearly ten months in the heart of the country of the Zulus, and that I have been in every respect too well informed to have any doubt upon the subject.[62]

Even if one were to suspect Delegorgue's credulity about some features of Zulu despotism, the description of his experience in Zululand would still convey the limitations of the perspective represented by Morris's statements and also would suggest that there is another way of looking at Mpande.

His reign is the most problematic of all, raising some of the most interesting questions, for he was something between a despot *manqué* and a limited monarch. Careful inspection of the evidence contradicts the interpretation that dismisses him as an incompetent, apathetic king, and it reveals a complex and prudent policy, which realistically did not pit Zulu strength against European technological power, yet worked to preserve the integrity of Zulu institutions in new conditions. It was a period of replenishment, and, in Morris's own words, "The kraals were flourishing, and the cattle had long since made good the losses from the Boer depradations. All the men between twenty and sixty years of age were enrolled in regiments which could be mobilized in a few days, and the nation was more powerful than it had ever been before." [63] One may reflect on the wisdom of the policy of those fruitful years by considering how the destruction of the political and social equilibrium established in Mpande's reign brought the ruin of the Zulu kingdom.

In Mpande's relation to subordinate chiefs as well as to the rest of his subjects, many features of the despotic style remained. It is true that the way of formulating policy began to change, the kingship, in this respect, approaching a kind of limited monarchy, and political life in general assumed a form that is more typical among Bantu-speaking people. In great questions of policy—especially military policy—the king convened councils, ascertained the prevailing opinion, and adopted it as his own.[64] This trend became institutionalized so that in later Zulu history the king had no effective power that was not supported by public opinion.[65] Another kind of limitation began to develop in Mpande's reign also, for the king was known to declare publicly that he was obliged in his actions to conform to law.

In practice, however, the despotic style persevered, so that Mpande's reign was full of contradictions. Gluckman describes one situation in which legal formality was reversed by despotic practice:

> The Zulu king Mpande once had to judge on a claim for a large herd of cattle between the rightful heir who had been born in Swaziland after his father had fled there during the wars of Shaka and the father's brother who subjected himself to Shaka. The king found in law for the young man, though the uncle, a favourite of his pleaded that he was being ruined. But the king insisted that he had to obey the law. That night he told the uncle that he would send a troop to wipe out the young man and his family, so that the uncle would become rightful heir.

Hearing of the plot, the king's son warned the young man, who was a friend, and complained to his father. Confronted with the contradiction between the policy of legality and despotic practice, the king replied that he was ignorant of the plot and that it had been hatched by his councillors.[66]

Mpande was responsible for other violent actions of a familiar nature. Bryant described how the king dispatched his younger half brother:

> Upon certain information laid by one Tekwane, of this presumably innocent brother he feigned to be suspicious—the more

so because the mother of Ggugqu had been, in the paternal family, of senior rank to his own. Ggugqu and his mother were accordingly stabbed to death in their home, his wives disembowelled and his children battered lifeless.[67]

Like his predecessors, Mpande was known to eliminate great men in the kingdom, although he was more circumspect and looked for pretexts. During his sojourn with Mpande, Delegorgue's residence was ransacked by a thief. The king blamed the local chief, Suzuwana, who should have reported the incident. Delegorgue believed, "Evidently Panda caught at anything that might embroil Suzuwana; for Suzuwana had the grave defect of being rich." [68]

When the thief was caught, he was killed, and Delegorgue commented, "killed for the crime of theft by housebreaking: a dreadful punishment, no doubt, for so small an offence; but under Panda there is no prison, no bastinado, nothing but death, whatever be the degree of crime." When Delegorgue discussed the severity of punishments with the king, he was told that death was a more humane punishment than the European practice of incarceration, and, he added, "When a criminal is killed everyone is quiet." The loss of a warrior was nothing, he claimed, showing that he retained the despotic notion of his subjects as the king's instruments to be disposed at will. As he told the visitor, "My men, my warriors, everybody knows, are more numerous than grasshoppers; and when a grasshopper falls to the ground, do you miss one from the swarm?" [69]

In the same vein, David Leslie related a story told to him by an old headman about a recent event at the royal kraal:

A regiment of soldiers were going through some evolutions before Panda. One of them happened to wear his hair a little longer than ordinary, which the King having noticed, he flew into a violent rage, and ordered the man out, and had him killed immediately. The only comment he made on this was "it was perfectly right: what were the people for, unless to be killed when the King chose?" [70]

Although the powers of chiefs and induna increased during Mpande's reign, the officers of the king were still officially expected to act exclusively as his agents. As Delegorgue observed, "They are responsible for the spirit animating their subordinates, and the smallest negligence exposes them to a sentence of death." [71]

He also pointed out that the Zulu ruler still thought of himself as a terrorist, for "does he not claim the titles of Great Master, Great Destroyer? He is great only in so far as he inspires fear." [72] The disposition toward violence within the system, he believed, was not to be imputed to the character of the Zulu people but to that of the king who was in command, "for the chiefs of the Zulus have been wholly bloodthirsty, and from the time but exclusive of Senzangakona, each of them has given proof that he has been imbued with the conviction that he could reign only by terror." [73] Mpande, he was convinced, could not be excluded from the terroristic pattern of his predecessors. Shaka, Dingane, and Mpande, he observed, "when seizing the reins of government, promised to exercise power with moderation; but each of them, as soon as he believed himself to be firmly seated, set himself to rage in the most cruel manner, in order to spread terror everywhere, and to reign grandly by dint of terror." [74]

The despotic system had contracted, but terroristic rule, considerably limited in scope, remained. Generally regarded as the mildest of Zulu rulers, Mpande still declared flatly to Sir Theophilus Shepstone, Chief Native Affairs Commissioner of Natal, "The Zulus are only ruled by being killed." [75]

It should go without saying that the Zulu despots did not rule exclusively by terror, for the systematic political use of violence does not by itself govern men. The system of power included other methods as well—authority, economic redistribution, rewards, persuasion, magic, and other techniques familiar to legitimate rulers. The pattern of violence, however, reacted to fundamental conflicts and it inhibited resistance. It made government possible—or at least set the conditions in which a certain kind of government was possible. During the latter part of Mpande's reign and during Cetshwayo's, however, that government changed. When Cetshwayo, the last of the Zulu kings, repeated the statement that the Zulu were ruled by being killed, he did not mean the same thing.

CHAPTER IX

PASSAGE

FROM

DESPOTISM

THERE IS NO WAY to abstract the Zulu system from the history of European influence and to plot a hypothetical trajectory of its despotism. There is no way, moreover, of knowing whether the terror would have continued or abated, although Dingane showed no sign of ever abandoning it. It is true that decentralization and limitation proceeded under Mpande, but in the absence of Europeans, Mpande would not have occupied the throne in the first place.

The ambiguities of Mpande's reign were the contradictions of a system in transition. As the Zulu nation was flourishing in restless peace and the political structure was changing from despotism to the form of a kingdom, Mpande began to accept the limitations imposed by Boer and British pressures. Within the state he initiated less and seemed to lapse into political passivity. Yet, despotism was not a thing of the past, although its manifestations were sporadic and its range diminished. When the king ordered executions and confiscations, in cases that were doubtful or not serious, rumor was allowed to reach the victims, permitting them to escape, leaving their property to be collected for the king. In serious cases, secrecy was observed and the executions were carried out. In an attempt to control the flow of the refugees, Mpande kept up a traffic desert. Farrer wrote that the king "had a space of country left unoccupied, fifty or sixty miles broad, along the whole frontier line; and any Zulu caught thus attempting to cross the boundary was taken back and put to death." In 1854, the Lieutenant-Governor of Natal warned Europeans against the familiar practice of enticing refugees, not only because it violated the authority of the king but also because it caused "much loss of life to the unfortunate refugees themselves. . . ." [1] Undoubtedly, the number of fugitives from Mpande was exaggerated, and many of the people flowing into Natal were probably refugees of the *Mfekane* (see page 111) trying to return home.

Although Mpande never abandoned the violent practices of the despotic style, the range or extent of his power decreased, and induna and chiefs who lived away from the center assumed more power. Rich and powerful men were still being killed by the king, although the second half of his reign was indeed comparatively milder than the first, but those who escaped the violence managed to build strong local organizations and to exert conciliar pressures on the monarch. One strong territorial chiefdom had its origin in a kraal toward the north created by Shaka and placed under Ngqengelele, whose son Umnyanana was later made Principal Induna by Cetshwayo. Another to the northeast in the land of the Ndwandwe had originated as a territory placed in charge of Shaka's cousin, Maphita—son of Senzangakhona's brother—who consolidated and preserved substantial power, to be used ultimately by his son Zibhebhu for rebellion and to defeat the restored king, Cetshwayo, in 1883. Maphita, whose future had been uncertain under the vigilance of Dingane, had thrown in his lot with Mpande against the latter, and for that reason, lived in peace under Mpande and gathered strength. Another strong northern section with growing independent tendencies was led by Uhamu, son of a wife Mpande had married to "raise seed" for his deceased brother. The seed grew up to defect from Cetshwayo and to aspire to the throne. In addition, a number of southern chiefs were emerging as well, and the relation between chiefs and ruler was changing, for the degree of domination ensured by the destructive vigilance of Shaka and Dingane was a thing of the past.

In the process of decentralization, some of the initiative for terrorism had passed to the witch finders, or *izanusi*, whose powers were restored under Mpande. They worked as powerful forces in the service of social and political conformity, reducing ambition and deviance, for individuals who stood out risked being condemned as *abathakhati*, or evildoers, and held responsible for illness and misfortune. Refugees from Zululand found more oppression in their life in Natal, and they declared that their fear of the witch detectors kept them from returning. The diviners were controlled by the territorial and local chiefs. It was observed that they, "who seem to be the cause of so much bloodshed . . . look upon themselves as instruments of power in the hands of the Chiefs." [2]

As political events settled into the routine of a kingdom, the issue of succession emerged for the first time in the history of the state. Mpande's way of handling the issue encouraged the forces of decentralization and the growth of territorial concentrations. To the Boers, he had presented Cetshwayo as his principal son, but years later he publicly showed partiality to Mbuyazi, a son by his favorite wife. The home kraals of the rival princes were placed eighty miles apart, Mpande explaining the separation by the statement that "two bulls cannot live in the same kraal." Since people were more free to move about than in the previous regimes and since the territorial units were acquiring a new meaning, powerful and popular chiefs once again gathered followers, and the Zulu state was divided into rival parties, each supported by subordinate chiefs, with Cetshwayo's people eventually outnumbering Mbuyazi's three to one. Conflict between them in 1856 led to civil war fought in a single decisive battle in which large numbers of men, women, and children were killed. In consequence, Cetshwayo became the de facto regent until he assumed the throne on his father's death.

Mpande undoubtedly had not anticipated civil war, and unless we accept the notion of his stupidity, a plausible explanation of his conduct in dividing Zululand by pitting son against son is the story told by John Dunn, who had helped Mbuyazi but later became a confidant of Cetshwayo, receiving a chiefdom from him. Dunn's statements must be taken with caution, for ambition led him to betray the king and to seek power from the British, and one cannot expect his point of view to show Cetshwayo in a favorable light. Dunn claimed that Mpande told him that

although Cetshwayo and Umbulazi [Mbuyazi] fought for my place, I gave the preference to neither. The one in my heart is yet young, and I am afraid to mention who he is, even to you. Of the two that have been killing each other—Cetywayo and Umbulazi—Cetywayo was my favorite, but it was not he whom I intended to take my place.[3]

According to this version, then, Mpande had hoped to establish Mbuyazi as a counterforce to the growing power of Cetshwayo. Instead, Cetshwayo consolidated his power, even to the extent of having another young half brother killed in his father's presence.

While Cetshwayo was recognized informally as the "real" power in Zululand, he did not destroy the formal authority of his father. Cetshwayo himself in an autobiographical statement declared: "I only went up and lived in the Ulundi kraal when my father got too old and feeble to rule, and I was called upon to take up the reins of Government of Zululand, which was ended by the Zulu War of 1879."[4] While Leslie was visiting Cetshwayo's kraal, formal permission was received from the king for the prince's age regiment to assume the head ring— the symbol of male seniority—and to marry. Cetshwayo responded by calling in the neighboring regiments for a feast and ceremonial dance in honor of the occasion.[5] Although several initiatives had passed from Mpande, he retained the integrating functions, expressed by symbolic and political acts.

The most important symbol of historical and social unity was the sacred coil, or *inkatha*, which was contained in a python's skin and kept by the ruler. It contained substances collected from the bodies of kings and warriors combined with secret medicines, and it grew in size with each generation, passing down from Shaka to Cetshwayo. It symbolized the unity of the state, and its circular form was "believed to have the power of collecting up all traitors and disaffected subjects, and joining them together with the rest of the nation in affection for the king." [6] Appropriately, when the kingdom fell the coil was destroyed, burned by the British in 1879.

Mpande also retained several despotic prerogatives, the most important of which was the right to kill. Leslie recognized but minimized its importance, writing: "Cetchwayo is the actual king, although all the outward semblance is allowed to his father. The power to kill a few people whenever the freak seizes him is simply considered nothing—merely a toy given to please him." [7] People flew like lightening to obey the king's commands, Leslie observed; those who displeased him were ordered to be killed or beaten, "and instantly fifty ready fellows dart out, only too happy to execute his commands." The same author was aware of the continual presence of violence—obviously less intense than in the previous regimes—and understood that the Zulu accepted it:

> I have said before that it is seldom their offences are punished with death, yet it must be borne in mind that death is always hovering over them; but, although they know this to be the case, they think no more of their end by order of their chiefs, or by violence, than most of ourselves do of "shuffling off this mortal coil" in the quietude of our beds and through natural causes.[8]

Finally, another integrating function retained by Mpande was the maintenance of the military system, which cut across all lines of territory and kinship, holding the state together, although warriors no longer resided permanently in military kraals but served there for periods of active duty. Mpande enrolled at least thirteen new age regiments in his thirty-two-year reign, but there were no wars to fight. Mpande was limited by the physical proximity of the Boers and by the diplomatic pressure of the British to desist from aggression. Shaka's lament haunted the kingdom: "Now where will you wage war?" Besides the tragic civil war, the only sizable campaign of his reign was a march against the Swazi, to give untried regiments a chance to wash their spears and to allow Cetshwayo to distinguish himself. One result of this campaign was a message from Shepstone for Mpande to refrain from future aggression; another consequence was to enhance the prestige of Cetshwayo. The more belligerent chiefs and the generals who had been trained under Shaka, restive under Mpande, turned to the prince as the hope of the future.

CETSHWAYO

The extent to which Cetshwayo was responsible for acts of violence against his own people is not clear, because the record is distorted by political emotion. The Zulu ruler's right to kill became a burning issue for the British, and apart from the territorial disputes, it was a crucial issue that provoked the War of 1879, which brought the ruin of the Zulu state. The ultimatum addressed to the Zulu on the brink of the war actually struck at two factors that integrated the state: royal prerogatives—including the right to kill and the right to control marriage—and the military system. The British, who preferred to ignore the evolution in Zulu political life, regarded both as despotic institutions. If Cetshwayo had submitted to the ultimatum, the Zulu system would have suffered gradual disintegration.

Ultimately, the reasons for the catastrophe may be found in the structural crisis of the Zulu state, a crisis that existed in all primitive states that were in an environment controlled by European power. The immediate political source of the War of 1879, however, was apparently the provocation given by Sir Bartle Frere, who was appointed Governor General of Cape Colony and High Commissioner of Native Affairs for South Africa in 1877, four years after Cetshwayo had been crowned King of the Zulu. The kingdom had survived and flourished as long as a balance of power was preserved by British efforts to support Zulu independence at the same time British policy contained Zulu expansion and limited Boer inroads on the frontier. The independence of the kingdom, however, was inconsistent with the colonial policy of the Disraeli government and the plan of Lord Carnarvon, the Colonial Secretary, to establish a confederation in South Africa. Shepstone supported the plan for his own reasons, looking covetously at the Zulu lands and prepared to sacrifice his presumed friendship for the Zulu state by using its property to obtain relief from the financial burdens of the Transvaal, the bankrupt Boer republic he had just annexed for the Crown. Frere, experienced as Governor of Bombay and a member of the Indian Council in England, pursued a policy of uniting the South African states after the Indian model and other recent confederations, intending to establish a single central government in which all Europeans would cooperate and by which the blacks would be protected and controlled, with the causes of their unrest ameliorated. To this end, the independence of the Zulu state would have to be destroyed. The justification for Frere's program was presented as moral outrage against the Zulu king's violence against his own people —taking the form of an official obsession with "blood-thirsty and barbaric despotism"—and a political fear of the "celibate man-slaying machine," which became his term for the Zulu impi. These provided the excuse for invading Zululand, along with the claim that Cetshwayo had violated his coronation promises, which, it was affirmed, had the force of legal limitations on his power.

The notion that Zulu despotism could not coexist with a European colony had been expressed by Fynn during Dingane's regime. At that time, the despot's monopoly of trade and the insecurity of life and property were given as reasons for the incompatibility between the two systems. Under Mpande, however, trade had been opened, although the ruler imposed greater and lesser restrictions from time to time. Nevertheless, Mpande had been regarded as an independent sovereign, enjoying a British policy of nonintervention.[9] Although the relative strengths of Zulu and British forces had been reversed since Dingane's regime, Sir Bartle Frere made use of a current war scare, and in the propaganda for his campaign reintroduced the anxieties for European safety which had been expressed historically by the settlers of Port Natal. He also added a new issue: a moral obligation to make the Zulu people secure from royal violence. The reorganization of the state being carried on by Cetshwayo he interpreted as an effort "to break loose from all restraint and to re-establish the régime of Chaka's unmitigated barbarism." The defenders of Cetshwayo contended that Frere grossly exaggerated allegations of "atrocious barbarities" on the part of the king, whom he called a "ruthless savage" and "ignorant, bloodthirsty, aggressive despot. . . ." who was "anxious to emulate the sanguinary fame of his uncle Chaka."[10] He also contended that chiefs and people hated their oppression, and that given the opportunity they would abandon Cetshwayo. A number of border incidents not unusual or disturbing in themselves were exaggerated by Frere as evidence of an immediate menace to the safety of Natal. Linking the incidents to the charge that the king's continual use of violence breached his coronation promises, Frere fashioned the pretext for the British invasion of Zululand. For our purposes, the historical changes in the nature and scope of the king's violence as well as the problem of its social functions may be explored by examining Cetshwayo's 1873 coronation and the issues of the dispute that surrounded the ceremony and its implications.

Mpande, it will be remembered, had actually been installed by a foreign power. Chief of a breakaway segment, he was placed on the throne by the Boers and his legitimacy was later confirmed by the rest of the Zulu nation's placing itself under his authority after Dingane's death. In return for their support, the Boers had stipulated a number of conditions to Mpande, including the restrictions that no one should be executed for the charge of sorcery and that no defenseless persons—women, children, or aged—should be killed.[11] These limitations were soon forgotten, however; no European power ever challenged Mpande's internal sovereignty.

After Mpande's death, fearing that the British might some day support a rival prince against him—as Mpande had been supported by the Boers against Dingane—Cetshwayo requested British confirmation of his royal authority, and Shepstone performed the office with elaborate gravity, turning the occasion into a coronation and placing a tinsel crown on the king's head. The requirements of Zulu legitimacy had been fulfilled already, since Masiphula, principal induna under Dingane as well as Mpande, had previously installed Cetshwayo as king. During the ceremony Shepstone, who was an impressive orator in the Zulu tongue, read off a number of declarations—to which voices were raised in a kind of ritual assent—among them the statement, "the indiscriminate shedding of blood shall cease in the land." He also stipulated conditions of legality: open trial of the accused, public examination of witnesses, the right of appeal, as well as the provisions that no life should be taken without consent of the king after the right of appeal has been exercised and that fines should be substituted for the death penalty in minor crimes.

John Dunn, who attended Cetshwayo closely before, during, and after the ceremony, described the king's reaction. He said that Cetshwayo was disappointed in Shepstone's performance, which he took as "nothing but a lecture of advice." The king felt, however, that his original intentions had been satisfied: "He had been proclaimed King by Masipula before the arrival of Mr. Shepstone, and now this had merely been confirmed by him, and now he was the acknowledged King of the country by the Natal Government, as well as by the Zulus." [12] Even Shepstone had a limited view of the effect of the king's "promises," admitting, "To have got such principles admitted and declared what a Zulu may plead when oppressed, was but sowing the

seed which will still take many years to grow and mature." [13]
Four years later, the nature of the "coronation" was reinterpreted. The declarations, Frere insisted, were conditions precedent for the British recognition of Cetshwayo's authority, and the breach of those conditions a justification for invasion. However, looking back on the king's conduct and the British response to it, Rider Haggard observed:

> He has never adhered to these coronation regulations, or promises, as they have been called, and the probability is that he never intended to adhere to them. However this may be, I must say that personally I have been unable to share the view of those who see in the breach of these so-called promises a justification of the Zulu war. After all, what do they amount to, and what guarantee was there for their fulfillment? They merely represent a very laudable attempt on the part of the Natal Government to keep a restraining hand on Zulu cruelty. . . . The Government of Natal had no right to dictate the terms to a Zulu king on which he was to hold his throne. The Zulu nation was an independent nation, and had never been conquered or annexed by Natal.[14]

Cetshwayo's intentions concerning his prerogative to kill may be inferred from an incident that took place immediately after the disputed ceremony. Taking advantage of the confusion when a fire broke out in the royal kraal, a man stole some narcotic patent medicine from the king's possessions and was soon detected. The execution, taking place almost before Shepstone had time to return to Natal, was performed in the old style and described by Dunn:

> The poor fellow lay on the ground for a short time, for he had only been stunned. His arms had been twisted right round behind his head and tied together straight over his head. As soon as he recovered his senses he prepared to march. Having often witnessed a similar scene he knew, from terrible experience, the routine. So he got up of his own accord, and without being told, took the path to the place of execution, and was

followed by about half-a-dozen men, who had been told off to go and finish him.[15]

On this occasion Dunn made some observations on the place of violence in the structure of controls, suggesting that the Zulus scarcely feared death—yet, only death would control them:

> This pilfering showed what little fear these people have for death, well knowing that on the slightest thing being found in their possession, and which belonged to the King, death followed for a certainty. . . . The Zulu is only to be ruled by fear of death, or the confiscation of his entire property.[16]

Dunn's testimony would support the belief that the king's violence matched that of his predecessors in its amount and scope:

> many a squabble I had to prevent my people being taken away and killed—life was held very cheap in Zululand in those days, and if Cetywayo has, in some future day, to give an account of all the lives he has taken in cold blood, he will have a heavy score to settle. . . . Shortly after the killing of the Chlorodyne man, one of Pande's old servants was put to death and this was the opening of the ball of killing without trial which was usual in Cetywayo's reign.[17]

Dunn's picture made Cetshwayo resemble the despots, but there was no agreement about the amount of violence in his regime, and the defenders of Cetshwayo claimed that reports were exaggerated. Cornelius Vijn, a young Dutch trader who stayed with Cetshwayo in the period after Dunn had deserted the king and joined the British forces, and who remained at the royal kraal throughout the war, declared:

> During my four years' experience I never heard that the King was killing many people, nor do I believe that he has killed to anything like the extent to which he has been credited. . . . I deny emphatically, and totally disbelieve, that Cetshwayo was,

a bloodthirsty tyrant; though he had, of course, to enforce from time to time the laws of his country, and, if he had not done so, where should I have been, who owed my safety to the order maintained by the King?[18]

Although there was a great difference of opinion over the number of executions, the king never denied that he killed, upholding his prerogative, incensed by the efforts to curtail his sovereign right, and justifying it on the grounds of functional necessity. On one occasion, he threatened to execute a number of girls who had evaded the rules concerning the permission to marry, which was still controlled by the king. How many girls were actually killed is not known, but it is clear that the rumors which had reached Natal were exaggerated. An official inquiry from the lieutenant-governor sent the king in a rage, and his reply must be treated cautiously because it was carried back by a messenger who belonged to the faction that was hostile to Cetshwayo. However, the words recorded in the Parliamentary Blue Book read as follows:

Did I ever tell Mr. Shepstone I would not kill? Did he tell the white people I made such an arrangement? Because if he did he has deceived them. I do kill; but do not consider that I have done anything yet in the way of killing. Why do the white people start at nothing? I have not yet begun; I have yet to kill; it is the custom of our nation, and I shall not depart from it.

Why does the Governor of Natal speak to me about my laws? Do I go to Natal and dictate to him about his laws? I shall not agree to any laws or rules from Natal, and by so doing throw the large kraal I govern into the water. My people will not listen unless they are killed; and, while wishing to be friends with the English, I do not agree to give my people over to be governed by laws sent to me by them. . . .

Go back and tell the white men this, and let them hear it well. The Governor of Natal and I are equal; he is Governor of Natal, and I am Governor here.[19]

The message was greeted with feelings of outrage, but it provides a clue to the king's understanding of the functions of royal violence, a clue that we can find if we proceed beyond the manifest defiance of the communication and inquire into what Cetshwayo meant by the statement—so similar to words of Shaka, Dingane, and Mpande—that "my people will not listen unless they are killed."

Allowances may be made for distortion by a hostile messenger, but the communication resembles a statement reported by Bishop Schreuder, who described an interview in which Cetshwayo claimed that Shepstone had omitted in his report to the queen the fact that in transactions between Shepstone and Cetshwayo, the latter expressly "had reserved to himself the right of killing people who kill others . . . who sin against or steal the king's property. . . ." And most significant, "it was his constant endeavour to prevent the Zulus killing one another." On other occasions, he had explained that executions were a deterrent to secession, and Dr. Mann, writing in 1873, said that the most extreme measures of relentless cruelty were adopted to arrest the wholesale exodus with which the king was threatened.[20] In another message to the Lieutenant-Governor of Natal, after a destructive fight had broken out between two Zulu regiments, Cetshwayo explained that warnings to his soldiers were not enough, and that "he cannot rule them without sometimes killing them, especially as they know that they can run to Natal."[21]

These statements need not be interpreted as the pronouncements of a violent despot, for they resemble the principles of the Swazi ruler, who was a constitutional monarch. When the Swazi king died, the queen regent unsuccessfully requested permission from the Crown to practice the custom of "killing off," for, as she put it, "it is a time for people to cry, and by killing people it would cause grief and lamentation." When the permission was refused, the principal induna, Jokova, observed that preventing the queen from killing her subjects was inconsistent with the declaration that the Crown respected the integrity of the Swazi as an independent state. He said: ". . . you talk about the independence of the Swazie Nation. We do not see that unless you allow us to rule in our own way there is any independence at all. Our way of ruling ourselves is to kill each other, and what shall the rule be if we are not allowed to kill?" [22]

The British efforts to exaggerate Cetshwayo's violence and to distort his behavior were documented in the Bishop of Natal's critique of the Parliamentary Blue Books, and by his daughter, Frances Colenso, in her two-volume work, *The Ruin of Zululand*. In the latter work, she observed:

> It had long been proved that Cetshwayo's previous rule had *not* been the cruel and tyrannical one which the apologists for our invasion of Zululand in 1879, had tried to make it out. The devotion of his people to him during the war, and, afterwards, when they suffered ill treatment, and even torture, rather than betray him to his pursuers, their persistent entreaties for his restoration and joy at his return were sufficient to establish this point, without the fact that there were only six cases in which a person had been killed by Cetshwayo's order during his whole reign, each of the six being a man convicted of some crime, or Undabuko's touching statement made in 1881, "there has never been known one like him among us Zulus before, so good, so kind, so merciful. Our fathers, who were old when we were born, all say so; and we, who have grown up with him . . . we have seen no one like him. For those three Kings who were brothers, our fathers, they killed people, great and small, and for a little thing, a mere nothing—it was their custom. But he is of an entirely different nature; he shrank from shedding blood.[23]

Among Europeans, the dispute over the king's violence ran to two extremes. The defenders of Cetshwayo wanted to understand the killings as a primitive custom of negligible consequence which had been exaggerated by colonial hawks. Haggard commented:

To admit that the Zulu king has the right to kill as many of his subjects as he chooses, so long as they will tolerate being killed, is one thing, but it is certainly surprising to find educated Europeans adopting a line of defence of these proceedings on his behalf that amounts to a virtual expression of approval, or at least of easy toleration.[24]

But the opposing party, led by Frere and his supporters, wanted to make Cetshwayo appear as sanguinary as Shaka, and they argued that unless the British intervened, the Zulu state would return to its previous condition of terroristic despotism and military aggression.

Frere's stereotype of a "bloodthirsty, barbarian despot" with absolute control of a "celibate man-slaying machine" bore scant resemblance to the complex realities of the Zulu state and took no cognizance of the significant changes that had taken place in the society since Shaka and Dingane. For one thing, the world view of the ruler had changed from that of a despot acting out fantasies of omnipotence to that of a king struggling with limitations. Under the rule of the first two despots, the boundaries of the state had never been seriously challenged, nor had their power been restrained by the authority of induna or councils, and the terror had effectively inhibited the roles of subordinate chiefs. Under Mpande, the situation and the political structure changed substantially. The state was forced to constrict under Boer and British pressure, and the external environment was no longer tractable but largely controlled by Europeans. Internally, councils developed and expanded their influence, induna assumed wider roles, and a new generation of territorial chiefs emerged, some having inherited their power. Of the three men who were great northern chiefs when Cetshwayo became king, two were the sons of men originally placed in control of the territories. In general, the territorial chiefs were living according to new expectations and were reshaping their relationships to the center, organizing local resources and people with growing independence and reducing the central power.

Some old ideals and expectations endured to make the people chafe at the constrictions of the state. Patience had worn out with the continuous Boer inroads on the boundaries. Moreover, it was difficult to maintain an energetic military organization when there were no wars to fight. Chiefs and headmen thought of themselves as providers, and men wanted to be blooded warriors, but there was not enough cattle to satisfy appetites and ideals and there were no enemies to kill. The plight was familiar and had been expressed long before—even under Dingane. As Leslie once heard an old man give the eloquent lament:

> But how can I give you meat, if I have no oxen? How can my young men and girls get milk, if I have no cows? We are at peace; we are becoming women. Surrounding nations will say that we are no longer warriors, but women: we fight no more, but dig the ground; our assegais have become hoes, our men have no hearts![25]

Recognizing the yearnings and discontents, Cetshwayo formulated a policy that ensured solidarity. As Gibson pointed out, the nation was well united and none of the chiefs opposed Cetshwayo.[26] At his installation, however, he could not be entirely certain of their loyalty, and before the ceremony he lived through some anxious moments when it appeared that conflict might break out between the followers of rival chiefs, or that the king might be seized and carried off by one of the northern factions. Dunn even wondered if Cetshwayo were indeed the favorite of his own party—the Usuthu. He was convinced that only the show of a "good stand of arms" by the Usuthu force intimidated the rival factions and prevented bloodshed.

At the beginning of his reign, then, even a superficial inspection of the conditions of his power made it clear that Cetshwayo was anything but a despot. But he drew universal enthusiasm with subsequent policy: resistance to the Boers and an increase of military strength. He asked the British for permission to wash his spears in the blood of the Swazi—a request that was denied. When Shepstone appeared in the Transvaal with a military escort, Cetshwayo massed his impi on the border, hoping to help his white "father" demolish the Boers. When, instead, Shepstone annexed the Republic, the king's feelings descended to a bitterness that increased until it found full expression in the 1879 war.

Officials in Natal said that violence was directed toward stopping the stream of refugees and enforcing rules such as the restrictions on marriage, and that it was felt by the Zulu living in Natal. A magistrate wrote, "It is really terrible that such horrible savagery could take place on our own borders. Our Kafirs will never civilize so long as the Zulu Chief remains unrestrained in his barbarous acts towards his people." [27] Cetshwayo's policy of reorganizing and tightening the state was intrepreted by Frere as a regression to Shaka's system.

Yet, the king was not only restrained but supported by chiefs, induna, and the Great Council. With regard to the great induna, Binns observes that they

> wielded enormous influence, governing their subjects with a rod of iron, and should they disagree with the policy of the King would quickly rise against him in open rebellion. It says much, therefore, for the wisdom of Cetshwayo that he was able to sense their feeling, to gain their confidence and carry forward a policy that won their almost unanimous support.[28]

John Dunn described Cetshwayo's respect for the consent of the induna in the disposition of cattle and land. With regard to cattle,

> he himself would not take any number from any particular kraal, without first consulting the Indunas in charge of such cattle, even if he wanted any for slaughter. In the same way he would not part with any of the land of the country without first consulting the leading men, and only, with their consent, could he do so.[29]

Cetshwayo's relationship to the induna when he was king had been carried over from the time he exercised power as heir apparent and de facto regent. When Dunn tried to get him to sell some land, the induna objected, saying that they feared it would encourage encroachment by the white men on Zulu territory. Dunn reported:

> Cetywayo turned to me, and said, "You hear? I can say no more—the Indunas have conquered me." Thus ended our land scheme, all this proving that the King was ruled by the voice of the Indunas in matters of cattle and land. Cetywayo though not King at the time, yet had all the power of a King.[30]

This aspect of the king's power is dramatically different from the despotic control of all property in the days of Shaka and Dingane. Moreover, the evidence indicates real limitation by the authority of the induna and not merely a device for the king to shift onto them the responsibility for his own decisions. In this vein, Samuelson, once an interpreter for Cetshwayo, wrote of the "autocratic disposition" of the king, but immediately qualified it with the following anecdote:

> One day he attempted to lord it over his induna Mkosana ka Zangqwana, who had been an Induna of King Mpande. This man was an imposing gentleman, with large round eyes, and when Cetywayo tried to sit on him, he sat on Cetywayo. He said: "King, I was once Induna of your father, and I claim the right to say what I have to without interference." Cetywayo then kept quiet and listened, and was reasonable thereafter.[31]

It is sometimes observed that even Shaka never proceeded with great matters of state without consulting his chief officers and making sure of the approval of his people. But his relation to them was different: Shaka's power was not bound by chiefs and people, whereas Cetshwayo really was limited by their interests and wishes. The two great induna were called "the two eyes, ears, or arms of the monarch." Yet, under Shaka, those eyes, ears, and arms were understood to be conditions of despotic power. Under Cetshwayo, they were indispensable for his functioning and not replaceable by substitutes—the organs without which he was nothing. They shared executive power. Shaka had acted upon his induna, appointing, disposing, and substituting more or less at his will. Cetshwayo interacted with his officers, within limits that were apparent to all.

The unity of the state and tensions among officers and between segments were controlled in part by the custom that required chiefs, subchiefs, and heads of kraals to reside at the king's court for a period that varied from weeks to months. The officials that were present constituted the *amaphakhati,* or the king's circle. When some left, others arrived, so that the king and his permanent staff were kept informed of needs and events in all districts, and the circle functioned as a continuous representative group. Serious tensions were kept in check by the threat of violence. The king had the power at any time to assemble a major force to put down conflict or to arrest a flight.

At the time of Frere's ultimatum, the king's violence—or the threat of it—the military organization, and the royal control of permission to marry were not isolated institutions, and in all probability Frere and Shepstone were not ignorant of their structural importance. Together those institutions helped to integrate the state. Frere's demands struck at all three. Within a month, his ultimatum required, the army must be disbanded, executions must be confined to legal procedures familiar to Europeans, and every young man must be free to marry as he wished.

The pretext for Frere's order was based on the alleged "laws" announced at Cetshwayo's coronation:

> These laws for the well-being of the Zulu people were the conditions required by the British Government in return for the countenance and support given by it to the new Zulu King. . . .
> They cannot be broken without compromising the dignity, the good faith, and the honour of the British Government. . . .
> The indiscriminate shedding of blood has not ceased, and . . . the killing of Zulu people has gone on as if no promise had ever been made, and no law ever proclaimed.[32]

The Zulu deputies responded to the ultimatum by declaring that no one was being put to death without cause and that persons accused of sorcery were being protected by new procedures and safeguarded as never before. To Frere's claim that the people were groaning under Cetshwayo's oppression, one of the induna said simply, "Have the Zulu complained?"

British forces entered Zululand, struggling with enormous problems of logistics and troop movement. The prowess and eventual defeat of the Zulu army drew mixed reactions throughout the world—admiration, surprise, regret. Cetshwayo was captured and imprisoned, and the Wolseley plan of multiple partition effectively destroyed the Zulu state while changing economic forces in the heart of South Africa altered the social conditions that had made the state possible. Zululand was divided by the Wolseley settlement into thirteen independent "principalities," ruled by men known to be hostile to the Usuthu—the royal party—or especially amenable to British control. Few of the chiefs at the head of each principality could pretend to legitimate Zulu authority, the settlement installing what today one would call "quisling" governments, establishing conditions for insoluble conflict within each principality and setting unit against unit. Even though the Zulu in large part preferred to be ruled by the British Crown, expecting it as a result of conquest, than by the "quisling" chiefs, the Crown was unwilling to take on the expense of administration and withdrew from direct control. Leaving little more than a British Resident as general supervisor of the settlement, the scheme required of the people no more than due submission to the chief of the territory in which they chose to live. To several chiefs, however, the meaning of due submission allowed exploitation, destruction, and confiscation. The system needed a supreme authority to control or at least co-ordinate the actions of the chiefs. Bloodshed was inevitable, and after conflict broke out, Haggard was moved to observe, "Cetshwayo's rule, bad as it was, was perhaps preferable to the reign of terror we have established under the name of a settlement." [33] The restoration of

Cetshwayo came to be viewed as a solution, supported even by the Boers, who were anxious to end the turbulence.

The Disraeli cabinet fell only seven months after the Zulu settlement was imposed. Cetshwayo went to England, appealed to the queen, mobilized British opinion in his favor, won a new settlement and a restoration for himself. Although Gladstone had condemned the Zulu War and had denounced Tory imperialism, his subsequent administration did nothing effective to reverse the trend in Zululand, although it restored its king. The restoration collapsed, for new social conditions and political realities, as well as the limitations of the new settlement, would not support a Zulu kingdom.

It was ten years after the first ceremony that Shepstone met Cetshwayo again to crown him King of the Zulu. The British imposed fifteen conditions on Cetshwayo's rule, which, Frances Colenso observed, deprived him of "all that constituted kingly authority" and left him without power over his people and no means of enforcing obedience.[34] From the beginning, Shepstone and the others who staged the restoration worked against the king's authority. Bishop Colenso's daughter assembled the evidence to show, "Every precaution, in fact, was taken to prevent a large and enthusiastic gathering of Zulus to greet the King on landing." According to Mnyamana, the restored prime minister and other witnesses, the people were told that " 'if any Zulu showed his face on the shore, the soldiers would speak to him with bullets.' " The threat was effective, and the absence of a crowd was interpreted by Shepstone in the official reports to mean "little enthusiasm created amongst the Zulus by the reappearance of their King." The European public was informed, "as the *Natal Mercury* telegraphed home to the *Times*, 'Zulus do not want, and never have wanted, the King.' " Subsequently, "every incident was made to tell in some way against Cetshwayo. Plainly 'the King could do no right,' and if by chance, he did a thing for blaming which no reason could be found, his *motive* was immediately called in question."[35]

The restoration scheme divided Zululand into three parts,

with Cetshwayo's kingdom bounded by a native reserve in the south and west and by Zibhebhu's chiefdom in the northwest. The preservation of the latter independent territory recognized and accepted the implacable hostility between Zibhebhu and the king, and the native reserve provided a refuge for those who were unable or unwilling to live under either. The kingdom was burdened with many serious problems: one was the deprivation of the chiefs who had been installed by the Wolseley settlement, although five of the thirteen were willing to welcome their former king. Formal restoration would have to be followed by the recovery of real authority, and how to cope with resistance without the regimental organization and without the old means of coercion—both were forbidden by the terms of the restoration—was to prove an insoluble problem. The situation was full of contradictions, and the limitations of the restoration scheme made royal power ineffective. The center would not hold.

Besides the political defects, there were social problems as well. The Wolseley settlement had succeeded in loosening the traditional ties of the young men to the Zulu state, strengthening, institutionalizing, and making a dominant trend of the impulses that had in the past attracted a minority of the Zulu people to European spheres such as Port Natal. The trend provided a ready source of workers for the labor-hungry Europeans who were transforming the economy of South Africa. The defeat of the Zulu impi in war and the new freedom to marry changed warriors into laborers, and as Shepstone put it succinctly, they had learned that "shillings were better weapons than assegais wherewith to capture property." Ten years before, the system would have contained the impulse or prevented the need to work for wages—even if the men had formed the desire to change their habits, it "would have been looked upon as revolutionary, and punishable, and would have been sternly repressed." Shepstone justified the change by saying that the anxieties of a Zulu warrior were scarcely offset by the reward, which was perhaps no more than the opportunity to steal a goat.[36] Eventually, Europeans would commonly express the view that the Zulu were better off as agricultural and industrial laborers under European economic control than as warriors in the old system.

Cetshwayo spoke to Shepstone about the limitations of his authority. Without the power to kill, he could not exact obedience, and he feared not only for the integrity of the kingdom but also for his own life. But there was no meeting of minds. Cetshwayo was talking about the minimal requirements for a king to rule; Shepstone professed to see the limitations as a bulwark against despotism. He repeated the conditions of the restoration. They prohibited the establishment of military kraals or of any military system. In addition, Shepstone wrote:

> I proceeded to say that they would all see, that although Cetshwayo would again be placed in the exalted seat that gave him the same right to rule over the people within the territory assigned to him, it was not the same seat that he had occupied before, it did not empower him to kill without full and fair trial, or upon the irresponsible declarations of witch doctors, or to interfere with girls marrying or being given in marriage, or to exact military service in any way. . . .[37]

Besides these internal limitations, the external conditions of the restoration were also designed to prevent the return of the old system, with Zibhebhu counterpoised on one boundary and a native reserve open to refugees on the other.

Shortly after the restoration, hostilities broke out on the border of Zibhebhu's territory. Probably because he wished to avoid subsequent British sanctions, Cetshwayo never revived the latent regimental organization, and it is probably also the case that he was not in control of the mobilization or of the action that followed. The king's forces, assembled in loose tribal divisions, outnumbered Zibhebhu's men about three to one, but the latter chose to make a stand on terrain exceptionally favorable to the smaller army. The king's men fought awkwardly and seemed unable to function without regimental organization and tactics. They were soon rendered helpless, routed, and crushed. According to the record, Zibhebhu lost some ten men, but the slaughter of the king's forces in headlong flight exceeded anything known to Zulu history. More men were lost in that engagement than in any battle Zulu warriors had ever fought.

As the conflict with Zibhebhu continued, the royal kraal was attacked and put to the torch. Cetshwayo fled to the native reserve and in February 1884 he was found dead. The British military surgeon, forbidden by the king's people to make an autopsy, recorded the cause of death as heart disease, but it was said that Cetshwayo had been poisoned.

Internecine conflict between sections of the Zulu people did not end, and in 1887 the Imperial Government formally annexed Zululand, which became part of Natal in 1897. The unity of the Zulu state was forever banished to the imagination. For the Zulu people, the reign of Shaka, despite its perpetual violence and ceaseless destruction, remained their time of greatest glory. As Thomas Mofolo declared in his fascinating novel, "Even today the Mazulu remember how that they were men once, in the time of Chaka, and how the tribes in fear and trembling came to them for protection. And when they think of their lost empire the tears pour down their cheeks and they say: 'Kingdoms wax and wane. Springs that once were mighty dry away.' " [38]

CHAPTER X

THE

STRUCTURE

OF TERRORISTIC

DESPOTISM

For Africans as well as Europeans, feelings about the past are hinged to attitudes in the present, and today some Zulu people think of the olden times as a golden age, whereas others rejoice in the end of "barbarism." [1] The former tend to lament the passage of despots and kings. Gluckman reports:

> During the time of the kings, the State bulked large in the people's lives. In council and on the battlefield only could high ambitions be satisfied. . . . To-day old men talking of the kings get excited and joyful, chanting the king's songs and dances, and all Zulu tend, in conversation, to slip into tales of the king's wars and affairs at his court. . . . The old Zulu generally shake their heads over the harsh rule of the past; and then speak of the glories under it. [2]

For those who have felt nostalgic for the lost grandeur, the despotic regimes contain the brightest moments of Zulu history, and the terror is merely a shadow in the imperial radiance. The feeling reflects the memory that the despots retained the consent of their people not only at the zeniths of power, when support was enthusiastic, but even in periods when the sense of glory was overshadowed by the feeling of oppression, and even

when the terror seemed to have expanded beyond all limits.
In Africa, as elsewhere, thoroughgoing despotism was rare,
for limited monarchy was the rule in traditional states, the king
exercising his power in a network of restraints imposed by custom, by councils of chiefs, and by public opinion. As Lord
Hailey observed in his survey of African systems:

> Above all the indigenous Chief has normally had no executive
> force at his disposal. It is only rarely (as for example in the
> case of some of the Zulu kings) that the Chief has been able
> to maintain a military organization of which he is the absolute
> head. Usually he has depended on the agreement of his tradi-
> tional councillors in arriving at a decision on matters affecting
> the tribe, and has only been able to implement it in action by
> availing himself of the goodwill of the heads of kin or other
> groups.[3]

In the evolution of the Zulu kingdom, after the era of despotism
had passed and the style of life had changed, the king as well as
his chiefs liked to be popular; they expected to discuss political
issues with their people and would not risk the disaffection of
councils or commoners. And if the voice of the people were
against anything the ruler was determined to carry out, it was
said, he had to give it up.[4] The king could no longer depend on
the use of systematic violence within a sealed border, and he
found milder methods to cope with resistance and to secure voluntary consent. Despite residues of despotic practice, the exercise of power shifted from violence to the principles of responsible leadership.

Still, one should not assume that the despotism had lacked
principles of its own. An inclination to identify violence with
disorder leads many observers to think of repetitive violence exclusively as a product of disorganization, and they do not stop
to inquire if it might be sometimes the principle of a certain
kind of order. In the despotic system, irresponsible leadership
as well as violence amounted to much more than the consequences of institutional breakdown—a common explanation.

They arose not from the haphazard wreckage of traditional controls but from the half-conscious logic of a social design that superseded the traditional chiefdoms.

Paradoxic as it may appear on the surface, the caprice of the despot, which included his use of violence, was a highly styled irrationality at the center of a unique social and political order. In Africa the despotic system was a collective experiment—unconscionably expensive with respect to the loss of human lives —and one might say it succeeded in special conditions, if one judged the results in its own terms. The role of the terroristic despot emerged as an adaptive social invention, both solving a crisis of social integration and avoiding the predicaments of a responsible monarch. Stabilized by cherished values and moved by a collective fantasy at least as powerful as any modern ideology, the social and emotional forces of terroristic despotism constructed a coherent style of political conduct and a unique political culture.

Before Dingiswayo, the hundreds of independent chiefdoms that occupied Zululand lived in comfortable autarky, tending herds and gardens, and as the Zulu say, "picking the eyes" of the country as a carrion bird might pick the eyes of a dead beast and go on to the next, leaving the carcass behind—that is, using only the most fertile land but not cultivating it intensively, and then moving on to the next location—and settling according to their needs. Relations among the autonomous political communities ranged from amity to raiding and war, but destruction was limited by the casual methods of warfare and by the freedom to move away. Serious tension within each chiefdom was usually resolved by fission, splitting and separating the followers of senior and junior brothers or of rival uncle and nephew, creating independent units that became new communities. Nguni chiefdoms at this time seem to have been constructed with the chief's lineage at the core, associated with more remote kinsmen and with other unrelated families as well. The structure depended on feelings of loyalty to the chief—frequently intense—and the sense of obligation to obey his commands, but powerful ones attracted followers, whereas inadequate chiefs lost them. Ultimately, the size of the community depended on the ability of the chief to fulfill his people's needs. An effective chief could rely on obedience and respect. He collected taxes and redistributed wealth, initiated important activities, organized labor for collective tasks, mobilized warriors for defense or attack, settled disputes, and maintained order. Yet, he had no permanent staff to execute his will, and his authority could not be described as a legitimate monopoly of force. In times of stress, his ability to hold the chiefdom together was limited to his own skill with threats, coercion, rewards, or diplomacy. Apart from political allegiance to the chief, cohesion was produced by social factors. A specialized political apparatus, which might be used to bind the community, did not exist.

The opportunities for the free movement of these fissiparous chiefdoms were probably reduced when the frontier guarded by Europeans in the Cape checked the southward course of Nguni migration. As the population increased rapidly and the crowding effect intensified, chiefdoms fought more, and the fighting was taken more seriously. Dingiswayo, with his new military organization, ended the conflict, drawing the independent chiefdoms within range under his suzerainty. Even if the story of his explicit intentions is not historically true, one must acknowledge it as an illuminating myth and recognize that the initial foundation of the state was established in opposition to the older tendency to conflict and fission.

Around Dingiswayo's time, clusters of chiefdoms began to form into larger polities throughout Southeastern Africa. The military innovations of Dingiswayo not only transformed the Mthethwa chiefdom into a primitive state but also created conditions in which the central political authority had greater control of the community and its environment than ever before. The disciplined regiments formed a large political staff to execute his will. Their increased strength and importance also contributed to social cohesion, since they cut across the lines of kinship, reducing the tendency to fission. Moreover, they provided a means for coercive political integration, deterring potential refugees, for fugitives could be cut down by pursuing impi. The relations of neighboring communities to the new state were defined by the ruler—they were to retain internal sovereignty, pay tribute, keep the peace, but lose external sovereignty.

The arrangement was not stable. Neighboring chiefs had pledged fealty to Dingiswayo, but there was no means to perpetuate the system, and any successor would probably have faced a new test of strength. Moreover, the conquered chiefs could not be expected to ignore the military innovations and the new political form. The success of the Mthethwa state was bound to stimulate imitations and a fresh contest for hegemony.

When Shaka succeeded Dingiswayo, he changed the structure. Merging the Mthethwa with his ancestral community, the Zulu chiefdom, and installing his own favorite as Chief of the Mthethwa, he created the Zulu kingdom. However, Shaka never intended to accept limitations appropriate to a traditional king, and he soon established himself as a despot, working to establish in the political imagination of the Zulu people the image of an omnipotent destroyer-provider.

The structure of a kingdom holds different forces in dynamic tension, balancing by some constitutional arrangement the powers of chiefs and king, the claims of kinship groups and the royal prerogative, the conciliar and the monarchical principles. The potential resistance of chiefs, clans, and councils reinforces a network of limited power. In contrast, the structure of a despotism reduces chiefs to subordinate officers and councils to instruments, isolates the bonds of kinship, and destroys or weakens corporate groups other than the state. In the Zulu system, persons, relations, and events with a potential for limitation impinged on the despot from time to time, but their effect was isolated, scattered, and systematically deprived of the conditions necessary to organize them as institutional restraints. In the First Fruits rites the despot was criticized, but the ceremony was limited to a single annual event. His mother and aunts exercised influence, but it never approached the restraining authority of roles such as that of the Swazi queen mother. Chiefs surrounded the despot in the royal kraal, but their conduct was limited to reverence and praise. He paid close attention to military councils, but devised techniques to keep them divided and to neutralize their political influence. In the holocaust after Nandi's death, a commoner told Shaka that the violence was excessive, and he responded by ending it, but there were few other occasions in which public opinion was even expressed. When members of the elite did remonstrate or quarrel with the despot, it was not to limit his power but to urge him to more fierce, predatory, or belligerent action. Thus, independent action of chiefs and induna was channeled in a single direction, never limiting or moderating the sovereign's power. Resistance emerged to public expression only when it held the ruler to the norms of the despotic system or reinforced the image of the great destroyer-provider.

Shaka also changed the state's relationship to former vassal chiefdoms as well as other communities. Those that did not voluntarily become members of the Zulu state were defined as enemies and destroyed, and their cattle were seized; any men who survived were incorporated into the impi. All the warriors were organized in a single military establishment, led by officers appointed by the despot, and the new solidarity of regiments replaced the old solidarity of clan and lineage. Even the king's women were bound in regimental organizations. The new community was to be a vast predatory organism directed by a single will. In it there was no place for conventional resistance, opposition, or even different identities.

Previously, violence had been restricted to fights, feuds, raids, and warfare, separating people and maintaining distance between groups tightly integrated by kinship relations. Against outsiders, violence might be supported and find a social basis for expression, but every primitive community—bands, tribes, and chiefdoms—lived by norms that prohibited or limited violence within it. As Sahlins has described the rules of tribal societies:

> The closer the relationship the greater the restraint on belligerence and violence, and the more distant, the less the restraint. . . . Violence is inhibited centripetally, among contiguous, closely related groups, but is directed centrifugally against distant groups and neighboring peoples.[5]

Hierarchic communities provide more opportunity for internal violence than egalitarian tribes.[6] Where lineages are ranked, for example, nobles may claim a right of violence against commoners who offend them, and, of course, a chief may exercise the power of life and death over people who violate norms, or, under certain conditions, he may even be able to mobilize a force of men to eliminate opponents. Nevertheless, such instances are not usually frequent, and the limitations on violence found in tribal societies *mutatis mutandis* still apply to chiefdoms as well.

Since the rules that limit violence are confined to the boundaries of the political community, tribal warfare has the capacity for terrorism, with violence turned outward. In the case of wars between tribes, E. R. Service has observed:

> Tribal warfare by its nature is inconclusive. Ambush and hit-and-run raids are the tactics rather than all-out campaigns, which cannot of course be economically sustained by a tribal economy and its weak organization. . . . Continual threat, sniping, and terrorization which will discourage and harass the enemy is the typical form of action. In fact, terrorization, or psychological warfare, seems to be at its highest development in tribal society. Headhunting, cannibalism, torture of prisoners, rape, massacre, and other forms of atrocious nerve-warfare are probably more effective means to the end at the tribal level than is true combat.[7]

In East Africa, Southall observed that the fighting of chiefdoms was more destructive than the warfare of chiefless societies:

> the improved political organisation resulting from chiefship led, in a sense, to more widespread violence, and even to more severe forms since the chiefless communities do not seem to have burned and plundered one another in their fighting, as Alur chiefs did when enforcing discipline among clans which failed to keep the peace. . . . Increase in the scale and efficiency of political organisation seems always to have carried with it the seeds of more destructive warfare. . . .[8]

In warfare, chiefdoms had the power not only to drive weaker groups away from territory they invaded, but also to defeat them and, up to the limit of its resources and capacity for redistribution, to incorporate the survivors. Nevertheless, in Zululand before Dingiswayo, warfare was limited to hit-and-run raids and often to inconclusive battles. Dingiswayo, limited by his attitudes as well as his resources, left the conquered chiefdoms alone as soon as they had accepted his suzerainty. Under Shaka, the Zulu army fought decisive engagements, and the potential for terrorism in primitive warfare—observed even on the tribal level—was developed and refined by Shaka, raised to a new level of organization, and used in wars of extermination. With the augmented resources of a primitive state, Shaka reversed Dingiswayo's policy, extended military terrorism, and fought total wars, still seizing cattle but destroying communities and incorporating large bodies of men. Furthermore, under Shaka and Dingane violence was directed not only against the external enemy but also against the enemy within—potential rebels and sorcerers. Shaka created an entirely new structure by directing the terror inward, using it to shape a culture of despotism with its associated political relations and social order.

The productive unit of traditional Nguni society was the kraal, a kind of household economy in the Aristotelian sense, in which the men tended cattle and the women raised crops. Wealth was measured in cattle, which served as a medium of exchange, as ritual animals, and as the source of meat and milk curds, which together with corn made up the diet. The highest value was set on cattle, and their husbandry absorbed the energies of the male population. The kraal economy supported a chief, who drained off a comfortable surplus by levying taxes, confiscating property, collecting legal fines, and receiving presents, but who also redistributed much of the surplus by giving grants of meat and beer, by holding feasts, and by lending and giving away animals. Nevertheless, an impressive amount of the surplus remained undistributed, constituting the chief's wealth, bracing his political power, and symbolically helping to define his position in the community. The surplus was also increased occasionally by cattle seized in raids, which also expanded the herds of his favorites.

In Shaka's day the economy was transformed by the enormous surplus seized by the impi. There was no point in distinguishing any longer between the royal herds and the property of individuals, for in principle the despot owned all property—others merely held cattle in precarious possession. Plunder was the major source of wealth. In the area controlled by Shaka, the policy of destroying or routing communities decreased the population, accumulated cattle, and added more men to the machinery of destruction—to seize more cattle, to incorporate more warriors, and to destroy more communities. Since no organized force in Shaka's time would resist the impi, the functional and territorial boundaries of the state depended on the physical limitations of the army's striking range. The Zulu state grew as an enormous military parasite, living off the wreckage of destroyed and plundered communities. Stresses in the system tended to emerge in periods of inaction, and when there were no battles to fight, Shaka complained that the army was devouring him.

The great wealth seized in Shaka's devastations was used for two major purposes. It maintained the standing army and it supported the royal kraal with its several branches and the despot's staff. Under the old system, the young, unmarried warriors, who had executed the chief's commands, had foraged for themselves and, except for a few of the chief's oxen slaughtered each week, were not maintained by the state. Under Shaka and Dingane the great surplus of captured wealth, providing meat and milk for the warriors as well as hides for shields, was also a major instrument in the despot's control of honors and rewards. Moreover, regimental colors were designed as a matching pattern of headdress, shields, and distinctive cattle markings. Large numbers of the cattle were consigned as regimental treasuries, and undoubtedly the competition among military units was stimulated by the desire of each to increase its herd.

In addition to supporting the regiments, the enormous herds served to shape the culture of the royal kraal and to define symbolically the nature of the despot and of the state. The idea of a chief and his chiefdom conveys a ruler and system limited by resources and by political restrictions. The culture of despotism, in contrast, conveys an impression of limitless power and infinite wealth. Shaka insisted that his men and his wealth were beyond computation. When the royal herds and the impi were paraded before Fynn, the Englishman was challenged to count them. A large drove passed in review for the test, and Fynn came up with a specific number in the thousands. He was greeted by a roar of laughter. The usual explanation for the response is that the Zulu were not familiar with the decimal system of counting and did not understand how he could arrive at the sum, but it is also clear from the context that the laughter greeted his attempt to state Shaka's wealth in finite terms. The property of the despot, which included the people as well as the cattle, was always officially described as limitless: numerous as the stars in the sky or the blades of grass on a hill or the grasshoppers in a field. The idiom of the despotic culture reiterated ideas of infinite resource, omnipotence, omniscience, and irresistibility. These attributes were always in the air, chanted by the people and perpetually intoned by specialists whose office was to sing the praises of the despot.

The historical passage from limited chief to paramount chief and finally to absolute despot produced an intellectual revolution with marked changes in Nguni ideas of power and society. The sources of the conscious ideas may in all probability be traced to unconscious fantasies about domination and submission, which may be universal and which may be exaggerated by a pattern of socialization that makes the weight of authority a prominent force in childhood experience. In Nguni culture, of course, the significance of fathers and senior men in the practice of child rearing is crucial. But that culture includes the Swazi people too, and the Swazi state avoided despotism. What is important is not the existence of fantasies about power, for they are probably universal, but the way they are cherished, elicited, acted out collectively, shaped by cultural forces, and given social expression. There is no need here to speculate about the psychic origins of despotic ideas, but it is probably more useful to suggest their source in human fantasy than to postulate, as Murdock does, their historic diffusion from a geographical focus in the Sudan with features borrowed from Pharaonic Egypt. Rather than imagine "a mental blueprint of a despotic political structure, transmitted from generation to generation as a part of traditional verbal culture," one might turn to universal emotional forces which in appropriate conditions are encouraged, expressed, and reinforced.[9]

Regardless of its source, the reality of a "mental blueprint of a despotic political structure" inferred by Murdock cannot be denied. In this blueprint, to describe the official idea of the despot's power as "absolute" is probably an understatement, for his rule aspired to infinity in all respects. The collective fantasy expressed by the blueprint—even though practice often wandered far from principle—was of an omnipotent, omniscient being, irresistible and terrible, whose awful majesty dominated the entire system, leaving no act or intention beyond control. Religious powers to control the divine ancestors and the unseen world accompanied his imagined domination of the physical world. His name was used only as a sacred oath or to recite a litany of praises, deeds, and epithets. His will initiated and co-ordinated everything, and violent acts merely punctuated his power and reminded the subjects of his grandeur. As Fynn put it, "daily examples of his might and ferocity were necessary to keep them in a state of awe."

The vulnerability of such an inflated image and the tension between private belief and public definitions encouraged continual violence. Trivial acts threatening the image—sneezing, belching, making him laugh—drew a murderous response. Shaka's greatest anxiety was to find medicines that would keep his hair from turning gray, for the signs of aging and the notions of weakness associated with them were not consistent with the official image. Certain symbolic acts were prohibited to anyone but the despot. Washing one's body on the back of a dead elephant was a forbidden act, Andrew Smith explained: "for a subject to practice it is esteemed one of the most heinous crimes he can commit; its being calculated to confer on him that strength which may enable him effectively to resist his sovereign." [10] Dingane was acutely sensitive to any sign of disrespect and reacted violently to imagined slights. Atrocities and apparently wanton destruction symbolically contributed to the picture of omnipotence, irresistibility, and arbitrary decision.

As the despot conveyed the impression of irresistible power, everyone else in the royal kraal, which was the symbolic and administrative center of the state, worked to create an atmosphere of total submission. Their ritual, obsequious approach to the despot, groveling in the dust before him, perpetual adulation, consent and, at his order, even participation, in their own destruction, and all the rites and expectations previously described were parts of the same grand performance. The royal kraal staged dramatically the solitary theme of the state, exhibiting countless scenes of the great destroyer-provider and the people, who were his instruments and his "dogs." The names of the royal kraals advertised the performance: Shaka's "Place of Great Slaughter," Mpande's "Place of the Irresistible One," Dingane's "Place Surrounded by Elephants." In a little book on Zululand, Farrer observed that "the name of Dingan's kraal signified 'the rumbling sound of the elephant.' Such names are thought to inspire a salutary terror." [11]

In the principal royal kraal, at the center of the state, both terror and glory were found at their highest pitch. Grandeur, wealth, provisions, the participation in greatness, and pride of state bound the people to the center. The terror did not stimulate flight, but instead inhibited resistance. Flight took place not at the center but at the periphery, where the terror was least.

Keen observers remarked how the personality of the despot affected the behavior of his kraal. Fynn observed that "the personal dispositions of the kings themselves are reflected in the very styles in which their subjects are wont to dance and sing." [12] However, this sensitivity to the ruler's disposition was part of a larger configuration, interlinked with the discipline of the regiments and the grandiose fantasies of the principal royal kraal. The underlying fiction—one is tempted to say, the single principle that makes the system intelligible—was that the state was like a single body: the body of the despot, moved by his feelings, fluctuating according to his emotional vicissitudes, regulated by his will. This principle, acted out by the Zulu but not formulated in so many words, was not merely a descriptive analogy or an organismic metaphor, but a mode of orientation and a mainspring, giving the state its structure and its destiny. Moreover, it had the force of an implicit *Grundnorm*, a touchstone of legitimacy. Therefore, it is not enough to say that the state was "like" the ruler's body, but rather that according to the rules that may be inferred from the phenomena of collective life, the Zulu felt that the state *ought* to be the body of the despot—who was imagined as the great destroyer-provider—responding to his emotions and controlled by his will. This notion of the ruler and of the nature of his power was a collective idea, a social pattern of expectations to which the despot was bound and to which he was returned when he strayed from its demands. Thus violence and caprice were not simply his idiosyncratic deviations from legitimate rule, but essential elements in the living "constitution."

This polity is so directly opposed to Western ideas of the political process that its mechanism has eluded perception and understanding. Irrationality and arbitrary decision are generally considered as departures from political order, and usually analysts of despotic regimes want to search for structures that hold the system together *despite* the ruler's caprice. According to familiar conventions of political thought, it is difficult to conceive of a regime that is integrated *by* the ruler's arbitrary behavior, for we tend to exclude violence and irrationality as organizing principles. From Plato to Hegel, many Western theorists have wanted to exclude irrationality from the concept of the political and to identify the political process with reason, peace, and universality. In this way of thinking, the political process is regarded as a means of social rationalization that begins with conflicting, selfish, irrational impulses (*chez* Hobbes and others) and orders them, or begins with selfish particular interests and organizes them in larger, more universal structures (*chez* Hegel and others). The bias, useful as it may be for normative theory, ignores the possibility that an alternative order, undesirable as it may be to us, can be created by a process that is committed to irrationality, violence, and particularity. According to this "constitution," no action is legitimate unless it is expressed as a decision or an impulse of the despot.

Western ideas of constitutionalism emphasize restraint, limitation of power, and juridical defense. Political communities voluntarily giving up their sovereignty to constitute a larger state accept their new limitations not only because they will receive material advantages but also because they agree with the rules and values of the larger community. According to familiar ideals, the formal relations between leaders, subordinate leaders, and citizens are expected to follow accepted procedures that are rational, impartial, universal, predictable, and consistent with the rule of law. In contrast, to illustrate the rules and values of an ideal despotic "constitution," one might, half seriously, imagine the following preamble:

"We, the people of the Despot, including the greater and lesser officers chosen by him and the formerly sovereign chiefs who have submitted to his will, rejoicing in the terrible majesty and radiant grandeur of the Master who has thrown his shield over us, in order to form a more perfect union, to conquer all peoples who do not submit, and to gather the wealth of the land which is his by right and by power, do pledge our lives, our honor, our children, and our efforts to magnify his glory, to immolate our wills in his service, to render ourselves, all people, and all things to dust at his command."

In contrast to the Western liberal idea that the state functions as a rational system of co-operating agents and agencies, the despotic constitution works on the theory that all conduct should emanate from a single will. The despot is the physical symbol of the unity of the state, the rules prescribe that the system ought to work as if it were an organism moved by his command, and the people orient their conduct to anticipate, to register, and to respond to the nuances of his moods and decisions.

Even within the principal royal kraal the illusions of despotic omnipotence and popular submission were contradicted by physical and human limitations, but continual violence and the enchantment of the grand performance drew attention away from the discrepancies between fiction and reality. The great kraal and secondary royal kraals—to which the despot moved his retinue from time to time—served as models of the polity, but the degree of control, so to speak, remained inversely proportional to the distance from the center. In small communities, headmen were known to execute their own people for violations of state rules because they feared Shaka's wrath if they failed to do so. The despot's network of spies and informers and the fear of being "eaten up" by a detachment of impi on police duty maintained control over widely scattered kraals. The weakness in the system was to be found in potential concentrations of power and in the potential independence of former chiefdoms formally incorporated in the system but less perfectly integrated than the conquered peoples who had been absorbed at the center.

If Shaka had expanded his domain by making the defeated communities territorial chiefdoms and simply subordinating the chiefs, the structural weakness would have been much greater. But his changes were more thoroughgoing. He transformed the corporate structure of the territorial units. Having changed from a country of herders and peasants to a primitive garrison state, Zululand was subdivided into command areas, in which military induna shared authority with territorial chiefs, who were often royal kinsmen. The *amakhanda*, or military kraals, served as headquarters of the regiments as well as administrative centers. The queen mother or royal uncle, brother, or aunt represented the personal interests of the despot and, of course, extended his "eyes and ears." The induna in charge of administrative and military operations were commoners who owed their appointments and their futures exclusively to the despot, without independent access to power, wealth, or honor. The crosscutting arrangement of territorial and military jurisdictions reduced the power of all local chiefs and officers. Each territorial chief lacked exclusive authority over all the people in his area because all the warriors, regardless of their original homes or residences, came under the jurisdiction of military kraals. Most of these establishments were located near the principal royal kraal, and at the center the despot moved in an area that was functionally and physically different from any ordinary territorial subdivision. Only rarely were military command and territorial authority vested in the same chief. After conquest, if the men of a community were not scattered and redistributed in different age regiments but left in a single geographical area, Shaka's practice was to place them under the authority of an *ikhanda,* new or old. Two known exceptions to the policy proved the political sagacity of the rule, for they both gave rise to instances of rebellion, secession, and defiance that challenged the fiction of omnipotent despotism.

Early in the history of the Zulu state, Mzilikazi, one Chief of the Kumalo, a people as large as the original Zulu chiefdom, declared his allegiance to Shaka, and his community was left politically intact, Mzilikazi eventually joining Shaka's general staff as a trusted induna. Poised between the large, fierce Ndwandwe chiefdom and the ruthless Zulu state, the Kumalo had been playing a deceptive but precarious game to preserve independence. One section of the Kumalo, under their chief, Donda, had surrendered to Dingiswayo but had also tried to maintain good relations with Zwide. However, he gave Shaka crucial intelligence about Ndwandwe operations, perhaps saving him from a trap and from Dingiswayo's fate, for which Zwide retaliated with a massacre, killing the chief and his heir. The Ndwandwe then attacked another section of the Kumalo, ruled by Mashobane, who was also slaughtered. Mashobane's son, Mzilikazi, escaped destruction and became a favorite of Zwide, from whom he later defected to become a favorite of Shaka. Finally, around 1822, Mzilikazi defied Shaka, and with his Kumalo subjects and fragments of other chiefdoms, gathered the nucleus of a state that began a devastating journey through the highveld, ending as the Matebele (Ndebele) nation in Rhodesia.

The other exception, the Qwabe, which was the largest chiefdom to remain in Zululand—larger than the original Mthethwa-Zulu nucleus of the state—eventually produced the rebellion that redefined the political structure of Dingane's regime. The chief, Pakatwayo, died when the Zulu defeated the Qwabe, but Shaka left the issue of succession to the chiefly lineage, and according to Bryant, the new chief, Nqetho, was "the most important personage among the Qwabe people." Bryant also claimed that the removal of Pakatwayo, the conquest of the

Qwabe, and the "incorporation" of Pakatwayo's people into the Zulu nation "were the most significant of Shaka's positive triumphs to date." [13] Yet, the incorporation proved to be imperfect, for after Shaka's death, Nqetho disclaimed allegiance to Dingane and removed his Qwabe from Zululand altogether. Thus, no independent corporate structure or tribal concentration remained in Zululand. Beyond effective striking range of the impi, new states formed, several of them composite kingdoms swollen by refugees of the *Mfekane*—the dislocations wrought by Shaka and the devastations of the uprooted peoples. Moshesh, founder of the Basuto nation in the west, Sobhuza, King of the Swazi in the north, and Faku, Chief of the amaMpondo in the south, all acknowledged Shaka's hegemony, offered tribute, and tactfully avoided conflict with the Zulu. Within the Zulu state, the structure of controls was uneven, with the ideal despotism of the royal kraal at the center and less perfect integration at the periphery. Even near the center, observers noted tension and latent conflict which was inhibited by the terror and not expressed. Intense nationalism lived side by side with passive but smoldering resignation to conquest. A statement in the *Cape Records* went so far as to claim that the community governed by the despot was "composed partly by Zulus and partly of the remains of tribes that have been vanquished, all of which are filled with an inveterate hatred to the conquerors, and are only at present restrained from showing it by the severity which is extended to any who may be bold enough even to insinuate their dislike." [14] Fynn explained the stresses that appeared under Dingane: "The Zulu nation is composed of a multitude of tribes. These were combined by Shaka into a single nation, a nation which he alone had the ability to control. Under Dingane a number of the tribes became insubordinate, he being regarded by the tribes that had been annexed as having no claim on their allegiance." [15] The terror, therefore, worked to inhibit the potential resistance that endured in fragments of tribal identities. Chiefs in charge of territorial units were required to attend the despot in the royal kraal for periods of time and to experience the terror. The periods of attendance reminded them that their fate as agents of the despot, receiving plunder and participating in glory, was preferable to that of a fugitive chief struggling for independence. The motivation to resist was destroyed by the emotional impact of the violence. At the same time, the terror provided for chiefs and people a conscious rationalization and justification for nonresistance, for the mystique of the despot's grandeur and irresistibility supported the idea that before such power human opposition could not stand.

The destruction and terrorization of the chiefs have been documented in the previous chapters, but it is epitomized in an episode drawn from the regime of Dingane. Gibson gleaned the particulars of the incident from men who had heard of it from their fathers, but he claimed that "of its authenticity there is no doubt." As Gibson wrote:

> It is probable that some difficulty was felt in exercising sufficient control over the different sections of the people and the chiefs who immediately ruled them. The method resolved upon for dealing with the situation, whatever it may have been, was the removal of the chiefs. To this end a great feast was appointed, and a general invitation extended to these. There was a great assemblage at Umgungundhlovu, and a vast concourse of people. Many cattle were slaughtered, and other provisions supplied, and the numerous groups which dotted the precincts of the kraal gave themselves over unsuspectingly to enjoyment. In the meantime, certain regiments had been disposed so as to surround the kraal and this assembly, and emissaries were appointed, furnished with a list of the doomed. These then traversed the grounds, accompanied by bands of executioners to whom they pointed out the victims as they were found. Chief after chief fell under their clubs. No one knew who might be pointed out next, and great was the consternation amongst the living as the day advanced. Many men of high distinction died that day, and those who found themselves alive at its close were filled with thankfulness.[16]

The terror worked not only against the expression of residual independence on the part of tribal groups and fragments of chiefdoms, but also against forces in the corporate structure that moved toward new kinds of autonomy. Over the course of time, induna and favorites originally appointed by the despot might have consolidated their personal authority and the power of their families. As the terror abated, they did. Although inhibited by Shaka and Dingane, this tendency was not checked by Mpande, so that at the end of his reign, when his son, Cetshwayo, succeeded to the throne, as Binns writes, the power of many of the great induna was similar to that of the feudal barons in early English history.[17] The same tendency toward decentralization and feudalization may also be observed in the evolution of the Matebele (Ndebele), originally established along the lines of Zulu military despotism. Omer-Cooper points out:

> The Ndebele . . . arose out of a secession of part of the army [of the Zulu]. For them state and army were identical and the military towns were the divisions of the whole people. Hence the tendency for the regiments to take on a permanent hereditary character and lose their original nature as age groupings to become territorial administrative divisions with the *indunas* coming to fulfil the role of territorial chiefs in the pre-*Mfecane* tribal system.[18]

Still, to inhibit the resistance of particular chiefs and to prevent a general reversion to a segmental structure with fissiparous trends were not the only functions of the terror. It also served to retain the despotic form, working against tendencies of political change. On the one hand, the terror kept the system from breaking up or decentralizing. On the other hand, preserving at the center the image of the great destroyer-provider, it prevented an evolution into a kingdom.

CHAPTER XI

DESPOTISM

WITHOUT

TERROR

. . . the craving for universal unity is the
third and last anguish of men.

—Fyodor Dostoyevsky,
The Brothers Karamazov.

ABSOLUTE POWER lends itself to fantasy and myth—inspired in
men who try to explain it as well as those who experience its
impact. It also inspires theoretical misconceptions that should
be corrected if we are to understand the work of terror in despotic states.

One common error about despotism is to take it for granted
that only the sovereign has a vital interest in preserving his
arbitrary power and that everyone else in the state is a passive
instrument. It is one of the screening illusions projected by the
despotic formula and acted out in the drama of the royal kraal.
It is also rooted in a tradition of Western social thought and
carries implications that I shall try to reveal. The following
chapter will deal with the actual relationships and the social
choice behind the illusion.

Another misapprehension, propagated by Montesquieu
among others, identifies despotism with the principle of terror.
It confuses one alternative method with a whole political system. To define an entire genus—despotism—by the character-

istics of one species—terroristic despotism—is essentially a fallacy of composition. If we comprehend that it is possible to have despotism without terror, then we see despotism emerge as a political structure like others, which may or may not include the method of terror. Consequently, terror may be understood as a particulate process—that is, as a mechanism not identified with any single political order.

The origin of the European idea of despotism may be found in Plato's and Aristotle's concepts of the master-slave relation and their belief that despotic systems were merely extensions of that relationship. Montesquieu took the idea a step further and described the workings of despotic constitutions, but he retained the notion that only the despot was active and free. The natural self-interest of secondary powers, he implied, could move only in one direction—toward *limiting* the power of the despot, thereby transforming the system into a monarchy. According to that way of thinking, if the system were to remain despotic, the only logical function for officers of the despot was in the role of passive agents. In the line of thought that extends from Montesquieu to Tocqueville and Taine to the latter-day pluralists, "despotism" stands for the absence of mediation between a single, arbitrary center of power and an inert, atomized population.

Hegel expressed similar ideas about despotism. That form of government was either degenerate monarchy, ruled by the unmediated caprice of the sovereign, or else—in its Oriental form —the first stage of political evolution. With the government of ancient China, Hegel believed, history began. In the Oriental state only the despot was free, but that freedom was simply caprice—either ferocity or mildness through an accident of nature—and not based on a rational principle. The ruler was the "substance" of the state, and his subjects merely the "accidents." Hegel refused to recognize despotic systems as constitutions, for he believed that a "constitution" mediated among and integrated parts that had a certain degree of independence. Furthermore, in Asiatic despotism, Hegel thought, the individual had no subjectivity or inner life, and he experienced the act of obedience not as a personal union with a community of which he was a part, but as a response to an external alien power.

Marx, in his theory of despotism, differed from predecessors because he emphasized the economic features and because he perceived the despotic state as one mode of community organization in primitive conditions. He paid less attention to the behavior of the despot and more to the way the despotic organization fulfilled collective needs. In any primitive society, co-operative relationships organized in communal form were the precondition for using the soil and its products. Only through the community could men appropriate, own, possess, or reproduce the material conditions of life. Nevertheless, the community might be organized according to either a more democratic or a more despotic form. Historically, these forms corresponded to what Marx conceived as the Germanic model, in which independent households that were complete centers of production associated in loose, tribal federations, or the model of highly integrated, Oriental despotism. Each alternative was not a free option but a system determined by climate, geography, and other impersonal forces. In the Germanic type, the community had its "real being" in the assemblies, based on the relations among individual landowners. Later, in the classical world, the community would be objectified in the physical presence of the city. In the Asiatic form, which Marx considered the most durable and stable, the entire community was objectified as a person—yet, the despot was but the *manifest* expression of a deeper communal solidarity. In *appearance*, Oriental despotism projected the ruler as the all-embracing unity that stood above all productive social relations, and it presented him as the sole owner of everything. In the political illusion created by the system, the representative of the higher unity appeared to mediate between men and the natural conditions of labor and to dispense as a grant the wealth that men received or possessed. On the surface, Oriental despotism appeared to negate property, but the foundation of the system was common or tribal property. The surplus product went to the community as a whole, rendered as tribute to the despot and as collective labor for the glory of the community. Since the individual never became an owner but only a possessor, he was to all intents and purposes the property, or even the slave, not of a single person, but of the entity that embodied the unity of the social order.[1] Marx's theory of despotism, therefore, contradicted that of Montesquieu. For Montesquieu and his followers, the despot atomized society and destroyed the solidarity of all relationships except for the bond between ruler and subjects. For Marx, despotism was a manifest expression of a deeper communal solidarity.

It is not possible to go into Karl Wittfogel's dispute with Marx's statements—which were really never very extensive—about Oriental despotism, except to observe one important difference between the two approaches. According to Wittfogel, "hydraulic societies" burdened by the technical necessities of regulating a crucial supply of water, developed political systems in which the head of the state dominated social life through a managerial elite and a bureaucratic apparatus. Wittfogel sees a monolithic absolutism in which an autocrat manipulated officials and held the population in "total submission" and "total loneliness" through "total terror." He does not examine the relation between despot and staff but simply repeats the old ideas of the nature of that bond. Despotic states had no "appropriate mechanics of outside control and internal balance," and they lacked any "lawful means of resisting the government." No lesser offices or "balanced oligarchy" shared the power, and Wittfogel does not explore the question of how and why the officials co-operated with the despot. There is no point in asking the same question about the people, since we may assume that in his view they were totally paralyzed by the terror. The officials, it appears, were entirely victims of manipulation, for Wittfogel does not detect any voluntary consent in their co-operation. He claims that "under absolutist conditions the holder of the strongest position, benefitting from the cumulative tendency of unchecked power, tends to expand his authority through alliances, maneuvers, and ruthless schemes until, having conquered all other centers of supreme decision, he alone prevails." That tells us little about the process, for he includes absolutism in the initial conditions: the proposition merely asserts that under "absolutist conditions," the ruler made himself absolute. Even though decisions might for a time have been made by persons below the ruler, the absolutism was not reduced, for the influence of the staff differed "qualitatively from the institutional checks of balanced power," and the ruler was under "no compulsion" to accept the suggestions of administrators and councillors. Finally, "despite significant bureaucratic attempts to subordinate the absolute sovereign to the control of his officialdom, the ruler could always *rule*, if he was determined to do so. The great monarchs of the Oriental world were almost without exception 'self-rulers'—autocrats." [2]

Wittfogel's theory is based on a concept that does not differ significantly from the old idea of the master-slave system, and that notion seems to be confirmed by the fantasies acted out in the royal kraal of a despotic state. But the concept of despotism suggested by Marx leaves open the precise relationship between despot and subjects and implies that the manifest behavior in despotic regimes was but a surface representation prescribed by a political formula. If the community solidarity *appeared* in the form of a solitary overlord with absolute power, then it must have been the political work of the entire community, cooperating in a specific manner to produce the illusion.

In previous chapters, we have explored the social functions or the objective consequences of a terroristic despotism, noting how the violence eliminated resistances, prevented fission and disintegration, and inhibited limitations on the central power. Until now, we have paid little attention to the motives of those who chose to co-operate with the regime.

In a limited monarchy, the close associates of the king—usually his nearest kin and highest officials—exercised some powers over the monarch. By their conditional obedience and conditional resistance, they held him to the working consensus that defined the ways in which his power should be exercised. The system of co-operation was stabilized by the smooth interaction of legitimate resistances and institutionalized counter-resistance. In a chiefdom governed by a secret association, the collegial solidarity and conditional rivalry of the peers kept each official—both in the public realm and in the invisible order—to the traditional rules. In a terroristic despotism, the team of men in the directorate likewise held the sovereign to the working consensus. The terror eliminated whatever challenged, opposed, or limited the absolute power of the sovereign —that is, all the actions that are commonly recognized as resistance. But the terror did not remove one special kind of conditional resistance from the directorate—indeed, one that helped to stabilize the system. The directorate continued to exert pressure on the ruler when he showed signs of giving up despotic power—when he deviated from the expected policy of a terroristic ruler, diminished his own authority, permitted limitations on central power, or spoiled the image of the omnipotent destroyer-provider. Since it does not move toward limited monarchy but away from it, this form of resistance—the only kind possible in a terroristic despotism—has not been detected by writers in the "pluralist" tradition.

The stock definition of an absolute ruler denies the existence of any regular constraints on him; all restrictions are perceived as forces that would temper his rule. As Sidgwick put it in standard form, "What is meant by calling him 'absolute' is that there is no established constitutional authority—no human authority that his subjects habitually obey as much as they obey him—which can legitimately resist him or call him to account." [3] It assumes that the only constraints officials cared to place on a despot would make his power less. The unimpeded natural action of secondary powers presumably would limit the central power. Fallers writes, "The arbitrary authority of despots is checked, not by ideology alone, but by groups of persons (perhaps acting in the name of ideology) who, by pursuing their common interests, establish patterns of rights and obligations which diffuse and restrict power." [4] In conventional Western theories of despotism, there is no hint that the self-interest of officials might be to protect the ruler's absolute power and not to diminish it. Therefore, when the officials in a despotism showed no sign of wanting to curtail the ruler, their behavior is usually assumed to spring from forced passivity rather than from commitment and voluntary co-operation. But self-interest is always shaped by the options and by points of view. In terroristic despotism, groups of persons pursuing their common interests and supported by ideology worked to uphold the absolute, unchecked power of the sovereign. The secondary powers in such a state *wanted* the ruler to be omnipotent— sometimes against the will of the despot himself.

The error of the "pluralist" stereotype—and I use the label here not as a precise classification, but as a shorthand expression to cover a number of different approaches that have the fallacy in common—is to assume that the mere presence of secondary powers implies that they would "naturally" exercise their authority to limit the central power. But that natural inclination is not a universal political tendency. Force produced a great deal of the subordination in a despotic state and terror inhibited the familiar resistances, but it is also true that chiefs and ministers by consent gave up their capacity to share, filter, check, and mediate the ruler's power. Still, they did "call him to account," only using their controls to reinforce his absolutism, or even to "force" him to remain a despot.

Some despots, then, were restrained from becoming limited monarchs. Others, however, remained despots, but exercised absolute power without depending on violence. For examples of this type, we may consider nineteenth-century Buganda in East Africa, which was making a transition away from violent rule, and Jimma Abba Jifar in Ethiopia, a case of despotism without terror.

Before the reign of Suna, Buganda had not yet achieved imperial proportions, and dynastic disputes kept the kingdom in turmoil. As C. C. Wrigley says in an essay on the Christian revolution in Buganda, "the history of Buganda in the latter part of the eighteenth century is a chronicle of almost incessant intestinal strife." [5] Despotic power, consolidated by Suna and continued by his son, Mutesa, inhibited that conflict and stabilized the regime. According to Henry Stanley's Ganda informants, the leading chiefs removed the prince designated by Suna as his heir because of his violent propensities and selected "the mild-spoken large-eyed boy" who was to be known as Mukabya and Mutesa. The new kabaka

> soon found reasons for slaying all his brothers, and, having disposed of them, turned upon the chiefs, who had elected him Emperor of Uganda, and put them to death, saying that he would have no subject about him to remind him that he owed his sovereignty to him.

> According to his father's custom, he butchered all who gave him offence. . . . Frequently, when in a passion, he would take his spear in hand and rush to his harem, and spear his women until his thirst for blood was slaked. [6]

Having read Speke, Stanley expected to find "a wholesale murderer and tyrant . . . a savage despot, whom Speke and Grant left wallowing in the blood of women . . ." when he visited Buganda in 1875. Instead, thirteen years after Speke's visit, Stanley found "an intelligent and distinguished prince . . . [and] witnessed with astonishment such order and law as is obtainable in semi-civilised countries." [7] The transformation, Stanley thought, was wrought by the doctrines of Islam, which had been recently introduced. After becoming a Muslim, the kabaka presumably "became more humane, abstained from the strong native beer which used to fire his blood, and renounced the blood-shedding custom of his fathers." [8] Like other Victorian observers, Stanley was convinced that such a change could come only from outside the system. A

Ganda historian, however, granting that Islam "had got a great hold on the kabaka" and that "he had studied the Koran diligently," [9] still claimed that the kabaka was converted from terrorism by his own *katikiro*, or prime minister. As Ham Mukasa gave the traditional story:

> Mutesa . . . started as a very bad ruler, and his first name, Mukabya [one who makes people wail] signifies how badly hated he was. But his Katikiro Kaira, himself a reformed man, realised the grave responsibility of such a rule of harsh punishments and reckless living, and he was instrumental in reforming the young Kabaka. One day Mutesa paid a visit to Kaira, and they talked about many things that were not good to do in a Kingdom, and they discussed what a peaceful Kingdom would be like. During the course of their conversation, Mukabya suddenly remarked, "and my name Mukabya strikes terror among my people. I will henceforward be called Mutesa, the peacemaker." From that day onwards, he was known as Mutesa and his conduct changed to suit the name.[10]

In this account of the conversion, the previous condition of Buganda is explicitly compared to the Zulu system, where the "King used to kill people as he wished." [11] Among the reforms imputed to Mutesa, "he taught his men that it was wrong to kill people in the way people were killed in Buganda," and he stopped the practice of informing:

> He taught chiefs to be truthful and to stop slandering other people for he realised that he had killed too many chiefs for nothing, simply because they were falsely reported to him. He discovered that wrong reports were due to jealousy. He found that every chief that was doing good work was the victim of a bad report from the other chiefs. Therefore he prohibited reporting to him.

Stanley, it is well known, converted the kabaka to Christianity, but apart from the religious issues, one gets the impression that Mutesa was a ruler in search of enlightenment, and that both the Europeans and the Arabs with their new doctrines and technology promised an expansion of knowledge and power. Mutesa also abolished the slave trade, and Stanley himself reported that the king abandoned Islam for Christianity because the Europeans he met were opposed to slavery, and their conduct was therefore consistent with their doctrines, whereas the Arabs came to Africa to trade in slaves.[12]

Although he occasionally lapsed into acts of violence, Mutesa chose to abandon the policy of terrorism with which he had begun his reign. It is clear, however, that he did not give up despotism. Kenneth Ingham, an historian of Uganda, writes that Mutesa recognized in despotic power "the spirit which united the Baganda against the outside world."[13] The despot was the sole representative of their unity: "The focal point of the sense of community was the office of kabaka or king. . . ."[14] The chiefs were creatures of the despot; land and labor were disposed by him, and his absolute authority was accepted without question:

> The complete and willing surrender of all individual rights, even the power of life and death, to an arbitrary ruler suggests a whole-hearted acceptance of the kabaka as the personification of Buganda and the Baganda, and the view is supported by the character of the nicknames given to him. The whole theme of those titles is that of the uncontrolled power of the kabaka.[15]

Mutesa died in 1884, and the last years of his reign were marked by signs of internal disunity. Unwittingly, the despot, whose rule prevented the old kind of discord and fission, had played host to new and unsettling ideas which were to destroy the political formula of despotism. Although Mutesa grew cool to the missionaries, and his successor was openly hostile to them, it was too late to check their influence. As Ingham observes, Islamic and Christian ideas, taken up with great fervor, undermined "the near-divinity which hedged the kabaka's position as the symbol of Buganda and its people." Religious teachings inspired new attitudes toward power: the "content was theological [but the] impact was political." [16] After Mutesa's death, the state disintegrated into factions which were represented by the Christian, Muslim, and traditional Ganda religious positions.

In desperation, Mwanga, the successor to the throne, chose to return to a terroristic policy, which he carried out erratically. His despotic claims, however, found insufficient support, and as Wrigley says, "whereas the rule of Mutesa had been a despotism based broadly on consent, the rule of Mwanga was a tyranny that was becoming intolerable both to the mass of the people and to the senior chiefs." [17] Some of the kabaka's praetorian units were armed with guns, but a large number of the men in them had become converts to Christianity, and his control grew more and more precarious. To the Christians, Mwanga alternated between repression and conciliation, but he remained convinced that the converts in the land, whose loyalties reached out to foreign powers, menaced the independence of the state. In 1886, he arrested and burned to death forty or more Christians, whose martyrdom then solidified the Christian opposition. Two years later, Mwanga was overthrown by the united forces of the Christian and Muslim factions. The Christian party, divided in Protestant and Catholic sections, held together through civil war, and after three kings had passed in rapid succession, occupied the capital late in 1889, and restored Mwanga to the throne. The new order made him "little more than a puppet in the hands of those who had restored him, and his replacement in 1897 by his two-year-old son did no more than underline the degeneration of the monarch's power." [18] That replacement followed a last attempt by Mwanga to lead non-Christian forces in a war to overthrow the power of the Christian chiefs. The ruler was now a figurehead, and an oligarchic "party" of Christians, which included competing Protestant and Catholic sections, collectively made the decisions about the shape and destiny of the state.

Thus, before its revolutionary transformation to a modern

kind of monarchy, Buganda under Mutesa had been moving toward despotism without terror, although it is not certain whether the choice to abandon continual violence was indigenous or inspired by foreign religious attitudes. At any rate, whatever the source of Mutesa's conversion, the despot had the means, through institutions that depoliticized the princes and through exclusive control of administrative offices, to hold absolute power and to prevent resistance without using violence. Despotic power could hardly survive the new conditions, even without external political dangers, however, for Christianity and Islam inspired factions and created new bonds of solidarity among the people within them. The new sense of brotherhood and its perils led many to cleave together in subcommunities rather than to spy on one another and to compete for favors from the despot.

Despotism thrives in a society that is shredded by suspicion and mutually destructive competition. In Buganda, where the people were ambitious, competitive, and suspicious, ruthless and destructive rivalry had affected everyone, high and low. Fallers describes the social effects of "*kuloopa*—malicious talebearing by ambitious rivals, a practice which in Buganda had been developed into a high art." [19] The subjective alliance with the ruler—preferred to solidarity among peers—which is found in all despotic systems, was also observed in Jimma Abba Jifar. As Lewis detects it in the relations among officials, there was "more profit in spying on one's neighbors and gaining the king's favor through carrying tales than in banding together to resist the king." [20]

A Galla Monarchy, the book by Herbert Lewis describing Jimma Abba Jifar from 1830 to 1932, before it was absorbed in the empire of Ethiopia, gives a clear picture of despotic organization without terror. Lewis has been criticized for his theory of the historical origins of the kingship in Jimma, but his reconstruction of the political system has not been challenged.[21]

Under minimal restraints, the ruler of Jimma exercised unlimited authority, primarily through his appointment and control of officials. As Lewis indicates, "The kingdom of Jimma Abba Jifar was highly centralized, and the kings of Jimma had an impressive record of avoiding the pitfalls of monarchical rule. The regime may, therefore, be called 'despotic' or 'absolutist.' " [22] The ruler would seek advice but was not required to follow it. He was not restricted by councils: "relations between the king and his advisors were relatively informal and unstructured. This was a major element supporting the king's despotic control, for a king's council may be one of the strongest limitations on his power." [23] Thus, the despot of Jimma was not encumbered by the legitimate resistances found in a limited monarchy.

From all accounts, there was not much violence in this despotism. The death penalty was rarely inflicted and confined to people accused or even suspected of conspiracy against the king.[24] Such cases were scarce, for rival brothers who toyed with conspiracy went into exile. In cases of murder, the judicial procedure worked to substitute monetary settlement for execution.

The despotism, then, was maintained not by violence but "through a number of institutions, processes, and customs." The despot held exclusive powers to appoint all the officials, and he commanded a force of 1500 mercenaries, which was larger than any other force under a single command. None of the provincial governors could maintain armed men, and the ruler's entire standing army of 2000 kept order, provided labor for public tasks, and occasionally acted as executioners. He also controlled the administration, which distributed functions in a way that limited the power of any single official. In Lewis's words:

> The governmental structure formed an organic system, the units of which could not be readily removed from the whole and simply reproduced in isolation. Having established government by ministries the king, as the individual through whom all the ministries were integrated, remained unique and supreme.[25]

Although the state had a history of dynastic disputes, there is no record of any rebellion from outside the royal family—not by nobles or provincial governors or anyone else. Since corporate kin groups were not politically important, the king felt little pressure from his own relatives, and he could also expropriate the land of a noble without incurring the hostility of a large group of people.

Despotism without terror, therefore, is not a contradiction in terms but a logical alternative and an historical reality. Furthermore, the political arrangements in a despotic state are not the work of one man. The defense and preservation of arbitrary but legitimate absolute power depend on a system of co-operation, which is a compact that includes the sovereign, his lieutenants, and the entire community.

The notion of an arbitrary, absolute ruler who governs without positive co-operation from his people is a myth and a fantasy—a magical figure, which Freud analyzed in *Totem and Taboo*. That chimerical despot possesses the power imagined in the master of the royal kraal—dramatized for a time in the Zulu state. In Victorian fantasy, that fierce animal driven exclusively by lust and aggression, classically pictured by Atkinson as a "more or less human ancestor . . . the unsocial head of a solitary isolated group," [26] is a figment of the unconscious.

With typical Victorian innocence of African realities, Henry Sidgwick comfortably proclaimed:

> In the general history . . . of political institutions it is a peculiar characteristic of certain portions of the white race or races of men, that they have maintained, in advanced stages of civilisation, a different method—at once more artificial and more orderly—of avoiding evils of arbitrary rule; while at the same time endeavouring to maintain the unity of resolution and action which is necessary for the efficient performance of governmental functions. This is what we call the constitutional method.[27]

We shall discuss constitutional methods further in Chapter XIV. Sidgwick would have been surprised to learn that the varieties of constitutional method in the wide range of African communities were probably more subtle, resourceful, and complex than their counterparts in European history. He would have been even more surprised to learn that his Victorian contemporaries shared with the men in the Dark Continent the fantasies surrounding "evils of arbitrary rule."

CHAPTER XII

THE CHOICE
OF TERROR

Violence and war try to settle in a short time, and
by a sudden dissipation of energy, difficulties that ought
to be dealt with by the subtlest analysis and
the most delicate tests—for the object is to reach a state
of unforced equilibrium.

—Paul Valéry, *History and Politics.*

ONE CORNER of the mind remains ungratified by explanations
that would submit human choice as the cause of complex phenomena. For ages, mythology occupied that corner, and when
men sought explanations for ruinous events, they often rested
content with statements that traced their origins to the character of gods or heroes or to "necessity," a greater force beyond
the gods. Rationalists of another age, more innocent than we
are about the nature of modern thinking, assumed that mythology could be shed like larval skin, and that the reason of mankind, once liberated, would penetrate the darkest recesses of
social life unencumbered by archaic dreams. Now we know better. We understand that it is the disposition of reason to be
caught napping, and we have added to the labors of rational
activity the task of plucking the thread of fantasy from the fabric of explanation. Therefore, we no longer take the trouble to
feign dismay over daily evidence that neither Plato, nor the
illuminati, nor the Victorian eminents, managed to strip myth-
making from explaining, and we expect to find the mythopoeic

process ever creating and deceiving. We are also more patient with myth, recognizing its creative energy, than were our predecessors, and we think that although the mythic component can never be purged from the process of rational explanation, still its influence may be controlled. Nevertheless, fantasies and myths about terroristic despotism, while elaborating some insights about the psychological forces associated with that form of rule, have obscured its social processes and governmental structure.

The realm of the unworldly is not the only source of misleading explanations that conclude with "character" or "necessity." One naturalistic point of view would deny human responsibility for efforts to initiate, maintain, or terminate the process of terror because it regards that process deterministically, as an inescapable sequence of events. Another perspective, in the manner of "great-man theory," would attribute full responsibility to a solitary "hero." Neither extreme takes sufficient cognizance of the social relationships in the process.

In the deterministic idiom, writers often describe epochs of terror as great upheavals larger than human motivations, or as vast tidal convulsions, and treat those times as cosmic, unavoidable calamities. One may suspect that in some underground way, the psychological association between natural disaster and massive political violence has some influence on the fatalistic interpretation of terroristic regimes.

However, it is on psychological rather than on social grounds that a connection may be established between reigns of terror and natural disasters, although the emotional issues in the experience of terror must be reserved for the next volume. In some respects, the impact of massive violence on a population does resemble the effect of great natural catastrophes such as earthquakes. After these cataclysms, people are stunned, social relations disrupted, and the emotional climate filled with inhibition and guilt. The feelings of guilt and sense of supernatural vengeance have no place in the scheme of naturalistic determinists who use the metaphors of cataclysm to describe reigns of terror, but they are constant realities in the social experience of disaster. In the eighteenth century, a young Encyclopedist and disciple of Montesquieu, Nicolas Boulanger, who is an important but unremembered theorist of despotism, based his explanation of despotic systems on great natural disasters and the emotions that followed in their wake. He went so far as to trace the principles of terroristic despotism in the empires of the Orient as well as Africa, the New World, and Europe, to the reactions of ancient peoples to natural cataclysms.[1]

Strangely, Boulanger's study of despotism may have a significance resembling that of Freud's *Totem and Taboo:* in it, what is questionable historically may be true psychologically. In curious, unexpected ways, empirical studies of disaster two centuries later, give fresh relevance to Boulanger's work, which has otherwise barely survived as an antiquarian remnant. Martha Wolfenstein shows in her study of natural disasters that "in the moment of being struck by an overpowering force there seems often to be the feeling of an agency that acts with intent." Victims tend "to react to disaster as if it were a punishment." Wolfenstein explicitly makes a connection to the behavior observed among victims of terrorism, referring to the feelings of eastern European Jews about their persecutions by the Nazis.[2] The literature recording the impact of concentration camp experience gives further support to the connection.

The experience of victims living through natural disasters is different from the language of those who use disaster as a metaphor to describe terrorism. The environment of disaster victims is filled with a vague but tragic sense of guilt, and they try to find someone to blame. Manifesting an irrational desire to detect moral agency in nonhuman causes, their thoughts are the reverse of rational attempts to understand human violence as an impersonal sequence of destructive events.

In a similar vein of inevitability, some writers who do not deny that terrorism is a choice still avoid the issue of moral responsibility by regarding the decision as an inescapable policy. They come up with judgments that resemble the following improvisations: "The crisis in France was so acute that Robespierre had no choice but to initiate the Reign of Terror"; or "The only way for Stalin to modernize Russia and to open the Siberian wilderness was through terror and forced labor." To the contrary, the argument in this book, based in part on the histories of simple societies, explains the policy of terror as a response to crises of integration and as one social choice among alternatives. A social choice is neither an inescapable event nor a solitary decision.

When policy is studied as a pattern of collective decisions within a range of alternatives, it is vain to seek deterministic explanations or to construct predictive models. One tries to estimate probable actions—projecting them into the future or tracing them in the past—and to search for law-like regularities. One can try to come to some conclusions about specific choices: to discover the rule by which past actions could have been performed and to reconstruct the logic by which decisions could have been made.

Sometimes it is possible to discern alternatives that remain open and to understand the ones that are closed, but it requires precise imagination and a great deal of information to guess, much less to predict, the choice to be made between alternatives that are open. When people say that an alternative is "closed," the statement has several possible meanings. One is that physical conditions prevent certain actions from taking place. Another meaning is that the choice is physically possible, but outside the interest of the actor, or beyond his imagination, or beyond the cultural experience of his supporters. A third meaning is that the choice would have to cope with a higher degree of social resistance than other alternatives. In this case, the "closure" is not final but conditional. If a political leader commits himself to the choice in question and mobilizes men and resources to overcome the resistances, he may "open" the alternative.

When leaders make crucial choices and when they open new or closed alternatives, they are often regarded historically as great men or heroes. Sidney Hook writes that "heroic action can count decisively only where the historical situation permits of major *alternative* paths of development." [3]

Yet, Hook admits that a "heroic" leader does not work alone. He depends on a circle of lieutenants, an apparatus, or a "machine"—that is, a staff of men who are disposed to co-operate in his ventures and who are paid off by material and emotional privileges. Hook declares:

> The event-making figure in history obviously can achieve nothing by himself alone. He is dependent upon a narrow group of lieutenants or assistants who constitute a "machine," and upon a much broader group in the population. . . . [He] brings his machine into play to take over and administer social functions, pulverize opposition, and consolidate military influence. As far as possible the machine reduces all potential centers of resistance and draws into its periphery all independent institutions. . . . [But] just as he uses the machine to bring other social groups in line, the hero uses these social groups, tamed but resentful over the privileges lost to the machine, to keep the latter in tow.

In the relationships to staff and people, Hook emphasizes the freedom of the heroic figure, and he declares that even though the hero needs to satisfy group and social interests, he can choose to promote specific interests and to suppress others. [4] He would probably consider the "machine" as a condition but not as a part of the policy of terrorism, and anyone following that approach would be inclined to assign responsibility for the policy exclusively to the hero-despot.

Hook concludes that the "hero in history is the individual to whom we can justifiably attribute preponderant influence in determining an issue or event whose consequences would have been profoundly different if he had not acted as he did." [5] He intends to take a position that rejects both determinism and great-man theory as exclusive principles of historical interpretation, but an analysis following his approach would scarcely avoid explaining the epochs of terroristic despots by the actions of the heroes, which is not much different from conventional descriptions of those regimes. Though Hook's approach is not objectionable, it is inadequate for our purposes, and it actually lends weight to the "great-man" interpretation of despotism, for it draws attention away from the mechanism of social choice. We shall take a different direction, and to clarify the policy of terror as a social choice, examine the relationships between the terroristic despot and the members of the system.

In a chiefdom governed by a terroristic secret order, it is clear that the directorate was a *team* of men who co-operated as peers, sharing the crucial decisions and enjoying supreme power, prestige, and the conviction that their efforts upheld the legitimate order. Their political solidarity was not impaired by internal rivalries for prestige, and as a group they strove to eliminate anyone—high or low—who strayed from the working consensus that was in effect the living constitution of the chiefdom.

In a terroristic despotism it is less obvious that the directorate was a team because the awful radiance of the despot eclipsed his associates. Moreover, both the ideological fantasy within the system and European theories of despotism have simplified the nature of the regime and obscured the relationships. Since the living constitution of this regime, described in Chapter X, required that political decisions should be validated as impulses of the ruler, it was scarcely in order for anyone to ponder the roles and functions of the officials. When Dambuza, a principal induna, accompanied by a lesser officer, was condemned to death by the enemies of Dingane, he did not plead that he was a mere instrument compelled to follow orders, but simply refused to discuss his responsibility. He was accused by Mpande and the Boers of instigating massacres and advising Dingane to commit atrocities. Delegorgue reported that Dambuza, "a man so devoted as willingly to give up his life to serve Dingaan," when pressed to make admissions of his own responsibility, "was silent on his own behalf" and defended the innocence of his comrade, the lesser induna. Finally, he insisted "that he had but one master, that it was his duty to remain faithful to that master till the last." [6]

The people as well as the induna were rewarded for loyalty and co-operation. They received material benefits as well as the emotional gratification of participating in greatness without limit. In the Zulu case, we have seen how the cattle taken from the kraals of victims of the terror were redistributed. Fallers also shows that in Buganda during the despotic period, "consent and legitimacy were secured, not so much by constitutional restraint upon the Kabaka, as by a nation-wide psychic and material 'pay-off' in the shape of the spoils of war." [7] Chiefs benefited especially, but the entire nation shared in the compact with the despot:

> A faithful chief, particularly one who had extended the boundaries of the kingdom, would be rewarded by being given *carte blanche* to plunder the estates and assume the office of one who had fallen into disfavor. This "pay-off" to the king's loyal servants goes far toward explaining the legitimacy which the *Kabaka* enjoyed, despite his arbitrariness and cruelty. In fact, there was a definite "pay-off" for the nation as a whole: the ever more frequent wars against neighboring peoples, in which more than one hundred thousand men might take part, were essentially raids for plunder, in which everyone who took part received a share. In addition, the nation as a whole received the psychic satisfaction which came from national aggrandizement at the expense of their neighbors. In the context of this ideological and economic commitment to aggressive expansion, the despotic behavior of the *Kabaka added* to his legitimacy, rather than the reverse. [8]

A number of people, particularly members of the directorate, co-operated as a matter of voluntary choice, meaning that they preferred the system to any alternatives. The pains and dangers did work against universal enthusiasm, however. Even when arbitrary power rested on firm ideological and emotional foundations, specific arbitrary acts stimulated resentment and feelings of hostility, and therefore the terror was a political co-ordinate to absolute power, preventing the withdrawal of support. Yet, when the terror inhibited resistance, passive submission was not the only alternative to voluntary co-operation.

Hannah Arendt observes that as terror atomizes people and renders them inert, some other force is needed to set them in motion. In totalitarian systems, she suggests, ideology provides the motor, supplementing the paralyzing effect of the terror. Terroristic despotism has its own kind of ideology, we have seen, but another process, which may be named the "forced choice," works to secure active co-operation. The "forced choice" depends in part on the violence that also initiates the process of terror, but it is analytically distinct from the terror, and it may be understood—if we recall the definitions of Chapter II—as violence to change the conditions of control. Although we are referring to a single set of violent acts, we must understand that it contributes to different processes which must be distinguished because each can exist independently. The "forced choice" does not affect those who co-operate voluntarily—such as the men in the directorate and a great number of ordinary people—and its major effect is not to *inhibit* resistance. Instead, it motivates those who neither resist nor co-operate voluntarily, and it transforms passivity into active co-operation.

The method creates a social condition that closes alternative chances to act until the individual must choose between two evils, both of which would be rejected in an "open" situation. As people move to avoid the more noxious alternative, the struggle mobilizes their energies, and they actively co-operate with political authority to gain the positive increment of the lesser evil. The incentives to co-operate may be increased if the increment appears as a relative advantage, and if an individual must compete with his fellows to seize it. In that case, the subjective alliance he makes with the officials shatters the solidar-

ity of his own social group and reinforces his active co-
operation with despotic power.

Chester Barnard, in his study of formal organizations, recognized that a social system may offer adequate incentives for co-
operation by "the creation of coercive conditions." One familiar practice, which may include murder, exploits the subjective
impact of forced exclusion, which is used

> as a means of persuasion *by example*, to create fear among those
> not directly affected, so that they will be disposed to render
> to an organization certain contributions. It presents realistically
> the alternative either of making these contributions or of fore-
> going the advantages of association. The grades of exclusion
> are numerous, beginning with homicide, outlawing, ostracism,
> corporal punishment, incarceration, withholding of specific
> benefits, discharge, etc.[9]

Barnard understood that force may be used when authority
does not secure voluntary co-operation, and that force creates a
new authority when the coercion is accepted. Coercive authority offering a "forced choice," then, may also elicit active co-
operation:

> Contributions secured by force seem to have been often a
> necessary process of coöperation. Thus slavery is the creation
> of conditions by force under which bare subsistence and pro-
> tection are made sufficient incentives to give certain contribu-
> tions to the organization; although often it has been the result
> of conditions not purposely created, that is, slavery has been
> sometimes a voluntary means to being admitted to benefits of
> coöperation otherwise witheld. However, usually slavery is evi-
> dence of an unstable efficiency, except when it can be combined
> with other incentives (as in forced military service).[10]

The mixture of incentives adds stability, and, Barnard
thought, "it is generally accepted that no superior permanent
or very complex system of coöperation can be supported to a

great extent merely by coercion." [11] In terroristic despotism, the material and psychic "pay-off" as well as the "forced choice" did provide a mixture of incentives to stimulate and to organize active support. For those who withdrew support or might oppose the arbitrary power of the despot, the terror did the rest.

The differential pains and dangers in the system as well as the competitive, individual pursuit of relative advantage were organized in the service of despotic power. By the mechanism of "forced choice," the dangers of attachment to the central military apparatus could be offset by conditions that encouraged territorial chiefs to be rapacious and punitive. If membership in the despot's central military force provided a few privileges as well as immunity from the local controls, the desire to escape the reach of his local chief could mobilize a man's enthusiastic loyalty to the center.

Although rivalries and suspicions sometimes threatened to breach the compact, in a stable directorate the lieutenants guarded the despot's absolute power, and the despot preserved the lives and privileges of his highest officers. During the last days of Dingane, the organization held together until the despot executed Ndlela, his chief induna. Only then a group of the other induna invited the Swazi to kill the despot.

The members of the directorate were committed to the principles of despotism and received its greatest advantages. The rest of the people were all targets of the terror. Some were specialized executioners or informers. The others, to escape designation as victims and to grasp some relative advantage, might become spontaneous informers or even agents of violence. An acute crisis, such as the mourning for Shaka's mother, might force the choice on everyone of being either executioner or victim, with the chance of becoming both.

Violence and fear do not stabilize a political system or secure active co-operation. The secret of terroristic organization in states—which have structural dissociations not found in chiefdoms—combines the process of terror with the "forced choice" and the competitive struggle for relative advantage. If A fears that B may inform on him, then to avoid that danger and to acquire B's cattle, A may arrange to have B executed. Similarly, in a concentration camp the terror is not sufficient to make the inmates exercise power over one another in the service of the camp guards. However, if men are divided by an imposed system of invidious identities with different privileges in a milieu of danger and privation, the mechanism of forced choice changes their incentives. Under those conditions, the slimmest increments can enlist men to co-operate, and the gain of two cigarettes with the added chance of some immunity from violence can motivate a man to punish or to exercise control over a fellow prisoner.

In primitive despotisms, the "pay-off" provided incentives for voluntary co-operation. The "forced choice" worked against passivity and stimulated active, if not free, co-operation. The terror inhibited resistance. Despotism without terror found ways to eliminate resistance without using violence. Other kinds of states—limited monarchies—worked by balancing resistances. A despotism without terror resembled limited monarchy in its use of nondestructive institutional modes to cope with resistance. Nevertheless, any despotism was different from a limited monarchy because a solitary ruler made all the important decisions and enjoyed unconditional obedience, sharing power with no one and governing without the strictures of conditional resistance. Therefore, monarchy and despotism found different ways to achieve equilibrium. Monarchy balanced resistances, whereas despotism prevented them. Varieties of social choice, within the range of cultural and ecological alternatives, yielded different patterns, but the common purpose of them all was to shape a political community that would master successive crises of integration.

CHAPTER XIII

CRISES OF

INTEGRATION

All ancient communities ran the risk of being overthrown
by a very slight disturbance of equilibrium . . .
—Henry Sumner Maine, *Ancient Law.*

SMALL COMMUNITIES organized as bands remained in ecological conditions that did not permit expansion or coalescence with other units. Some larger communities, living in more settled conditions with economies that could support specialized political roles, prevented them from emerging, developing mechanisms to inhibit and destroy concentrations of power, resisting hierarchical organization, and remaining stateless. Other societies, moving along a different course of historical development, permitted or encouraged concentrations of power, which were associated with larger, more inclusive systems of organization and new structural problems.

The movement from simple and egalitarian to complex and hierarchical organization, integrating clans and tribes into chiefdoms, and chiefdoms into kingdoms, was a process and not a completed event. Each stage or level of organization, then, might be marked by a crisis of integration which was often managed but not permanently resolved, and each system worked out a strategy—more or less successful—to preserve its union and to reduce the opportunities for dissolution. Unless the process of integration, which was a matter of invention or partial imitation, controlled or relieved tensions and latent conflict, the compound might disintegrate under stress. Violence was one choice among many techniques of force and persuasion that could be employed to deal with the resistances underlying tension and conflict. As long as clan, tribal, or chiefdom identities endured in parts of the compound, the form of their survival remained a central issue, for their strength and mode of expression helped to determine the potential for dissolution. If their energies were absorbed in ritual and other symbolic modes or if they were restricted to narrow channels of social action, their expression might not disrupt the social order. If they were expressed through political action, however, they might be experienced as resistance by the central authority, and, if so, some method would be devised to cope with them. One response was to organize them in a constitutional order that balanced, mediated, and stabilized conflicting forces. The alternative action was to destroy them wherever possible and to inhibit their expression by a pattern of violence.

The irresistible power sought in a regime of terror, where systematic violence worked to maintain power relations that were free from resistances and reciprocal controls, served more than one purpose, but one crucial function carried more weight than the others. The power relations maintained by the process of terror, expressed in ideal form as unchallenged command and unconditional obedience, were used to solve crises of social integration. West African chiefdoms, examined earlier in this book, provide examples of how such power relations—or at least approximations to the ideal—were organized by secret associations in some stateless societies. Zulu despotism offers another example of how they were organized in a state and how the ideal was expressed symbolically and shaped into a political culture.

The dynamics of these crises of integration are not vastly different in modern societies, but in primitive conditions they were closer to the surface and more often exposed. As Walter Goldschmidt has pointed out, Western man "has been habituated for centuries to take political integration for granted." But anyone "concerned with social systems in the broader context" is challenged by a number of questions that rarely occur to social scientists whose attention is confined to modern social organization:

> Why have political integration at all? Or again, in order to have political integration, what special functions must be performed in a society that lacks writing (and hence documents), centralized economic industries (and thus manifest economic advantages), an effective weapon technology (and thus a serious difficulty in concentrating power), and other such elements that tend to give support to modern unified political systems.[1]

I shall argue that the alternative solutions to problems of integration were not inexorable products of historic events or in any sense inevitable. They were deliberate social choices.

Deliberate choices were not necessarily intentional. A choice was deliberate if men were free to follow another course of action, but such a choice does not imply that they necessarily intended or even foresaw the consequences. Furthermore, a social choice was always made not by a solitary individual but by a team of men who had options. As I describe some of the abundant ways that African rulers and their people found to deal with crises of integration without resorting to terror, I do not suggest that all of those methods were available to rulers such as Shaka and Dingane, who chose violent counter-resistance. The choice of terrorism was implied in a larger pattern of experiencing and acting, but that configuration was one option, within cultural limits, in a range of alternative patterns.

Other systems resembled the Zulu in the use of terror, either externally to reduce military resistance or internally to inhibit political resistance. A number of marauding communities organized on military lines carried on external terrorism, but their potential for internal terrorism depended on structural crises and problems of social integration.

THE MARAUDING COMMUNITY

In 1568, the Jaga people, who may have originated in the interior of Central Africa, invaded the coastal area in marauding bands, almost destroying the kingdom of Kongo, and disrupting the whole of West Central Africa. Vansina compares the movement of the Jaga to "the Nguni build-up which led to Shaka's Zulu empire." The Jaga lived in fortified camps, permanently organized for war, killing their own infants to avoid impediments on the march, but incorporating the older boys and girls of devastated communities into their camps. They were sudden, devious, and irresistible, organized in flexible units that could be dispersed or concentrated. By superior discipline and the total militarization of life they were able to defeat chiefdoms much more populous than their own. Like the Zulu, they were the terror of their region, and "it is this terror, more than any other factor, which seems to explain the success of the Jaga." [2] Internally, however, the Jaga camps bore little resemblance to the Zulu state.

Although information about the internal organization of the Jaga is scarce, one interesting source is an account by Andrew Battell, an English sailor in a privateer who was captured by the Portuguese in Brazil around 1590, transported to Africa, and around 1601 lived for somewhere between sixteen and twenty-one months with the Jaga, gaining an intimate knowledge of their daily life. He described them as cannibals who ate the adult bodies of their enemies and who also practiced human sacrifice. The camp was organized under twelve captains commanded by a general, who was also referred to as the Great Jaga. Captured boys and girls seemed to be the only source of increase in the population, for in a period of fifty years the camp had grown to sixteen thousand strong, but only the dozen captains and about the same number of women were of original Jaga stock. [3] The boys captured in war were disgraced by a collar hung around their necks until they redeemed themselves by taking an enemy's head, which admitted them to the ranks as soldiers. The historian Ravenstein concluded that "Jaga" was not the name of a people, but a military title "assumed by the leaders of predatory hordes of very diverse origin, in order to inspire terror in the hearts of peaceful tribes; just, as in more recent times, certain tribes in East Africa pretend to be Zulu for a like reason." [4]

Battell did not report pervasive terror within the community, and since Jaga life was totally absorbed in warfare, it is not surprising that the forms of violence mentioned by him were confined to military operations, military discipline, or ritual. The Great Jaga dispensed executions as well as exhortations. Every night the general would mount a high scaffold and make a warlike oration to encourage his people, but at other times he destroyed those who were accused of shrinking from the fight as an example to the others. Battell said that those who "are faint-hearted, and turn their backs to the enemy, are presently condemned and killed for cowards, and their bodies eaten." [5] The Jaga were not a state and scarcely a society—in a quainter idiom they would have been called a "predatory horde." Since they did not carry on many of the activities common to societies and states, they did not require complex organization. Their crises of integration, therefore, were limited in kind, and they had neither the need nor the means for complex types of internal terrorism.

We have more information about the Matebele in Southeastern Africa, originally a marauding community, led by Mzilikazi, the Kumalo chief who had become one of Shaka's trusted generals and fled from him to crush his way north to the Transvaal and then to Rhodesia, where he established an empire of his own. He imitated Shaka in most respects and combined military terrorism with an internal regime of terror, holding together a vast domain in a stratified state that included many people of diverse cultures. [6]

Two Extremes: Terroristic Despotism and the Segmentary State

Nevertheless, all the states that had gathered, like the Matebele, in flights from Shaka did not preserve the model of terroristic despotism. The Fort Jameson Ngoni began in 1821 as a command of armed fugitives under the leadership of Zwangendaba, formerly a subchief in Zwide's Ndwandwe kingdom, which had been defeated and scattered by the Zulu. These Ngoni thrust their way to the Delagoa Bay region, eventually settling in what is now Zambia.[7] Unlike the Matebele, who established a terroristic despotism in which irresistible central power inhibited the powers of chiefs and lieutenants, they constructed a decentralized, segmentary state in which the lords of territorial segments exercised extensive authority, limited only by the balance of the powers held by their peers, who controlled the other segments. Although the Ngoni remained a dreaded military force, their problems of internal organization were not settled by terror, and they found other methods to cope with diminishing solidarity and crises of integration.

Originally, the Ngoni were organized in agnatic lineages and age sets. Large numbers of captives were absorbed directly into the lineage structure. This practice differed from that of the Zulu, who accepted captives as equals but not as fictive kinsmen, and it differed radically from that of the Matebele, who enforced a tripartite caste system. The expanding lineages of the Ngoni grew beyond kin organizations to become residential, territorial segments, and the heads of the lineages became regional governors under the paramount chief. Under each lord of the segment, a corps of lieutenants, related to him by real or fictive kinship, governed the subordinate units. New units were formed as the need arose, and the lord split up his numerous wives into separate bevies, each bevy under the leadership of a senior wife, assisted by junior co-wives, all their adult sons, lieutenants, and dependants. Through a process of continual segmentation familiar to tribes, new units remained an integral part of the primal segment, and "with the passage of time every flourishing segment became subdivided internally into several inferior segments." [8]

The men fought in age regiments which were drawn from all the segments and made up the army. However, in contrast to the Zulu type of regimental system, where only the king had the authority to mobilize age sets, the head of a major segment could mobilize the warriors who belonged to his unit and send them on raiding expeditions. Therefore, the lord of each segment, as long as he was sure of his people's loyalty, commanded an army as effective as any other force in the state. Although the paramount chief could mobilize all the regiments, he had no specially recruited retainers, specialized force, or corps of bodyguards. On national raids, the armies were mobilized and commanded by a senior lieutenant from the segment of the paramount chief's great wife.

Partial decentralization may also be observed in the exercise of the death penalty. Senior lieutenants sometimes executed people without referring the matter to the paramount chief. When news of the incident reached him, the latter would praise the lieutenant for acting in the paramount's interest or else abuse him for usurping his powers, warning him to be more careful in the future. In general, the paramount chief and his staff of lieutenants did not hold a monopoly of coercion, but they supervised the exercise of power by the lords of the great segments and their lieutenants, regarding many forms of independent action as threats to the unity of the state. The powerful lord of a major segment might strike out for independence, and an ambitious lieutenant might found his own segment and eventually his own state, but a premature move would result in certain death for treason. [9]

Crises of integration in the Ngoni state erupted when scarcity or conflict transformed the ordinarily peaceful lines of segmentation into lines of fission, resulting in cleavage and the secession of a unit, which tried to assume an independent political identity. A decision to break away prevailed against forces that bound each segment to the state: kinship ties, the age regiments, resources provided by the paramount chief, and the menace of external enemies always ready to pounce on small groups that had abandoned the security of the state. Competitive relationships among the great lords as well as the vigilance of the paramount chief kept the ambitions and the movements of each under scrutiny. However, as Barnes observes, "there was no central power posed against the provincial lords, as in some societies." The constraint was provided by the massing effect, complementary opposition, and the balance of power among segments. As Winans describes a similar segmentary state, "the center cannot and does not claim a monopoly upon the exercise of authority but must operate in a field in which it depends upon the oppositions among lesser foci to give it overwhelming force." [10]

In one sense, however, the state was held together by armed force. A segment breaking away would protect its flight by armed combat and would try to get a safe distance to form a new state ringed by its no-man's-land. Those who were left behind would assemble a military force to pursue and destroy the refugees. If the fugitives succeeded in escaping, the leader assumed the role of the paramount chief, received the royal salute, and initiated his own first fruits ceremony. [11]

The well-known instability of affiliations and political structures throughout traditional African society may be explained by the conditions that sped the formation, fission, and disintegration of independent communities. For seceding groups, withdrawal was more of a political and military issue than an economic problem, for in simple pastoral and agricultural societies it was not difficult for them to become self-sufficient—any subcommunity large enough to risk secession was usually capable of supporting itself. In Southern Africa at least, before the influx of Europeans, the availability of vacant land, the abundance of animal and plant edibles to consume in flight—except in the Zulu traffic desert—and the relative ease of finding a haven with a friendly chief all contributed to the movement and transfer of peoples. Moreover, every local ruler held authority that covered the important collective functions—ritual, economic, executive, judicial, and sometimes military. With this control of a wide range of activities, local communities were largely autonomous in many respects and miniature replicas of the government of the state. Therefore, they could exist, if necessary, by themselves.[12]

Subordinate units in any society are partial systems which may be described as incomplete and dependent. The effect of their subordination is to limit their purposes or the ways in which they may operate.[13] In modern societies, economic specialization and division of labor reinforce dependence and incompleteness. In primitive conditions, it was potentially easier for a subordinate unit to achieve economic, military, and political autonomy. Terroristic despotism and the segmentary state dealt with this potential by fundamentally different kinds of action. In the former, latent drives toward independence on the part of chiefs and wealthy men were systematically inhibited by a pattern of recurrent violence exercised by a special staff commanded by the despot. In the latter, the paramount chief acted by urging loyal subordinate chiefs to mobilize their staffs to move against the offender only after an overt act of independence had come to the paramount's attention and the first signs of fission were already manifest.

In contrast to the Ngoni, therefore, a terroristic despotism like the Matebele state under Mzilikazi did maintain a "central power posed against the provincial lords." Imitating the Zulu system, this central power did not confine itself to striking down men who had actually plotted or committed acts of opposition, rebellion, or secession, but instead kept the headmen and chiefs who potentially might commit such acts in a state of paralysis by terror. The missionary, Mackenzie, who lived among the Matebele, wrote:

The head men lead perhaps the most wretched lives under this wretched government. The private soldier has little in possession or enjoyment, but he has also little care. The officer, on the other hand, knows that jealous eyes are upon him. His equals in rank and station covet his possessions, and regard the favours which he receives from the chief as so much personal loss to themselves. Therefore the head men are continually plotting and counter-plotting against one another. "We never know," whispered one of them to me, having first looked carefully around to see if we were quite alone, "we never know when we enter our house at night if we shall again look upon the light of the sun." As a matter of fact such men seldom fall asleep sober, they every night call in the aid of boyalwa (beer) to deepen their slumbers. One day a small wiry man was introduced to me at Inyate by one of the missionaries. He was asked where he had been the night before, and with a smile mentioned the name of a certain village. . . . I was told after he left that this was one of the chief's executioners; and from the frequency of his domiciliary visits, he was called by the Matebele "the chief's knife." . . . Waiting in the neighbourhood till his victim has drunk the last cup of beer, he gives him time to fall into that stupor of sleep and drunkenness out of which he is never to awake. The chief's knife has his assistants, who are in readiness to "mak' siccar" any bloody work; for Moselekatse could not carry out his paternal administration with only one "knife." According to the testimony of one of the missionaries, it is nothing for him to send in one night four or five different parties of vengeance, to hurry the inhabitants of four or five villages into eternity.[14]

The Ngoni and the Matebele may be understood as two states with similar historical origins and similar political cultures which chose diametrically opposite kinds of political structure. In the segmentary state of the Ngoni, the power of the hereditary ruler of each segment bordered on autonomy, and the authority of the paramount chief was limited and problematic. The relationship between the paramount and the chiefs of the segments tended toward symmetry, reciprocity, and approached equality. As Fallers has said, "The authority of the paramount over the whole state depends on his ability to maintain a balance of power among the subordinate units. . . . It is the paramount's ability to confront a rebellious segment with the juxtaposed power of another, more loyal segment that enables him to maintain such limited authority as he enjoys." [15] He negotiated and mediated among segment heads more often than he commanded. The very lineage principles that provided solidarity and support for the paramount chief also limited his authority. Lineage structures promoted divisions and problems. Still, they were the most common source of pluralism in African kingdoms. Fallers concludes that they were the political substructure that most often limited the authority of rulers and that they provided the means for a political expression of group interests.

In contrast to the limited authority of the paramount chief in a segmentary state, the power of a ruler like Mzilikazi, the despot of the Matebele, was officially limitless, and his relationship with subordinate chiefs was asymmetric, unilateral, and exclusively defined as command and obedience. The subordinate chiefs had no staffs or resources of their own, and far from feeling secure in their positions, they trembled with terror. The despot had a specialized staff—the "king's knives"—to control them by systematic violence, and this control in part depended on divisions among the chiefs, their destructive rivalry, suspicions, mutual plots, and the rewards each expected when he managed to betray a rival chief or headman.

It is true that every ruler acted through a staff of men who potentially had the capacity to limit his powers by claims of their own. Nevertheless, terroristic despotism was the exception to the rule enunciated by Fallers, who cites M. G. Smith and others to support his assertion that "political power cannot be monopolized by a ruler, however despotic." [16] Ruler did depend on staff, and vice versa, but they "depended" in different ways, and hence they were not mutually dependent. The despot's staff did not share his power, yet actively supported his monopoly. In other kinds of state, the officers of the king—with allowance for different degrees of activity and participation—were a different kind of executive staff, with varying degrees of capacity to press claims of their own.

LIMITED MONARCHIES

The segmentary state, of course, was not the only alternative to terroristic despotism, and between decentralized and despotic extremes, most primitive states varied within a wide range of constitutional monarchy.[17] In those states, the power of the king was confined within an elaborate system of informal restrictive institutions and formal checks and balances. Three types of structure we have considered, then, excluded terrorism from their patterns of internal control. The elementary, undeveloped nature of a marauding community such as the Jaga provided few occasions for internal terror. The uncentralized structure of a segmentary state such as the Ngoni provided no means to carry out terroristic rule. A constitutional monarchy such as the Swazi, prevented both terror and arbitrary government through the mechanism of a balanced polity.

In many monarchies, however, the restrictions on royal power did not necessarily freeze the pattern of government. Individual kings were more or less successful in contending with the forces that restricted them, and they devised techniques to counteract resistances. In many cases, the complexity of institutions worked in their favor. The basic elements in the labyrinthine structure of large states may be detected in the microcosm of a typical chiefdom: the head of a privileged lineage ruling through councils and through agents obliged or disciplined to obey. Still, under the conditions of larger states, with specialization, proliferation, dissociation, and central co-ordination, the ruler might expand or protect his power by using one part of the system to block or to neutralize the resistance of another. As we shall see, a number of alternatives to violence were available to him in his struggle with resistances and restrictive institutions.

CHAPTER XIV

ALTERNATIVES

TO TERROR

. . . unholy Rage, sitting within on cruel weapons,
his hands bound behind him with a hundred knots
of bronze, roars with a savage, blood-stained mouth.

—Vergil, *The Aeneid.*

ORDINARY CHIEFDOMS and states worked through a synthesis of
monarchic and conciliar principles. The head of the community represented its unity. He also initiated, co-ordinated, and
adjudicated. Moreover, he presided over councils, which tested
policy and deliberated problems. The councils, which included
representatives of subdivisions—usually corporate groups organized as lineages or as territories—assessed realities, discussed complications, explored the rules, anticipated consequences, registered objections, encouraged, criticized, warned,
and remonstrated. Through formal or informal means, the
councillors clarified and expressed the resistances in the system.

In the primitive state, the most common sources of resistance
besides the councils were to be found in the king's lineage or
the royal clan, in parts of the executive staff, and in the territorial subdivisions. Actions by popular assemblies were rare and
less important, except as expressions of public opinion, and
popular revolts, of course, were virtually unknown. The nature
and limits of resistance were a constant issue, for as everyone

knew, acute resistance would threaten the unity of the state and could lead to disintegration.

This chapter will probe the dimensions of different political solutions to the crises of integration implicit in resistance, comparing the violent methods of terroristic systems with less destructive alternatives. The analysis will confine itself to states and not take up the problems of chiefdoms. In the course of the exploration, to help clarify the alternatives and keep them in context, some states that were terroristic despotisms at certain moments in their histories will be compared briefly with limited monarchies that had similar cultures to begin with, and in many cases the same ecology.

THE STRUCTURE OF RESISTANCES

For present purposes, and from the standpoint of the ruler, resistance may be understood as defective co-operation of greater or lesser degree, or as some kind of behavior, intentional or not, that renders authority incomplete. One kind may be called *inertial* resistance: repetitive behavior without specific orientation to the authority of the ruler, which unintentionally prevents the execution of a command or the implementation of a decision. The other kind of resistance is *reactive*, specifically oriented to political authority, and it may be classified according to degrees of force: (1) challenge, which may take the form of warning, protest, remonstrance, or rebuke; (2) disobedience of specific commands, obstruction, refusal to cooperate with certain decisions, or retaliation in some other sphere; (3) withdrawal of support or an attack on the entire authority of the ruler—usually described as secession and rebellion. In most cases, actions of the last kind, the most serious form of resistance, were led by princes of the royal blood.

Royal Kinsmen. Kings generally ruled in the company of close relatives and with the assistance of kinsmen more remote. In some cases, the relatives differed from other servants only by virtue of their special loyalty, but in others they actually dominated political life, and the king's role amounted to little more than a presiding officer of the royal lineage's corporate organization. Schapera claims that a forceful and energetic ruler could dominate his subjects

> ruling in effect as a dictator—but at the cost of some painful disputes with his closest relatives. On the other hand, a weak chief . . . became the virtual puppet of certain royal headmen, whose influence over him created an opposition which led to much subsequent trouble.
> Tribal politics is in fact made up to a considerable extent of quarrels between the chief and his near relatives, and of their intrigues against one another to command his favour. . . . They are entitled by custom to advise and assist him in his conduct of public affairs, and they actively resent any failure on his part to give them what they regard as their due.[1]

Certain principles, such as ritual access to spirits of the royal ancestors, or the sacred quality of a blood line, or ownership of magical regal insignia defined the right and the power to rule, and these principles extended tó an entire descent group, with rules of selection determining the choice of the specific individual who held the highest office. Since royal authority was usually vested in a ruling family, the senior members, unless physically prevented or disqualified by rules, tended to share the highest power, and their own relatives in turn tended to concentrate prerogatives and power. The near kin of the king and their own nearest kin almost always enjoyed high rank, served as intimate councillors to the throne, and often worked as the chiefs of major territorial divisions, with local branches of the royal family occupying the subchieftaincies. The case was different for federations and certain kinds of decentralized kingdoms, but in the more unitary forms, the most important agents of the king were usually members of his family. Even the Zulu despots, who had unconditional control of appointments, relied on a network of relatives, placing brothers, mothers, wives, uncles, and aunts in charge of regimental headquarters. But in the limited monarchies of the Bantu-speaking peoples, the king's brothers and uncles had the right to be consulted on all major issues, exercised influence as his private advisors and public councillors, acted for him *in absentia*, and governed districts. The king could do little without their active support, but their solidarity proved to be his greatest source of strength.

Besides placing his close kinsmen in charge of major operations, the king allied himself to important men by marriage, taking wives from the families of those who controlled large followings and marrying off sisters and daughters to others. With the infusion of the lines of administration with kinship and affinal ties, overlordship was sweetened by the more intimate bonds of family relationship.[2] Hilda Kuper reports that any wise Swazi king recognized the value of kinship: "It extends through the nation, linking him by blood and marriage with chief and commoner, wealthy and poor. The success of a chief's reign depends to a great extent on his treatment of his kinsmen and their friendship towards him."[3] In a matrilineal society such as the Bemba, the heirs of the ruler were his brothers and nephews (sisters' sons). Still, his own sons, father's relatives, and other persons related by marriage were favored. Patrilineal kin held important positions, reinforcing the Bemba ruler's grip on the political system.[4]

In stable kingdoms, the royal descent group cherished the office of kingship and the formulas that sustained it. The group served as guardian of the mythic charter of royalty, and the senior uncles and aunts were living archives of political history, genealogy, ritual, and protocol. Therefore, to maintain the cultural forces that invigorated legitimacy, the king needed the princes, princesses, and grandees, and they needed him.[5] Finally, people all over the country took a lively interest in the palace when they could boast familial connections with royal affairs, especially when rank conferred honor and inspired the hope of advantages. When the king's relatives through blood and marriage pervaded the kingdom, royal rank could have a strong integrating effect.

Specific conditions, of course, determined the effect, for the presence of a large number of royal kinsmen might also turn into a force of disintegration. In the kingdom of Kongo in West Central Africa, every male descendant of the early kings could make a claim for succession to the throne; after 1540, succession was limited to descendants of Affonso I. In a space of two hundred years, those descendants had become so numerous that they made up an entire social class known as the *infantes*, from which an electoral college chose the king. The factionalism among the *infantes* pervaded the state, and the number of eligible candidates increased exponentially with each generation, diminishing the stability of the political order.[6]

At the same time that any king's relatives were his most important social base, they were also potentially the greatest source of fission, the most dangerous fomenters of disruption, and, in conditions of conflict, the agents of disintegration. Schapera has observed that the political community was "basically an unstable unit; and the most frequent causes of its breaking apart are the behavior of the chief and the ambitions of his near kin." Intrigues against the king were often made by the people closest to him, and in proverbs, princes were referred to as poisoners, restless subjects, or the king's killers. Thus, the most obvious locations for the close agnates of the king—at the palace or in the provinces—were also the most dangerous. At the palace they might be kept under surveillance, but it would have been uncomfortable for the king to have his most eligible replacements immediately at his elbow. In the provinces, comfortably distant from the king, a prince could live expansively in royal style, but the life of a kinglet was full of temptations to turn a subordinate chiefdom into an independent kingdom.

The great powers and privileges of the king inspired envy, Schapera observes, which in turn created rivals who coveted the office, and politics consisted largely of dynastic disputes. Richards agrees that "the survival rate of African kingdoms is inevitably low" and that of royal dynasties even lower.[7] The discontent of commoners passed into these disputes, for, as Schapera points out, the only ways in which commoners normally could show their opposition was to support one of the king's rivals or else to join the forces of a seceding prince.[8] Communities found it necessary, then, to work out some mechanism to control the twin dangers of rebellion and secession inherent in the role of the princes.

The kinds of resistance the king might experience from royal kinsmen would usually take one of the following forms: (1) They conspired to assassinate him or else mounted an attack, engaging in civil war to seize power. (2) They seceded and established a separate, independent political community. (3) They remained under his authority but acted in some way to reduce, limit, or obstruct his power. (4) As a corporate group they pressed material claims beyond limits approved by the king. Therefore, each ruler needed methods to protect himself and the throne from ambitious brothers, uncles, or other rival princes; to prevent fission; to guard against inroads on his power; and to keep within limits the demands of his relatives for material resources. Since the king relied on the support of his kin, he had obligations to them which were rendered equivocal by his dual position—unless some procedure changed his status, he was both the head of the royal corporate group and the head of the state. Since royal persons considered him their special property, they might feel resentment and betrayal when the king made decisions on behalf of the entire community that seemed to neglect their interests.

In the terroristic alternative, the despot killed the most eligible successors to the throne and relied on the process of terror to inhibit the remainder of the royal family. Shaka and Dingane did not permit sons to live; Dingane and Mpande liquidated brothers. In Buganda, early in the nineteenth century when the reign of each kabaka augmented the central power, the princes were kept away from affairs of state and a number of rulers had them executed.[9] They were burned, starved, or strangled to avoid spilling royal blood, which was sacred. When the first European observer visited the Buganda court, Speke noted that extensive violence at that time was directed against intimate associates of the kabaka, especially wives and servants. Nevertheless, not only despots contrived the destruction of royal persons. Schapera lists a number of rulers who were not despots but who killed sons, pregnant wives, and brothers, yet he concludes that "on the whole such practices are not very common, and although in all divisions many instances are known of chiefs killing brothers or other near kin the victims were usually true rebels or conspirators and not merely potential rivals." [10]

In most cases, eligible candidates for the throne were expected to survive, and communities invented ways to regulate succession that were imperfect but not less stable than methods of violence. There was no way to avoid risks or choices between procedures and no way to rear a future king without providing occasions for conflict and faction. Each set of rules minimized the chances of conflict from one source but consequently risked potential resistance from another direction. None eliminated the chance of fission, but the consequence of each procedure was to determine, if fission was at hand, the lines along which division would take place: between the partisans of uncle and nephew, brother and brother, or father and son. For instance, let us compare the Nguni and Sotho models. In the latter system, the heir often reached manhood early in his father's reign. The ruler, therefore, might use his son as a deputy, but unless safeguards were introduced, the practice gave occasion for conflict between father and son. The Nguni pattern usually offered a safeguard against this kind of conflict, because the great wife of the ruler was not married until he was well established in office, which meant that the heir was usually not old enough to challenge the king before he died. The procedure might mean difficulties for the heir, however. The regent might have been the late king's younger brother, who ruled until the new king reached majority, or perhaps the elder brother of the heir. In some communities, the split—if it emerged—took place between the regent and the heir. In others—the Venda, for example—it was rare for the regent to refuse to give up his power, but the period of regency allowed time for conspiracies on the part of other sons of the late king, who might try to displace the heir through factional intrigue.[11]

In some systems, the potential resistance of pretenders to the throne was allowed to materialize and to exhaust its violent energy before each new ruler was installed, through the institution of the accession war. In the kingdom of Ankole, which was located in the present state of Uganda, the procedure required that the strongest son of the late king should rule the state. Therefore, the brothers and their followers were expected to fight until the lone survivor claimed the royal insignia. A mock king, who was a commoner, was chosen to keep a semblance of order until the accession war, which might last for months, came to an end, and then he was killed. The great chiefs who guarded the borders of the country stayed out of the war, and tried to keep a minimum of order. When the surviving prince took the throne, he stood alone in the royal line without opponents. The accession war thus fit into the body of Ankole beliefs and practices, "the general function of which was to maintain the continuity of kingship as an essential part of political co-operation and to eliminate, as far as possible, competition and discord as permanent elements of political leadership."[12]

An unusual device protecting the nation from fission and civil war was the divided succession and rotation in the Nupe kingdom. The descendants of the Fulani conquerors in Nupe (in Nigeria) established three royal houses, and these three families eliminated the other relatives from the succession, paying them off with less important offices. The three dynasties then succeeded to the throne in strict rotation, and for them it seemed to be the only solution for a ruling group that came to power in great numbers, organized in groups of partisans and jealous kinsmen.[13]

An arrangement that has shown reasonable success in avoiding both violence and fission may be found in the Swazi kingdom. To avoid conflict between the king and his sons, the first son was never the heir, and to protect the solidarity of the royal group, the successor was not known until the council chose him after the king's death. A number of commoners known as *tinsila* were made blood brothers of the king and they guarded the physical contacts with his own kinsmen. A regent was never full brother of the late king, and after the king's death the queen mother was expected to be continent and to bear no more children. Princes were given responsibility over territorial divisions and expected to satisfy their appetites for authority in the service of the king. The Swazi system managed to balance the forces of authority and potential resistance, and they explicitly criticized the Zulu for the coercive element in their line of succession. Swazi laws of succession "demonstrate a conscious attempt to overcome the lines of fission that are likely to endanger the unity of the group" and to avoid the violent excesses of the Zulu experience.[14]

Taking their course against the will of the established powers, assassination, rebellion, and secession are ultimate forms of resistance in any political system. Lesser forms, however, with limited scope and restricted purposes might be institutionalized in systems that did not have a despotic constitution. In limited monarchies, some of these formalized resistances were expressed by persons whose office gave them the privilege, under certain conditions, of controlling, challenging, or punishing the king. According to the working consensus in these monarchies, even though he might employ formal or informal means to counteract them, the king could not deny his consent to the expression of legitimate resistances. In one instance, the king was obliged to consent to his own execution when, in the Oyo kingdom (West Africa), the head of the Council of State, under certain conditions, commanded him to take poison.[15]

Sometimes the highest privilege of conditional and limited resistance was held by a female relative of the king, who was expected to have the utmost loyalty to him and, of course, could never replace him. In the systems of the Swazi, Ashanti, and probably Buganda, the queen mother—for the Venda it was the senior paternal aunt—could scold or rebuke the king. Similarly, in Swaziland and other kingdoms, the ruler's brothers and uncles, serving as his chiefs, as members of his council, or as personal advisers, could act against him by reprimanding or imposing fines on him or by withdrawing co-operation. Yet, acts of resistance were held within institutional limits, and when the queen mother plotted against Mbandzeni, a King of the Swazi in the nineteenth century, he ordered her execution.

Since the political acts of royal kinsmen could destroy the entire system of co-operation, kingdoms devised various modes of counter-resistance to direct and control their energies. As alternatives to violent methods, which destroyed resistance or inhibited its antecedent conditions by the process of terror, monarchies made rules to deprive royal persons of authority, or else designed structures to limit, neutralize, or balance their powers.

Excluded from all offices of state, the "princes" of the royal clan in Dahomey enjoyed lives of "gilded domesticity." They did no work—except as spies for the king—but were supported by taxes and royal slaves, and were provided with wives by the king. Their very compensation for political deprivation reduced them to a slothful position.[16] In Buganda, when princes were no longer killed, they were disqualified from the succession and not permitted to hold office, but given land enough to maintain them in comfort. Only a prince who was born while his father was the kabaka was a "prince of the drums" and eligible to succeed the king; all the others were called "peasant princes" or "princes thrown away." When a new king was installed, his brothers were publicly informed that their sons could never occupy the throne, and at the ceremony an official turned to all the princes and proclaimed, "You are peasants; fight if you wish and we will put you to death." Still, since the sufficiency of disqualifying rules was not trusted, it was forbidden for a prince "to become the guest of any chief, or to attach himself to his retinue, because it was feared that in such a case the chief might espouse his cause, and try to place this prince upon the throne. . . ."[17]

In some states where princes were not deprived of all political authority, their potential for resistance was limited by balancing their powers, i.e. appointing commoners to office, some as chiefs of a number of territorial subdivisions and others as the highest officers in the central administration. In the Soga kingdoms (in Uganda), princes of the blood were believed to possess an inherent fitness to rule, and some of them governed territorial divisions of the state, which they turned into principalities with a considerable degree of autonomy. The king, however, appointed commoners to govern some of the territorial units and also filled his entire administrative staff with commoners, who were bound to him personally as clients and who depended on him for their positions. Soga lore explicitly stated that kings trusted their client-chiefs and not the princes. Controlling the machinery of government and holding all the king's offices, the commoners balanced the princely powers and, since they had no hereditary right to rule, protected the king against usurpation. On a smaller scale, the men of royal blood who governed territories maintained their own staffs of client-chiefs to control their jurisdictions and to defend them against the ambitions of rival kinsmen.[18] Similarly, among the Swazi, the highest ministerial posts in the government and other offices on all levels were filled by commoners. The king was careful "not to give too much power to male kinsmen," and he maintained a balance between the rights of the royal clan and the commoners.[19] Furthermore, in the Ngwato state (in Botswana), a heterogeneous society, a principle of hereditary rule ran throughout the entire political system, and administrative authority in each unit was vested not so much in the principal person but in the whole family of which he was the head. The state was divided in sections with a royal headman in charge of each, and sections were divided into wards; some were royal wards originally founded by the sons of the paramount chief, and others were headed by faithful commoners who had royal herds in their care. In the councils, the paramount chief worked with close paternal relatives as well as headmen who were commoners. The common headmen, however, were bound closer to him than anyone else:

> They were dependent upon him for their entire subsistence, and therefore of necessity were among his most loyal adherents. They were looked upon as and proved themselves his strong supporters against the intrigues of his uncles and brothers, and, since they could never be potential rivals for the chieftainship, he came to rely more and more upon them, until in time they became the most influential group assisting him to govern. . . .[20]

One way of preventing the secession of princes in charge of subdivisions was for the king and his hereditary councillors to fill the chiefdoms in order of seniority with princes of the blood who traveled from post to post according to regulations. Their circulation excluded the chance of making hereditary office a local matter, and it bound the princes to the throne because they hoped to ascend to a series of chieftainships in order of seniority. The Bemba followed this scheme.[21] Another alternative was to turn the royal kin into something like a proto-bureaucracy, in which titles and positions depended on progressive elevation in rank. In this way, they became royal personnel rather than princes and grandees, and their careers depended on rotation in office and the ladder of promotions, which bound them to the system. In the Kede state, a riverine community which was a vassal of the Nupe kingdom in Nigeria, the exalted monarch (the *Kuta*), who had a strong economic position and a large retinue, filled the most important offices in the state with his blood relatives. His titled "councillors" were hereditary and always drawn from a number of different families who "owned" the offices, but the so-called delegates, who governed the various Kede settlements and colonies along the Niger and Kaduna rivers, were all recruited from the family of the *Kuta*. Their graded ranks followed a strict order of precedence and promotion, ascending through posts with increasing power, importance, and remuneration. The lower rungs of the ladder were occupied by new recruits from the chiefs' kin without titles, but the higher ranks depended on gradual promotions, which were determined by the *Kuta* in consultation with a board of notables. The penultimate promotion was to the office of deputy to the *Kuta*, and since this officer was also the heir apparent to the throne, he was usually the most senior titled relative of the *Kuta*, in most cases a brother or nephew. The system of graded promotions, with the highest promotion to the throne itself, and the scheme of rotation in office, preventing any official from establishing independent control of a subdivision, overcame the weaknesses in royal kinship ties and turned them into a bulwark of power for the *Kuta*. The weakness of the system, Nadel thought, lay in the fact that it allowed no legitimate check on that power, and he concluded that the only way in which a more equitable balance could have been achieved was through the illegitimate or extra-institutional means of feuds or factional splits in the hereditary ruling class.[22] Other systems to be found in West and Central Africa used different methods of constructing palace bureaucracies and of filling ladders of titled offices, occupied by a mixture of royals, nobles, and commoners, to bind and balance the royal kin.

In some cases, a simple rule could change the relationship of the king to his kinsmen and relieve some of the resistances in the system. In Bunyoro (in Uganda), for example, a new king was formally detached from the royal clan and one of his brothers appointed as the head of the clan. In this way, the king was identified with the entire kingdom and responsibility for the claims of the royal descent group transferred to someone else.[23]

In general, it may be said that the most effective kinds of nondestructive counter-resistance that a king could mount against his relatives depended on his capacity to make appointments to central and territorial offices. However, it is true that the control of resources or the deterrent effect of his possession of superior weapons (such as Arab guns) or the exclusive control of ritual functions could also be imposing sources of strength.

Typical examples of two different kinds of stable dynastic rule, relatively untroubled by rebellion and secession, that managed the resistances of the royal kin without violence may be found in the Swazi kingdom and in Jimma Abba Jifar, the Galla despotism in Ethiopia.[24] Lewis believes that the position of the royal family in Jimma Abba Jifar stood in the middle ground between the extremes represented by two systems in Uganda—the Soga kingdoms and Buganda, which were neighbors. As Margaret Fallers has observed, the Soga rulers gave their sons control over territorial divisions and villages, and since these grants tended to become hereditary, the princely enclaves moved in the direction of fission and secession. In contrast, the princes of Buganda were excluded from politics, eliminating royal leadership from the causes of fission.[25] In neither the Soga nor the Ganda case, Lewis believes, "was the monarch as free as the king of Jimma to make the personally most advantageous use of his kinsmen."

In Jimma, the great, extended family of the king did not constitute a corporate group with unique political identity and an independent claim to resources. He used his relatives as agents and advisers and rewarded loyalty with position and wealth, but he "was not politically bound to the members of his own family and descent group."[26] His brothers remained men of power, often the rulers of provinces, but if they gave offense by signs of rivalry with the king or if they in any way threatened the unity of the kingdom, they were exiled. The exiled brothers of kings lived pleasantly in the kingdoms of the area, establishing connections by marriage with other royal families, and they played significant roles in their host communities. Perhaps the practice of exile and the comforts of that life reduced the desperation of potential rivalry in Jimma and eased the pressures toward fission. Furthermore, in Jimma, the king's freedom from restraints enabled him to maintain a stable dynastic structure without significant resistances from his relatives.

In the Swazi kingdom, however, stability was achieved by finding an equilibrium that transformed resistances into constitutional limitations and by finding a system of shared powers that satisfied the interests of the princes and balanced the claims of royals with the powers of commoners. Although the highest princes ruled territories and the royals constituted a privileged, corporate group, the monarch's control of resources, ritual, and appointments was more than sufficient to prevent fission or decentralization in the Swazi kingdom.

The Executive Staff. We noticed that observers of Zulu despotism after Shaka occasionally detected signs of disagreement in matters of policy between the ruler and his great induna, but it seemed that as long as those ministers did not contradict the principle that the ruler was an omnipotent, irresistible destroyer, they survived without suffering violence. Indeed, in the issues that divided despot and ministers, the ministers seemed to take more often than not a position that would urge the ruler closer to the despotic ideal, and never sought to impose constitutional limits on his power. The Zulu despots respected their principal ministers, and in Buganda, where the kabaka "had the power of killing each and every individual in the kingdom," the prime minister was one of the few persons who by tradition were immune from execution.[27] When this immunity was violated, his execution was not open like the others, but disguised as accident or illness. The open violence raging in the courts of terroristic despots, such as the Zulu rulers before

Cetshwayo, and such as the kabakas of Buganda—at least through the early reign of Mutesa I in the middle of the nineteenth century—struck lesser officials and servants in particular. During the worst excesses, the kabaka put to death his own children, brothers, and sisters, but it was noted that servants as well were killed "for next to nothing."[28] The kabaka was considered a fierce destroyer of his people and likened to the queen of the termites who fed upon her subjects. Other sayings also dramatized the destructive nature of the royal office: "Just as the blacksmith's shop has coal burning all the time yet no ashes accumulate, so it is with the king who always kills people and yet they go to him." And "The king is a net which is everywhere, and may kill you whether or not you go to him." The king walked abroad with a band of executioners near him, who were ready to kill or bind anyone he pointed out.[29]

Although it is clear that he misunderstood a great deal of what he saw, John Speke, the first of the European visitors, was shocked by the slaughter in the Buganda court. The slightest violations of instruction or etiquette incurred the death penalty, and in other cases people were executed without having committed any offense. Speke wrote that no one could utter a word until he was spoken to, "and a word put in out of season is a life lost." As he sat by the king's side, the son of the chief executioner himself—one of the highest officers of state—was led off for execution for some imperfection in his salute to the kabaka. There was no escape from the dangers of court life, it seemed, and Speke believed that "their very lives depend upon their presenting themselves at court a certain number of months every year, no matter from what distant part of the country they have to come."[30] Many of the attendants were the sons of chiefs or the sons of their subordinates. The principal route to high rank in Buganda was through service as a page in the court of the kabaka, but since life in the palace was fraught with danger in addition to opportunity, it was not uncommon for a chief to send a child of a subordinate in place of his own.[31]

Evidently, there were some limits to the power of the

kabaka: the prime minister and the queen mother exercised influence, and the concept of the "good king" expressed at the accession ceremony reflected some norms of kindness and justice.[32] Moreover, in the history of Buganda, the people rose in rebellion at certain offenses and overthrew the kabaka. Lucy Mair has objected to the notion of his "omnipotence," observing:

> If one asks whether the Kabaka of Buganda was feared, that is another question, and the answer is yes. But this does not make a man omnipotent; it simply secures the subservience of those who are near enough to him to be within reach of his anger and of the punishments that he can inflict.[33]

Subservience is one style of obedience without resistance, and one must infer that a function of the kabaka's violence was to inhibit the potential resistances—including petty obstructions and delays—of his own executive staff. By specialization and dissociation, one part of the staff could be used for destructive action against the rest. This unit was the executioner's division, trained as specialists in violence and disciplined to destroy on command anyone, regardless of rank, condition of life, and social relationship.[34] Thus, the staff of the kabaka included the usual organs of command and administration and a distinct organization for violent counter-resistance.

Milder kings worked out a repertoire of alternative nondestructive methods that Herbert Lewis has called "the strategy of monarchical rule." He observed:

> In order to succeed in the struggle with his administrators, a king must wherever possible apply techniques designed to control them. His aim must always be to limit the scope for independent action of his officials. One means to this end is to restrict each subordinate to as small a sphere of operation as is practical in any particular case. The more limited and closely defined is the jurisdiction of any individual, the more dependent he will be.[35]

The various procedures to deal with administrative resistance by supervision, rewards, penalties, and reorganization are universal and probably too familiar to bear repetition here. One unusual method, however, should be mentioned, not merely because the example is picturesque, but because it exposes the dynamics of political co-operation.

A form of resistance against a chief, we have noted, was for the elders to refuse to co-operate in some essential task. Logically, then, an equally effective counter-resistance would be for a king, whose functions were essential to the co-operative system, to go on strike. Eugen Zintgraff, the first explorer to write a book about the Grassfields region in the Cameroon, witnessed such an action in 1889 and recorded it in his description of the Bali of Bamenda. Garega, the King of the Bali, who had ambitions of uniting the Grassfields under Bali hegemony, was a shrewd ruler who was very clever in sensing the wishes of his people, and he never issued an order without being certain that it would be carried out. He kept a council of fifty or sixty older men in constant session to help run the government. His behavior gave the appearance of ferocity, but it stopped short of destruction. Zintgraff wrote, "Garega's power over his people is unlimited. Open resistance to commands is nil; more than once I saw the old king break his spear in fury over the bent back of some unpunctual sub-chief." [36] If covert resistance mounted to an intolerable degree, the king withdrew and refused to co-operate until he was begged to return:

> Where he came up against some passive resistance from a less enlightened section of his entourage, he took what might seem to us a rather unusual way out, namely, a temporary resignation and retirement. Seeming tired of the burden of the government he would retire alone to a distant farm, sit down in a retired place and wait there in pique for hours. It often needed many prayers from his followers, who searched for him everywhere, before he would consent to return to his duties and naturally he required unqualified and ready obe-

dience before he agreed to return. His return was consequently a victory march.[37]

The Councils. The conciliar function organized several practices. Bearing and transmitting information, advising, and working as part of the administrative process, it served the needs of the ruler. However, councils also enjoyed an independent authority, which was older than chiefs and kings. This authority was based on the special legitimacy of seniority, with its characteristics of sagacity, responsibility, preservation of norms, agency for tradition, and proximity to the ancestors. Councils, then, were not merely royal mechanisms but also instruments for the ancient authority of eldership. In the course of the struggle between monarchic and conciliar forces, the outcome could take one of several forms: absolute monarchy, limited monarchy with councils restraining the king, or an aristocracy with a figurehead king. To turn to European experience for one example of the victory of the conciliar principle, until the end of the Roman Republic the great council known as the Senate retained its original *auctoritas,* but also managed to keep the originally monarchical executive power in its hands, controlling resources and ritual, administering the state, and remaining the source of initiative, prestige, and decision.

In Africa, the terroristic despots did not eliminate councils from the government, but destroyed their power of resistance. Shaka attacked the source of their independent authority, and his early campaign to destroy the old men had great political significance, for it struck at the social roots of eldership and conciliar power.[38] Shaka replaced the traditional councillors with military officers. He asked his councils for advice but manipulated their responses, punishing those who disagreed with him, and he divided the organizations, playing one off against the other. He also forbade them to meet without him, under pain of death.

In ordinary states, where councils played an active role, the ruler presided over two or three types, and in most cases these groups exercised judicial as well as executive and deliberative functions. Schapera generalized, "The existence of these councils greatly limits the Chief's actual exercise of his power. . . . In order to get anything done, he must first gain the goodwill and support of his advisers and councillors, who play a considerable part in restraining his more arbitrary impulses. Any attempt to act independently of them is not only regarded as unconstitutional, but will also generally fail." [39] Every day the ruler consulted some or all of his intimate privy council, a probouleutic—that is, responsible for preliminary deliberation —informal kitchen cabinet, which met in closed session. One member of this group served as his mouthpiece and regular intermediary with the political community. Councils were not, however, static organizations with immutable functions and powers, as one may conclude from the history of the *Great Lukiiko*, the present legislature of Uganda, which began as a gathering of chiefs who assembled daily in the palace to talk over whatever business the kabaka chose to set before them.

On the next level sat a wider, more formal council, which included chiefs and headmen, convened regularly on certain occasions and summoned in emergency when the ruler wanted to sound out public opinion. Decisions made in this council usually had the force of law. Finally, in some systems, the widest council was a full assembly of all the initiated men.

The nature of resistances expressed in council differed from one level to the next, but in its special idiom each clarified what was expected of the ruler and also challenged his deviations. Intimate councillors criticized and warned, while the higher councils might even bring formal action against him—in the Tswana state, the paramount chief could be brought to public trial and punished for his transgressions. Although matters rarely reached that stage, the Tswana chief might also be fined for contempt of the council's authority if he failed to carry out its deliberate wish.

The ruler was usually expected to take the sense of the meeting. In the event of a difference between king and council, the matter was held in abeyance. In case of a deadlock, in the Tswana system, a committee made up of the most influential men would visit the ruler and "persuade him to agree with the people." If the deadlock endured, the council might refuse point blank to carry out his suggestions.[40]

In the open councils, there were few obvious limitations on free discussion. Kuper shows that in the General Council of the Swazi kingdom "no one is prohibited from attending and speaking at the meetings," and the members of the Inner Council "do not fear expulsion if they speak freely, and they openly criticize when they feel that is necessary." [41] Rulers not only shunned being exposed in the councils for their shortcomings, but also avoided taking a position that contravened majority opinion. Sometimes their original positions were modified or even reversed in the course of debate, and there was no way to avoid public discussion of policy, for it was a highly prized activity. Europeans observed that the indigenous peoples of Southern Africa believed passionately in the importance of "talking over" disputes and that they were extraordinarily gifted in the art of discussion,[42] which corresponds to the "love of palaver" observed in West African communities.

Nevertheless, chiefs and kings came up with some modes of counter-resistance against the councils that are familiar political techniques. Through their control of appointments to councils—where that control was not limited or excluded by a principle of hereditary succession to conciliar positions—rulers might pack the council with favorites, ensuring their own support. Moreover, the king's close advisers, who were familiar with the issues and who had the advantage of predigesting matters on the agenda would find ways to dominate the proceedings, to push their opinions, or to argue around the opposition. They might also have sent influential emissaries beforehand to lobby with chiefs who could be expected to oppose the king's recommendations. Furthermore, there were often hidden restrictions to the official freedom of speech and debate. Public opposition might provoke later reprisals from the ruler or the king's men. An influential person who was secure in his position or angry enough might speak his mind without worrying about the consequences, but ordinary men struggling to grasp advantages and to avoid deprivations would think twice about risking the king's wrath. Just as no ruler would go against the conciliar expression of public opinion with impunity, no man would take a public stand against the king without good reason and ample support. Intimidation limited the resistances of the councils, for fear sometimes operated as an inhibiting force in the relation between the councillors and the throne.

Finally, it should be recognized that the members exercised influences outside the council place. When royal marriages were planned—especially when the great wife of a Nguni king was being chosen—councillors played an active part in the negotiations, including the complex economic task of collecting cattle for the bridal payment. Furthermore, before the installation of a successor to the throne, leading councillors who considered the heir apparent an unsuitable candidate might intrigue against him to select a junior relative who was more satisfactory in their eyes. Therefore, the despots Shaka and Dingane, by refusing to marry and to produce heirs, removed from the potential control of councillors an entire sector of political life.

Territorial Chiefs. The structure of primitive communities, which made fission and separation an easy matter, had another side to it. As Omer-Cooper indicates, the same structure could "lend itself to a process of aggregation as easily as to one of fragmentation." A conquered chiefdom might simply be attached to a hierarchy of territorial units, with its head becoming a subchief, and indeed a number of great states grew up in this manner.[43] The question of whether the movement of aggregation would prevail over the pressures toward fission, however, depended not on the structure of the units but on the resistances within them and the counterforces devised to contain or inhibit these resistances.

As we have seen, Shaka did a great deal to redesign the corporate structure of the state in order to minimize the autonomy of subdivisions. The reorganization was effective but insufficient, and in Dingane's reign the most important targets of the terror process were the chiefs. Loyalty to the local chiefs remained a threat to the stability of the larger system. In Buganda, too, the kings had reorganized the system over many generations, and Fallers suggests that in the course of development the Ganda state may have resembled the Zulu nation. At one time the most important officers in Buganda were held by the hereditary heads of lineages and clans, who also "owned" the land, but the government eventually passed into the hands of chiefs who were appointed by the kabaka, who were controlled by him exclusively, and who were loyal only to him.[44] Yet, even though these chiefs made up a proto-bureaucracy, in all probability the old temptations remained and their potential resistance was discerned, for they were struck by the terror observed in the early part of Mutesa's reign. Roscoe wrote:

> the King might cause any one of his chiefs to be bound, detained, or put to death at his pleasure. A chief would enter the court apparently high in favour, and then some trifling circumstance might alter everything; he would be seized, bound, and dragged away by the police with cuffs and blows, and with every mark of indignity, to be put into the stocks until the King's final decision was known. . . .
>
> The King often brought a spurious charge against a chief who was becoming rich. . . .[45]

And as Fallers describes the relation between the Ganda king and his chiefs:

> By the middle of the nineteenth century, the kingdom was governed by a corps of chiefs who owed their positions largely to the personal grace of the Kabaka, who might appoint, dismiss and transfer them at will. Every young man aspired to a career in the service of the Kabaka, around whom was woven a cultural tissue of arbitrary fierceness and power. A chief might

one day stand at the pinnacle of wealth and influence, the ruler of a large district and the recipient of lavish tribute from his people and estates from his king; next day, having incurred the monarch's disfavour, he might be stripped of property and office, lying in stocks, the object of scorn and physical tortures of a most imaginative kind.[46]

In the cases of Buganda, Matebele, and Zulu, violence was part of a continual process of terror to inhibit the chiefs, but similar uses of violence against them by other rulers fell short of terrorism. A king, upon taking the throne, might execute a set of chiefs whose resistance he feared, but after replacing them he might rule without extensive violence. Thus, in the history of Ruanda, King Rwaabugiri destroyed a group of chiefs to eliminate them as rivals and to establish absolute power, but this action was apparently not a policy of terror—contrary to what the historian Vansina suggests (referring to it as *"cette politique de terreur"*)—or if it was, it must have been a brief episode, for the exercise of power afterwards did not depend on continual violence.[47]

There were three kinds of territorial chief. One was a prince of the blood; another, a governor appointed by the king. (We have already discussed a number of ways in which kings controlled their royal kinsmen and the members of their executive staff.) The third kind represented the people the chief governed, usually by hereditary right, and he was often referred to as the "owner of the land." It was more difficult to incorporate chiefs of this kind into the kingdom. If they were removed and replaced by a prince or a king's man, the people of the territory might be stirred by resentment to secede and to replace him with a chief of their own line. On the other hand, if the original chief were retained, his unique power over the people made his relation to the king tentative and problematic. For this reason in many systems, chiefdoms on the periphery were not really integral units of the state but only vassals or allies who merely paid tribute and formally accepted the king as an overlord.

If the leader of a community claimed legitimate authority, dispensed wealth and honor, administered ritual, maintained order, and interacted with the representatives of other communities without the consent or participation of another office, he enjoyed the powers of a sovereign chief. On the other hand, if a king claimed the right to define that leader's authority so that his legitimacy derived from the higher office, or if the king managed to control resources or to participate in the other functions, that mediation defined the community leader as a subordinate chief. In all systems—despotisms as well as limited monarchies—a constitutional agreement or working consensus specified the nature and scope of chiefly authority. Actions that exceeded the boundaries established by this mutual understanding were defined as illegitimate resistance. The range within the boundaries or the extent to which higher authority could *specify* the manner in which local chiefs might perform their functions indicated the degree of subordination. As the range of choice within the boundaries shrank and the central control of specificity increased, the number of actions defined as illegitimate resistance expanded correspondingly. Nondestructive methods of coping with the potential resistance of chiefs worked by confining their jurisdictions through political means or by controlling the social bases of their power.

Apart from legitimacy and ritual, the most important source of chiefly power was the control of resources. Subordinate chiefs did not lose this power, but they could not determine how it would be used. Food, labor, cattle, and commodities moved up the hierarchy of chiefs in the form of taxes, tribute, and gifts, and a great deal of it flowed down again in the form of hospitality and largesse. The right to take or receive wealth and the obligation to redistribute some of it belonged to both the subordinate and the sovereign chief. As Fallers points out, "the most important thing was *control* over goods and services, and this the chiefs possessed to a marked degree, just as they possessed control over people." [48] The ownership of wealth conferred prestige, which was often one source of power, but that was a matter separate from the control of resources. Hypothetically, a poor man who was able to allocate resources would have power without wealth. The distinction between ownership and control of resources explains in part why terroristic despots preferred to keep their chiefs in modest circumstances. If a chief were to wax rich, his affluence not only gave him prestige, which was a source of personal power, but also a surplus that might be used as independent resources. However, the degree to which any king was able to control the resources of local communities helped to determine the limits on the chiefs, and the measure of the king's receipts was an index of territorial subordination.

Political methods of confining the chiefs usually designed hierarchies of overlapping jurisdictions, and tangled skeins of official functions with complexities that only the king's power could resolve. Furthermore, to deny certain functions, such as fiscal or military operations, to the territorial heads fragmented their authority and made them depend on other officials who exercised those functions, thereby rendering their power incomplete. Other means of controlling the chiefs, as we have already noted in the case of royal kinsmen, were to place them on career ladders that depended on the king and to rotate them through a cycle of offices in different territories.

The power of the king over his chiefs was strengthened when the political processes that selected them were dissociated from the groups they administered. Lloyd Fallers reiterates this principle, which was previously asserted by M. G. Smith, and states it as a distinction between administration (defined as the execution of policy) and politics (defined as the struggle for power and for the right to determine policy). As he puts it:

> There remains an important difference between a state each of whose servants is the legitimate political representative of the people he governs and one in which the official is chosen through processes distinct from his unit of administrative responsibility, however political these processes may be.[49]

The principle may be stated in another way, making it relevant to the problem of power and resistance. If a state contains factions or corporate groups strong enough to influence policy and to select chiefs, the influence of these groups and their struggle for power constitute potential resistances to the authority of the king. If the units these chiefs administer are identical with the corporate groups engaged in the struggle over policy, then the resistances will be located in the administrative system, weakening the capacity of the king to execute policy in those units. If the corporate groups or factions struggling over policy and influencing appointments are different from the units of administration, however, then the king's control over those resistances is less crucial to his administrative effectiveness in the territorial divisions.

In contrast to the Zulu, whose example they often consciously tried to avoid, the Swazi kings tried to cement their relations with the hereditary rulers of conquered groups by respecting them and satisfying their interests. The Dlamini—the royal clan of the Swazi—"emphasized the sanctity and power of hereditary chieftainship," and this policy received its impetus from Mswati, "the greatest of the Swazi fighting kings." Hilda Kuper writes:

> as long as a chief or his heir survived, the Dlamini ruler acknowledged him as the foundation on which the conquered group could be rebuilt. Mswati reinstated heirs of certain clan chiefs in the districts of their fathers, once their allegiance was assured. In this way he made staunch allies of once powerful enemies. This transition in attitude and behaviour resulted from the treatment the future chief received from the Dlamini king, the building up of economic and political interdependence and the creation of bonds of kinship and friendship.[50]

The later Swazi kings, finding their domain already disposed in well-established local units, did not interfere with local overlords or change their boundaries without good reason. Stability was cherished from one reign to another, and everyone recognized that for a king to shake up the traditional units, which had been loyal to his father, would be to introduce resentment and disorder. Only to correct insubordination, to solve violent quarrels between adjoining areas, or to bestow unusual honors on especially distinguished men, did a king intrude on the lands of an established chief.[51] For the most part, to control the powers of the chiefs, kings relied on the balances in the political system.

The Lunda people, deep in the savanna of Central Africa, worked out a remarkably effective system to stabilize relations between the central government and the provincial chiefs. Without a regular standing army and with very little military strength, the Lunda formed expanding states which spread dramatically over a large part of Africa in the seventeenth century. Neighboring states simply exploited defeated chiefs and overtaxed them, but the Lunda system proved to be a desirable mode of aggregation: chiefs joined its territorial complex voluntarily or with little resistance, and Lunda colonies, Vansina declares, became neutral places "from the point of view of the non-Lunda residents in an area, a place where one could go for arbitration, a place to which one was ultimately subjected without the use of force." [52] The first kings with their kinsmen and retinues superimposed a state on the foundation of land-owning kinship groups and integrated the local leaders into the political system as a separate category of land-owning chiefs. The Lunda struck a delicate but stable balance between the central power and the governed territories by institutionalizing the clear distinction between the formerly sovereign chiefs, who were subsequently named the "owners of the land" or "lords of the countryside," and the "political chiefs" governing districts and representing the king and the palace authorities. As a proverb explained, the political chief was the cinder that the wind carried away, but the owner of the land was the ember that remained. Political chiefs exercised authority over the residents of the administrative districts but not over the soil. The country lords never surrendered title to the land, and they retained ritual functions and much of their traditional authority over persons in their jurisdictions, but they handed over taxes and rendered other obligations to the political chiefs.[53] In this dual system, the institutions of positional succession and perpetual kinship guaranteed the integrity of the country lord's position and strengthened the relationships among the political chiefs and the high titleholders in the central government. Vansina has shown that throughout the Lunda empire, "the whole political structure rested on the twin mechanisms of positional succession and perpetual kinship," and these mechanisms were so flexible and adaptive that they "could be diffused without necessitating any changes in the existing social structures, which explains why so many Central African cultures could take over the system with little or no cultural resistances. . . ."

For the sake of illustration, in order to clarify these institutions, let us imagine the heads of two chiefdoms who were full brothers. Perpetual kinship means that the relationship between the heads of those communities would always be defined by fraternal rights and obligations. Positional succession means that whoever succeeded to the position of chief in one unit, even though he was biologically merely a distant cousin, would legally become the brother of the other chief. The heir took on the social identity of his predecessor, acquiring his name, kinship connections, property, and political office. As Vansina observes, the practices served as an "integrative mechanism which is social in its idiom but which is often mainly political in its purposes and effects." [54] The device satisfied interests of the country lords but limited their action, and in the central government it framed a network of stable expectations that linked the political chiefs to higher officials and to the king. With their respected positions as "owners of the land," the country lords had more incentive to support the political system than their counterparts in some other states, who were downtrodden tributary chiefs.

Social Institutions and Inertial Resistance. The collective fantasy of terroristic despotism, which performed many functions of a modern ideology, encouraged the ruler to bring all kinds of social behavior under his control. Therefore, conduct that was regulated by inclinations and principles outside the political sphere could be defined as resistance, and he might act to break its autonomy.

In the Zulu case, the despots took pains to control sexual behavior, marriage, and the family, and to reduce the social power of kinship. The later Zulu kings, working in conditions of limited monarchy, co-operated with the pressures to restore the traditional rights to marry. The family eventually returned to the province of custom, and kinship institutions recovered authority.

The control of magic was more obviously relevant to the political sphere, for diviners and witch finders could interfere with the ruler's decisions, and his officers were vulnerable to their activities. The locus of magical power fluctuated with political vicissitudes: Shaka and Mzilikazi broke the independent power of witch finders, and Mpande decentralized their terror, allowing them to rise again under the territorial chiefs. In the country of the Matebele, the heir of Mzilikazi, his son Lobengula, used the societies of witch finders "as the principle means of removing his private enemies" and to build up his own despotic regime. According to one observer, "on the pretext of sorcery, hundreds, nay thousands of innocent people who had incurred [his] suspicion, or who had acquired too great a popular influence, were 'smelt out' and butchered." [55]

The logic of terroristic despotism inclined toward the control over details of behavior that seemed devoid of political significance. At one time in Buganda, the kabaka ordered every man to wear a bead on his wrist, on pain of losing his head, and every woman a bead strung to her waist, on pain of being cut in half. Speke described a perpetual stream of petty offenders, mainly palace women, being dragged off to execution each day. He actually intervened to save one victim when, "by some unlucky chance, one of the royal wives . . . plucked a fruit and offered it to the king . . . but he like a madman, flew into a towering passion, said it was the first time a woman ever had the impudence to offer him anything, and ordered the pages to seize, bind, and lead her off to execution." [56] Besides what seem to be minor infractions of etiquette, Speke recorded a number of prohibitions that were enforced by the death penalty:

> No one even dare ever talk about the royal pedigree, of the countries that have been conquered, or even of any neighbouring countries; no one dare visit the king's guests, or be visited by them, without leave. . . . Neither can any one cast his eye for a moment on the women of the palace, whether out walking or at home, lest he should be accused of amorous intentions. Beads and brass wire, exchanged for ivory or slaves, are the only article of foreign manufacture any Mganda can hold in his possession. Should anything else be seen in his house—for instance, cloth—his property would be confiscated and his life taken.[57]

Some of these controls were implicit in the despot's monopoly of economic life, and some of the executions were probably carried out, as Speke surmised, "merely that his guests might see his savage power," but the range of controls over details of ordinary behavior suggests that the despot *sought* to determine specificity in the entire conduct of life. The ubiquity of royal violence gave every action within striking range of the palace a political orientation, defining many kinds of social deviance as political resistance, and the news of executions reminded the people with perpetual shocks that no transaction escaped political jurisdiction.

Legitimacy of Resistance. In terroristic despotism, then, systematic violence worked not only to paralyze the resistance of secondary powers, but also to inhibit social deviation, for social practices not under control might indeed have led to problems of co-ordination and to crises of integration. Almost anything could be defined as resistance, and no form of resistance was officially permitted. Physical destruction was the uniform mode of counter-resistance.

All other kinds of government handled resistance in a different manner. On the one hand, many actions that drew forth violence in the despotic regimes were not defined as resistance in limited monarchies. On the other hand, in a certain range, some resistances were defined as legitimate forms of political action and incorporated into the system of power. Whereas the rules of terroristic despotism demanded zero resistance and unconditional obedience, the institutions of limited monarchy, within certain restrictions, called for conditional obedience and conditional resistance. The king ruled without opposition as long as his actions conformed to the working consensus. When he moved outside its limits, certain officials exercised their own legitimate power against him. In the Swazi kingdom, for example, if the king abused his privileges, the queen mother could not only act as a check, but also might become the leader of an organized opposition.

In a system that endowed officers below the king with secondary powers, their legitimate resistance temporarily interfered with co-operation. The consequence of their resistance was to modify the action of the ruler, thereby restoring cooperation. Moreover, the structural consequence of institutionalizing and giving legitimate force to secondary powers was to establish a most effective kind of counter-resistance. Just as defining the powers of the king kept them within limits, identifying and naming resistances, formalizing the manner in which they were to be exercised, confined their force, made them predictable, prescribed their scope, and tended to control their disruptive potential. Conflict in the state emerged when the king and his secondary powers strove to occupy incompatible positions. When the structure of powers and resistances was stable, the king, his agents, and all incumbents chose to accommodate their actions to the working consensus and took compatible positions, each accepting mutually defined limitations and respecting the powers of the others. The stability of a limited monarchy depended on the smooth, cooperative interaction of legitimate resistances. In terroristic despotism, the constitution achieved stability when resistance came to an end.

CHAPTER XV

THE

STRUCTURE OF

COUNTER-RESISTANCE

Let us go and wage war
Resistance is ended;
From whom did you hear
That resistance was ended?
Iyoyi
From whom did you hear
That resistance was ended?
—from Shaka's war song
in R. C. Samuelson, *Long, Long Ago*.

A POLITICAL COMMUNITY is a system of co-operation before it can be anything else. In hierarchical communities such as chiefdoms and states, men in authority initiate and judge the course of interactions. Their subordinates sometimes experience political decisions as acts of force—that is, as commands against their will bearing unfavorable consequences for their own lives or for the community as a whole. They may react to unfavorable situations and render authority incomplete by performing isolated acts of resistance or by pursuing highly integrated political activities. Groups resist not only to oppose specific policy but also to preserve their vitality and to defend their internal social environment against disruption.

Resistance can suspend co-operation or make it defective. The forms of resistance—including criticism, challenge, disobedience, rebellion, and secession—may hinder, interrupt, or threaten to destroy the system of co-operation. Any form is a specific mode of adaptation to unfavorable circumstance, but the general purpose of all kinds of resistance is to re-establish a favorable situation.

We have briefly considered typical acts of resistance above on pp. 16–17. Many of these acts depend on a social process, which is essential to the more resolute forms of resistance. Moreover, organized resistance carried on by factions or by other groups with solidary relationships goes through phases of the process, depending on the endurance and severity of the force it opposes:

(1) The alarm reaction, before resistance is planned and carried out.

(2) The stage of action—or negative adaptation to the force—when resistance achieves maximal strength. Usually at this stage the establishment modifies the initial force. It withdraws the original command or else reinforces the initial decision with persuasion, with additional coercion, or with violence. If the resistance is successful, this stage is final.

(3) The stage of exhaustion, when the resistors lose the capacity to oppose or to maintain relationships within the group. The stress is too long or too acute if the relationships change detrimentally or if the group succumbs to the environment.

The alarm reaction is the initial stage that sets the conditions of resistance. At that time the undesirable command is rejected, and resources are mobilized to punish or countercontrol the establishment. It is often a moment of rapid communication and intense interaction, creating new ties and solidifying old relationships. It is also a time for recruiting allies, mending fences, working together, co-ordinating activities, getting resources, making agendas, suspending some activities and integrating others, and planning strategy. As Simmel recognized, perceiving the establishment as an opponent increases solidarity in the resisting group.

The relation between force and resistance may be understood in dynamic terms as political stress. It is a relation with balances of energy that shift as each side counteracts the other. Resistance elicits from the establishment a response that may be understood as political work, which either removes, modifies, or supports its initial force. The response is often necessary, because ordinary activity cannot go on without co-operation.

When the dimensions of resistance portend minor disruption, or if resistance is limited to specific aspects of co-operation, the establishment can afford to deal with it by watchful neglect, avoiding the danger of changing the milieu in which the co-operative systems exist. For example, if demonstrators protesting the activities of military forces, an economic organization, or a university limit the resistance to criticism and challenge and if their action remains external to the co-operative system in question, visible counter-resistance may be avoided. If their action interferes with the system of co-operation or if the protest manages to persuade members of the organization to withhold co-operation, however, active counter-resistance of one kind or another is inescapable.

Some systems, we have seen, tolerate little or no resistance. Every political order has, besides the rules that specify who will exercise power and through what procedures, an informal code that tells how the establishment will deal with resistance. The code is meant for ordinary stress, but an acute crisis or prolonged, intense conflict is bound to change the style of counter-resistance.

One response that precludes counter-resistance is for the establishment to yield and to withdraw voluntarily the command originally defined as an act of force by the resistors. If a group has a co-operative relationship with the establishment prior to its alienation by an act of force, then, unless new factors are introduced, the voluntary withdrawal of force restores co-operation. However, if the establishment fails to respond before the resistance moves to the peak of adaptation in the second phase, the interactions, relationships, and mobilization in the dissident group may create a new social reality for the members. Conditions of the second phase may stimulate the group to new perceptions and new expectations which make it impossible for them to return to the old compact. Then fewer alternatives remain to the establishment besides counter-resistance by coercive means or by violence.

Men in authority are generally sensitive to the cost of "giving in," assuming without much reflection that yielding to resistance necessarily compromises power. They pay less attention to the social cost of counter-resistance. Nevertheless, as the executive organ of the state, a government has the executive responsibility to be found in any social system—namely, the function of inventing and maintaining incentives for people to co-operate.[1] Depleting the opportunities for voluntary co-operation does not destroy co-operation, but it changes the nature of the system. It leaves few resources besides the coercive apparatus of the state. The loss of voluntary co-operation induces a mood of desperation and a conviction that co-operation must be maintained at any cost. It increases the temptation to depend on the "forced choice" game of incentives and on the violent removal—ultimately, the violent inhibition—of resistance. In extreme cases, transformation of the entire society may be the price of counter-resistance.

In general, there are two kinds of counter-resistance: one is *reactive*, the other *preventive*. Both kinds have one form that depends on voluntary decisions and another that employs force or violence. The persuasive kind of reactive counter-resistance works by arguments, flattery, promises, bribery, tokens, rewards, "buying off" leaders of the opposition, negotiation, bargaining, exchanging advantages, or any sort of influence causing men to withdraw resistance voluntarily. The second kind of reactive counter-resistance employs coercion or force and threatens or executes penalties of one kind or another in order to secure an involuntary withdrawal of resistance or simply in order to crush resistance by armed strength.

The nonviolent kind of preventive counter-resistance works

through programs to anticipate needs, or by social institutions that reduce the occasions for conflict. Another mechanism is provided by constitutional orders that factor out resistance from broad areas of social interaction and confine its expression to specialized procedures in formal political institutions. In monarchies, political stress may be contained within the structural opposition between the throne and other institutions such as a Council of State. In modern states, when factions become political parties, they agree to formalize their resistances and confine their expression to behavior defined by the rules. This arrangement channels resistance, identifies it with specific issues, ventilates it in the drama of public debate, expresses it in parliamentary maneuvers, and holds it within the bounds of electoral procedures. The institution of "loyal opposition" in parliamentary systems confines resistance to legitimate actions, makes it predictable, and promises that the manner of its expression will not endanger the system of co-operation. When a parliamentary system breaks down, it often means that social reactions to an unfavorable situation could no longer be abstracted and confined to the forms of established political institutions. In that case, the breakdown of the old forms of preventive counter-resistance could call forth new reactive counter-resistance.

The other kind of preventive counter-resistance, which depends on recurrent violence, is the system of terror, which inhibits the social process of resistance. In an emotional environment of extreme fear, the interactions and relationships that bolster individual courage or encourage group solidarity cannot survive. People are afraid to meet together and are afraid even more to examine their mutual interests and express discontent. The alarm reaction of the first phase is lost in the general atmosphere of fright. Indeed, people live in a condition of perpetual alarm, which—instead of stimulating—actually inhibits the work of resistance. The perpetual danger from within the community depresses activity not officially sanctioned and it renders personal relations unpredictable. Interactions of the second phase do not begin to emerge unless people are insulated in some way from the corrosive effect of the terror. The impact of continual violence from authority figures on the unconscious mind, the psychodynamics of terror, and the effect on social behavior—as well as possibilities for insulation from the terror—are matters for the next volume.

In this inquiry, we have seen that in West African chiefdoms controlled by secret associations, the fear of visitation from unpredictable, terrifying spirits is sufficient to inhibit many kinds of resistance, although the degree of terror is comparatively lower than its intensity in states. In terroristic despotisms, all resistance is explicitly forbidden, and it is socially inhibited by the ruler's agents of violence. We have explored the dynamics of primitive systems—where resistance tends to be less specialized and more clearly associated with crises of integration—to seek a general explanation of *why* societies establish regimes of terror.

A rational, systematic answer to the question, "why," should give either a genetic or a functional explanation. I have tried to provide both by describing the historical genesis and subsequent development of terror in the Zulu case, and by analyzing the functions of terror in chiefdoms and states. I have also argued that terror is a social invention and a political choice within a range of alternatives. I did promise, however, to go further and to reveal the conditions in which a political system supports the choice of terror. Accordingly, I list five conditions necessary for the maintenance of a terroristic regime, which may also be understood as functional prerequisites.

(1) A shared ideology that justifies the violence. In West Africa, religious ideas about the authority of ancestral spirits licensed the destructive acts of the secret orders. In terroristic despotism, the collective fantasy about the omnipotence of the great destroyer-provider legitimated his violence; victims were dismissed as evildoers. A state of emergency is often the justification in modern conditions. The French Revolutionaries described the Terror as the tyranny of the people against the tyr-

anny of kings; victims were defined as aristocrats or as enemies of the Revolution. Nazi ideology justified the violence of the master race against its foes. Soviet terror was officially defined as the weapon of the proletariat against the class enemy. Legitimacy suppresses outrage.

(2) The victims in the process of terror must be expendable —that is, their loss cannot affect the system of co-operation. If the violence liquidates persons who are needed for essential tasks, or if replacements cannot be found for their roles, the system of co-operation breaks down.

(3) Dissociation of the agents of violence and of the victims from ordinary social life. This double dissociation removes violence from social controls and separates the victims from sources of protection. Victims are often defined as unpersons or as outsiders beyond the pale.

In West African chiefdoms, masked action episodically dissociated the secret officials from ordinary controls. Although some chiefdoms of this kind remained bicentralized and relatively unchanged for centuries, this type of dissociation was not always an historically stable mode. Centralization introduced specialized staffs, which often superseded the ancestral spirits as forces of counter-resistance.

In terroristic states, the agents of violence are structurally detached, often living apart and usually organized as independent social units—armies, corps of executioners, alien mercenaries, special police, etc. In the Nazi state, the SS and the Gestapo were organized as specialists in terror, even dissociated structurally from other staffs of violence such as the army and the police. In societies simpler than states and chiefdoms— and in most chiefdoms—the terroristic alternative to dealing with resistance does not emerge because of the limitations inherent in the structure of executive action and because there are no mechanisms for dissociation.

(4) Terror must be balanced by working incentives that induce co-operation. Hannah Arendt has argued that ideology provides the motor in totalitarian systems to overcome the

paralysis of terror.[2] We have examined the "pay-off" and the "forced choice" in terroristic despotism. Terror works against the refusal to co-operate, but it is not a substitute for co-operation itself.

(5) Co-operative relationships must survive the effect of the terror. Perpetual fear, suspicion, and unpredictable behavior can rupture the traditional bonds of kinsmen, friends, and fellow workers. If the impact of the terror destroys the network of relationships that supports collective activities and political interactions, the entire co-operative system will break down. The terror can destroy itself by tearing apart the social organization necessary to maintain it. The traditional social network must survive the violence, or substitute relationships must be introduced, if both the society and the terror are to endure.

This vulnerability of social relationships is well known. In the ancient world, Plato recognized that despotism destroyed the bonds of friendliness and fellowship.[3] Leo Lowenthal has described how terror in the totalitarian state dehumanizes and atomizes, depriving men of the psychological means for direct communication at the same time it drives them into collectivities integrated by force.[4] In his study of terror in the Soviet Union, Barrington Moore has observed:

> If everybody in a society is marked as an actual or potential scoundrel, all sorts of vital social relationships will break down. . . . Terror ultimately destroys the network of stable expectations concerning what other people will do that lie at the core of any set of organized human relationships.[5]

Therefore, the kind of co-operation in which people associate and work together without being friends or trusting one another in the first place would endure the terror best. Since they are already co-operating without friendship and trust, the mode of co-operation is less vulnerable to the erosion of personal relations under the terror. Curiously, then, a society in which people are already isolated and atomized, divided by suspicions and mutually destructive rivalry, would support a system of terror better than a society without much chronic antagonism. If co-operative relations do not survive the deterioration of social ties under the terror, the system will break down. These five conditions refer to things that must happen and situations that must exist if systematic terrorism is to endure. Conversely, in the absence of any one of them, the terror would not be possible.

Through the process of terror, a regime may overcome the threat of resistance and secure co-operation. Some rulers resort to violence because their societies appear doomed by the obstacles to co-operation, but others inaugurate terror systems even while their people are engaged in enthusiastic co-operation.

Fortified by terror, men have invented a way to escape the eternal problems of unity and division and have also built their rulers a monumental defense against the pains of justice, limits, and renunciation. But this stronghold is only one of the ramparts societies have raised in many terrible shapes throughout human history. It is the cruelest form of the common barrier that marks the difference between what men need and what they get.

NOTES

CHAPTER I

1. The "causal" relation in some cases is not obvious. It is far from simple in such instances to evaluate the contributing factors. Despite the difficulty, extracting "causes" from events is a matter for historical and sociological judgment. One need not conclude from the dense complexity of social processes that all reasoning about sufficient conditions ought to be abandoned.

2. Forms of terrorism in this general category are examined in Brian Crozier, *The Rebels: A Study of Post-War Insurrections*, London, 1960, and in E. J. Hobsbawm, *Primitive Rebels: Studies in Archaic Forms of Social Movements in the 19th and 20th Centuries*, Manchester, 1959. See also the League of Nations documents regarding the work of several committees, international conferences, and conventions for the repression of terrorism. The list may be found in Hans Aufricht, *Guide to the League of Nations Publications: A Bibliographic Survey of the Work of the League, 1920–1947*, New York, 1951. For a study of the international legal and political issues associated with this kind of terrorism, see Jerzy Waciorski, *Le terrorisme politique*, Paris, 1939.

3. See Paul Radin, *The World of Primitive Man*, New York, 1960, Chs. 6, 8.

4. There is no need to locate the terror process in a voluntaristic theory of social action. That it happens to elude the definition of "social action" does not diminish its sociological importance. One should heed Weber's observation that "sociology, it goes without saying, is by no means confined to the study of 'social action' "; moreover, Weber pointed out that reactive behavior "may well have a degree of sociological importance at least equal to that of the type which can be called social action in the strict sense." Max Weber, *The Theory of Social and Economic Organization*, trans. by Henderson and Parsons, New York, 1947, p. 114. For Weber's own reflections on the relation between reactive behavior and meaning-oriented action, see *Wirtschaft und Gesellschaft*, 4. Aufl., Tübingen, 1956, 1 Hbd., pp. 11–13.

5. *Combat*, 1946, trans. by Dwight Macdonald, reprinted in *Liberation*, February 1960.

CHAPTER II

1. Jan Huizinga, *The Waning of the Middle Ages*, trans. by F. Hopman, New York, 1954, Ch. I.

2. Marc Bloch, *Feudal Society*, trans. by L. A. Manyon, Chicago, 1961, p. 411.
3. Ibid. p. 127.
4. E. E. Evans-Pritchard, *The Political System of the Anuak*, summarized in Lucy Mair, *Primitive Government*, Baltimore, 1962, p. 75.
5. Ibid. p. 197.
6. Thorstein Veblen, *The Theory of the Leisure Class*, New York, 1953, p. 31.
7. Paul Tillich, *Love, Power, and Justice*, New York, 1961, p. 46.
8. *The Sociology of Georg Simmel*, trans. and ed. by Kurt H. Wolff, Glencoe, Ill., 1950, pp. 181 ff.
9. Ibid. pp. 186–87.
10. J. B. S. Hardman, "Intimidation," *Encyclopedia of the Social Sciences*, Vol. VIII, p. 239. Cf. the same author's article, "Terrorism," ibid., Vol. XIV, p. 575, in which he describes terrorism as "the method or theory behind the method whereby an organized group or party seeks to achieve its avowed aims chiefly through the systematic use of violence."
11. Theodor Mommsen, *The History of Rome*, 4th ed., trans. by W. P. Dickson, 4 vols., New York, 1891, Vol. III, p. 105.
12. Stanley M. Elkins, *Slavery: A Problem in American Institutional and Intelletual Life*, Chicago, 1959, Ch. III.
13. Kenneth M. Stampp, *The Peculiar Institution*, New York, 1956, Ch. IV.
14. Ibid. pp. 171–74.
15. Ibid. pp. 183–87.
16. Marcus Terentius Varro, *Rerum Rusticarum* I. xvii. 1. See also Edmund H. Oliver, *Roman Economic Conditions to the Close of the Republic*, Toronto, 1907.
17. Hannah Arendt, "What Was Authority?" in *Authority*, ed. by C. J. Friedrich, Cambridge, Mass., 1958, p. 91.
18. Clarence Marsh Case, *Non-Violent Coercion*, New York, 1923; see also Joan Bondurant, *Conquest of Violence*, Princeton, 1958, p. 9.
19. Leo Kuper, *Passive Resistance in South Africa*, New Haven, 1960, p. 72.
20. General Karl von Clausewitz, *Vom Kriege*, 13. Aufl., Berlin und Leipzig, 1918, pp. 3–4. The translation is my own; emphases in the original are removed.
21. Ibid. pp. 19, 5.
22. Ibid. p. xxxi.
23. Ibid. p. 6.
24. Heinrich Oppenheimer, *The Rationale of Punishment*, London, 1913, p. 172.
25. Ibid. pp. 175, 174.
26. Thomas Hobbes, *Leviathan*, ed. by William Molesworth, *The English Works of Thomas Hobbes*, Vol. III, London, 1839, p. 300.
27. Ibid. p. 297, italics omitted.
28. Ibid. p. 299.

CHAPTER III

1. A. N. Whitehead, *Adventures of Ideas*, New York, 1933, p. 56.
2. Bertrand Russell, *Power: A New Social Analysis*, New York, 1962, pp. 27, 57.
3. Dorothy Emmet, "The Concept of Power," *Proceedings of the Aristotelian Society*, Vol. 54, 1954, p. 13.
4. José Ortega y Gasset, *Concord and Liberty*, trans. by Helene Weyl, New York, 1946, pp. 34, 35.
5. John L. Myres, *The Political Ideas of the Greeks*, New York, 1927, p. 158.
6. Herodotus, *Histories* III. 83; Aristotle, *Politics* 1277b.
7. Aristotle, *The Metaphysics* V. 1013a, trans. by W. D. Ross, 2nd ed., London, 1948.
8. *Metaphysics* 1013a, 1046a, trans. by Richard Hope, Ann Arbor, Mich., 1960, pp. 104, 182. The Hope translation prefers "power" to the word "potency," which is found in older translations.
9. As indicated later in the chapter, I have extended the conception of power proposed by Felix E. Oppenheim in *Dimensions of Freedom: An Analysis*, New York, 1961.
10. *Metaphysics* 1019a, trans. by Hope, p. 105.
11. R. M. MacIver, *The Web of Government*, New York, 1947, p. 77.
12. Russell, *Power*, p. 25.
13. Oppenheim, *Dimensions of Freedom*, p. 100.
14. Ibid. Chs. 4, 5.
15. Ibid. Ch. 2.
16. Ibid. p. 40.
17. Ibid. p. 52.
18. William Foote Whyte, *Street Corner Society*, 2nd ed., Chicago, 1961, p. 258.
19. George C. Homans, *Social Behavior: Its Elementary Forms*, New York, 1961, p. 386.
20. Tacitus, *The Complete Works*, trans. by Church and Brodribb, New York, 1942, pp. 712–14.
21. Eric A. Walker, *A History of Southern Africa*, 3rd ed., London, 1957, p. 112; cf. *Cambridge History of the British Empire*, Vol. VIII, p. 41 ff.
22. *From Max Weber: Essays in Sociology*, trans. by H. H. Gerth and C. Wright Mills, New York, 1946, p. 251.
23. A. Andrewes, *Probouleusis*, London, 1954, pp. 6, 9.
24. *Cambridge Ancient History*, 1st. ed., Vol. II, Ch. xvii; N.G.L. Hammond, *A History of Greece to 322 B. C.*, London, 1959, pp. 67, 140.
25. Aidan W. Southall, *Alur Society: A Study in Processes and Types of Domination*, Cambridge, Eng., [1953].
26. *Metaphysics* 1015a, b.

27. Max Jammer, *Concepts of Force: A Study in the Foundations of Dynamics*, New York, 1962, p. 37.
28. *Nichomachean Ethics* 1110b.
29. Jammer, op. cit. p. viii.
30. Tillich, *Love, Power, and Justice*, p. 7.
31. Jammer, op. cit. p. 264.
32. In Sophocles, *Oedipus at Colonus* 373, Ismene tells exiled Oedipus that at Thebes, each of his sons is attempting to grasp both *arché* and *kratos* of the throne.
33. Hesiod, *Theogony* 385.
34. Aeschylus, *Promethus Bound* 34, 402, 150.
35. The fact that the official rules limited speech to only two persons on stage, it should go without saying, is hardly a complete or sufficient explanation for Bia's silence.
36. Aeschylus, *Prometheus Bound* 42.
37. Ibid. 50, 10.
38. Charles E. Merriam, *Political Power*, Glencoe, Ill., 1950, p. 21.
39. MacIver, *The Web of Government*, p. 16.
40. C. Wright Mills, *The Power Elite*, New York, 1956, p. 171.
41. *Kautilya Arthasastra*, trans. by R. Shamasastry, 7th ed., Mysore, India, 1961.
42. *From Max Weber*, p. 124.
43. For a brief summary of the controversy over the date of Manu, see D. Mackenzie Brown, *The White Umbrella: Indian Political Thought from Manu to Gandhi*, Berkeley, 1953, p. 27.
44. *The Laws of Manu*, trans. by G. Bühler, *The Sacred Books of the East*, Vol. XXV, London, 1886, p. 219.
45. Ibid. p. 221.
46. Ibid. pp. 219–20.
47. Ibid. pp. 218–19.
48. Ibid. pp. 314–15.
49. H. G. Creel, *Confucius and the Chinese Way*, New York, 1960, p. 222. The contrast between Legalism and Orthodox Confucianism is also described by the philosopher Fung Yu-lan, *A Short History of Chinese Philosophy*, New York, 1960, pp. 164–165.
50. Creel, op. cit. pp. 215–16. Fung Yu-lan considers Han Fei-tzu as the "culminating representative" and "the last and greatest theorizer of the Legalist school . . ." op. cit. p. 157.
51. Creel, op. cit. p. 239.
52. Fung Yu-lan, op. cit. pp. 160, 164.
53. Ibid. p. 158, italics added.
54. T. A. Sinclair, *A History of Greek Political Thought*, London, 1961. p. 24.
55. The dependence of power on co-operation is cogently argued in E. E. Harris, "Political Power," *Ethics*, Vol. LXVIII, 1957, pp. 1–10.

56. *African Political Systems,* ed. by M. Fortes and E. E. Evans-Pritchard, London, 1961, pp. xiv, xxiii.
57. Max Weber, "Politik als Beruf," *Gesammelte Politische Schriften,* 2. Aufl., Tübingen, 1958, p. 494, my translation.
58. *From Max Weber,* p. 78.
59. Compare *Theory of Social and Economic Organization,* pp. 154–56 with Max Weber, *Wirtschaft und Gesellschaft,* 4. Aufl., 1. Hbd., Ch. i, §17, pp. 29–30.
60. Weber, *Theory of Social and Economic Organization,* p. 132, italics added.
61. Ibid. p. 152, italics added.
62. Reinhard Bendix, *Max Weber: An Intellectual Portrait,* New York, 1962, p. 290.
63. David Easton, "Political Anthropology," *Biennial Review of Anthropology 1959,* ed. by B. J. Seigel, Stanford, 1959, pp. 213, 218–19; *The Political System,* New York, 1953, p. 153, n. 2.
64. R. M. MacIver, *The Modern State,* London, 1926, pp. 222, 223, 225, 230.
65. See Aristotle, *Politics* 1315b, and Fritz Hartung, *Enlightened Despotism,* trans. by H. Otto, London, 1957.
66. *Politics* 1314a.

CHAPTER IV

1. E. R. Service, *Primitive Social Organization,* New York, 1962.
2. For a criticism of this usage, see Morton H. Fried, *The Evolution of Political Society,* New York, 1967, pp. 164 ff.
3. A. I. Richards, "African Kings and their Royal Relatives," *Journal of the Royal Anthropological Institute,* Vol. 91, 1961, p. 143.
4. Claude Lévi-Strauss, *Tristes Tropiques,* trans. by John Russell, New York, 1964, p. 300.
5. Colin Turnbull, *Wayward Servants,* New York, 1965, p. 184.
6. Laura Bohannan, "Political Aspects of Tiv Social Organization," in *Tribes Without Rulers,* ed. by John Middleton and David Tait, London, 1958, p. 58.
7. Paul Bohannan, "Extra-processual Events in Tiv Political Institutions," *American Anthropologist,* Vol. 60, 1958, p. 6.
8. Ibid. pp. 1–12.
9. Paul Stirling, *Turkish Village,* New York, 1965, Ch. 7.
10. Paula Brown, "Patterns of Authority in West Africa," *Africa,* Vol. 21, 1951, p. 267.
11. S. F. Nadel, *A Black Byzantium,* London, 1942, p. 47.
12. Ibid. pp. 58–63.
13. Southall, *Alur Society,* p. 195.

14. Ibid. p. 188.

15. Service, *Primitive Social Organization*, pp. 161, 159.

16. Southall, *Alur Society*, p. 237.

17. Jean Buxton, "The Mandari of the Southern Sudan," in *Tribes Without Rulers*, p. 80.

18. Henri A. Junod, *The Life of a South African Tribe*, 2 vols., Neuchatel, Switzerland, 1912, Vol. I, p. 381, italics removed.

19. Ibid. pp. 397, 402.

20. A. I. Richards, "The Political System of the Bemba Tribe—North-Eastern Rhodesia," in *African Political Systems*, p. 106.

21. Ibid. p. 110.

22. Service, *Primitive Social Organization*, p. 148.

23. Mair, *Primitive Government*, p. 108.

24. Ibid. p. 122.

25. Robert H. Lowie, *The Origin of the State*, New York, 1927, pp. 76, 93.

26. Ibid. pp. 103–4.

27. Lowie, "Some Aspects of Political Organization among the American Aborigines," *Journal of the Royal Anthropological Institute*, Vol. 78, 1948, p. 20.

28. Diedrich Westermann, *Die Kpelle: Ein Negerstamm in Liberia*, Göttingen, 1921, pp. 89 ff.

29. Lowie, *The Origin of the State*, p. 83.

30. Ibid. p. 90.

31. Ibid. pp. 101, 111.

32. Ibid. p. 91.

33. Lawrence Krader, *Formation of the State*, Englewood Cliffs, N. J., 1968, p. 41.

34. Hutton Webster, *Primitive Secret Societies*, New York, 1908, pp. 108–9.

35. Kenneth Little, "The Mende Chiefdoms of Sierra Leone," in *West African Kingdoms in the Nineteenth Century*, ed. by Daryll Forde and P. M. Kaberry, London, 1967, pp. 255, 257–58.

36. Cf. Stanley Diamond, "Dahomey: A Proto-State in West Africa," unpublished Ph.D. Dissertation, Columbia University, New York, 1951, p. 3.

37. Meyer Fortes, "The Structure of Unilineal Descent Groups," *American Anthropologist*, Vol. 55, 1953, p. 26.

38. Leo Strauss, *On Tyranny*, New York, 1963, pp. 11, 17–18.

39. G. P. Lestrade, "Some Notes on the Political Organisation of the Bechwana," *South African Journal of Science*, Vol. 25, 1928, p. 428.

40. G. P. Lestrade, "Some Notes on the Political Organisation of the Venda-Speaking Tribes," *Africa*, Vol. 3, 1930, p. 309; Brown, "Patterns of Authority in West Africa," loc. cit. p. 267.

41. Marshall D. Sahlins, "The Segmentary Lineage: An Organization of Predatory Expansion," *American Anthropologist*, Vol. 63, 1961, pp. 331–32.

42. Webster, *Primitive Secret Societies*, p. 74.

43. Ibid. p. 75.

44. George W. Harley, "Notes on the Poro in Liberia," *Papers of the Peabody Museum*, Cambridge, Mass., Vol. 19, No. 2, 1941, p. 31.

45. Marcel Mauss, "Une catégorie de l'esprit humain: La notion de personne celle de 'moi,'" *Journal of the Royal Anthropological Institute*, Vol. 68, 1938, p. 272.

46. C. A. Valentine, *Masks and Men in a Melanesian Society*, Lawrence, Kansas, 1961, pp. 2–3, 48.

47. Peter Morton-Williams, "The Egungun Society in South-Western Yoruba Kingdoms," *Proceedings of the Third Annual Conference of the West African Institute of Social and Economic Research* (1954), Ibadan, 1956, p. 92.

48. D. O. Hebb, "On the Nature of Fear," *Psychological Review*, Vol. 53, 1946, pp. 259–76; *The Organization of Behavior*, New York, 1961, p. 243.

CHAPTER V

1. Brown, "Patterns of Authority in West Africa," loc. cit. p. 270.

2. Kenneth Little, "The Political Function of the Poro," Part I, *Africa*, Vol. 35, 1965, p. 349.

3. George W. Harley, "Notes on the Poro in Liberia," *Papers of the Peabody Museum*, Vol. 19, 1941, pp. 7, 3.

4. Ibid. p. 31.

5. George Schwab, *Tribes of the Liberian Hinterland*, Papers of the Peabody Museum, Cambridge, Mass., 1947, p. 163.

6. Ibid. pp. 167, 168, 170.

7. George W. Harley, "Masks as Agents of Social Control in Northeast Liberia," *Papers of the Peabody Museum*, Vol. 32, No. 2, 1950, p. viii.

8. Little, "The Political Function of the Poro," loc. cit. p. 355.

9. George W. Harley, *Native African Medicine*, Cambridge, Mass., 1941, pp. 20, 38.

10. F. W. Butt-Thompson, *West African Secret Societies*, London, 1929, pp. 27–28.

11. "Masks as Agents of Social Control," loc. cit. p. vii.

12. "Notes on the Poro," loc. cit. pp. 3, 6, 7, 31.

13. Ibid. p. 31; "Masks as Agents of Social Control," loc. cit. pp. viii–ix.

14. The "coercive," "arbitrary," and authoritarian nature of Poro values is discussed in J. L. Gibbs, "Poro Values and Courtroom Procedures in a Kpelle Chiefdom," *Southwestern Journal of Anthropology*, Vol. 18, 1962, pp. 341–49.

15. Harley, "Notes on the Poro," loc. cit. p. 32.

16. Harley, "Masks as Agents of Social Control," loc. cit. pp. 16–17.

17. Henry Sumner Maine, *Ancient Law*, first published 1861, London, 1954, p. 110.

18. "Masks as Agents of Social Control," loc. cit. p. 42.

19. Ibid. p. 43.

20. Ibid. pp. 10, 42.

21. Harley, *Native African Medicine*, pp. 30, 34, 147, 150.

22. Harley, "Notes on the Poro," loc. cit. p. 10.

23. Ibid. p. 11.

24. "Masks as Agents of Social Control," loc. cit. p. 43.

25. M. G. Smith, "On Segmentary Lineage Systems," *Journal of the Royal Anthropological Institute*, Vol. 86, 1956, p. 54.

26. Southall, *Alur Society*, p. 228.

27. Schwab, *Tribes of the Liberian Hinterland*, p. 171.

28. H. U. Hall, *The Sherbro of Sierra Leone*, Philadelphia, 1938, p. 5.

29. Kenneth Little, "The Political Function of the Poro," Part II, *Africa*, Vol. 36, 1966, pp. 66, 70.

30. Kenneth Little, "The Mende Chiefdoms of Sierra Leone," in *West African Kingdoms*, pp. 249, 257.

31. Ibid. p. 258.

32. W. H. Bentley, *Pioneering on the Congo*, London, 1900, Vol. 1, p. 283; P. C. Lloyd, "The Traditional Political System of the Yoruba," *Southwestern Journal of Anthropology*, Vol. X, 1954, pp. 366–84.

33. E. M. Chilver and P. M. Kaberry, "The Kingdom of Kom in West Cameroon," in *West African Kingdoms*, p. 127.

34. Peter Morton-Williams, "The Egungun Society in South-Western Yoruba Kingdoms," loc. cit., p. 101.

35. Morton-Williams, "An Outline of the Cosmology and Cult Organisation of the Oyo Yoruba," *Africa*, Vol. 34, 1964, pp. 255–56.

36. Morton-Williams, "The Yoruba Kingdom of Oyo," in *West African Kingdoms*, p. 58.

37. Morton-Williams, "The Yoruba Ogboni Cult in Oyo," *Africa*, Vol. 30, 1960, p. 367.

38. Morton-Williams, "The Yoruba Kingdom of Oyo," op. cit. p. 42.

39. Ibid. pp. 54, 55.

40. Morton-Williams, "The Yoruba Ogboni Cult in Oyo," loc. cit. p. 34.

41. Webster, *Primitive Secret Societies*, pp. 99, 100, 110.

42. Ibid. p. 121.

43. Morton-Williams, "The Egungun Society in South-Western Yoruba Kingdoms," loc. cit. pp. 102–3.

CHAPTER VI

1. See Max Gluckman, *Analysis of a Social Situation in Modern Zululand*, Manchester, 1958.

2. George McCall Theal, *History and Ethnography of Africa South of the Zambesi*, London, 1907, Vol. I, pp. 76–78. Theal was the author of many

volumes on South African history, including a standard work, *History of South Africa from 1795 to 1872*, 4th ed., 5 vols., London, 1915.

3. For a recent classification of the forms of kingship, see J. Vansina, "A Comparison of African Kingdoms," *Africa*, Vol. XXXII, 1962, pp. 324–35.

4. I have tried to follow the rules of current orthography in the spelling of Zulu words. The reader's natural phonetic inclinations will come close enough to the Zulu names and terms that appear in this volume. The most important exception, besides the click sounds, is the use of the letter *h*, which gives an aspirated quality to the consonant it follows. Therefore, combinations such as *ph* and *th* are not the fricatives *f* and *th*, and should be pronounced as aspirated *p* and *t*. The reader may simply drop the *h* and pronounce *Mthethwa, Thembu, Thonga, Usuthu*, etc., as *Mtetwa, Tembu, Tonga, Usutu*, etc. The click sounds, represented by *x*, *c*, and *q*, have no equivalent in European languages.

5. See J. D. Omer-Cooper, *The Zulu Aftermath*, London, 1966; W. F. Lye, "The Difaqane: The Mfecane in the Southern Sotho Area, 1822–24," *Journal of African History*, Vol. VIII, 1967, pp. 107–31; E. A. Ritter, *Shaka Zulu: The Rise of the Zulu Empire*, New York, 1957.

6. H. F. Fynn, *The Diary of Henry Francis Fynn*, ed. by James Stuart, and D. McK. Malcolm, Pietermaritzburg, 1950, p. 20; John Bird, *The Annals of Natal*, Vol. I, Pietermaritzburg, 1888, p. 67; Theal, *History of South Africa*, Vol. I, p. 488. Walker says that Theal's figure of two million may be too high, but does not offer an alternative estimate; see Walker, *A History of Southern Africa*, p. 176.

7. I. Schapera, "The Old Bantu Culture," in *Western Civilization and the Natives of South Africa*, London, 1934, pp. 5–6. Another estimate is that Shaka's domain included 100,000 souls and an area of 80,000 square miles, but Max Gluckman thinks these figures are too low: "The Kingdom of the Zulu," in *African Political Systems*, p. 26. As far as the size of Shaka's army in the field is concerned, other estimates range from Bryant's figure of 20,000 to Fynn's count of 50,000 in the victorious attack on Sikunyana's Ndwandwe army.

8. A. T. Bryant, *Olden Times in Zululand and Natal*, London, 1929, p. 4.

9. N. J. Van Warmelo, "The Nguni," Introduction to A. M. Duggan-Cronin, *The Bantu Tribes of South Africa*, Cambridge, Eng., 1939, Vol. III, i, p. 9; Omer-Cooper, *The Zulu Aftermath*, p. 13. Soga objected to this classificatory use of the "Nguni" name, especially as it appeared in the work of Bryant, and preferred a much more restricted usage; see Soga, *The South-Eastern Bantu*, Johannesburg, 1930, pp. 82–83.

10. Shula Marks, "The Nguni, the Natalians, and their History," *Journal of African History*, Vol. VIII, 1967, pp. 531–32.

11. Cf. Monica Wilson, "The Early History of the Transkei and Ciskei," *African Studies*, Vol. XVIII, 1959, p. 174.

12. Despite their obvious inaccuracies about the dates of migrations, the published collections of traditional history are useful for many purposes,

if one understands their limitations. Each records one version of the tradition as remembered by old people at the time it was collected. A collection written by an African is the work of John Henderson Soga. His books, *The South-Eastern Bantu* and *The Ama-Xosa: Life and Customs,* Lovedale, [1931], reflect the memories of the Zulu's southern neighbors around 1920. J. Y. Gibson, *The Story of the Zulus,* London, 1911, was collected around the turn of the century. A. T. Bryant, *Olden Times in Zululand and Natal* is a remarkable document—a rambling but monumental history—written in a colorful style that makes it sometimes difficult to extricate the legend from Bryant's fantasies. Ritter, *Shaka Zulu* is another useful source that must be read with caution, but some of the informants, it is said, had lived in Shaka's presence, and the author claimed familiarity with the Zulu royal family's unwritten history.

13. Arnaldo Momigliano, "An Interim Report on the Origins of Rome," *Journal of Roman Studies,* Vol. LIII, 1963, pp. 107–8.

14. Bird, *Annals,* Vol. I, pp. 3–4.

15. Monica Wilson, loc. cit. pp. 172, 178.

16. Radiocarbon analysis of a sample from western Swaziland indicates a date of A.D. 410. The excavator writes, " 'The date suggests that the South African Iron Age may have begun somewhat earlier than hitherto supposed.' " B. M. Fagan, "Radiocarbon Dates for Sub-Saharan Africa: V," *Journal of African History,* Vol. VIII, 1967, p. 525.

17. Walker, *History,* p. 115.

18. Cf. S. F. N. Gie, *Cambridge History of the British Empire* (cited hereafter as *CHBE*), Vol. VIII, vi, 148–52.

19. Cf. W. M. Macmillan, *Bantu, Boer, and Briton,* London, 1929, p. 4.

20. The work of Fynn and Isaacs is invaluable, for they become intimates of Shaka. They learned the language, spent a great deal of time in his company, witnessed important civic and military events, and wrote about the details of his regime as participant-observers.

Besides other books cited in the previous notes, my description of Zulu despotism and the careers of Shaka and Dingane draws heavily on the following sources: John Bird, *The Annals of Natal;* H. F. Fynn, *The Diary of Henry Francis Fynn;* Nathaniel Isaacs, *Travels and Adventures in Eastern Africa,* 2 vols. (first published 1836), Cape Town, 1936–37; A. T. Bryant, *A History of the Zulu and Neighbouring Tribes,* Cape Town, 1964; J. Y. Gibson, *The Story of the Zulus;* W. C. Holden, *The Past and Future of the Kaffir Races,* reprinted ed., Cape Town, 1963; Joseph Shooter, *The Kafirs of Natal and the Zulu Country,* London, 1857; A. F. Gardiner, *Narrative of a Journey to the Zoolu Country in South Africa,* London, 1836; Thomas Arbousset, *Relation d'un Voyage d'Exploration au Nord-Est de la Colonie du Cap de Bonne-Espérance,* Paris, 1842; Percival R. Kirby, ed., *Andrew Smith and Natal: Documents Relating to the Early History of that Province,* Cape Town, 1955; Cape of Good Hope, *Report and Proceedings of the Government Commission on Native Laws and Customs,* Cape Town, 1883; E. J. Krige, *The Social System of the Zulus,* 2nd ed., Pietermaritzburg, 1950;

Adulphe Delegorgue, *Voyage dans l'Afrique Australe*, 2 vols., Paris, 1847.
21. Bird, *Annals*, Vol. I, p. 163.
22. *Olden Times*, p. 91.
23. Soga, *The South-Eastern Bantu*, p. 390.
24 *Olden Times*, pp. 94–95.
25. Fynn, *Diary*, p. 39. A similar description of the post appeared in W. F. W. Owen, *Narrative of Voyages To Explore the Shores of Africa, Arabia, and Madagascar*, 2 vols., London, 1833, Vol. I, p. 73. However, Fynn accepted the story of the traveling European physician as the explanation for the source of Dingiswayo's ideas. He believed the man was Dr. Cowan, who in 1806 left Cape Town with a party and headed northeast; see *Diary*, p. 5. Fynn's other account in Bird, *Annals*, Vol. I, p. 62, was both vague and inaccurate about the date. Mackeurtan recognized the language barrier as an obstacle, but believed that if Dingiswayo saw "Dr. Cowan's twenty Hottentot soldiers under Lieutenant Donovan," then "the whole matter becomes quite clear." On the contrary, nothing becomes clear, for it is not easy to understand how the mere spectacle could suggest the complex innovations. Cf. Graham Mackeurtan, *The Cradle Days of Natal*, London, 1930, p. 118.
26. Omer-Cooper, *The Zulu Aftermath*, p. 169.
27. Marks, "The Nguni, the Natalians, and their History," loc. cit. pp. 532–33.
28. Omer-Cooper, op. cit. p. 2.
29. Fynn, *Diary*, p. 10.
30. *Olden Times*, p. 79.
31. Bird, *Annals*, Vol. I, p. 156.
32. Cf. W. M. Macmillan, *Bantu, Boer, and Briton*, p. 14.
33. *Olden Times*, pp. 99, 641–642. Omer-Cooper claims that Dingiswayo was not the "sole inventor" of the age regiment system either, for it was being used simultaneously by the neighboring Ndwandwe and Ngwane, op. cit. p. 175.
34. Theal, *History*, Vol. I, p. 435; Walker, op. cit. p. 175.
35. An old Mthethwa prophet mentioned thirty chiefs who acknowledged the supremacy of Dingiswayo. Shooter, *Kafirs of Natal*, p. 250.
36. *Olden Times*, p. 63.
37. A. T. Bryant, *A Zulu-English Dictionary*, Pinetown, Natal, 1905, p. 643.
38. *Olden Times*, p. 171.
39. Ibid. p. 537; *History of the Zulu*, p. 84.
40. W. F. W. Owen, *Narrative of Voyages*, Vol. I, Chs. 4, 6. A year later, the sloop *Jane* with Henry Francis Fynn aboard as supercargo, joined the British ships in the Delagoa Bay area. Fynn remained for six months visiting the inland chiefs and their people. On one journey, before he fell ill with fever and was treated successfully by African doctors, he visited a Zulu kraal; *Diary*, pp. 42, 45.
41. Bryant, *Olden Times*, Ch. 55.

42. Isaacs, *Travels and Adventures*, Vol. I, p. xx.
43. James Stuart, Preface to Fynn, *Diary*, p. xii. Cf. Bird, *Annals*, Vol. I, p. 104.
44. Gibson, *Story of the Zulus*, pp. 21–22.
45. Ibid. p. 37.
46. Donald R. Morris, *The Washing of the Spears*, New York, 1965, p. 67, italics mine.
47. Ibid. p. 79, italics mine.

CHAPTER VII

1. Bird, *Annals*, Vol. I, p. 76.
2. Ibid. p. 78.
3. Fynn, *Diary*, p. 78.
4. Ibid. pp. 28–29.
5. Ritter, *Shaka Zulu*, p. 319.
6. Isaacs, *Travels and Adventures*, Vol. I, p. 62.
7. Ibid. p. 92.
8. Holden, *Past and Future of the Kaffir Races*, p. 41.
9. Isaacs, *Travels and Adventures*, Vol. I, pp. 253–54.
10. Ritter, *Shaka Zulu*, p. 45; Bird, *Annals*, Vol. I, p. 164.
11. Bryant, *History of the Zulu*, pp. 4, 48.
12. Bird, *Annals*, Vol. I, p. 158; Bryant, *Zulu-English Dictionary*, "Historical Sketch," p. 49*.
13. "Enclosure No. 1: Lieut.-Gov. Scott's Despatch No. 12," Bird, *Annals*, Vol. I, p. 139. See also Fynn, *Diary*, p. 18.
14. Robert Payne, *Zero: The Story of Terrorism*, New York, 1950, pp. 136, 244.
15. Bryant, *Olden Times*, p. 132.
16. Fynn, *Diary*, p. 89.
17. Ibid. p. 126; Isaacs, *Travels and Adventures*, Vol. I, p. 128.
18. Ibid. p. 160; Fynn, *Diary*, p. 130.
19. Ibid. p. 145.
20. W. S. Ferguson, "The Zulus and the Spartans: A Comparison of their Military Systems," *Harvard African Studies*, Vol. 2, Cambridge, Mass., 1918 (pp. 197–234), p. 228.
21. Fynn, *Diary*, p. 19; Bird, *Annals*, Vol. I, p. 66.
22. Ibid. p. 157.
23. Ferguson, loc. cit. p. 229.
24. Fynn, *Diary*, p. 123.
25. Ibid. p. 148.
26. Isaacs, *Travels and Adventures*, Vol. I, pp. 150, 267, 205.
27. Fynn, *Diary*, p. 286.
28. Isaacs, *Travels and Adventures*, Vol. I, p. 100.
29. Fynn, *Diary*, p. 127; Bird, *Annals*, Vol. I, p. 89.

30. Isaacs, *Travels and Adventures*, Vol. I, p. 114.

31. Fynn, *Diary*, p. 152.

32. Gluckman, "The Kingdom of the Zulu," loc. cit. p. 31.

33. Thomas Mofolo, *Chaka: An Historical Romance*, trans. by F. H. Dutton, London, 1931, p. 137.

34. Max Gluckman, "The Rise of a Zulu Empire," *Scientific American*, Vol. 202, April 1960, p. 168. A book is expected from Gluckman on the rise of Shaka and his assassination by Dingane, expanding the first part of his Mason Lectures. It is hoped that the book will explicate his views on the subject.

35. Bryant, *Olden Times*, p. 573; Ritter, *Shaka Zulu, passim.*

36. Fynn, *Diary*, p. 295; Ritter, *Shaka Zulu*, p. 11.

37. Morris, *The Washing of the Spears*, pp. 46, 91–92, 54, 117.

38. Fynn, *Diary*, p. 137.

39. Ritter, *Shaka Zulu*, Ch. 11.

40. Mofolo, op. cit. p. 162.

41. Ibid. pp. xii–xiii.

42. H. Rider Haggard, *Nada the Lily*, first published 1892, London, 1958, p. ix.

43. Isaacs, *Travels and Adventures*, Vol. I, p. 133.

44. Ibid. pp. 270–71.

45. Fynn, *Diary*, p. 136. The survivors of the shipwrecked *Stavenisse* in the seventeenth century observed that it was the custom for men to abstain from intercourse with their wives during the period of mourning for chiefs, Bird, *Annals*, Vol. I, p. 43; mentioned by Omer-Cooper, op. cit.

46. Krige, *Social System of the Zulus*, pp. 38, 118–19.

47. Fynn, *Diary*, p. 24.

48. Isaacs, *Travels and Adventures*, Vol. I, pp. 129–32.

49. Ibid. p. 133. Isaacs's difficulties with the Zulu language were noted by A. T. Bryant, *The Zulu People as They Were before the White Man Came*, Pietermaritzburg, 1949, p. 720.

50. Dudley Kidd, *The Essential Kafir*, London, 1904, pp. 139, 148.

51. Schapera, "The Old Bantu Culture," loc. cit. p. 33; Bryant, *The Zulu People*, p. 698.

52. Cf. E. E. Evans-Pritchard, "Sorcery and Native Opinion," *Africa*, Vol. IV, 1931, p. 36; *Witchcraft, Oracles and Magic among the Azande*, London, 1937, p. 394.

53. Krige, *Social System of the Zulus*, p. 321.

54. Kidd, *Essential Kafir*, p. 176.

55. Isaacs, *Travels and Adventures*, Vol. I, p. 86.

56. Bryant, *Zulu-English Dictionary*, p. 607; also see C. M. Doke and B. W. Vilakazi, *Zulu-English Dictionary*, 2nd ed., Johannesburg, 1958, p. 781.

57. Shooter, *Kafirs of Natal*, p. 141.

58. Kidd, *Essential Kafir*, p. 176.

59. Cape *Government Commission on Native Laws and Customs*, Part I, p. 6.

60. Krige, *Social System of the Zulus*, pp. 297–99.

61. James Macdonald, "Manners, Customs, Superstitions, and Religions of South African Tribes," *Journal of the Anthropological Institute*, Vol. XX, November 1890, pp. 115, 139.

62. Kidd, *Essential Kafir*, p. 177.

63. *Nada the Lily*, p. 68.

64. Ritter, *Shaka Zulu*, Chs. 10, 19.

65. H. W. Garbutt, "Native Witchcraft and Superstition in South Africa," *Journal of the Royal Anthropological Institute*, Vol. XXXIX, 1909, p. 536.

66. Ritter, *Shaka Zulu*, p. 105.

67. Kidd, *Essential Kafir*, p. 114.

68. Henry Callaway, *The Religious System of the Amazulu*, Springvale, Natal, 1868–70, Part III, p. 390.

69. Ibid. p. 340.

70. Isaacs, *Travels and Adventures*, Vol. I, pp. 276, 280.

71. Bird, *Annals*, Vol. I, p. 96.

72. Cf. Callaway, loc. cit. p. 348; Krige, *Social System of the Zulus*, p. 325.

73. Fynn, *Diary*, p. 29.

74. Walker, *History of Southern Africa*, p. 112.

75. Fynn, *Diary*, p. 14.

76. Ibid. p. 30; Isaacs, *Travels and Adventures*, Vol. I, pp. 37, 60.

77. Ibid. p. 113.

78. Fynn, *Diary*, pp. 27–28.

79. Isaacs, *Travels and Adventures*, Vol. I, p. 284; Ritter, *Shaka Zulu*, p. 50.

80. Bryant, *Olden Times*, p. 125.

81. Ferguson, "The Zulus and the Spartans," loc. cit. p. 230.

82. Isaacs, *Travels and Adventures*, Vol. I, p. 198.

83. Ibid. p. 89.

84. Bryant, *Olden Times*, p. 413.

85. Isaacs, *Travels and Adventures*, Vol. I, p. 158.

86. Cf. Gluckman, "The Kingdom of the Zulu," loc. cit. p. 33.

87. Isaacs, *Travels and Adventures*, Vol. I, p. 133.

88. Fynn, *Diary*, p. 18.

89. Bryant, *Olden Times*, p. 626; Gibson, *Story of the Zulus*, p. 33.

90. Cf. E. R. Service, *Profiles in Ethnology*, New York, 1963, p. 308.

91. Fynn, *Diary*, pp. 134–35.

92. Barrington Moore, Jr., *Political Power and Social Theory*, Cambridge, Mass., 1958, p. 35.

93. Isaacs, *Travels and Adventures*, Vol. I, pp. 199, 203.

94. Bird, *Annals*, Vol. I, p. 91; Fynn, *Diary*, p. 137.

95. Ibid. p. 139.

96. Isaacs, *Travels and Adventures*, Vol. I, p. 204.

97. Holden, *Past and Future of the Kaffir Races*, p. 36.

98. Bryant, *Olden Times*, pp. 626, 659.
99. Ibid; Ritter, *Shaka Zulu*, p. 336; Fynn, *Diary*, pp. 156–57.
100. Isaacs, *Travels and Adventures*, Vol. I, p. 259.
101. Ibid. pp. 260–61.
102. Bird, *Annals*, Vol. I, p. 99.
103. Fynn, *Diary*, p. 163.
104. Ritter, *Shaka Zulu*, p. 319.
105. Ibid.
106. Ibid. pp. 334–35.

Chapter VIII

1. *Andrew Smith and Natal*, p. 77.
2. Isaacs, *Travels and Adventures*, Vol. II, p. 7.
3. Ibid. pp. 29–33, 104–5, 192, 234.
4. Peter Becker, *Rule of Fear: The Life and Times of Dingane King of the Zulu*, London, 1964, p. 13.
5. Mackeurtan, *Cradle Days of Natal*, p. 154.
6. Fynn, *Diary*, pp. 162–63.
7. Max Gluckman, *Analysis of a Social Situation in Modern Zululand*, p. 33.
8. *Andrew Smith and Natal*, pp. 42, 86.
9. Gardiner, *Narrative of a Journey to the Zoolu Country*, p. 93; Bird, *Annals*, Vol. I, pp. 300, 303.
10. Fynn, *Diary*, p. 165.
11. Becker, *Rule of Fear*, p. 64.
12. Fynn, *Diary*, p. 163.
13. *Rule of Fear*, p. 83.
14. Bryant, *Olden Times*, p. 76.
15. See Bryant, "The Zulu State and Family Organization," *Bantu Studies*, Vol. II, 1923, pp. 47–51.
16. Bryant, *Olden Times*, p. 71, italics added.
17. Ibid. p. 159.
18. Bird, *Annals*, Vol. I, p. 337.
19. Gardiner, *Narrative*, p. 54.
20. *Andrew Smith and Natal*, p. 54.
21. Gardiner, *Narrative*, pp. 203–4.
22. "Journal of George Champion," in Bird, *Annals*, Vol. I, p. 206.
23. Delegorgue, *Voyage dans l'Afrique Australe*, Vol. II, p. 244, trans. in Bird, *Annals*, Vol. I, p. 484.
24. Delegorgue, *Voyage*, Vol. II, pp. 244–45, my translation.
25. *Andrew Smith and Natal*, p. 43.
26. Isaacs, *Travels and Adventures*, Vol. II, p. 107.
27. Gardiner, *Narrative*, p. 94.
28. Isaacs, *Travels and Adventures*, Vol. II, p. 183.

29. Bird, *Annals*, Vol. I, p. 353.
30. Fynn, *Diary*, p. 232.
31. Isaacs, *Travels and Adventures*, Vol. II, pp. 230–31.
32. Ibid. p. 231.
33. Ibid. p. 232.
34. Bird, *Annals*, Vol. I, p. 480.
35. Gardiner, *Narrative*, pp. 45–46.
36. Ibid. p. 276.
37. *African Political Systems*, pp. 33–34.
38. Bird, *Annals*, Vol. I, p. 480.
39. Isaacs, *Travels and Adventures*, Vol. II, p. 242.
40. Max Gluckman, *Rituals of Rebellion in South-East Africa*, Manchester, 1954; *Custom and Conflict in Africa*, Glencoe, Ill., 1955, p. 127.
41. Fynn, *Diary*, p. 175.
42. Isaacs, *Travels and Adventures*, Vol. II, p. 12.
43. Ibid. p. 203.
44. Fynn, *Diary*, p. 189.
45. Ibid. p. 228.
46. Ibid. pp. 214–15.
47. Gardiner, *Narrative*, p. 407.
48. Ibid. p. 108.
49. Ibid. p. 127.
50. Fynn, *Diary*, p. 212.
51. Omer-Cooper, *The Zulu Aftermath*, pp. 44–45.
52. Daniel Pieter Bezuidenhout, *Orange Free State Monthly Magazine*, December 1879, in Bird, *Annals*, Vol. I, p. 368.
53. See Gluckman in *African Political Systems*, p. 26.
54. Becker, *Rule of Fear*, p. 257.
55. Bryant, *Olden Times*, p. 679.
56. Morris, *The Washing of the Spears*, pp. 151, 192, 197.
57. *Voyage dans l'Afrique Australe*, 2 vols. Some relevant sections are translated in Bird, *Annals*, Vol. I.
58. Bird, *Annals*, Vol. I, p. 558.
59. Ibid. pp. 715–16.
60. "Report of the Landdrost of Tugela on the Embassy to Panda," in Bird, *Annals*, Vol. I, p. 541.
61. Morris, *The Washing of the Spears*, p. 151.
62. Bird, *Annals*, Vol. I, pp. 560–61.
63. Morris, *The Washing of the Spears*, p. 204.
64. Delegorgue in Bird, *Annals*, Vol. I, p. 481.
65. See Cape *Government Commission on Native Laws and Customs*, Part I, pp. 4–21.
66. Max Gluckman, *Custom and Conflict in Africa*, p. 40.
67. Bryant, *Olden Times*, p. 43.
68. Bird, *Annals*, Vol. I, p. 713.
69. Ibid. p. 715.

70. David Leslie, *Among the Zulus and Amatongas,* Glasgow, 1875, p. 69.
71. Bird, *Annals,* Vol. I, p. 481.
72. Ibid. p. 485.
73. Ibid. p. 491.
74. Ibid. p. 480.
75. This statement was transmitted to the author in a letter from the late E. A. Ritter and appears here with permission of his daughter, Miss Carsten Ritter. Mpande made the statement to Shepstone in the presence of Sir Marshall Clark, who passed it on to Mr. Ritter's father, Captain C. L. A. Ritter.

CHAPTER IX

1. J. A. Farrer, *Zululand and the Zulus,* London, 1879, pp. 32–35.
2. R. C. A. Samuelson, *Long, Long Ago,* Durban, 1929, p. 223.
3. John Dunn, *Cetywayo and the Three Generals,* ed. by D. C. F. Moodie, Pietermaritzburg, 1886, p. 10.
4. Samuelson, op. cit. p. 218.
5. Leslie, *Among the Zulus and Amatongas,* p. 62.
6. Samuelson, op. cit. pp. 401–2; Krige, *The Social System of the Zulus,* pp. 243–44.
7. Leslie, op. cit. p. 80.
8. Ibid. p. 69.
9. Farrer, op. cit. p. 32.
10. See Bishop Colenso's preface to Cornelius Vijn, *Cetshwayo's Dutchman,* London, 1880, pp. ix–x.
11. Farrer, op. cit. pp. 28–29.
12. Dunn, *Cetywayo and the Three Generals,* p. 50.
13. C. T. Binns, *The Last Zulu King,* London, 1963, p. 70.
14. H. Rider Haggard, *Cetywayo and his White Neighbours,* London, 1890, p. 12.
15. Dunn, op. cit. p. 54.
16. Ibid., pp. 49, 54.
17. Ibid. pp. 29, 56.
18. Vijn, *Cetshwayo's Dutchman,* pp. 80–81.
19. Great Britain, *Parliamentary Papers,* 1877, Vol. LX, C. 1748, p. 216.
20. Farrer, op. cit. pp. 72, 68, 42.
21. *Parliamentary Papers,* 1878, Vol. LVI, C. 2079, p. 96.
22. Great Britain, *Accounts and Papers,* 1890, Vol. XII, C. 6201, p. 47.
23. F. E. Colenso, *The Ruin of Zululand,* Vol. II, London, 1885, p. 407.
24. Haggard, *Cetywayo and his White Neighbours,* p. 14.
25. Leslie, op. cit. p. 35.
26. Gibson, *The Story of the Zulus,* p. 121.
27. *Parliamentary Papers,* 1877, Vol. LX, C. 1748, p. 216.
28. Binns, op. cit. p. 78.

29. Dunn, op. cit. p. 56.
30. Ibid. p. 57.
31. Samuelson, op. cit. p. 231.
32. Dunn, op. cit. pp. 84–85.
33. Haggard, *Cetywayo and his White Neighbours,* p. 57.
34. Colenso, *Ruin of Zululand,* Vol. II, p. 369.
35. Ibid. pp. 299–302, 358.
36. *Parliamentary Papers,* 1883, Vol. XLIX, C. 3616, pp. 57–59.
37. Ibid. p. 53.
38. Mofolo, *Chaka,* p. 198.

CHAPTER X

1. Cf. Hilda Kuper, *An African Aristocracy,* London, 1947, p. 8.
2. Max Gluckman, "The Kingdom of the Zulu," *African Political Systems,* pp. 31, 46.
3. Hailey, *An African Survey: Revised 1956,* London, 1957, pp. 31–32.
4. Cape of Good Hope, *Government Commission on Native Laws and Customs,* Part I, pp. 5–19.
5. Marshall D. Sahlins, "The Segmentary Lineage: An Organization of Predatory Expansion," *American Anthropologist,* Vol. 63, 1961, pp. 331–32.
6. Cf. Fried, *The Evolution of Political Society,* p. 143.
7. Elman R. Service, *Primitive Social Organization,* p. 115.
8. Southall, *Alur Society,* p. 146.
9. Cf. G. P. Murdock, *Africa: Its Peoples and their Culture History,* New York, 1959, pp. 36–37.
10. *Andrew Smith and Natal,* p. 52.
11. J. A. Farrer, *Zululand and the Zulus,* p. 67.
12. Fynn, *Diary,* p. 164.
13. Bryant, *Olden Times,* pp. 391, 201.
14. Bird, *Annals,* Vol. I, p. 265.
15. Fynn, *Diary,* p. 164.
16. Gibson, *The Story of the Zulus,* pp. 48–49.
17. C. T. Binns, *The Last Zulu King,* p. 78.
18. Omer-Cooper, *Zulu Aftermath,* p. 172.

CHAPTER XI

1. Karl Marx, *Pre-Capitalist Economic Formations,* ed. by E. J. Hobsbawm, New York, 1965.
2. K. A. Wittfogel, *Oriental Despotism,* New Haven, 1957, Chs. 4, 5; the quotations are from pp. 103, 106–7.
3. Henry Sidgwick, *The Development of European Polity,* 3rd ed., London, 1920, p. 10. The same definition is adopted by K. V. Rangaswami

Aiyangar, *Considerations on Some Aspects of Ancient Indian Polity,* 2nd ed., Madras, 1935, p. 69.

4. Fallers, "Despotism and Social Mobility," *Comparative Studies in Society and History,* Vol. II, 1959, p. 30.

5. C. C. Wrigley, "The Christian Revolution in Buganda," *Comparative Studies in Society and History,* Vol. II, 1959, p. 36.

6. H. M. Stanley, *Through the Dark Continent,* 2 vols., London, 1899, Vol. I, pp. 295–96.

7. Ibid. pp. 151, 152.

8. Ibid. p. 296.

9. Ham Mukasa, "Speke at the Court of Muteesa I," *Uganda Journal,* Vol. 26, 1962, p. 97.

10. Ham Mukasa, "The Rule of the Kings of Buganda," *Uganda Journal,* Vol. 10, 1946, p. 141.

11. Ibid. p. 143.

12. Stanley, loc. cit. p. 254.

13. K. Ingham, "Some Aspects of the History of Buganda," *Uganda Journal,* Vol. 20, 1956, p. 3.

14. Ibid. p. 1.

15. Ibid. p. 2.

16. Ibid. p. 4.

17. Wrigley, "The Christian Revolution in Buganda," loc. cit. p. 41.

18. Ibid. p. 45.

19. Fallers, "Despotism and Social Mobility," loc. cit. p. 20.

20. H. S. Lewis, *A Galla Monarchy,* Madison, Wis., 1965, p. 120.

21. See the review by Eike Haberland and the rejoinder by Ronald Cohen, *American Anthropologist,* Vol. 69, 1967, pp. 124–26, 745.

22. Lewis, *A Galla Monarchy,* pp. 4, 80, 114.

23. Ibid. p. 88.

24. Ibid. p. 112.

25. Ibid. p. 119.

26. Andrew Lang and J. J. Atkinson, *Social Origins* and *Primal Law,* London, 1903, p. 220, italics removed.

27. Sidgwick, op. cit. p. 11.

Chapter XII

1. Nicolas Antoine Boulanger, *Recherches sur L'Origine du Despotisme Oriental,* London, 1762.

2. Martha Wolfenstein, *Disaster: A Psychological Essay,* Glencoe, Ill., 1957, pp. 200–201.

3. Sidney Hook, *The Hero in History,* Boston, 1955, p. 109.

4. Ibid. pp. 166–69.

5. Ibid. p. 153.

6. Bird, *Annals,* Vol. I, pp. 568–71.

7. L. A. Fallers, *The King's Men*, London, 1964, p. 6.
8. Fallers, "Despotism and Social Mobility," loc. cit. p. 21.
9. Chester I. Barnard, *The Functions of the Executive*, Cambridge, Mass., 1962, p. 149.
10. Ibid. pp. 183, 149–50.
11. Ibid. p. 150.

CHAPTER XIII

1. Walter Goldschmidt, Foreward to Edgar V. Winans, *Shambala: The Constitution of a Traditional State*, Berkeley, Calif., 1962, pp. xiv–xv.
2. Jan Vansina, *Kingdoms of the Savanna*, Madison, Wis., 1966, pp. 66–69.
3. E. G. Ravenstein, ed., *The Strange Adventures of Andrew Battell of Leigh in Angola and the Adjoining Regions*, London, 1901, p. 33.
4. Ibid. pp. 149, 153.
5. Ibid. p. 28.
6. See Peter Becker, *Path of Blood*, London, 1962.
7. J. A. Barnes, *Politics in a Changing Society*, London, 1954, pp. 7 ff.
8. Ibid. p. 11.
9. Ibid. pp. 36, 60.
10. Winans, *Shambala*, p. 157.
11. Barnes, *Politics in a Changing Society*, pp. 58–59.
12. Cf. Schapera, *Government and Politics in Tribal Societies*, London, 1956, pp. 25, 77, 199.
13. Barnard, *The Functions of the Executive*, p. 98.
14. John MacKenzie, *Ten Years North of the Orange River*, Edinburgh, 1871, pp. 325–26.
15. Lloyd Fallers, "Political Sociology and the Anthropological Study of African Polities," *European Journal of Sociology*, Vol. IV, 1963, p. 320.
16. Ibid. p. 324.
17. See Jan Vansina, "A Comparison of African Kingdoms," *Africa*, Vol. XXXII, 1962, pp. 324–35.

CHAPTER XIV

1. I. Schapera, "The Political Organization of the Ngwato," *African Political Systems*, p. 79.
2. Schapera, *Government and Politics in Tribal Societies*, p. 108; *The Bantu-speaking Tribes of South Africa*, p. 180.
3. Kuper, *African Aristocracy*, p. 60.
4. Richards, "The Political System of the Bemba," *African Political Systems*, p. 89.

5. A. I. Richards, "African Kings and their Royal Relatives," *Journal of the Royal Anthropological Institute*, Vol. 91, 1961, pp. 138–39.

6. Vansina, *Kingdoms of the Savanna*, pp. 42, 139.

7. Richards, "African Kings and their Royal Relatives," loc. cit. p. 136.

8. Schapera, *Government and Politics in Tribal Societies*, pp. 56, 153, 157, 169, 202, 207.

9. L. A. Fallers, "Despotism and Social Mobility," loc. cit. pp. 17–18.

10. Schapera, *Government and Politics in Tribal Societies*, pp. 173–74.

11. G. P. Lestrade, "Some Notes on the Political Organisation of the Venda-Speaking Tribes," *Africa*, Vol. III, 1930, p. 319.

12. K. Oberg, "The Kingdom of Ankole in Uganda," *African Political Systems*, pp. 157–59.

13. Nadel, *Black Byzantium*, p. 88.

14. Hilda Kuper, *African Aristocracy*, Ch. VII; *The Swazi: A South African Kingdom*, New York, 1964, Chs. 2–3.

15. See above, p. 105.

16. Diamond, *Dahomey*, p. 81.

17. John Roscoe, *The Baganda*, London, 1911, pp. 188, 190.

18. L. A. Fallers, *Bantu Bureaucracy*, Chicago, 1965, pp. 134–37.

19. Kuper, *African Aristocracy*, p. 60.

20. Schapera, "The Political Organization of the Ngwato," loc. cit. p. 78.

21. Richards, "African Kings and their Royal Relatives," loc. cit. p. 147.

22. S. F. Nadel, "The Kede: A Riverain State in Northern Nigeria," *African Political Systems*, pp. 175–78.

23. John Beattie, *Bunyoro: An African Kingdom*, New York, 1960, p. 30.

24. See above, pp. 275–77.

25. M. C. Fallers, *The Eastern Lacustrine Bantu*, Ethnographic Survey of Africa, East Central Africa, Part XI, London, 1960, p. 67.

26. Lewis, *A Galla Monarchy*, pp. 79, 76.

27. Sir Apolo Kagwa, *The Customs of the Baganda*, ed. by M. M. Edel, New York, 1934, pp. 82–84.

28. Ibid. p. 84.

29. Ibid. pp. 20–21, 170.

30. John H. Speke, *Journal of the Discovery of the Source of the Nile*, Edinburgh and London, 1863, pp. 323, 324, 340.

31. Fallers, "Despotism and Social Mobility," loc. cit. p. 22.

32. L. P. Mair, *An African People in the Twentieth Century*, New York, 1965, pp. 181–82.

33. Mair, *Primitive Government*, pp. 139–40.

34. Kagwa, *Customs of the Baganda*, pp. 170–71.

35. Lewis, *A Galla Monarchy*, p. 15.

36. Eugen Zintgraff, *Nord-Kamerun*, Berlin, 1895, trans. in *Zintgraff's Explorations in Bamenda, Adamawa and the Benue Lands 1889–1892*, ed. by E. M. Chilver, Buea, Cameroon, 1966, p. 8.

37. Ibid.

38. For the importance of age and seniority in traditional societies, see

Schapera, *Western Civilization and the Natives of South Africa*, pp. 20–21.

39. Schapera, *The Bantu-speaking Tribes of South Africa*, p. 184.

40. Lestrade, "The Political Organisation of the Bechwana," loc. cit. p. 431.

41. Kuper, *African Aristocracy*, p. 63.

42. Cape of Good Hope, *Government Commission on Native Laws and Customs*, Part I, p. 45.

43. Omer-Cooper, *Zulu Aftermath*, p. 20.

44. Fallers, *The King's Men*, pp. 5–6.

45. Roscoe, *The Baganda*, p. 259.

46. Fallers, *The King's Men*, p. 6.

47. Jan Vansina, *L'évolution du royaume rwanda des origines à 1900*, Bruxelles, 1962, p. 71.

48. Fallers, "Despotism and Social Mobility," loc. cit. p. 23.

49. Fallers, "Political Sociology and the Anthropological Study of African Politics," loc. cit. pp. 323–25.

50. Kuper, *African Aristocracy*, p. 15.

51. Ibid. p. 46.

52. Vansina, *Kingdoms of the Savanna*, pp. 82–83.

53. Fernand Crine, "Aspects politico-sociaux du système de tenure des terres des Luunda septentrionaux," in *African Agrarian Systems*, ed. by Daniel Biebuyck, London, 1963, pp. 157–72.

54. Vansina, *Kingdoms of the Savanna*, pp. 27, 82. Cf. Max Gluckman, *Politics, Law and Ritual in Tribal Society*, Oxford, 1965, p. 120.

55. H. M. Hole, "The Rise of the Matabele," *Proceedings of the Rhodesia Scientific Association*, Vol. XII, 1912–13, p. 140.

56. Speke, *Journal*, p. 394.

57. Ibid. p. 345.

CHAPTER XV

1. See Barnard, *The Functions of the Executive*.

2. "Ideology and Terror: A Novel Form of Government," reprinted in Hannah Arendt, *The Origins of Totalitarianism*, 2nd ed., New York, 1958, p. 474.

3. Plato, *Laws* 697.

4. Leo Lowenthal, "Crisis of the Individual: Terror's Atomization of Man," *Commentary*, Vol. I, 1946, pp. 1–8.

5. Barrington Moore, Jr., *Terror and Progress USSR*, Cambridge, Mass., 1954, pp. 175–76.

SELECTED

BIBLIOGRAPHY

Aeschylus, *Prometheus Bound*, London, 1926.

Andrewes, A., *Probouleusis*, London, 1954.

Arbousset, Thomas, *Relation d'un Voyage D'Exploration au Nord-Est de la Colonie du Cap de Bonne-Espérance*, Paris, 1842.

Arendt, Hannah, *The Origins of Totalitarianism*, 2nd ed., New York, 1958.

———, "What Was Authority?" in *Authority*, ed. by C. J. Friedrich, Cambridge, Mass., 1958.

Aristotle, *The Metaphysics*, trans. by W. D. Ross, London, 1948; trans. by Richard Hope, Ann Arbor, Mich., 1960.

———, *Nichomachean Ethics*, London, 1926.

———, *Politics*, London, 1932.

Aufricht, Hans, *Guide to the League of Nations Publications: A Bibliographic Survey of the Work of the League, 1920–1947*, New York, 1951.

Barnard, Chester I., *The Functions of the Executive*, Cambridge, Mass., 1962.

Barnes, J. A., *Politics in a Changing Society*, London, 1954.

Beattie, John, *Bunyoro: An African Kingdom*, New York, 1960.

Becker, Peter, *Path of Blood*, London, 1962.

———, *Rule of Fear: The Life and Times of Dingane, King of the Zulu*, London, 1964.

Bendix, Reinhard, *Max Weber: An Intellectual Portrait*, New York, 1962.

Bentley, W. H., *Pioneering on the Congo*, 2 vols., London, 1900.

Binns, C. T., *The Last Zulu King*, London, 1963.

Bird, John, *The Annals of Natal*, 2 vols., Pietermaritzburg, 1888.

Bloch, Marc, *Feudal Society*, trans. by L. A. Manyon, Chicago, 1961.

Bohannan, Laura, "Political Aspects of Tiv Social Organization," in *Tribes Without Rulers*, ed. by John Middleton and David Tait, London, 1958, pp. 33–66.

Bohannan, Paul, "Extra-processual Events in Tiv Political Institutions," *American Anthropologist*, Vol. 60, 1958, pp. 1–12.

Bondurant, Joan, *Conquest of Violence*, Princeton, 1958.

Boulanger, Nicolas Antoine, *Recherches sur L'Origine du Despotisme Oriental*, London, 1762.

Brown, D. Mackenzie, *The White Umbrella: Indian Political Thought from Manu to Gandhi*, Berkeley, Calif., 1953.

Brown, Paula, "Patterns of Authority in West Africa," *Africa*, Vol. 21, 1951, pp. 261–78.

Bryant, A. T., *A History of the Zulu and Neighbouring Tribes*, Cape Town, 1964.

———, *Olden Times in Zululand and Natal*, London, 1929.

———, *A Zulu-English Dictionary*, Pinetown, Natal, 1905.

———, *The Zulu People as They Were before the White Man Came*, Pietermaritzburg, 1949.

———, "The Zulu State and Family Organization," *Bantu Studies*, Vol. II, 1923, pp. 47–51.

Butt-Thompson, F. W., *West African Secret Societies*, London, 1929.

Buxton, Jean, "The Mandari of the Southern Sudan," in *Tribes Without Rulers*, pp. 67–96.

Callaway, Henry, *The Religious System of the Amazulu*, Springvale, Natal, 1868–70.

Cambridge Ancient History, 1st ed., Vol. II, Cambridge, Eng., 1923.

Cambridge History of the British Empire, Vol. VIII, Cambridge, Eng., 1929.

Cape of Good Hope, *Report and Proceedings of the Government Commission on Native Laws and Customs*, Cape Town, 1883.

Case, Clarence Marsh, *Non-Violent Coercion*, New York, 1923.

Chilver, E. M., *Zintgraff's Explorations in Bamenda, Adamawa and the Benue Lands, 1889–1892*, Buea, Cameroon, 1966.

———, and P. M. Kaberry, "The Kingdom of Kom in West Cameron," in *West African Kingdoms in the Nineteenth Century*, London, 1967, pp. 123 51.

Clausewitz, Karl von, *Vom Kriege*, 13. Aufl., Berlin und Leipzig, 1918.

Colenso, F. E., *The Ruin of Zululand*, 2 vols., London, 1885.

Creel, H. G., *Confucius and the Chinese Way*, New York, 1960.

Crine, Fernand, "Aspects politico-sociaux du système de tenure des terres des Luunda Septentrionaux," in *African Agrarian Systems*, ed. by Daniel Biebuyck, London, 1963, pp. 157–72.

Crozier, Brian, *The Rebels: A Study of Post-War Insurrections*, London, 1960.

Delegorgue, Adulphe, *Voyage dans l'Afrique Australe*, 2 vols., Paris, 1847.

Diamond, Stanley, "Dahomey: A Proto-State in West Africa," unpublished Ph.D. dissertation, Columbia University, New York, 1951.

Doke, C. M., and B. W. Vilakazi, *Zulu-English Dictionary*, 2nd ed., Johannesburg, 1958.

Dunn, John, *Cetywayo and the Three Generals*, ed. by D. C. F. Moodie, Pietermaritzburg, 1886.

Easton, David, "Political Anthropology," *Biennial Review of Anthropology, 1959*, ed. by B. J. Siegel, Stanford, 1959, pp. 210–62.

———, *The Political System*, New York, 1953.

Elkins, Stanley M., *Slavery: A Problem in American Institutional and Intellectual Life*, Chicago, 1959.

Emmet, Dorothy, "The Concept of Power," *Proceedings of the Aristotelian Society*, Vol. 54, 1954, pp. 1–26.

Evans-Pritchard, E. E., "Sorcery and Native Opinion," *Africa*, Vol. IV, 1931, pp. 22–55.

———, *Witchcraft, Oracles and Magic among the Azande*, London, 1937.

Fagan, B. M., "Radiocarbon Dates for Sub-Saharan Africa: V," *Journal of African History*, Vol. VIII, 1967, pp. 513–27.

Fallers, L. A., *Bantu Bureaucracy*, Chicago, 1965.

———, "Despotism and Social Mobility," *Comparative Studies in Society and History*, Vol. II, 1959, pp. 11–32.

———, *The Kings Men*, London, 1964.

———, "Political Sociology and the Anthropological Study of African Polities," *European Journal of Sociology*, Vol. IV, 1963, pp. 311–29.

Fallers, M. C., *The Eastern Lacustrine Bantu*, Ethnographic Survey of Africa, East Central Africa, Part XI, London, 1960.

Farrer, J. A., *Zululand and the Zulus*, London, 1879.

Ferguson, W. S., "The Zulus and the Spartans: A Comparison of their Military Systems," *Harvard African Studies*, Vol. 2, Cambridge, Mass., 1918, pp. 197–234.

Forde, Daryll, and P. M. Kaberry, eds., *West African Kingdoms in the Nineteenth Century*, London, 1967.

Fortes, M., and E. E. Evans-Pritchard, eds., *African Political Systems*, London, 1961.

Fortes, Meyer, "The Structure of Unilineal Descent Groups," *American Anthropologist*, Vol. 55, 1953, pp. 17–41.

Fried, Morton H., *The Evolution of Political Society*, New York, 1967.

Fung Yu-lan, *A Short History of Chinese Philosophy*, New York, 1960.

Fynn, H. F., *The Diary of Henry Francis Fynn*, ed. by James Stuart and D. McK. Malcolm, Pietermaritzburg, 1950.

Garbutt, H. W., "Native Witchcraft and Superstition in South Africa," *Journal of the Royal Anthropological Institute*, Vol. XXXIX, 1909, pp. 530–58.

Gardiner, A. F., *Narrative of a Journey to the Zoolu Country in South Africa*, London, 1836.

Gibbs, J. L., "Poro Values and Courtroom Procedures in a Kpelle Chiefdom," *Southwestern Journal of Anthropology*, Vol. 18, 1962, pp. 341–50.

Gibson, J. Y., *The Story of the Zulus*, London, 1911.

Gluckman, Max, *Analysis of a Social Situation in Modern Zululand*, Manchester, 1958.

———, *Custom and Conflict in Africa*, Glencoe, Ill., 1955.

———, "The Kingdom of the Zulu," in *African Political Systems*, pp. 25–55.

———, *Politics, Law, and Ritual in Tribal Society*, Oxford, 1965.

———, "The Rise of a Zulu Empire," *Scientific American*, Vol. 202, 1960, pp. 157–68.

———, *Rituals of Rebellion in South-East Africa*, Manchester, 1954.

Great Britain, *Accounts and Papers*, 1890, Vol. XII, C. 6201.

Great Britain, *Parliamentary Papers*, 1877, Vol. LX, C. 1748; 1878, Vol. LVI, C. 2079; 1883, Vol. LXIX, C. 3616.

Haggard, H. Rider, *Cetywayo and his White Neighbours*, London, 1890.

Haggard, H. Rider, *Nada the Lily* (first pub. 1892), London, 1958.

Hailey, Lord, *An African Survey: Revised 1956*, London, 1957.

Hall, H. U., *The Sherbro of Sierra Leone*, Philadelphia, 1938.

Hammond, N. G. L., *A History of Greece to 322 B.C.*, London, 1959.

Hardman, J. B. S., "Intimidation," *Encyclopedia of the Social Sciences*, Vol. IV, New York, 1937, pp. 239–42.

――, "Terrorism," *Encyclopedia of the Social Sciences*, Vol. VII, New York, 1937, pp. 575–79.

Harley, George W., "Masks as Agents of Social Control in Northeast Liberia," *Papers of the Peabody Museum*, Cambridge, Mass., Vol. 32, 1950, No. 2, pp. v–xiv, 3–44.

――, *Native African Medicine*, Cambridge, Mass., 1941.

――, "Notes on the Poro in Liberia," *Papers of the Peabody Museum*, Vol. 19, 1941, No. 2, pp. 3–36.

Harris, E. E., "Political Power," *Ethics*, Vol. LXVIII, 1957, pp. 1–10.

Hartung, Fritz, *Enlightened Despotism*, trans. by H. Otto, London, 1957.

Hebb, D. O., "On the Nature of Fear," *Psychological Review*, Vol. 53, 1946, pp. 259–76; *The Organization of Behavior*, New York, 1961, p. 243.

Heer, Friedrich, *Sieben Kapitel aus der Geschichte des Schreckens*, Zürich, 1957.

Herodotus, *Histories*, London, 1960.

Hesiod, *Theogony*, Oxford, 1966.

Hobbes, Thomas, *Leviathan*, in *The English Works of Thomas Hobbes*, ed. by William Molesworth, Vol. III, 1839.

Hobsbawm, E. J., *Primitive Rebels: Studies in Archaic Forms of Social Movements in the 19th and 20th Centuries*, Manchester, 1959.

Holden, W. C., *The Past and Future of the Kaffir Races*, Reprint, Cape Town, 1963.

Hole, H. M., "The Rise of the Matabele," *Proceedings of the Rhodesia Scientific Association*, Vol. XII, 1912–13, pp. 135–48.

Homans, George C., *Social Behavior: Its Elementary Forms*, New York, 1961.

Hook, Sidney, *The Hero in History*, Boston, 1955.

Huizinga, Jan, *The Waning of the Middle Ages*, trans. by F. Hopman, New York, 1954.

Isaacs, Nathaniel, *Travels and Adventures in Eastern Africa*, 2 vols. (first pub. 1836), Cape Town, 1936–37.

Ingham, K., "Some Aspects of the History of Buganda," *Uganda Journal*, Vol. XX, 1956, pp. 1–12.

Jammer, Max, *Concepts of Force: A Study in the Foundations of Dynamics*, New York, 1962.

Junod, Henri A., *The Life of a South African Tribe*, 2 vols., Neuchatel, Switzerland, 1912.

Kagwa, Sir Apolo, *The Customs of the Baganda*, ed. by M. M. Edel, New York, 1934.

Kautilya Arthasastra, trans. by R. Shamasastry, Mysore, India, 1961.

Kautsky, Benedikt, and Eugen Kogon, *et al.*, "Vorträge and Diskussion über

'Terror,'" *Verhandlungen der Deutschen Soziologentage*, IX. Band, 1949, pp. 98–142.

Kidd, Dudley, *The Essential Kafir*, London, 1904.

Kirby, Percival R., ed., *Andrew Smith and Natal: Documents Relating to the Early History of that Province*. Cape Town, 1955.

Krader, Lawrence, *Formation of the State*, Englewood, Cliffs, N. J., 1968.

Krige, E. J., *The Social System of the Zulus*, 2nd ed., Pietermaritzburg, 1950.

Kuper, Hilda, *An African Aristocracy*, London, 1947.

——, *The Swazi: A South African Kingdom*, New York, 1964.

Kuper, Leo, *Passive Resistance in South Africa*, New Haven, 1960.

Lang, Andrew, and J. J. Atkinson, *Social Origins* and *Primal Law*, London, 1903.

Laws of Manu, trans. by G. Bühler, in *The Sacred Books of the East*, ed. by F. M. Müller, Vol. XXV, London, 1886.

Leslie, David, *Among the Zulus and Amatongas*, Glasgow, 1875.

Lestrade, G. P., "Some Notes on the Political Organisation of the Bechwana," *South African Journal of Science*, Vol. 25, 1928, pp. 427–32.

——, "Some Notes on the Political Organisation of the Venda-Speaking Tribes," *Africa*, Vol. 3, 1930, pp. 306–22.

Lévi-Strauss, Claude, *Tristes Tropiques*, trans. by John Russell, New York, 1964.

Lewis, Herbert S., *A Galla Monarchy*, Madison, Wis., 1965.

Little, Kenneth, "The Mende Chiefdoms of Sierra Leone," in *West African Kingdoms*, pp. 239–59.

——, "The Political Function of the Poro," Parts I and II, *Africa*, Vol. 35, 1965, pp. 349–65; Vol. 36, 1966, pp. 62–72.

Lloyd, P. C., "The Traditional Political System of the Yoruba," *Southwestern Journal of Anthropology*, Vol. 10, 1954, pp. 366–84.

Lowenthal, Leo, "Crisis of the Individual: Terror's Atomization of Man," *Commentary*, Vol. I, 1946, pp. 1–8.

Lowie, Robert H., *The Origin of the State*, New York, 1927.

Lye, W. F., "The Difaqane: The Mfecane in the Southern Sotho Area, 1822–24," *Journal of African History*, Vol. VIII, 1967, pp. 107–31.

——, "Some Aspects of Political Organization among the American Aborigines," *Journal of the Royal Anthropological Institute*, Vol. 78, 1948, pp. 11–24.

Macdonald, James, "Manners, Customs, Superstitions, and Religions of South African Tribes," *Journal of the Anthropological Institute*, Vol. XX, 1890, pp. 113–40.

MacIver, R. M., *The Modern State*, London, 1926.

——, *The Web of Government*, New York, 1947.

Mackenzie, John, *Ten Years North of the Orange River*, Edinburgh, 1871.

Mackeurtan, Graham, *The Cradle Days of Natal*, London, 1930.

Macmillan, W. M., *Bantu, Boer, and Briton*, London, 1929.

Maine, Henry Sumner, *Ancient Law* (first pub. 1861), London, 1954.

Mair, L. P., *An African People in the Twentieth Century*, New York, 1965.

Mair, L. P., *Primitive Government*, Baltimore, 1962.

Marks, Shula, "The Nguni, the Natalians, and their History," *Journal of African History*, Vol. VIII, 1967, pp. 529–40.

Marx, Karl, *Pre-Capitalist Economic Formations*, ed. by E. J. Hobsbawm, New York, 1965.

Mauss, Marcel, "Une catégorie de l'esprit humain: La notion de personne celle de 'moi,' " *Journal of the Royal Anthropological Institute*, Vol. 68, 1938, pp. 263–82.

Merriam, Charles E., *Political Power*, Glencoe, Ill., 1950.

Mills, C. Wright, *The Power Elite*, New York, 1956.

Mofolo, Thomas, *Chaka: An Historical Romance*, trans. by F. H. Dutton, London, 1931.

Momigliano, Arnaldo, "An Interim Report on the Origins of Rome," *Journal of Roman Studies*, Vol. LIII, 1963, pp. 95–121.

Mommsen, Theodor, *The History of Rome*, 4th ed., trans. by W. P. Dickson, 4 vols., New York, 1891.

Moore, Barrington, Jr., *Political Power and Social Theory*, Cambridge, Mass., 1958.

———, *Terror and Progress USSR*, Cambridge, Mass., 1954.

Morris, Donald R., *The Washing of the Spears*, New York, 1965.

Morton-Williams, Peter, "The Egungun Society in South-Western Yoruba Kingdoms," *Proceedings of the Third Annual Conference of the West African Institute of Social and Economic Research* (1954), Ibadan, Nigeria, 1956, pp. 90–103.

———, "An Outline of the Cosmology and Cult Organisation of the Oyo Yorbua," *Africa*, Vol. 34, 1964, pp. 243–61.

———, "The Yoruba Kingdom of Oyo," in *West African Kingdoms*, pp. 36–69.

———, "The Yoruba Ogboni Cult in Oyo," *Africa*, Vol. 30, 1960, pp. 362–74.

Mukasa, Ham, "The Rule of the Kings of Buganda," *Uganda Journal*, Vol. X, 1946, pp. 136–43.

———, "Speke at the Court of Muteesa I," *Uganda Journal*, Vol. XXVI, 1962, pp. 97–99.

Murdock, G. P., *Africa: Its Peoples and their Culture History*, New York, 1959.

Myres, John L., *The Political Ideas of the Greeks*, New York, 1927.

Nadel, S. F., *A Black Byzantium*, London, 1942.

———, "The Kede: A Riverain State in Northern Nigeria," in *African Political Systems*, pp. 165–96.

Oberg, K., "The Kingdom of Ankole in Uganda," in *African Political Systems*, pp. 121–64.

Oliver, Edmund H., *Roman Economic Conditions to the Close of the Republic*, Toronto, 1907.

Omer-Cooper, J. D., *The Zulu Aftermath*, London, 1966.

Oppenheim, F. E., *Dimensions of Freedom: An Analysis*, New York, 1961.

Oppenheimer, Heinrich, *The Rationale of Punishment*, London, 1913.

Ortega y Gasset, José, *Concord and Liberty*, trans. by Helene Weyl, New York, 1946.

Owen, W. F. W., *Narrative of Voyages to Explore the Shores of Africa, Arabia, and Madagascar*, 2 vols., London, 1833.

Payne, Robert, *Zero: The Story of Terrorism*, New York, 1950.

Plato, *Laws*, 2 vols., London, 1926.

Radin, Paul, *The World of Primitive Man*, New York, 1960.

Rangaswami Aiyangar, K. V., *Considerations on Some Aspects of Ancient Indian Polity*, 2nd ed., Madras, India, 1935.

Ravenstein, E. G., ed., *The Strange Adventures of Andrew Battell of Leigh in Angola and the Adjoining Regions*, London, 1901.

Richards, A. I., "African Kings and their Royal Relatives," *Journal of the Royal Anthropological Institute*, Vol. 91, 1961, pp. 135–50.

———, "The Political System of the Bemba Tribe—North-Eastern Rhodesia," in *African Political Systems*, pp. 83–120.

Ritter, E. A., *Shaka Zulu: The Rise of the Zulu Empire*, New York, 1957.

Roscoe, John, *The Baganda*, London, 1911.

Roucek, Joseph S., "Sociological Elements of a Theory of Terror and Violence," *American Journal of Economics and Sociology*, Vol. XXI, 1962, pp. 165–72.

Russell, Bertrand, *Power: A New Social Analysis*, New York, 1962.

Sahlins, Marshall D., "The Segmentary Lineage: An Organization of Predatory Expansion," *American Anthropologist*, Vol. 63, 1961, pp. 322–45.

Samuelson, R. C. A., *Long, Long Ago*, Durban, Natal, 1929.

Schapera, I., *Government and Politics in Tribal Societies*, London, 1956.

———, "The Old Bantu Culture," in *Western Civilization and the Natives of South Africa*, London, 1934, pp. 3–36.

———, "The Political Organization of the Ngwato," in *African Political Systems*, pp. 56–82.

Schwab, George, *Tribes of the Liberian Hinterland*, Papers of the Peabody Museum, Cambridge, Mass., 1947.

Service, E. R., *Primitive Social Organization*, New York, 1962.

———, *Profiles in Ethnology*, New York, 1963.

Shooter, Joseph, *The Kafirs of Natal and the Zulu Country*, London, 1857.

Sidgwick, Henry, *The Development of European Polity*, 3rd ed., London, 1920.

Simmel, Georg, *The Sociology of Georg Simmel*, trans. and ed. by Kurt H. Wolff, Glencoe, Ill., 1950.

Sinclair, T. A., *A History of Greek Political Thought*, London, 1961.

Smith, M. G., "On Segmentary Lineage Systems," *Journal of the Royal Anthropological Institute*, Vol. 86, 1956, pp. 39–80.

Soga, J. H., *The Ama-Xosa: Life and Customs*, Lovedale, Natal, 1931.

———, *The South-Eastern Bantu*, Johannesburg, 1930.

Sophocles, *Oedipus at Colonus*, London, 1912.

Southall, Aidan W., *Alur Society: A Study in Processes and Types of Domination*, Cambridge, Eng., [1953].

Speke, John H., *Journal of the Discovery of the Source of the Nile*, Edinburgh and London, 1863.

Stampp, Kenneth M., *The Peculiar Institution*, New York, 1956.

Stanley, H. M., *Through the Dark Continent*, 2 vols., London, 1899.

Stirling, Paul, *Turkish Village*, New York, 1965.

Strauss, Leo, *On Tyranny*, New York, 1963.

Tacitus, *The Complete Works*, trans. by Church and Brodribb, New York, 1942.

Theal, George McCall, *History and Ethnography of Africa South of the Zambesi*, London, 1907.

————, *History of South Africa from 1795 to 1872*, 4th ed., 5 vols., London, 1915.

Tillich, Paul, *Love, Power and Justice*, New York, 1961.

Turnbull, Colin, *Wayward Servants*, New York, 1965.

Valentine, C. A., *Masks and Men in a Melanesian Society*, Lawrence, Kansas, 1961.

Vansina, Jan, "A Comparison of African Kingdoms," *Africa*, Vol. XXXII, 1962, pp. 324–35.

————, *L'évolution du royaume rwanda des origines à 1900*, Bruxelles, 1962.

————, *Kingdoms of the Savanna*, Madison, Wis., 1966.

Van Warmelo, N. J., "The Nguni," in *The Bantu Tribes of South Africa*, ed. by A. M. Duggan-Cronin, Cambridge, Eng., 1939, Vol. III, Sect. I, pp. 9–17.

Varro, Marcus Terentius, *Rerum Rusticarum*, London, 1934.

Veblen, Thorstein, *The Theory of the Leisure Class*, New York, 1953.

Vijn, Cornelius, *Cetshwayo's Dutchman*, London, 1880.

Waciorski, Jerzy, *Le terrorisme politique*, Paris, 1939.

Walker, Eric A., *A History of Southern Africa*, 3rd ed., London, 1957.

Weber, Max, *From Max Weber: Essays in Sociology*, trans. by H. H. Gerth and C. Wright Mills, New York, 1946.

————, "Politik als Beruf," *Gesammelte Politische Schriften*, 2. Aufl., Tübingen, 1958.

————, *The Theory of Social and Economic Organization*, trans. by Henderson and Parsons, New York, 1947.

————, *Wirtschaft und Gesellschaft*, 4. Aufl., Tübingen, 1956.

Webster, Hutton, *Primitive Secret Societies*, New York, 1908.

Westermann, Diedrich, *Die Kpelle: Ein Negerstamm in Liberia*, Göttingen, 1921.

Whitehead, A. N., *Adventures of Ideas*, New York, 1933.

Whyte, William Foote, *Street Corner Society*, 2nd ed., Chicago, 1961.

Wilson, Monica, "The Early History of the Transkei and Ciskei," *African Studies*, Vol. XVIII, 1959, pp. 167–79.

Winans, Edgar V., *Shambala: The Constitution of a Traditional State*, Berkeley, Calif., 1962.

Wittfogel, K. A., *Oriental Despotism*, New Haven, 1957.

Wolfenstein, Martha, *Disaster: A Psychological Essay*, Glencoe, Ill., 1957.

Wrigley, C. C., "The Christian Revolution in Buganda," *Comparative Studies in Society and History*, Vol. II, 1959, pp. 33–48.

Zintgraff, Eugen, *Nord-Kamerun*, Berlin, 1895.

INDEX

(This index does not include names and titles in the notes, pp. 345-66.)